Feet and Footwear

Feet and Footwear

A Cultural Encyclopedia

MARGO DEMELLO

GREENWOOD PRESS
An Imprint of ABC-CLIO, LLC

A B C 🌐 C L I O

Santa Barbara, California • Denver, Colorado • Oxford, England

Library of Congress Cataloging-in-Publication Data

DeMello, Margo.
   Feet and footwear : a cultural encyclopedia / Margo DeMello.
     p. cm.
   Includes bibliographical references and index.
   ISBN 978–0–313–35714–5 (hard copy: alk. paper) — ISBN 978–0–313–35715–2 (ebook)
1. Footwear—Encyclopedias. 2. Shoes—Social aspects—Encyclopedias. 3. Foot—Encyclopedias. 4. Footwear industry—Encyclopedias. I. Title.
GT2130.D45   2009
391.4′1303—dc22   2009020843

13 12 11 10 9   1 2 3 4 5

This book is also available on the World Wide Web as an eBook.
Visit www.abc-clio.com for details.

ABC-CLIO, LLC
130 Cremona Drive, P.O. Box 1911
Santa Barbara, California 93116-1911

This book is printed on acid-free paper (∞)

Manufactured in the United States of America

Contents

List of Entries

Guide to Related Topics

LOCAL CUSTOMS, PRACTICES, AND BELIEFS

Acupuncture
Beliefs
Christianity
Concealment Shoes
Crush Videos
Fetishes
Foot and Shoe Adornment
Foot binding
Foot Massage
Foot Washing

Henna
Islam
Judaism
Pedicure
Proverbs
Reflexology
Shoe Etiquette
Sumptuary Laws
Wedding Shoes

MYTHOLOGY, FOLKLORE, AND FAIRY TALES

Achilles
"Cinderella"
Fairy Tales

"The Princess and the Golden Shoes"
"The Red Shoes"
"The Shoes That Were Danced to Pieces"

HEALTH AND MEDICAL ISSUES

Acupuncture
Amputation
Athlete's Foot
Blisters, Bunions, Calluses, and Corns
Club Foot
Diabetes
Disorders and Injuries
Flat Feet and Fallen Arches
Foot Care Products
Foot Odor
Foot Structure
Hammer Toe

Ingrown Toenails
National Podiatric Medical Association
Orthopedic Shoes
Orthotics
Plantar Warts
Podiatry
Polydactyly
Prosthetics
Reflexology
Toenails
Webbed Toes

TYPES OF SHOES

Athletic Shoes
Ballet Shoes
Birkenstocks
Boots
Bowling Shoes

Cleats and Spikes
Clogs
Cowboy Boots
Crocs
Dance Shoes

Earth Shoes
Espadrille
Flip Flops
Galoshes
Go Go Boots
Golf Shoes
High Heels
Huarache
Jack Boots
Jogging Shoe
Military Shoes and Boots
Moccasins
Motorcycle Boot
Orthopedic shoes
Orthotics

Overshoes
Platform Shoes
Pumps
Sandals
Skateboarding Shoes
Skates
Slippers
Sneakers
Snow Shoes
Sport Sandals
Stilettos
Uggs
Vegan Shoes
Wellington Boot

FAMOUS SHOE BRANDS AND SHOE MAKERS

Adidas
Birkenstocks
Blahnik, Manolo
Candie's
Choo, Jimmy
Cole, Kenneth
Converse
Dr. Martens
Dr. Scholl's
Earth Shoes

Ferragamo, Salvatore
Florsheim
Keds
New Balance
Nike
Red Wing
Reebok
Uggs
Vans

CULTURES AND SUBCULTURES

Africa
Alaska
Arctic Region
China
Classical Civilizations
Egypt
Europe
Greece
India

Japan
Korea
Middle East
Native America
Plains Indians
Rome
Southwest Indians
United States

MEDIA AND CELEBRITIES

Advertising
"Blue Suede Shoes"
Celebrity Endorsements
Grauman's Chinese Theatre
John, Elton
Jordan, Michael

Kinky Boots
Marcos, Imelda
Parker, Sarah Jessica
Sex and the City
Simpson, O.J.
Spice Girls

SHOE MAKING

Preface

Feet and footwear are enormously rich subjects for students of symbolism, ritual, magic, culture, and fashion. Currently, there is not a single overall reference book that covers the breadth and scope of the literature. This encyclopedia is the first of its kind to take a comprehensive look at the natural and cultural history of feet and footwear—shoes, sandals, boots, socks, and hosiery. It addresses feet from the perspective of anatomy, evolution, and medical science as well as the cultural and religious significance of feet across cultures and through history. It also looks at shoes: how they are constructed, the shoemaking industry, the fashions and trends in footwear, and the major people and groups associated with shoes. In addition, this encyclopedia addresses the historical and cross-cultural beliefs and practices associated with shoes and locates those practices and beliefs in art, film, literature, folklore, and history. Finally, the book addresses some of the major theoretical issues surrounding feet and their adornment.

This volume is aimed at general readers with an interest in the feet and footwear, as well as students and scholars who are doing more in-depth work on the social and cultural uses of feet and shoes. Readers with an interest in fashion, in podiatry, in religion, and in anthropology will all find something of interest in this volume. Most entries include a list of further reading on the subject for readers who desire more information, and included at the end of the book is a list of resources (including magazines, organizations, Web sites, and museums devoted to feet and shoes) as well as a comprehensive bibliography.

There are 165 entries in this encyclopedia that cover the basics of feet and footwear, the people and groups associated with them, the beliefs and practices surrounding them, and the laws and norms that have dealt with them over time. Major organizations and people in the shoe industry, famous brands, as well as celebrities associated with shoes have been included, with a special emphasis on North America. For the most part, however, the book covers societies spanning the world and going back into prehistory.

Entries are listed in alphabetical order. When a subject has multiple names associated with it, the most commonly used name (i.e., shoemaker) will be the name used for the entry, and other names (i.e. cobbler) will include a note directing the reader to the full entry. Additionally, each entry contains cross-referenced items in **bold** type as well as a list of related subjects at the end of each entry.

Each entry explains the term, gives an overview, and provides any historical or cross-cultural significance. Because of the speed with which the industry changes, there will doubtless be innovations and styles that have come out that are not included in this encyclopedia.

Acknowledgments

Every book, regardless of the author, includes the work and assistance of a great many people. I owe my first thanks to my editor, Kaitlin Ciarmiello, who offered me this opportunity and worked with me from beginning to completion.

This book includes photos and illustrations from a number of sources. The historical images are courtesy of the Library of Congress, the National Library of Medicine, HistoryPicks.com, and the Beinecke Rare Book and Manuscript Library. Additional photographs are from *Associated Press* Images, the Department of Defense, the Public Health Image Library of the CDC, PDPhoto.org, Jupiterimages Corporation, and BigStockPhoto.com. I am also grateful to the Bata Shoe Museum for providing five beautiful photographs of historical footwear from their own collection, and to Shoe Icons, who provided nine photos from their own collection. I am also grateful for the photo I received from Jeff Hayes of Rival Tattoo Art Studio in Albuquerque, New Mexico. Jeff is my tattooist and created a special tattoo of a Victorian shoe that he tattooed onto a client's foot specially for this book.

I am also grateful for the support, encouragement, and friendship I received from Bill Velasquez, who not only graciously and thanklessly took on the entire job of running the New Mexico activities of House Rabbit Society (an organization I help direct) over the past year, but who sent me links and information about shoes and feet throughout the year (and who one night showed me his wife Debbie's alleged webbed toes).

I also want to thank my parents, Robin and Bill, for their love and support in all of my activities. Finally, I want to thank my husband, Tom Young, for once again putting up with a frantic and desperate wife whose overeating and general level of stress increased as my book deadline neared.

Introduction

Feet and footwear carry not only the weight of the body, but a great deal of symbolic, social, and cultural weight as well. How we view and treat the foot, the kinds of footwear that we wear, and how we view our footwear tell us a great deal about society and culture. Feet, both bare and shod, are linked to our ideas about gender, sexuality, class, and culture. Thus we can read, through the history of footwear in a given society, the evolution of that society's ideas about men and women, about the working classes and the elites, and about work and leisure. Shoes ultimately signify individual identity, group affiliation, and social position.

Footwear refers to the coverings of the feet, usually referring to shoes, but also socks, leggings, and other coverings. The oldest forms of footwear were worn for protection, but as cultures became more sophisticated and societies became ranked, footwear came to be used to mark social status as well.

In 2005, researchers at Washington University, looking at the bones of ancient humans, located the earliest dates for the wearing of supportive footwear. Because people who go barefoot have stronger toes than those who wear shoes or sandals made with rigid soles, scientists theorized that either shoes or sandals were first worn 30,000–40,000 years ago by Homo sapiens in Eurasia because the skeletons left from that period demonstrate weaker toes than older skeletons. While primitive animal skin boots worn to protect the feet from the snow were probably worn as far back as 50,000 years ago in northern climates, they would have provided little to no foot support, resulting in toes that look no different than the toes of people who go barefoot.

The oldest forms of footwear would be the **sandal** and the **moccasin**, both of which date back to the Paleolithic, when our ancestors made simple clothing items using stone tools. Because shoes are made of materials that do not survive well in the fossil record, there are no records of early Stone Age shoes. Much of what we know about early footwear is speculative, although preserved footprints can indicate the presence of footwear. The oldest known shoes include a pair of 10,000-year-old sandals found in Oregon, made of grass and sagebrush bark woven into a sole and straps, and a pair of 9,000-year-old sandals from California, also made of vegetable matter. The oldest shoes made of animal skins were found with the "Ice Man," a 5,300-year-old fossil from the Tyrolean Alps. These shoes were stuffed with straw and moss for warmth and were similar to simple one-piece moccasins found in most northern cultures around the world.

Another relatively early form of footwear is the wooden **clog**, worn to protect the feet from wet or muddy ground. Clogs are carved out of a single block of wood

The Shoe Tree at Morley Field, Balboa Park, San Diego. Shoe trees are spontaneously created works of communal folk art, and are found throughout America. Often the shoes are inscribed with messages prior to being tossed into the tree. This tree fell down in 2008, and a new shoe tree has started to take its place. [Photo taken by the author]

and can last for many years, and thus are a good form of footwear for people who cannot afford to buy shoes of leather. With the development of welted shoe technology in Europe in the fifteenth century, new forms of shoes appeared, including the **pump**, originally worn by both men and women, and the Oxford **men's shoe**, which remain two of the most enduring shoe types around the world.

Feet, and the shoes that we wear on them, operate in the liminal spaces between the body and the physical space that surrounds it. Feet connect us to the world and allow us to move through that world. Feet are necessary for locomotion, and thus feet are often symbolic of travel or movement of various sorts. Shoes, too, take on this association, and thus Hermes, for example, the Greek god of travel, is depicted in a pair of winged shoes and is often depicted by the shoes alone. Thus, putting on a pair of shoes is symbolic of getting ready to move, while taking off a pair of shoes, or owning no shoes at all, represents staying put. Furthermore, having a lack of shoes implies having no mobility—either physical or social.

Because they are in contact with the earth, feet are subject to a whole host of beliefs and practices surrounding their impurity or their polluting qualities. This translates to cultural rules prescribing what should and should not be done with bare feet, shod feet, as well as shoes and has given rise to a variety of personal care products aimed at keeping the feet clean and odor-free.

Feet, and in particular, bare feet, are humble. They walk on the ground and, when the wearer cannot afford shoes or has removed his or her shoes, they imply humility or poverty. This explains why so many religious practices involve bare feet, foot washing, or the kissing of feet or shoes. Shoes, on the other hand, are vehicles for mobility and are strongly linked to class and status around the world. In fact, the history of footwear can be seen partly as a history of class division and development, with different forms of footwear in cultures around the world being limited to members of particular social classes.

Shoes are also symbolically powerful because of their close connection to their wearers. Throughout much of human history—because shoes were so expensive prior to the Industrial Revolution—many people wore the same pair of shoes for years, and even handed them down to their children. Because of this, the shoes of the dead often have special significance, leading to their use in a number of magic rituals and secular practices. On the other hand, most people today resist wearing second-hand shoes, perhaps because of their close association with their former wearers.

The fact that shoes are intimately connected to their wearers also explains why so many people are obsessed with shoes. Serious collectors own hundreds of pairs of shoes (or, like Imelda Marcos, thousands), and the average American woman owns 30 pairs. But whether one owns 30 or 1,000 pairs, buying shoes is a decision that is often fraught with significance, in part because shoes are seen as a

Jordanian protesters throw their shoes at a huge photograph of George W. Bush during a symbolic farewell to former U.S. President George W. Bush as the inauguration of new U.S. President Barack Obama took place in Washington, in Amman, Jordan, January 20, 2009. Dozens of activists gathered to throw shoes at a large photograph of George W. Bush, recalling Iraqi journalist Muntadhar al-Zeidi who threw his shoes at President George W. Bush during a visit to Iraq. [AP Photo/ Nader Daoud]

reflection of the personality of the wearer and because we will be judged by the quality and condition of our shoes. "Putting one's best foot forward" involves, at the most practical level, wearing shoes that signal one's status and class ambitions; the shoes that we wear act as calling cards and can seriously affect the way that we're treated. (Indeed, in China, traditionally, a matchmaker would bring a potential bride's shoes with her when searching out a good husband, since her shoes tell so much about the girl, her social position, and her upbringing.) And while the primary purpose of shoes is to protect the feet and allow for locomotion, we often purchase shoes with comfort, health, and even fit as our lowest priority. Instead, throughout history elites have worn stylish but impractical shoes, and today many people—but especially women—continue to choose shoes on the basis of how they look. They convey not only our status, but for women they enhance our sexuality as well.

This encyclopedia aims to not only cover the history and cross-cultural evolution of footwear, but to make the diversity of practices and beliefs about feet and shoes intelligible to the reader.

Further Reading Benstock, Shari, Suzanne Ferriss. *Footnotes: On Shoes*. New Brunswick, NJ: Rutgers University Press, 2001; Cosgrave, Bronwyn. *The Complete History of Costume and Fashion: From Ancient Egypt to the Present Day*. New York: Checkmark Books, 2000; Lawlor, Laurie. *Where Will This Shoe Take You? A Walk Through The History of Footwear*. New York: Walker & Company, 1996; O'Keeffe, Linda. *Shoes: A Celebration of Pumps, Sandals, Slippers & More*. New York: Workman Publishing, 1996; Rielle, Georgio and Peter McNeil, eds. *Shoes: A History From Sandals to Sneakers*. London: Berg Publishers, 2006; Steele, Valerie. *Encyclopedia of Clothing and Fashion*. Farmington Hills, MI: Charles Scribner's Sons, 2005; Yue, Charlotte and David. *Shoes: Their History in Words and Pictures*. Boston: Houghton Mifflin, 1997.

A

ACHILLES

The Achilles tendon is a tendon located in the back of the ankle in humans, named after a Greek mythological hero named Achilles.

Achilles, born to Peleus, king of the Myrmidons, and Thetis, a sea nymph, was featured in Homer's *Iliad*, which centered on the Trojan War in which Achilles was a warrior. The Trojan War (described in both the *Iliad* and the *Odyssey*, and perhaps based in part on reality) was fought for over nine years between the ancient city-state of Troy and the Greeks and was incited by the kidnapping of Helen, wife of the king of Sparta, by Paris of Troy.

In the *Iliad*, Achilles was a great warrior whose actions in battle ultimately sealed Troy's fate and led to its fall. In particular, his battle with Hector over Hector's killing of Achilles's friend Patroclus was legendary. While Achilles's death is not related in the *Iliad*, it is told in other tales and involves Paris, who incited the war nine years earlier.

Achilles's death, by a possibly poisonous arrow to the heel, makes sense when combined with one story of his birth, also not related by Homer. According to the unfinished poem *Achilleid* by Statius, Achilles's mother Thetis attempted to ensure her infant son's immortality by dipping his body into the river Styx; unfortunately, she held him by the back of his ankle, thereby leaving that small area of his body unprotected. (The *Iliad* itself contradicts this notion, since it tells of Achilles's wounding by Asteropaeus.) Following Statius's poem in the first century, many Greek and Roman stories included the now-popular account of Achilles's death by an arrow to the back of the ankle.

Today, "Achilles's heel" refers both to the tendon at the back of the ankle that takes its name from these legends and, since the mid-nineteenth century, to a severe weakness or vulnerability. German and Nordic folktales commonly feature such "Achilles's heels," such as in *The Song of the Nibelungs*, in which Siegfried's invulnerability stems from his bathing in dragon's blood except for a spot on his shoulder where a linden leaf fell, rendering him fatally vulnerable. This theme is also found in contemporary popular culture, most famously with Superman and his sole weakness for Kryptonite.

In anatomy, the Achilles tendon, located at the back of the ankle, is a fibrous tissue that attaches two muscles (the gastrocnemius and soleus) from the lower leg to the back of the heel, and is also known as the calcaneal tendon. It was first described as the "cord of Achilles" in 1693 by the Flemish anatomist Philip Verheyen (who dissected his own leg) in Corporis Humani Anatomia, and it is the strongest and thickest tendon in the human body.

The Achilles tendon is subject to injury because it must support not only the weight of a person but, during locomotion and depending on other factors, it might also support many times the weight of a person. Athletes are especially prone to injure the Achilles tendon and are advised to warm up and stretch before exercise in order to prevent tendon strain. The most common injuries among athletes include Achilles tendonitis, which is a soreness of the tendon, and Achilles tendon rupture, which involves the tearing of the tendon. Other potential causes of injury can include uneven leg lengths, changes in heel height (when switching between high-heeled and low-heeled shoes), and high or low arches. Wearing correct footwear, including prosthetic footwear or orthotics when warranted, is one way to minimize the possibility of injury or strain to this tendon.

> In archetypal symbolism feet represent mobility and freedom. In that sense to have shoes to cover the feet is to have the conviction of our beliefs and the wherewithal to act on them.
>
> CLARISSA PINKOLA ESTES

See also: Disorders and Injuries; Foot Structure; Orthotics; Orthopedic Shoes

Further Reading Strauss, Barry. *The Trojan War: A New History*. New York: Simon and Schuster, 2007.

ACUPUNCTURE

Acupuncture is an ancient Eastern medical technique that uses the insertion of needles into the body to cure illness.

Acupuncture is the practice of inserting very fine needles into the body at points called acupuncture points, or acupoints, in order to influence the physiological or emotional health of the body. Shen Nung, a third millennium BCE medical and agricultural scholar, came up with the theories that form the basis of modern acupuncture. He postulated that the body had an energy force running through it known as Qi, which includes spiritual, emotional, physical, and mental aspects. The Qi travels through the body along special pathways or meridians, and if the Qi is unbalanced or lacks strength, or if its travels are disrupted, ill health can occur. Shen Nung felt that the meridians come to the surface at specific locations in the body, which allowed them to be accessed in order to repair the Qi. These points of access are the acupoints, and they can be accessed via the use of needles as well as through acupressure and moxibustion, the burning of herbs over the skin. By balancing and repairing the Qi, the patient can be healed.

There were originally 365 acupuncture points, which were related to 14 original meridian lines. Each meridian line is correlated to an organ, the spine, or the abdomen, and today there are additional points and meridians that have been identified.

The foot has at least 34 acupuncture points, on both the bottom and the top of the foot. There are two points on the foot associated with the liver meridian, for example. Here, when acupuncture is applied to the point between the first and second toes on the top of the foot, or the webbing between the first and second toes, the liver meridian, or pathway, is stimulated. These points are used to deal with problems of urination and menstruation, genital problems, digestive problems, as well as irritability and pain.

Acupuncture, as well as other forms of Chinese medicine, is based on a very different understanding of health and the human body than western medicine. The western approach, for example, is oriented towards disease, with treatments aimed at eliminating or controlling disease. Western medicine sees diseases of the mind and body as being separate in origin and nature (and thus in treatment), resulting in a reductionist approach that views the body and mind as constituting a series

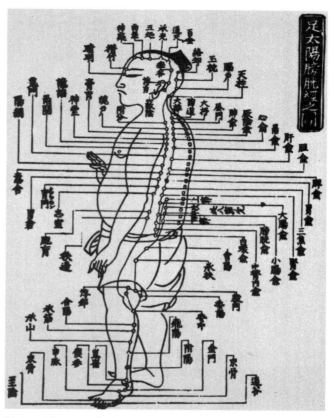

Human Figure with Acupuncture Points Indicated. Illustration from Early Chinese Medical Textbook, World Health Organization Photo. [Photo courtesy of the National Library of Medicine]

of parts that can be healthy or sick. Chinese medicine, on the other hand, is a holistic approach that focuses not on disease or pathology but on wellness and balance. It sees the body as divided into several systems of function that correspond to physical organs, and illness is a result of systems being out of balance or harmony. The diagnosis of illness, then, is not associated with a certain organ or part being diseased, but of a systemic disorder that must be treated on that basis.

Today, acupuncture is practiced not only throughout Asia but throughout the western world as well, by practitioners who either combine acupuncture with traditional western methods—in this case, the use of acupuncture is known as a complementary therapy—or by those who practice only traditional Chinese techniques.

According to a 2002 National Health Interview survey, 8.2 million Americans have used acupuncture. As a complementary therapy, it is used for pain control, anxiety, drug detoxification, stroke and palsy symptoms, muscle spasms, gastrointestinal disorders, headache, arthritis, and bone pain. Some veterinarians also use acupuncture to treat back and muscle pain, arthritis, epilepsy, nervous conditions, and gastrointestinal disorders in nonhuman animals.

Many western doctors reject the efficacy of acupuncture and attribute the apparent successes to the fact that some diseases and conditions will naturally go away on their own, or that some diseases are cyclical, or that patients who seek alternative treatments may be more invested in their health and in feeling better. In addition, some patients will "hedge their bets" by using acupuncture alongside of western treatments, and thus they cannot tell which treatment provided the cure.

Besides the points on the foot that are stimulated to relieve problems related to meridians throughout the body, acupuncture is also used to relieve problems related directly to the foot. Chronic foot pain has been relieved using acupuncture, according to recent studies, and stimulating acupuncture points on the feet can increase blood flow to the region.

Sujok is a Korean form of acupuncture developed in 1987 that focuses entirely on the hands and the feet. According to its adherents, hands (*su*) and feet (*jok*) are miniature versions of the entire body, with regions of the feet and hands corresponding to areas of the body, such as the big toe representing the head and the third and fourth toes representing the legs. Sujok proponents feel that the hands and the feet actually resemble the rest of the body, with the toes and fingers representing the protruding areas of the body both in appearance and in action. (For example, fingers and toes only bend in one direction, similar to arms and legs.) By stimulating points on the foot, one can control conditions of the entire body. The principle of Sujok claims that if body parts are similar, then an action on one part will necessarily work on the corresponding body part. In this way, Sujok is similar to sympathetic magic, and in particular the law of imitation, which states that performing an action on one item (say a voodoo doll) will have a corresponding result on the person that the item resembles. Sujok uses acupuncture as well as other eastern treatments like moxibustion (the burning of mugwort), and pressure therapy in order to provide healing.

See also: China; Disorders and Injuries; Reflexology

Further Reading Fleischman, Gary and Charles Stein. *Acupuncture: Everything You Ever Wanted to Know But Were Afraid to Ask.* Barrytown: Station Hill Press, 1998; Mann, Felix. *Reinventing Acupuncture: A New Concept of Ancient Medicine.* Philadelphia: Elsevier Health Sciences, 2000.

ADIDAS

Adidas is the largest sportswear manufacturer in Europe and one of the oldest athletic shoe companies in the world. Once known primarily as a European brand specializing in shoes for soccer and rugby, it is now an international brand that makes **athletic shoes** for every kind of sport.

Adidas Founder Adolf Dassler, himself an athlete, began making athletic shoes in 1920 in his mother's home. In 1924, he and his brother Rudolf formed the Gebruder Dassler Schulfabrik (shoe factory), which by 1927 had 100 employees. The company began placing **spikes** onto its running shoes, and by 1928 Dassler was giving away shoes to athletes, a gamble that paid off when its shoes were worn at the Olympic Games in Amsterdam and, in 1936, when African American runner Jesse Owens won four gold medals wearing Dassler shoes. Dassler shoes were the first athletic shoes to include an arch support.

During World War II, the Dassler brothers had a falling out that was said to be related to their different alliances during the war, with Rudolf fighting for the Nazis (and being captured by the Allies) and Adolf staying home and making boots for the Wehrmacht. After the war, Rudolf left the company to form Puma (which directly competed with Adolf's company, outfitting the West German soccer team with the Puma Atom, a soccer cleat, until Adidas took over the contract, which it maintains to this day). Adolf renamed the Gebruder Dassler Schulfabrik Adidas (the name comes from combining the first two syllables of Adi and Dassler). The two brothers never reconciled, and their rift split the town of Herzogenaurach as well.

By the end of the 1940s, Adidas was the leading athletic shoe manufacturer in the world, selling 11 different kinds of shoes, all with the company's now trade-marked Three Stripe logo. By the 1950s, Adidas had started its partnership with the German soccer team, which wore Adidas footwear in the 1954 World Cup, demonstrating a savvy use of sports teams to promote the company's brand. Over the next couple of decades, Adidas came to dominate international sports, with 75 percent of all athletes at the 1960 Olympic Games, 78 percent at the 1972 Games, and 89 percent at the 1984 Summer Games wearing Adidas. Adidas entered the American market in 1968 and dominated that market as well (aided by reductions in tariffs for imported products after 1966—and the introduction of the nylon mesh upper in 1970—until the rise of **Nike** during the 1980s and 1990s.

Adidas is also known for its aesthetic features in its shoes as well as its sportswear. Adidas's Three Stripe logo has always been somewhat of a status symbol among those who wear the products, and during the 1970s Adidas sportswear went mainstream, becoming part of popular culture and fashion, especially its logo tee shirt. By the time that rap music and hip hop culture took off in the 1980s and 1990s, Adidas was the brand of choice, a relationship cemented by Run DMC's 1986 song "My Adidas" and the rapper style of wearing Adidas shoes without laces. In the U.S. market, Adidas remains

Sports shoes of German sports goods maker Adidas-Salomon AG are put on display in a shop in Magdeburg, eastern Germany, on Thursday, February 7, 2002. Adidas-Salomon said that it met its 2001 targets of achieving 15 percent growth in net profit and five percent in sales. [AP Photo/Eckehard Schulz]

competitive today in part because of the brand's cachet among rappers, skateboarders, and hipsters, many of whom collect vintage Adidas. Adidas also started reissuing older shoe styles after celebrities like Madonna began wearing them, making them popular all over again.

Today, Adidas remains an industry leader. Annual revenues in 2007 were $15.6 billion, and the company, still headquartered in Germany, employs 25,000 people around the world. In 2006 Adidas acquired **Reebok**.

See also: Athletic Shoes; Celebrity Endorsements; Jogging Shoe; Nike; Reebok; Sneakers

Further Reading Fried, Gil, Steven Shapiro, Timothy DeSchriver. *Sport Finance*. Champaign: Human Kinetics Publishers, 2003; Haig, Matt. *Brand Royalty: How the World's Top 100 Brands Thrive and Survive*. London: Kogan Page Publishers, 2004; Smit, Barbara. *Sneaker Wars: The Enemy Brothers who Founded Adidas and Puma and the Family Feud that Forever Changed the Business of Sport*. New York: Ecco, 2008.

ADVERTISING

Advertising refers to the use of media to persuade the public to purchase goods or services, and the practice dates back thousands of years to at least the classical civilizations.

With the invention of the printing press in the fifteenth century, advertisements went from being locally produced and displayed to being tools that could be used to promote to the masses via flyers and—starting in the nineteenth century—newspapers and magazines. With new media technologies in the twentieth and twenty-first century, new forms of advertising were developed, including radio and television ads, e-mail and Internet ads, and ads tied to sporting and cultural events. Other forms of advertising include ads posted on buses, subways, bus stop benches, and gas pumps, as well as ads broadcast through cell phones, in movie theatres, and even via skywriting.

Shoes and other forms of footwear have been advertised by both dealers and retailers since the dawn of advertising, but shoe advertising exploded in the twentieth century. Newspapers were the first means of mass-market advertising for shoes, and local **shoe stores** ran ads to promote a line of shoes or a big sale, generally using hand-drawn images of the shoes. Stores also advertised their wares via window displays at the store itself as well as through techniques such as sandwich boards. Today, shoes are advertised by both shoe companies and shoe retailers, in magazines and newspapers, and on television, billboards, and the Internet.

Until the rise of **athletic shoe** advertising, led by **Nike**, shoe advertisements remained relatively consistent in message and tone over the years. Shoe makers and retailers promoted the quality of their shoes, the level of fashion (for women's shoes), and the price. As shoe companies became more competitive, creating a brand identity became important. Advertisements were geared towards selling a particular brand, with shoemakers and retailers joining together to pay for ads in fashion magazines. Ads began to deemphasize the shoe and promote the lifestyle associated with the shoe by showing not simply the photograph of the shoe, but images of models wearing shoes and engaging in activities associated with the shoes. Today, shoe advertising is increasingly about branding: creating brand awareness and turning product and company names into household words.

While at one time advertisements for shoes were aimed at informing the reader of the qualities of the shoe, in recent years shoe advertisements have become much more sophisticated, especially those that advertise athletic shoes. The athletic shoe market in the United States is worth $8.5 billion, so it's not surprising that the major companies involved would devote a great deal of money and creativity towards promoting their products.

Nike was the first company to really focus on creative advertising, using a strategy aimed at creating and maintaining brand loyalty among its customers. Nike achieved much of its success by enlisting the aid of celebrity athletes, who sign sponsorship agreements with the company and wear Nike products, with the distinctive swoosh logo, at public events. Starting in 1972 with tennis player Ilie Nastase, Nike has been endorsed by top athletes in virtually every sport, including such names as **Michael Jordan** and Tiger Woods, and even non-athletes like Spike Lee. The company has also sponsored sports teams and sporting events and has created Web sites for individual sports. One of Nike's most important marketing devices involves creating shoes and other forms of athletic wear branded with the name of an athlete, such as the Air Jordan shoes.

Henry Arthur Shoes, manufacturer of boots, shoes, and uppers. Ad from 1873. [Photo courtesy of the Library of Congress Prints and Photographs Division]

By sponsoring athletes popular with young people, and by targeting youth in particular with clever, humorous ads, Nike's advertising campaigns effectively harnessed consumers—especially young consumers—to become part of Nike's marketing campaign via the wearing of their logoed products. Nike's ads also excel because of its use—now common in the industry but pioneered by Nike— of close-up shots of athletes in action. Muscles, heavy breathing and sweat are prominent features of many of Nike's print and television campaigns, and, combined with the "Just Do It" slogan launched in 1988, ensured Nike's control over the athletic shoe market. (One-third of all sneakers sold are Nikes.). Many of Nike's consumers buy and wear their shoes for athletic purposes, but it is estimated that 80 percent of all Nike shoes are not worn for sports, demonstrating Nike's success in transforming athletic wear into fashion, and, ultimately, a mark of status.

Nike's advertisements, besides relying heavily on celebrity athletes and the fetishization of muscles, also derive much of their success from their creative and often controversial themes. One such ad ran during the 2000 Summer Olympics and featured runner Suzy Favor-Hamilton running from a masked man wielding a chain saw and ended with the tagline "Why Sport? You'll live longer." The ad was protested as demeaning towards women and also frightening for children, and it was pulled after just a couple of days. Other advertising techniques have been equally controversial, such as Nike's use of either non-licensed materials or legally licensed songs (such as the Beatles's "Revolution"), which nonetheless elicited heavy criticism and a lawsuit from Apple Records, the Beatles's record company.

Some of Nike's ads have been targeted by those who oppose Nike's reliance on offshore production facilities. For instance, in 1998 Marc Kasky, a consumer advocate, sued Nike with the claim that Nike's advertisements and public statements misrepresented the company's overseas factories and the labor conditions in those factories, and thus constituted false advertising. After a local court ruled against Kasky, the California Supreme Court overturned that ruling and wrote that Nike's ads constituted commercial speech and thus were not protected by the First Amendment.

Athletic shoe companies could be at risk for lawsuits that challenge their health and safety claims as well. Because athletic shoes like Nike, **Adidas**, and New Balance sometimes market their shoes with claims that their shoes can prevent injury to their wearers, consumers who wear the shoes and sustain injuries could react angrily. A 1997 study in the *British Journal of Sports Medicine*, in fact, found that shoes that are marketed as safe are used by athletes more aggressively than inexpensive shoes with no such claims, resulting in a greater frequency of injuries by creating a false sense of security.

Nike is not the only shoe company to produce edgy, controversial ads. Pearl Izumi, a producer of running shoes, developed a buzz-worthy print campaign in 2007 that opened with the line, "Ever notice how it's always runners who find dead bodies?" The ad ends with "In fact, if it weren't for runners, you wonder how many of these crimes would ever get solved. Better Lace 'em up. Because someone, somewhere is missing. So do your civic duty. Run like an animal." This campaign derived its humor from television shows like *Law & Order* that often open with runners finding dead bodies.

Other edgy shoe ads include the British **Dr. Martens** ads in 2007 that showed dead rock stars like Kurt Cobain and Johnny Ramone wearing Doc Martens. (The ads were pulled after customers registered their outrage and Cobain's widow, Courtney Love, protested.) **Candie's** print ads showed Playboy centerfold Jenny McCarthy sitting nude on a toilet, and **Kenneth Cole** ads promoted both Kenneth Cole shoes and condoms, with the caption that read: "Our shoes aren't the only thing we encourage you to wear."

Starting in 2002 an ad purporting to be a Nike-created ad circulated on the Internet, showing a Nike shoe at the scene of a bloody terrorist bombing with the caption that read: "You may not survive the blast, but your shoes will." It was not, in fact, a real Nike ad. Other shoe companies have been victims of similar hoaxes, including one in which a fake Puma ad made the Internet rounds, featuring models wearing Pumas engaged in sex.

Advertising sometimes backfires, as the case of a 1999 ad for athletic shoe retailer Just for Feet demonstrates. In the ad, a barefoot African runner is sedated by a group of white men who force Nikes onto his feet while he is unconscious. Widely panned as racist and insensitive, Just for Feet ended up suing the advertising agency and filed for bankruptcy within the year.

See also: Celebrity Endorsements; Dr. Martens; Nike; Shoe Stores

Further Reading Bartel Sheehan, Kim. *Controversies in Contemporary Advertising.* London: Sage, 2003; Jackson, Steven, David L. Andrews. *Sport, Culture and Advertising: Identities, Commodities and the Politics of Representation.* London: Routledge, 2005.Tungate, Mark. *Adland: A Global History of Advertising.* London: Kogan Page Publishers, 2007.

AFRICA

Africa is the second-largest continent in the world and is made up of 53 different countries. While these countries have very different cultural, religious, and linguistic backgrounds, there are some general statements that can be made about feet and footwear in Africa. Because it is made up largely of tropical and desert habitats, the climate tends to be warm-to-hot for most of the year throughout much of the continent. For this reason, **sandals** are the most common foot covering throughout much of Africa.

Made of **leather**, wood, pods, or bark, and often decorated with shells, straw, or beads, sandals provide protection from the ground yet keep the feet cool. Leather is taken from animal skins such as antelope, cattle, goats, and sheep. Untanned leather, or rawhide, is often used for the soles while tanned leather, or rope made from plant fibers, is used to attach the sandal sole to the foot, either as straps or as a toe loop. Sandals are often made out of two or three layers of rawhide forming the sole. The leather is often dyed a variety of colors using local vegetable dyes or **henna** and could be decorated with plant fibers, beads, or other materials. In many African cultures, men are responsible for both leather work and bead work, and would thus make shoes. In areas of Africa that are covered by sand, such as the Sahara desert, the soles are cut extra wide, similar to **snow shoes**, to keep the wearer from sinking into the sand and to protect the feet from the hot sand. Today, it is common for African shoes to be made partly from recycled material like tire treads or plastic liter bottles for the soles as well as the uppers.

Made from an old tire, the footwear of a Massai warrior from northern Tanzania is seen while he talks to the media in London ahead of the London Marathon race on April 11, 2008. The warrior is running in the London Marathon wearing his traditional outfits to raise money for his local community. [AP Photo/Sang Tan]

Closed shoes, made of leather and often decorated with beads, are found throughout Africa as well, but may have only been worn in Sub-Saharan Africa starting in the fifteenth century, thanks to the introduction of closed shoes through international trade. In North Africa, closed shoes and **boots** are much more common than in Sub-Saharan Africa and are more commonly associated with camel-riding cultures. In much

of Northern and Eastern Africa, **Islam** has become the dominant religion and has influenced shoe styles there. For instance, the *babouche*, or flat, open-backed slipper, is commonly worn in Morocco.

Wooden **clogs** arrived in Africa through trade with the **Middle East** and **India**, and elevated clogs were often worn by kings, such as among the Yoruba of Nigeria, in order to elevate them above the commoners. These clogs, also worn by commoners at festive occasions such as weddings, were carved out of beautiful woods like ebony and were highly adorned with silver leaf, silver bells, and beads. Some were elevated on stilts, such as the Japanese *geta*, the Korean *namakshin*, or the Middle Eastern stilted sandal.

Elites in Africa have traditionally worn much more elaborately made and decorated shoes than the masses, with royal family members wearing the most elaborate of all. Because rulers often controlled the distribution and use of decorative beads as well as the mediums of exchange like cowrie shells, it is not surprising that the shoes of the rulers would be elaborately beaded with geometric patterns, images of animals, and with masks, demonstrating the wealth, status, and power of the wearer. For instance, Ashanti royalty wore sandals decorated with gold leaf, and Yoruba royalty wore elaborately beaded boots. As new luxury materials like silk entered Africa, they were largely worn by the elites as well.

Shoes and clothing reflect not only social status, but age, occupation, and gender as well. Some African cultures had **sumptuary laws** that forbade certain classes from wearing certain types of footwear, or wearing footwear at all.

In addition, it was common in some African cultures prior to colonization for commoners to remove their footwear in front of the king or when in the royal palace as a sign of respect, a tradition that was also practiced in **Japan**. After colonialism, shoes became less expensive and more easily available, but it wasn't until the twentieth century that African elites lost their control over footwear and the sumptuary laws were overturned.

Many Africans today wear western shoes as well as clothing. Because of widespread poverty in Africa, a number of organizations devoted to fighting poverty in Africa are based around providing shoes to African children. Shoe4Africa, for instance, is a Kenyan organization that began in 1995 by providing shoes to Kenyan athletes. Tom's Shoes is a California-based shoe manufacturer that has a program called Tom's Shoe Drop in which the company will send a pair of shoes to South Africa or Argentina for every pair bought.

Some African cultures have particular **beliefs** about feet. For example, many African cultures feel that the feet of royalty should never touch the ground. This is the case among the Ashanti of Ghana, among the Edo of Benin, as well as among the Luba of Congo, whose king traditionally sat in a specially designed stool to ensure that his feet stayed off the ground. The Ashanti King also rested his feet on cushions, even when wearing sandals, in order to ensure that they never touched the ground, and servants carried additional pairs of sandals in case one of the king's shoes broke.

Africans hold some of the same beliefs and practices regarding feet and footwear that are found in other cultures. For example, in much of Africa both feet and shoes can have polluting qualities associated with them. It is customary in many parts of Africa to remove one's shoes before entering a home. In addition, showing the soles of one's feet to other people is unacceptable, even though many people go barefoot. Another traditional West African belief is that to prevent a ghost from entering a house, one must leave a pair of shoes at the door.

See also: Bata Shoe Museum; Beliefs; India; Middle East; Sandals

Further Reading Akinwumi, Tunde M. "Interrogating Africa's Past: Footwear Amongst the Yoruba," in Rielle, Georgio and Peter McNeil, eds. *Shoes: A History From Sandals to Sneakers*. London: Berg Publishers, 2006.Hall Strutt, Daphne. *Fashion in South Africa 1652–1900: AnIllustrated History of Styles and Materials for Men, Women and Children, with Notes on Footwear, Hairdressing, Accessories and Jewelery*. Amsterdam: AA Balkema, 1975;

ALASKA

Alaska is an American state that was first visited by European explorers in 1741, and first settled by Russians in 1784 for the purposes of fur trading. The original inhabitants of Alaska, once called Eskimo, constitute 11 different cultural groups, all of which are Athabascan. Today, Alaska has the highest percentage of Native American residents of any American state, with almost 16 percent of the population having indigenous origins. Because much of Alaska is subarctic, the climate is cool to very cold, and the footwear worn reflects the cooler temperatures. As with other cultures around the world, footwear styles reflect the unique cultural identity of the group wearing them and the characteristics of the individual making them.

Footwear, which includes **moccasins**, **boots**, and **snow shoes** (which are attached to moccasins), was traditionally made with tools made of stone, wood, and bone. Moccasins and boots are traditionally made of moose, deer, and caribou hide as well as from waterproof materials like seal skin, and they were often beaded, with women traditionally sewing and men doing much of the beading. Whether short or tall, traditional Alaskan footwear is constructed in the style of other **Native American** groups: from one or two pieces of animal skin, sewn or

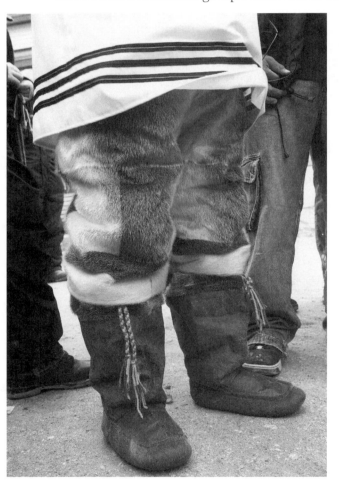

joined together. Winter shoes are lined with fur from sea otter, wolverine, or polar bear, although socks made by women of woven grass would also be worn for extra insulation. While moccasins are soft-soled, boots are generally constructed using a pre-made sole of bearded seal, walrus, or sea lion, which is fitted to the vamp and to the shaft of the boot, often with strips of leather tied around the leg.

Materials used to make shoes and clothing differ depending on local resources (with seals, otters, walruses, and sea lions being more available to coastal groups, for example, and bears or wolves being available to inland groups), but groups that had trade relationships with other tribes could also access materials from those tribes that were unavailable in their own area. Certain skins, like those of bears, are traditionally more highly prized as footwear because of the danger involved in hunting the animal.

Traditional seal skin boots worn in Alaska. [Copyright 2008 Jupiterimages Corporation]

Moccasins and boots worn for ceremonial purposes are typically more highly decorated than those worn for non-ceremonial occasions. Adornment of shoes, like on the rest of the clothing, is not purely decorative but has traditionally been used for magical-religious purposes in order to protect the wearer from harm. Hunters in particular need to have the protection of the spirits; without the spirit's goodwill, the animals could be withheld or the hunter could be put into danger. By decorating one's shoes with the proper images and symbols, one could assure the cooperation of the spirits and of the animals themselves. Even the shoe construction itself was a magical process, as the women who made the shoes imparted their own personal spirits into the shoes.

See also: Arctic Region; Beliefs; Boots; Moccasins; Native Americans; Snow Shoes

Further Reading Oakes, Jill, Rick Riewe. *Alaska Eskimo Footwear*. Anchorage: University of Alaska Press, 2007.

AMERICAN PODIATRIC MEDICAL ASSOCIATION

The American Podiatric Medical Association (APMA) is the professional organization of American podiatrists, with over 10,000 members. The organization acts as both an accrediting organization as well as an educational organization. Through the Council on Podiatric Medical Education, the organization accredits colleges of podiatric medicine and approves residency programs in medical schools. (Podiatrists must attend a podiatric medical school rather than a traditional medical school.) The APMA also provides a seal of acceptance on selected shoes, hosiery, and the like, and a seal of approval on health care products. In addition, it provides information to the public on foot health issues, on finding podiatrists, and on careers in **podiatry**.

The organization provides a public help line, brochures, and a Web site and also is frequently contacted by the press to provide tips on foot care in newspaper and magazine articles, and the APMA's seal of acceptance is used by the public to purchase, for example, the least harmful **flip-flop** brands.

The organization also puts on an annual conference and publishes a peer-reviewed journal, the *Journal of American Podiatric Medical Association*. The APMA also conducts surveys, including a 2008 survey in which 51 percent of women said they are willing to wear cute shoes no matter how much they hurt.

See also: Disorders and Injuries; Podiatry

Further Reading Alexander, Ivy. *Podiatry Sourcebook*. Detroit: Omnigraphics, 2007; Chang, Thomas. *Master Techniques in Podiatric Surgery*. Philadelphia: Lippincott Williams & Wilkins, 2004.

AMPUTATION

Amputation refers to the removal or loss of a limb through trauma or surgery or for purposes of punishment or body modification. Amputation is used to stop the spread of disease or gangrene and to remove a limb that has been crushed beyond repair. Ancient writings, artwork, and skeletal remains show that amputation has been used by medical and sometimes religious specialists for thousands of years. In addition, individuals have sometimes had to amputate their own limbs when a leg or an arm has been trapped, and the horror film *Saw*'s premise is that two men must saw off their own legs in order to escape death.

Prior to the modern era, amputation was the main treatment for leprosy, frost-bite, animal bites, and infectious diseases. Tools used for amputation included knives and saws for cutting, pliers and sometimes a crow bar for removal of the limbs, and hot iron to cauterize the blood vessels and stop the bleeding. In 1693, Philip Verheyen, after having had his leg amputated by a doctor because of infection, dissected the severed limb himself and, based on what he learned, published one of the most widely used anatomy texts of the period, *Corporis Humani Anatomia*. Verheyen also experienced what many contemporary amputees encounter after their surgeries—the sensation of having a "phantom limb," and the phantom pain that often accompanies it, which he described in a series of notes to his amputated leg in the early eighteenth century. Today, amputation techniques used by professionals are much more sophisticated and use a wide range of tools as well as more sophisticated techniques to control bleeding.

Prosthetic devices that replace the missing limb have also grown more sophis-ticated in the last century and have moved from simple pegs of wood strapped to a leg or an arm stump to modern lightweight metal and plastic prostheses that not only replace the missing limb but allow for a wide range of mobility as well.

Today, the most common reason for the amputation of a foot or toes is **diabetes**, which can permanently damage the blood vessels and nerves in the extremities, leading to dangerous infections and damage from being unable to feel one's feet. Once trauma or infection is severe, often the foot must be amputated to save the rest of the leg. Almost two-thirds of all non-accident related foot amputa-tions in the United States are due to diabetes. Other reasons include frostbite, gan-grene, cancer, and blood clots. Today, partial foot amputations are becoming more common and generally involve surgical reconstruction of the remaining foot, as well as a prosthesis to aid walking.

Some people also have what is considered to be a psychiatric disorder called apotemnophilia in which a person has the desire to remove a healthy limb. Many people who have this condition experience a strong drive, which often began in childhood, to have a limb removed, and they know exactly which limb must be removed in order to achieve satisfaction. Men and women with this condition are rarely able to find a doctor who will knowingly remove a healthy limb, although there are a handful of underground doctors who will perform these sur-geries. However, many apotemnophiliacs intentionally damage their limbs enough so that they must be surgically removed in order to save their lives or because the limbs are damaged beyond repair. A great many remove their own limbs, usually a small appendage like a finger or toe, and some convince sympa-thetic friends to do it for them.

Amputation has also been used at times as a form of punishment. For instance, Don Juan de Oñate, the colonizer of New Mexico for Spain in the late sixteenth century, punished the resisting Acoma Indian tribe by killing 800 people, enslav-ing hundreds of women and children, and amputating the left foot of every remaining adult man. In 1998, on the four hundredth anniversary of his arrival in New Mexico, the bronze statue of Oñate located outside of Española,

Man in chair having leg amputated, interior scene with surgeon and assistant, and spectator who has lost his left hand. Woodcut print, illustrated in Feldtbuch der wundtartzney. [Photo courtesy of the National Library of Medicine]

Peg Leg. Carved wooden limbs like this one have been used as prostheses for hundreds of years. [Copyright 2008 Jupiterimages Corporation]

New Mexico, was vandalized with its right foot sawed off. A note was left saying "fair is fair."

See also: Diabetes; Disorders and Injuries; Fetishes; Prosthetics; Torture

Further Reading Cristian, Adrian. *Lower Limb Amputation: A Guide to Living a Quality Life*. New York: Demos Medical Publishing, 2005; May, Bella. *Amputations and Prosthetics: A Case Study Approach*. Philadelphia: F.A. Davis Company, 2002; Veves, Aristidis, ed. *The Diabetic Foot*. New York: Humana Press, 2006.

ANIMAL FEET

Humans are animals, so human feet will share a number of similarities with nonhuman animal feet, especially mammal feet. Looking at animal feet as a whole illustrates both the wide variety of feet in the animal world and the evolutionary relationships between many animals, both human and nonhuman.

Vertebrate animals include both those that live in the water and those that live on land, and the limbs of both types of animals are adapted to living in those very different conditions. Water animals, for example, have fins rather than feet, while the feet and legs of land animals need to bear the weight of a two- or four-legged animal. The feet of most land animals, then, are designed to bear weight as well as to allow for locomotion.

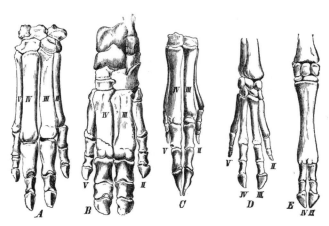

Illustration of five different animal foot skeletons. [Copyright 2008 Jupiterimages Corporation]

The locomotion of animals is obviously constrained by the structure of the feet and legs, among other characteristics. Terrestrial vertebrates, or tetrapods, move using legs and feet, as do insects, while invertebrates and legless vertebrates such as snakes crawl or slither. Finally, a handful of animals roll to get around.

Terrestrial vertebrates generally have four limbs, although in birds and some animals like kangaroos and humans, the forelimbs are not used for ground locomotion; only the hind limbs are used for walking or hopping. In most tetrapods, however, all four limbs are used for walking, leaping, and running.

Tetrapods have one of three types of feet: plantigrade, digitigrade, and unguligrade. Plantigrade animals like humans are relatively flat-footed in that the bottom of the foot bears the weight of the whole body. Digitigrade animals like dogs support their weight on their toes (which are correspondingly longer than in other animals), and unguligrade animals, or ungulates like cows and horses, support their weight on their hooves—literally the nails of their toes.

Most land vertebrates not only have legs and feet intended to hold the animal up and provide for locomotion, but most of those feet, excluding the ungulates, have five digits. In fact, five digits—found in animals as diverse as bipedal humans, quadrupedal squirrels, and swimming dolphins—appear to be the primitive trait in terrestrial vertebrates, while the hooves of ungulates is a derived trait, adapted to particular animals in a particular environment. (Birds, on the other hand, have four digits.) The fact that so many animals retain the five digits (and even ungulates display the five-digit characteristic when they are embryos) illustrates the fact that all of these animals share an ancestor—one with five toes. This is true even when all five digits serve no purpose—as in the fifth claw, or dew claw, of the dog.

Another difference between the feet of land animals has to do with the pads or lack of pads at the bottoms of the feet. Dogs, for example, have pads on the bottoms of their feet, which absorb stresses and protect the feet from damage. Many other animals do not, and some animals, such as water birds, have specialized

webbed toes that allow them to swim. Whether an animal has claws, nails, or hooves at the end of the digits is another difference. Primates are unique in that the claws found in so many other animals were replaced by nails, while the hands and feet grew more sensitive, with finger and toe prints, rather than pads, which allow for a much greater sense of touch as early primates developed grasping hands and feet.

As bipedalism evolved among our pre-human ancestors millions of years ago, the long, flexible toes found among other primates disappeared, replaced by shorter toes that do not grasp, but instead better support the full weight of a bipedal creature.

See also: Foot Structure

Further Reading Mason, George Frederick. *Animal Feet*. New York: William Morrow, 1970.

ARCTIC REGION

The Arctic Region includes the regions and countries that lie north of the Arctic Circle and that surround the North Pole, including Greenland, Iceland, the north-ernmost part of **Alaska**, Siberia, the northern territories of Canada, and a number of islands. Many of the indigenous people who live in this region are called Inuits.

Because of the severity of the temperatures in this region, footwear, like cloth-ing, is made largely of a combination of fur and waterproof skins, such as seal skin. **Moccasins**, **boots**, and **snow shoes** are the three most common foot coverings.

Moccasins are soft-soled shoes that are made with one piece of **leather** forming both the sole and the sides and top of the shoes. Made out of whatever animal skins are available (such as caribou, seal, or bear), they are decorated to reflect individual identity and cultural affiliation and often serve spiritual purposes as well.

Because of the severe cold, boots are worn more commonly than moccasins in the Arctic region. Boots in the northern parts of Greenland and Canada are known as *kamiks* and are made of seal skin and caribou skin, and sometimes dog skin. (Kamik also refers to the process of boot making.) They are always lined with fur for warmth, and **socks** of woven grass or fur are worn as well to insulate the feet and legs. In addi-tion, during extremes in temperature, the Inuit would layer their footwear with socks, an inner booty or slipper, followed by the boot and often an outer slipper as well. Often the leg skins of the animal are used to create the legs of the boot, and sometimes the leg and foot of the animal is used to create a fully seamless boot. Seal skin is pre-ferred in wetter climates while caribou is preferred in drier but colder climates. As in Alaska, bearded seal is a preferred material for the soles of the boots because it is waterproof.

Kamik making is a tradition taught for generations of Inuit by elders to youth and is a way in which important Inuit values are imparted to young people. Women are primarily responsible both for the construction of kamiks and for the preparation of the skins, using traditionally made bone tools and animal sinew as thread. Often fish oil is used to waterproof the kamik.

Decorations on kamiks reflect the individual artistry of the maker and often the status of the wearer as well, such as whether the wearer is male or female and one's specific cultural affiliation. Boots are decorated with embroidery, fur, and dyed sealskin appliqué.

Other indigenous groups living in the Arctic region include the Saami, who live in the northernmost regions of Scandinavia and western Russia, and the many groups who live in northern Siberia. Footwear styles of these groups are similar to those of the Inuits, due to the similar environmental conditions, and include short boots made of reindeer skin for the Saami (with grass worn inside for added warmth), and reindeer and seal skin boots in Siberia, decorated with many of the same techniques found among the Inuit, as well as beads. Like indigenous Alaskan boots, decorations in Siberia are used in part to connect the wearer to the spirit world, and in part to represent cultural affiliation.

Inuit Women's Kamik. Boots like these have been worn for hundreds and perhaps thousands of years by Arctic peoples. [Copyright © 2009 Bata Shoe Museum, Toronto. Photo: Hal Roth]

Snow shoes are also worn in the Arctic region. Snow shoes are constructed out of a large frame made of branches around which animal sinew or hide laces are woven to create a base on which a person walks. An individual attaches the snow shoes to their moccasins, which then allow the wearer to walk on top of snow, keeping the feet dry.

See also: Alaska; Beliefs; Boots; Moccasins; Native America; Snow Shoes

Further Reading King, JCH, Birgit Pauksztat, Robert Storrie. *Arctic Clothing of North America: Alaska, Canada, Greenland.* Montreal: McGill-Queen's University Press, 2005.

ATHLETE'S FOOT

Athlete's foot (or *tinea pedis*) is a fungal infection found on the feet caused by fungi called dermatophytes, which cause the skin to swell. It is related to other fungal infections like jock itch and ringworm. Symptoms include itching, redness, and scaly skin, usually between the toes but often on other parts of the feet as well. The Athlete's Foot is also the name of an **athletic shoe** store.

Athlete's foot is so named because in order for the dermatophytes to thrive, they need a warm, damp environment to live in—an environment that is typically found both within shoes as well as in locker rooms where athletes congregate before or after sports. In addition, walking with **bare feet** is the norm in locker rooms, public showers and pools, and saunas, making it even more likely to pick up or spread the condition. On the other hand, athlete's foot can be picked up from a variety of sources, including shoes, having direct contact with an infected person, and even from companion animals. Preventing athlete's foot involves wearing **sandals** or other foot protection when in public places, especially pools and locker rooms, and washing and drying feet carefully to keep feet clean and to prevent fungus from growing. In addition, wearing natural fiber **socks** and shoes that allow the feet to breathe are both ways to prevent contracting athlete's foot.

Athlete's foot can be diagnosed via testing at any doctor's office and is easily treatable with nonprescription topical anti-fungal medications; if the problem persists, an oral drug can be prescribed instead. Over-the-counter anti-fungal medications are easily available as powders, ointments, or sprays, so most people with mild cases simply treat the condition themselves.

See also: Disorders and Injuries; Foot Odor

Further Reading Copeland, Glenn, Stan Solomon, and Mark Myerson. *The Good Foot Book: A Guide For Men, Women, Children, Athletes, Seniors*. Alameda, CA: Hunter House, 2005; Vonhof, John. *Fixing Your Feet: Prevention And Treatments for Athletes*. Berkeley, CA: Wilderness Press, 2006.

ATHLETIC SHOES

Athletic shoes, sometimes called **sneakers**, tennies, or trainers, are shoes that are especially designed to wear during sports. Today, there are countless choices in athletic shoes, but for the most part shoes are made for the following sports: track and field (running, jumping, and other track and field sports), court sports (basketball, volleyball, tennis), field sports (soccer, football, baseball), winter sports (skating, hockey, skiing), outdoor activities (hiking and other outdoor activities), and specialty sports, which include golf, bowling, and bicycling, among others.

Each of these types of activities involves different movements, different environments, and different levels of stress on the feet. Court sport shoes, for example, are geared towards running back and forth and side to side on a hard surface, as in tennis or basketball, while **jogging shoes** are designed to support the feet while running in a straight line, and field sport shoes are spiked to help the feet gain traction on a grass field as in soccer.

Athletic shoes are made primarily out of breathable fabric and **leather** on the upper, with, most importantly, rubber (or sometimes plastic) soles. Rubber soles are lighter than the leather soles found in most shoes, provide traction and shock absorbency, and are waterproof and durable.

Athletic shoes as we know them today owe their existence to both the development of easy-to-use rubber, as well as the fitness movement that was spreading throughout England and the **United States** during the nineteenth century. The first rubber-soled shoes, called sandshoes or plimsolls, were made in England by the New Liverpool Rubber Company in 1876 (and were worn for croquet) and in the United States in 1892 by Humphrey O'Sullivan, based on technology perfected by Charles Goodyear. The U.S. Rubber Company, formed that same year, was the first company to sell shoes with rubber soles and heels under a number of brands, which in 1916 were consolidated under one name: **Keds**. The first Keds athletic shoe was sold in 1917, and were known as sneakers, because the rubber sole allowed the wearer to sneak up on another person. Another early line of athletic shoes were made by Dunlop Rubber in 1924. These shoes were all easily distinguishable from earlier shoes sold in the West in that until the mid-nineteenth century, shoes were leather-soled and had no differentiation between left and right shoes. The rubber soled shoes, with distinct shoes for right and left feet, were a huge innovation.

Spikes were another early development in athletic shoes that actually predated rubber-soled shoes. In the mid-nineteenth century spiked running shoes were developed by the first sports shoe company in the world, J. W. Foster and Sons (later to become known as **Reebok**) and by the end of the century, the Spalding Company. These shoes were made entirely out of leather, but with metal spikes on the bottom. This technology was taken a step further in 1925 by Adi Dassler, who created running and soccer shoes with spikes that became the foundation of his company, **Adidas**. Other sports popular at the time soon had their own shoes, too. Bicycle shoes with wide heels to grip the pedal were first introduced in the 1860s, for example.

Baseball is one of the oldest of the modern team sports, dating back to the mid-nineteenth century. The earliest baseball shoes were high tops made of canvas or leather, but were not specially made for the sport. Spalding made a kangaroo leather baseball shoe at the turn of the century, and kangaroo would remain a popular material for baseball shoes for the next few decades. During the twentieth century, spikes were added to baseball shoes, but they were outlawed in 1976, and replaced by plastic cleats in the 1980s.

Chuck Taylor All Stars were originally made for basketball

Athletic shoes are worn for a variety of sports as well as for leisure. These shoes are designed for walking. [Copyright 2008 Jupiterimages Corporation]

and were first released in the 1930s by **Converse**. Made of canvas with high tops to support the ankles, the style has changed very little over the past 80 years, although most basketball shoes today are made of leather rather than canvas, and soles are more cushioned than in the early years. The 1930s also saw the first formal tennis shoes, made by Adi Dassler in 1931.

Football shoes (or cleats), on the other hand, were not developed until 1948 by Puma—prior to that, football players wore leather boots with cleats—while modern soccer shoes weren't developed until the 1950s. European soccer teams originally wore leather boots (with cleats inserted) due to the cold weather in much of **Europe** while South American teams wore sandal-shoes. It wasn't until 1954 that the German national soccer team wore newer, lower shoes designed by Adi Dassler of Adidas, but it wasn't until the development of plastic shoes that the modern soccer shoe really developed.

The modern age of athletic shoes really began with **Nike**. Founded in 1964 by a former University of Oregon runner and track and field coach, Phil Knight and Bill Bowerman wanted to create a better running shoe, which they accomplished via innovations like rubber waffle soles, breathable nylon uppers, and cushioning in both the mid-sole and the heel.

Starting in the 1970s, athletic footwear developers started to draw on the expertise of podiatrists, who provided insight into the anatomy of the foot and how feet react to various stressors such as running, jumping, and side-to-side movement. Again, Nike led the way, beginning in the 1970s, developing new technologies like foam, air and gel cushioning in the heels, which allowed for much greater shock absorbency when running. Prior to this time, most people who wore athletic shoes still wore Keds and Converse shoes, neither of which was designed with support and shock absorbency in mind. Shoe developers began to take into account factors like pronation, supination, different foot widths, and motion control when designing new shoes. Women's athletic shoes are now designed with an eye towards the different physiological needs of men and women (as well as different aesthetic demands). Podiatrists developed technologies like arch supports and heel cradles, both of which were later incorporated into athletic shoes, beginning in the 1970s.

Nike and other major shoe companies like Adidas also began developing different types of shoes geared towards different types of sports. Even for runners, there is a wide variety of shoes now available, including those that emphasize cushioning, very lightweight shoes for short distance sprints, shoes which control for pronation and supination (i.e. motion control shoes), those that emphasize stability, and shoes for trail runners who run off-road. Highly specialized athletic shoes like cheerleader shoes, wrestling shoes, and aerobics shoes are now available as well as cross-trainers, which are designed and marketed to appeal to athletes who train in a variety of sports.

Nike was a leader in the athletic shoe industry in other ways as well, for it was Nike who first popularized the notion that athletic shoes can be worn for nonathletic purposes, leading to a surge in the 1980s of athletic shoe purchases and a new fashion trend in the United States, and then around the world. Athletic shoes have moved from being primarily about athletics to being about lifestyle. Nike also led the industry in terms of outsourcing its shoe production to third-world countries in order to cut costs. Today, no athletic shoes are made in the United States; instead, athletic shoes are now made in low-cost factories around the world, primarily in Asia.

Nike's shoes have also long been an important sign of social status, especially among youth, who overwhelmingly buy shoes endorsed by major athletes like the Air Jordan. Nike has also been an industry leader in terms of getting athletes to wear their brand, both while performing as well as outside of the athletic arena. Again, this has been about lifestyle—by encouraging consumers to buy products branded with names like **Michael Jordan** or Tiger Woods, consumers are picking a lifestyle that they want to be identified with rather than an athlete or even a sport, as most athletic shoe consumers do not wear the shoes for athletic purposes in the first place.

Nike's **advertising** has been instrumental in the change in status and popularity of the athletic shoe in American culture. By emphasizing the technological innovations of its shoes, the importance of fitness, and by promoting the idea that athletic shoes are a critical aspect of one's lifestyle and image, Nike has moved its shoes, and athletic shoes in general, into a prominent place in American culture. (Ironically, even though athletic shoe advertising emphasizes the technical innovations, such as the air cushioning systems, most people have no use for such features.)

Another thing that has changed in the athletic shoe industry and that has also been driven by advertising is the way new shoe models are introduced. Prior to the 1970s and 1980s, American shoe companies like Converse did not introduce new shoes very often, and the iconic Converse brand has looked much the same for decades. Today, shoes are produced the way that fashion is, with new models produced seasonally, encouraging consumers to clamor for new models. Aggressive marketing drives demand and thus sales.

Since the 1950s, athletic shoes have also been an important part of popular culture, with music, sports, and Hollywood icons starting new trends in footwear. Kurt Cobain's devotion to Converse One Stars (and his death in 1994 wearing a pair) propelled the brand to greater popularity among young fans of the grunge scene, and even led to a special "Converse Chuck Taylor Kurt Cobain" sneaker in 2008. Jeff Spicoli wore **Vans** slip-ons in 1981's *Fast Times at Ridgemont High*, creating a new trend among surfers, skateboarders, and those who wanted to emulate those lifestyles. Johnny Ramone of the Ramones famously wore Vans, All Stars were worn by the cast of *West Side Story*, James Dean wore Converse, Baby wore Keds in *Dirty Dancing*, rappers Run-DMC wrote a song called "My Adidas," and in 2008, while still the Democratic presidential nominee, Barack Obama had two pairs of sneakers inspired by him, one with his catch phrases "change" and "yes we can" emblazoned on them, and a second, with his photo and the caption, "a black man runs and a nation is behind him," molded onto the sole.

Ironically, while today we associate athletic excellence with athletic shoes, there have been some athletes in the modern era who have chosen to forego shoes altogether. Zola Budd was a long distance runner in the 1980s who ran **barefoot**, and Ethiopian Abebe Bikila won the 1960 Olympic marathon while barefoot—the first African to ever win a gold medal in the Olympic games.

Today, the athletic shoe industry is a $13 billion industry with 350 million pairs of shoes sold each year in the United States alone. Athletic shoes are sold in many more venues than nonathletic shoes, including sporting goods stores, specialty athletic shoe stores like Athlete's Foot and Foot Locker, as well as department stores, shoe stores, and, today, over the Internet.

Nicknames for athletic shoes include sneaker, trainer, basement, takkies, bubblegums or jumps (no name sneakers), daps, felony shoes, fishheads, go fasters, gutties, keds, kicks, plimsoll, runners, shoeclacks, sneaks, tennies, tennie-runners, trainers, and treads.

See also: Adidas; Celebrity Endorsements; Converse; Keds; Nike; Reebok; Sneakers; Shoe Stores; Vans

Further Reading Garcia, Bobbito. *Where'd You Get Those?: New York City's Sneaker Culture: 1960–1987*. New York: Testify Books, 2003; Gill, Alison. "Limousines for the Feet: The Rhetoric of Trainers," in Rielle, Georgio and Peter McNeil, eds. *Shoes: A History From Sandals to Sneakers*. London: Berg Publishers, 2006; Papson, Stephen, Robert Goldman. *Nike Culture: The Sign of the Swoosh*. London: Sage Publications, 1998; Vanderbilt, Tom. *The Sneaker Book: Anatomy of an Industry and an Icon*. New York: The New Press, 1998.

AUSTRALOPITHECUS FOOTPRINTS

Australopithecus is the genus name for hominids (or ancestral humans) who lived from about 4 million to about 2 million years ago in **Africa**. The fossils found of *Australopithecus* demonstrate that these creatures were the first truly bipedal species, in other words, the first primates that walk on two feet. Evidence of bipedality can be detected in the skull, the pelvis, the spine, the femur, the knee, and the feet.

The feet of nonhuman primates evolved with the same grasping capabilities of primate hands, so the bones are very long and the toes are grasping, with an opposable big toe. In addition, there is no arch. Human feet, on the other hand, have shorter toes, and the big toe is in line with the rest of the toes. Human toes cannot grasp, and human feet have an arch to help support the weight of the human body and to absorb the stresses associated with bipedal locomotion. All of these characteristics have been found in the fossils of some of our earliest ancestors, demonstrating when bipedalism first arose in the hominid line.

Anthropologists have identified at least six species of Australopithecines—the gracile or slender Australopithecines (*anamensis, afarensis, africanus* and *garhi*) and the robust Australopithecines (*robustus* and *boisei*), who are thought by some to belong to the genus *Paranthropus*, and who probably are not ancestral to modern humans. The gracile species lived from about 4 million to about 2.5 million years ago, while the robust species lived from about 2.5 million to about 1.5 million years ago.

Besides the fossil evidence, anthropologists Mary Leakey, Tim White, and Richard Hay made another important discovery in 1978 in Tanzania at a site called Laetoli. There, in preserved volcanic ash, they found an 80 foot long trail of footprints of two hominid ancestors, most likely of the species *Australopithecus afarensis*, dated to about 3.6 million years ago. The footprints have been identified as those of perhaps three individuals, with one of the individuals walking in the footprints of the other.

The footprints demonstrate clearly that their owners were bipedal given the position of the big toe parallel to the other toes, the relatively short toes (in comparison to existing nonhuman primates, but still longer than those of modern humans), the weight-bearing heel strike, and the presence of an arch. Analysis of the footprints also demonstrate the classic human gait in which the heel hits the ground first and the toe is used to push off for the next stride.

Since the original discovery of the footprints, other anthropologists have challenged a few of the claims made by Leakey and her team, such as whether *Australopithecus afarensis* had an arch or not. Others have challenged one of the earliest assumptions about the creatures who left the footprints: that they were a nuclear family unit walking to a watering hole, with the mother carrying an infant on her hip. Today, many scholars believe that the individuals were perhaps all walking at different times, interrupting the neat characterization found in many media accounts of the discovery that the footprints represented "the first family."

Since the Laetoli prints were discovered in 1978, another set of hominid footprints were discovered, in Johannesburg, South Africa. These are dated to 117,000 years ago and are the oldest known footprints found from anatomically modern humans.

See also: Animal Feet; Foot Structure

Further Reading Amato, Joseph Anthony. *On Foot: A History of Walking*. New York: NYU Press, 2004; Bowman-Kruhm, Mary. *The Leakeys: A Biography*. Westport, CT: Greenwood Publishing Group, 2005; Meldrum, D. Jeffrey, Charles Hilton, "From biped to strider: the emergence of modern human walking, running, and resource transport." American Association of Physical Anthropologists Meeting. Birkhäuser, 2004

BALLET SHOES

Ballet is one of the oldest European dance forms, dating back to the fifteenth century in Italy as *balletto*, performed originally by men. Balletto was introduced to France in the seventeenth century by Catherine de Medici, where it became a popular form of entertainment known as ballet in the French royal court, with the first formal school for ballet created in Paris by Louis XIV in 1661. Today, ballet is performed for audiences by ballet companies around the world. *Ballet Shoes* is also the name of a 2007 made-for-TV movie.

One of the unique features of ballet involves the highly formalized technique that takes years for dancers to master. Dance technique is based on the dancer's control of the body and utilizes five basic foot positions, all involving what is known as "turn out," in which the feet are positioned with heels together, feet forming a straight line, and the legs rotated outward from the hips. (Apparently, this position derived from a pose popularized by King Louis XIV, who often stood with his legs turned out to show off his shoes.) These positions form the basis of a large number of highly technical movements and poses, such as plié, arabesque, and pirouette. The feet are an especially critical component of ballet, especially for women, who often dance on the tips of their toes, which is known as *en pointe*.

In the earliest days of ballet in Italy and France, dancers, who were originally male, wore the shoes popular at the time while performing, which were heeled shoes. King Louis XIV himself danced in his high-heeled shoes with big buckles. It wasn't until the early eighteenth century, when women were allowed to dance, that dancers first began to perform in shoes without heels. Marie Camargo of the Paris Opera Ballet, like other female dancers of the period, began to add turns and leaps to her performances, and thus developed new costuming styles to conform to the new dance moves, including shorter skirts and flat leather slippers tied to the feet with ribbons, which became the iconic ballet slipper. By the late eighteenth century, after the French Revolution, aristocratic fashion began to change and noble women adopted the flat **slipper** as a form of fashionable footwear for balls and formal occasions, replacing the heeled shoes even for the wealthy. Today, male ballet dancers wear either flat leather slippers, or sometimes soft leather boots.

Pointe dancing was first popularized by Italian dancer Marie Taglione in 1832 in a dance called *La Sylphide*. She modified her ballet slippers by creating a reinforced toe. Because of the unique demands of dancing on the tips of one's toes, specialized pointe shoes are now worn by female ballet dancers who dance on pointe. Pointe shoes are made with a **leather**, cardboard, or plastic shank that

These pointe shoes will take a great deal of abuse during the few hours of their wear. [Copyright 2008 Jupiterimages Corporation]

supports the arch of the foot, and the box, or toe, is formed with alternating layers of cloth, paper, and paste that are molded into a flat platform. The shoe is covered with satin, with two suede sole patches for the bottom of the shoes. (They also come with two satin ribbons, which the dancer must sew onto her shoes.) After the dancer first wears the shoes, the heat of her foot combined with her sweat warms the box and helps the shoe to mold to her foot. In addition to dancing in the shoes, dancers break them in by pounding them against a hard object. Because of what they allow a dancer to do with her feet and body, pointe shoes have truly revolutionized ballet.

While pointe dancing developed during the early nineteenth century, it wasn't until the turn of the century that true pointe shoes were first developed. It was Italian shoe designers who began experimenting with shoes made of harder materials to provide better support for a ballerina's feet, but the modern pointe shoe is said to have started with Russian dancer Anna Pavlova's attempts to reinforce her own shoes to better support pointe work. Italian-American shoemaker Salvatore Capezio developed a specialty in pointe shoes, selling them to dancers around the world. Capezio's shoes were stiffer, with reinforced boxes and wider toes to provide dancers with better support. Capezio today makes dance wear and dance shoes for dancers around the world. Another early shoemaker was Jacob Bloch, a Russian immigrant to the United States who sold shoes to many Russian dancers and companies and whose company now rivals Capezio for control of the dance wear market.

Professional dancers must replace their pointe shoes after only hours of dancing because the shank and box will wear down, so dancers often order their shoes in bulk, favoring one particular designer and model. Pointe shoes retail for about $40–$120 per pair.

While many dancers still wear pointe shoes made in the traditional way, in the 1990s a new company, Gaynor Minden, developed a patent for a new method of forming the shank and box with elastomers rather than paper and paste. Elastomers are elastic polymers that, when used in pointe shoes, will not break like traditional shanks, nor will they soften like traditional boxes. According to the company, this makes the shoes last many times longer than traditional pointe shoes, and the shoes don't require a lengthy breaking-in period. Further, Gaynor Minden shoes are said to cut down injuries, and have the **American Podiatric Medical Association**'s Seal of Acceptance.

Dancing on pointe is challenging and hard on a dancer's feet. Because of this, dancers experience a number of injuries and conditions related to pointe dancing, including **blisters, bunions, calluses and corns**, thickened and bruised toenails, plantar fasciitis, **neuromas**, and **hammer toe**. More serious injuries are stress fractures to the feet. Having proper training and a properly fitted pointe shoe can cut down on these injuries.

Today in the Bondage Discipline Domination Submission (BDSM) and fetish community, a popular footwear choice is the ballet **boot**, a high-heeled (usually 7 inches) lace-up boot that is modeled on the pointe shoe, although without the reinforcement of the box. Wearing a ballet boot forces the foot to be *en pointe*, although

Day in the Life of a Ballerina's Foot

Since the mid-nineteenth century, dancing on the tips of one's toes, or *en pointe*, is an important part of classical ballet technique for female dancers. Pointe dancers wear specialized pointe shoes made with a stiff shank to support the arch of the foot and a reinforced toe box made of layers of cloth, paper, and paste. Dancing *en pointe* is challenging and hard on a dancer's feet, and dancers do not begin to train for pointe dancing until they are at least 11 years of age and their bones have hardened, to prevent foot injuries and deformities. Still, pointe dancers experience a number of injuries and conditions, including calluses, corns, bunions, blisters, bruises, cuts, injured toenails, plantar fasciitis, neuromas, hammer toe, heel spurs, tendinitis, and stress fractures. A classically trained pointe dancer typically trains for about six hours per day, including classes and rehearsals, and only begins to dance *en pointe* after at least six months of strenuous pointe training (which would follow years of classical training). A typical dance day will start with a warm up class that includes strengthening exercises at the barre, running through the positions, and running through the steps involving pointe work. The dancer will also go through a pair of pointe shoes after just hours of dancing, which means that much of a dancer's time involves purchasing, being fitted for, and breaking in new shoes, which could involve pounding them against a hard object, wetting them, and even cutting the shank. Dancers must also sew the ribbons on their shoes themselves. Before dancing, many dancers wrap their toes with sports tape and insert fabric, paper towels, or gel into the toebox to pad the toes. Dancers trim their toenails before every dance class and performance, but they do not trim the dead skin and calluses from their feet as they provide an additional layer of shock absorbency. If a dancer has a performance that evening, there will be another warm up prior to the performance. After dancing, dancers will rub dressing on their feet or ice their feet to help relieve the pain and treat their blisters, and many will take painkillers after performances. Dancers who work in professional companies will often have access to company doctors and masseuses who treat their feet on a regular basis.

it is partially supported by the stiletto heel. Many foot fetishists find this pose erotic, especially given the limited mobility it confers upon the wearer.

See also: Boots; Dance Shoes; Disorders and Injuries; Europe; Fetishes; Slippers

Further Reading Barringer, Janice, Sarah Schlesinger. *The Pointe Book: Shoes, Training & Technique*. Princeton, NJ: Princeton Book Company, 2004; Kassing, Gayle. *History of Dance: An Interactive Arts Approach*. Champaign, IL: Human Kinetics, 2007; Reyna, Ferdinando. *A Concise History of Ballet*. New York: Grosset & Dunlap, 1965.

BARE FEET

Bare feet are associated with a host of symbolic associations worldwide, and can represent sexuality, poverty, or humility. Bare feet are unclothed. As such, in societies in which footwear is customarily worn, they are often seen as erotic or shameful. For example, it was indecent to show bare feet in **China**, in Medieval and Renaissance **Europe**, and in Victorian Europe and America, either in person or in art. Perhaps for this reason, bare feet—seeing them, fondling them, kissing them—became erotic for many people in those same cultures. Even after it was no longer taboo to show feet in public, bare or even partially clad feet remain erotic to many. For instance, high-heeled, open-toed **sandals** reveal what is called "toe cleavage," the cracks between the toes, which many find sexually appealing, while open-backed mules are also erotically charged to many people.

In societies in which shoes are worn by many or most people, going barefoot is generally a sign of very low status. Slaves in ancient **Rome**, for example, went barefoot, as did the poor, while Roman citizens would never be seen outdoors unshod. Bare feet were also associated with poverty during the Middle Ages in Europe, and slaves in the New World often went barefoot as well. For those people who could afford shoes, often they could only afford one pair, and once that pair was worn out they went barefoot until they could afford another pair.

In art in cultures around the world, showing a person without shoes often indicates poverty, but it could also indicate another form of lesser status. Roman women, for instance, were often shown barefoot next to Roman citizens in shoes as a way of indicating their lack of freedom and mobility. The American term "barefoot and pregnant in the kitchen" is now used to point to women's traditional lack of opportunity as homemakers.

Ironically, while women who are barefoot are denied the opportunities of work and travel and self-expression, a woman who covets shoes has often been seen as a woman whose priorities are grounded in vain or selfish pursuits. For example, Saint Clement, an early Christian philosopher, noted women's love of sandals ornamented with gold and instead encouraged Christians to wear only shoes that are "in accordance with nature." On the other hand, Clement did not encourage women to go barefoot as that would be unsuitable; instead, women were to wear white shoes, while for men, going barefoot was encouraged as a sign of simplicity.

Artistic representations of bare feet may also represent innocence or childhood, which could be one reason why bare feet since the 1960s in the West has been associated with hippies. Going barefoot is also used by ascetics and other mystics, either because they've taken a vow of poverty or as a sign of humility. For instance, it is customary for Jews and some Christians to go barefoot when mourning, and pilgrims of all religions often embark on their pilgrimage in bare feet.

Foot washing is also associated with humility in **Christianity**. In the New Testament, Jesus washed the feet of his disciples as a way to serve them during the Last Supper. At the time that Jesus lived, servants would have washed their masters' feet, so Jesus's decision to wash the apostles' feet was a way of teaching humility. For Christians who practice this today, it is intended to bring them closer to Jesus and to fill them with a sense of humility and service, concepts that should hopefully be reinforced through other aspects of service to community.

Additionally, kissing the bare feet of a guru is a sign of love and respect in India, while in the Christian tradition the faithful kiss the (shod) feet of the Pope. Respect and humility are also demonstrated by the custom of walking barefoot around and near the monument of Gandhi in India. Removing one's shoes in the presence of a person of higher status is another way of showing humility and respect and demonstrating one's subordinate status. This was common in **Japan** during the Imperial period as well as in precolonial Africa.

Because shoes are in contact with the ground, they are considered impure in many cultures, which explains the norm of removing one's shoes before entering a home or sometimes a public or sacred space, as for Buddhists and Hindus. The Old Testament recounts that God told both Moses and Joshua to remove their shoes when on holy ground, demonstrating a Jewish proscription against shoes in sacred places as well. This proscription was practiced by ancient Greeks and Romans as well as by Incas and even the ancient Druids. Removing one's shoes and going barefoot in a place of God can also be seen as a sign of humility and is linked to the practice of removing one's shoes before a social superior.

Firewalking

Firewalking refers to walking barefoot over hot coals. It has been practiced in rites of passage in many cultures and as a test of an initiate's strength and courage. It has also been practiced by religious ascetics as a form of self-mortification and as a way of testing one's faith—if the walker is not burned, then God is with him. (And generally, the participant is not burned at all.) Today, firewalking, in which individuals walk barefoot over coals ranging from 800 to 1,500 degrees Fahrenheit, is used in motivational and self-help workshops, and some corporations have their employees walk on fire during team-building seminars to build confidence and community. Firewalking's power comes from the belief that to walk on hot coals implies the aid of a supernatural force, strong faith, or an individual's ability to focus their "mind over matter." However, physicists and others have since debunked the idea that to walk on coals demonstrates anything supernatural at all. Most scientists now feel that the reason that one is not burned when walking on coals has to do with the short amount of time that the foot is in contact with the hot coals (standing on coals would certainly result in a burn, while a brisk walk involves foot-coal contact of less than a second at a time), the fact that coal is not a very good conductor of heat, and the fact that the moisture on the bottom of the feet keeps the foot from burning.

In addition, feet touch the ground as well, so removing the shoes prior to entering the temple is symbolic of removing one's feet. That's why foot washing is practiced prior to entering a place of worship for Muslims and why Muslims wash their feet before prayers. But the norm of removing shoes before entering a home or temple is not about bare feet per se; in fact, in Japan, homeowners will provide sandals or slippers for the guest to wear while visiting them, and most Japanese wear special socks while unshod in their own homes. Feet, then, can either be pure or impure while shoes are more often the polluting agent.

Some athletes run or hike in bare feet, bucking the trend of wearing specialized athletic shoes while engaged in sport. For example, Zola Budd was a long distance runner in the 1980s who ran barefoot, and Ethiopian Abebe Bikila won the 1960 Olympic marathon while barefoot. Today, some westerners hike in bare feet.

See also: Beliefs; Christianity; Foot Washing; India; Islam; Judaism

Further Reading Frazine, Richard Keith. *The Barefoot Hiker: A Book About Bare Feet*. Berkeley: Ten Speed Press, 1993.

BATA SHOE MUSEUM

The Bata Shoe Museum is the largest shoe museum in the world, with holdings of approximately 13,000 shoes as well as a variety of shoe-related artifacts and images. It is located in Toronto, Canada, and was founded in 1995 by Sonja Bata, of the Bata Shoe Organization, an international shoe manufacturer.

The Bata Shoe Organization was founded in 1892 as the T. & A. Bata Shoe Company in the former Austria-Hungary Empire, which was then a world leader in mechanized shoe production. By the 1930s, Bata was the world's largest shoe distributor, with factories throughout **Europe**, America, and **India**. After Bata locations in Eastern bloc countries were nationalized in 1945, the company relocated to Canada.

Since the 1940s, Mrs. Bata, whose father-in-law founded the Bata Shoe Organization, had been collecting shoes and researching shoe history and culture. This led to her endowment in 1979 of the Bata Shoe Museum Foundation, which funds research into footwear and which supports the Bata Shoe Museum. Designed by architect Raymond Moriyama to resemble a shoe box, the museum houses a permanent collection of shoes and footwear-related items going back more than 4,000 years and hosts temporary exhibitions on subjects like **ballet shoes** or Native American footwear. The museum's mission is to "contribute to the knowledge and understanding of the role of footwear in the social and cultural life of humanity."

The museum's permanent collection is broken into cultural areas and includes historical and contemporary artifacts from **Africa**, **China**, **India**, **Japan**, **Korea**, Latin America, the **Middle East**, Native North America, and the Circumpolar region, as well as two exhibits covering Euro-America, including the Walk of Fame, featuring celebrity footwear. The flagship exhibit is called "All About Shoes: Footwear through the Ages," and covers 4,500 years of shoe history. Because the museum is located in Canada, the greatest collection of footwear comes from the Arctic Region and from Native North America.

The Bata Shoe Museum is the only place in the world where the history, anthropology, or fashion buff can find in one place lotus shoes used on the bound feet of Chinese women, ancient Egyptian **sandals**, Elton John's platform **boots**, and the moon boots worn by astronauts during space travel. The museum high-

> "Footwear tells the whole human story, it's all there, from the animal hides that pre-historic cave dwellers wrapped around their feet to the high-tech boots worn by astronauts."
>
> SONJA BATA, FOUNDER OF BATA SHOE MUSEUM

lights the social and cultural aspects of footwear, framing the shoes within the context of the cultures in which they were found and the beliefs associated with them. It also aims to counteract the trend of western shoe styles replacing indigenous shoes around the world by having **shoemakers** from around the world participate in the museum's exhibits, demonstrating traditional shoe techniques to the public. (Critics have noted the irony that the company largely responsible for replacing indigenous shoes with mass produced shoes also operates the largest shoe museum in the world devoted to the collection and understanding of native forms of footwear.)

The museum gets its shoes from donations from other collectors, through field work when researchers study the techniques of traditional shoemaking, from auctions, and through dealers. Old and distressed shoes are not restored by the museum staff; instead, they are carefully treated in order to preserve them in their present condition and to prevent any further damage.

In 2006, the museum was the victim of a theft, namely of a pair of $160,000 Indian jewel-encrusted mojari **slippers** as well as a gold toe ring and a gold ankle bracelet. The museum ultimately recovered the items.

The museum's motto, provided by Canadian author Robertson Davies, is *Per Saecula Gradatim*, Latin for "One Step at a Time."

See also: Africa; Beliefs; China; Concealment Shoes; India; Japan; Korea; Middle East; Native America

Further Reading Bata, Thomas John, Sonja Sinclair. *Bata Shoemaker to the World*. Toronto: Stoddard, 1990; Benstock, Shari, Suzanne Ferriss. *Footnotes: On Shoes*. New Brunswick, NJ: Rutgers University Press, 2001.

BELIEFS

Both feet and footwear are the subject of a wide variety of beliefs around the world. Shoes, for example, can be lucky and unlucky, dirty and erotic, and represent contracts and marriage. They are also, in most cultures, intimately connected to the wearer.

Religious and cultural beliefs about feet often revolve around the idea of purity and impurity. In many cultural traditions, shoes must be removed before entering a home, and some religions, such as Hinduism, require that shoes be removed before entering a temple or place of worship. For the Japanese, this has to do with practical issues like keeping dirt out of the home and protecting the delicate straw floor mats. In addition, removing one's shoes symbolizes removing one's worries and troubles.

In Hindu tradition, not only are shoes removed before entering a temple (Muslims share this practice, as do the Japanese), but when sitting, one's feet should never point towards another person. For Hindus as well as Muslims, feet are considered unholy, which is why a great insult would be to throw one's shoes at someone else. In addition, feet should never be used to touch people or books or other important objects. Feet touch the ground, which is unclean, and removing the shoes prior to entering the temple is symbolic of removing one's feet. On the other hand, the feet of gurus and the gods are holy, and one practice in **India** is to sprinkle water that has bathed a guru's feet on one's head.

Going unshod is often mandated in a number of religious contexts. Not only is it required to take off one's shoes before entering a Hindu, Buddhist, or Muslim temple (and Muslims remove their shoes before prayer in any context), but many religions require **bare feet** for pilgrims. Ascetics from a number of traditions wear no shoes as well. Removing one's shoes before entering a holy place, or engaging in a holy practice, is both a sign of respect and humility, and for ascetics, it can be a form of mortification as well. (This might be connected to the idea that removing shoes is also a sign of grief and mourning in many cultures.) These traditions date back to ancient times: entering a temple or conducting a ritual in shoes would have been unheard of among the ancient Hebrews, Greeks, Romans or Egyptians. On the other hand, sometimes special **sandals** that were not otherwise worn on regular ground could be worn in a temple. This practice was done both to prevent the dirt or other detritus of the profane world from contacting the sacred space and to prevent the holiness from being carried away on the soles of the shoes.

The notion that feet are dirty or impure is found in a number of religions and cultural traditions. In much of **Africa**, the **Middle East**, and parts of Asia, including **Korea** and Thailand, showing the soles of one's feet to others is not acceptable, and most cultures discourage the touching of one's feet to another person's body—especially the head.

Foot washing is a tradition found in many religions. Followers of **Islam** traditionally wash their feet (a practice called *wudhu*) before praying (as well as their hands, hair, and face). Feet must be washed three times. The reason for wudhu is that without purifying one's body, one's mind cannot be purified. In Buddhism, water for foot washing is one of the eight offerings traditionally made to Buddha, which allows the believer to purify one's negative karma and achieve the body of a Buddha.

In **Christianity**, on the other hand, foot washing has a slightly different meaning. The New Testament tells us that Jesus washed his disciples' feet as a way to serve them during the Last Supper. At the time that Jesus lived, servants would have washed their masters' feet, so Jesus's decision to wash the apostles' feet was a way of teaching humility. In addition, feet in the Christian tradition often symbolize walking the spiritual path, so feet washing (using water, which often symbolizes the word of God, as well as cleansing away false beliefs) can also be construed as Jesus's message to his disciples to continue on the path of righteousness after his death.

Beliefs surrounding shoes, on the other hand, often have to do with luck, perhaps because for much of history only the wealthy were able to wear shoes. Shoes can be lucky via the following: spitting in the right shoe; placing a penny or silver coin in the left shoe; placing dried mint in each shoe; wearing holes in the bottoms of the shoes; wearing salt or pepper in one's shoes; or burning an old shoe. Putting a hole in the shoe is often intended to release evil spirits, as in the Native American tradition. At other times, shoes do not bring luck in and of themselves, but can be embroidered with patterns that are lucky, as in **China**.

Animal feet, too, can bring luck. In the **United States** and China, rabbits are a sign of good luck, perhaps because they are so fertile. (Another theory holds that rabbits are considered good luck because if you catch one in a trap, it is a sure sign that other small game are also in the area.) According to this theory, the rabbit's foot (i.e., the part that generally got caught in the trap) was seen as especially lucky. The tradition of carrying a rabbit's foot dates as far back as the sixth century B.C.E. Hares' feet were thought to provide good crops, many children, and prosperity. An African-American belief is that a left rear foot that was removed from a rabbit killed during a full moon by a cross-eyed person and then carried in the left pocket was considered most lucky. The Welsh also believed that rubbing a rabbit's foot all over a newborn ensured the child's fortune.

Horseshoes, too, are historically thought to bring luck, with the most common belief being that if a horseshoe is nailed to a wall with the ends pointing upward, good luck will come to the owner of the dwelling. Conversely, if the horseshoe is hung with the ends pointing downward, luck will drain from the shoe, bringing bad luck. On the other hand, other cultures have reversed this set of beliefs and hold that the ends pointing downward bring luck onto the person. These theories may derive from ancient European beliefs about demons, witches, and fairies, and the horseshoe's ability to keep them out. Iron, for example, was known to ward off fairies and evil in general. Another explanation for the horseshoe's luck is that horseshoes are made by blacksmiths, who were once thought to have magical abilities because of their use of fire. (One explanation for the luck of the horseshoe has Saint Dunstan, a tenth century blacksmith who later became the Archbishop of Canterbury, being approached by a man with cloven feet—the devil—who requested horseshoes to protect his hooves. Dunstan caused the devil so much pain while nailing the shoes to his feet that he made him promise to never enter a house with a horseshoe hanging over the door.) In addition, the crescent shape of the horseshoe is common in amulets and magical symbols used by people who worshipped goddesses, and horseshoes often had seven nails in them, with seven being a lucky number to many people. Finally, like the rabbit, the horse has magical and religious associations in a number of cultures, such as among the ancient Celts, Teutons, and Slavs, all of whom worshipped horses. Horses play a part in the beliefs and mythologies of Buddhism and Hinduism as well.

Shoes can also be very unlucky: tying the laces together and hanging the shoes on a nail; putting one's left shoe on first; wearing someone's old shoes; tripping over a boot; getting a gift of shoes from a lover; putting stockings in one's shoes before bed; placing one's shoes higher than one's head; wearing one shoe at a time; borrowing someone's shoes; leaving shoes on a table; or wearing a broken shoelace—all of these practices will bring the wearer bad luck. Giving shoes for Christmas brings bad luck, but an English belief states that if you don't give shoes to the poor, that is also bad luck. Putting shoes on the wrong feet can kill one's parents in both **Japan** and Europe, and in Korea it is customary that on the first night of the New Year, people hide their shoes to keep ghosts from taking them, which brings bad luck for the year.

The shoes of the dead are generally thought to be unlucky, although there are a number of superstitions that conflict with this idea. Burning old shoes is often a way to get rid of dead spirits as well as to ward off witchcraft. Shoes and death are linked in other beliefs as well, such as in the tradition of burying a person with a pair of shoes, often new, so that the deceased will have comfortable shoes to wear in the afterlife. In ancient **China**, for example, "longevity shoes" were shoes embroidered with a lotus flower and ladder, that were worn by the deceased and would carry them through to the afterlife. Dead emperors wore jade shoes, and upon death the rest of the emperor's shoes were burned. Also in China, banging shoes against a door is a way to get a wandering soul to come back. Because of these beliefs, shoes often came to symbolize death itself. On the other hand, in many cultures, including the United States and Europe, it was common to leave one's shoes at death to one's children, since shoes were prohibitively expensive for the poor. This practice was not seen to be bad luck and, in fact, it is where the phrase "following in your father's footsteps" comes from.

Shoes can also aid in divination, allowing one to see a ghost, the identity of a future husband, the identity of a murderer, or the direction one is intended to travel, and spitting in one's *zoris* in Japan is a way to call the spirits of the dead. In other cultures, on the other hand, shoes are able to repel spirits because in many European traditions, spirits don't like leather and will stay away from shoes.

Shoes are especially thought to bring luck at weddings. Tying shoes behind the new couple's car brings luck in England and fertility in Transylvania. Further, if a bridesmaid gets one of the shoes, she will marry next. Throwing shoes after the couple as they leave the church will also bring them good luck, as would placing a coin into the bride's shoe. Bridegrooms in France often put coins in their shoes prior to their weddings as a way of preventing impotence via sorcery. The coins represented the groom's testicles; by putting them in the shoes, they ensured their safety.

There are a number of old English beliefs about shoes and the bridal bed, including the belief that the groom's left shoe should have the buckle removed to keep witches from interrupting the consummation. On the other hand, if the husband buckles the bride's shoe on the day of their wedding, she will control their relationship. In India it was once customary for the bride's red shoes to be thrown across the roof to let visitors know that the couple was inside on their honeymoon, while among the Zuni, a woman's fiancé made her wedding boot for her. It is no accident that the European fairy tale "**Cinderella**" has as its central symbol the glass **slipper**, which will, for Cinderella, ultimately represent her chances at happiness, love, and marriage.

It is thought by many that shoes are such common wedding symbols because they represent the bride's submission to her husband and the passing of authority over the bride from the father to the husband. Early English marriage custom included, for example, the father removing one of the bride's shoes and giving it to the groom. And in the ancient Jewish tradition, a widow who is expected to marry her brother-in-law can remove a shoe from his foot, releasing him from the obligation. In India, it is customary after a wedding for the groom to place his bride's foot on a grinding stone to reaffirm her fidelity. Even the tradition of throwing shoes after the couple (or tying them to the car) can be read as the transfer of authority over the bride from father to son-in-law.

Many beliefs about shoes are grounded in sympathetic magic. For instance, wearing the shoes of a woman who just gave birth brings fertility, and wearing the shoes of one's beloved for eight days will make him love you. This is also seen in the **Native American** practice of walking in an enemy's shoes in order to empathize with them. While one can see the wearing of an item of the other person's clothing as serving the same function, shoes are seen as much more personal and linked to the wearer than an item of clothing. All of these examples demonstrate the law of contagion—what the shoe was once in contact with will rub off on the new wearer. Placing a guest's shoe in the middle of the road when you want him to leave your home, on the other hand, is an example of the law of imitation: what you do to the shoe will likewise affect the wearer. Further examples include the Chinese tradition of embroidering the images of fierce animals on children's shoes to protect them from evil, or the Japanese tradition in which Samurai warriors made shoes out of bear fur so that they would inherit the strength of the bear.

Because shoes often have a protective quality, there is also a set of beliefs associated with the concealment of shoes within the walls of one's home. Shoes found embedded in the walls of European and American homes may be indicative of ancient beliefs that hiding old shoes in a house keeps evil away. Often those shoes are children's or babies' shoes, and thousands of "**concealment shoes**" have been documented in Europe and in the original colonies of the United States and Canada. While shoes have been found in a variety of areas in the home, they are usually placed at the entryways into the home (doors, windows, and chimneys), which are thought to be more vulnerable to danger. Other cultures may have these beliefs as well, as the Indian tradition of placing a shoe on top of the home for protection testifies.

Magical rituals also focus on feet, or even footprints. For instance, in India, performing a ritual over a beloved's footprint can win you love, while reciting a spell over the footprint of an enemy and cutting the print with a leaf will bring that person harm. Indians, probably more so than any other people, believe in the religious and magical power of footprints based on the belief in India that the foot represents the soul because it supports the weight of the entire body. Therefore, the footprints left by a holy person, or the Buddha, would be revered because they would still contain some element of the person who left them. Other cultures, too, see special significance in footprints, and many have myths that explain a natural formation by the fact that God stood in that spot, leaving his footprint. Those sites were then sacred sites to those people. For instance, in Botswana, the local creation myths tell of a hole in the ground where humans and animals first emerged; nearby the hole is the footprint of Matsieng, the creator God.

Shoes, not surprisingly, are associated with a number of beliefs about travel. For instance, throwing a shoe at someone when they are setting off on a trip was an English good luck tradition, while in Scotland throwing a shoe over one's house on Halloween demonstrates the direction you are intended to travel. In Japan, burning mugwort in a shoe will make an unwanted guest leave.

See also: Animal Feet; Bare Feet; Christianity; Concealment Shoes; Islam

Further Reading Cleary, Meghan. *The Perfect Fit: What Your Shoes Say About You*. San Francisco: Chronicle Books, 2005; Means Lawrence, Robert. *The Magic of the Horseshoe: With Other Folklore Notes*. Boston: Houghton-Mifflin, 1898; Monger, George. *Marriage Customs of the World: From Henna to Honeymoons*. Santa Barbara: ABC-CLIO, 2004.

BIRKENSTOCKS

Birkenstock is a German shoe manufacturer that makes **sandals** and shoes known for their comfortable contoured sole and distinctive appearance.

Birkenstock's history goes back to 1774 with a **shoemaker** named Johann Birkenstock who made shoes in Langenbergheim, Germany. The distinctive Birkenstock shoe was not developed until 1897, however, when Konrad Birkenstock, who owned two **shoe stores** in Frankfort, created a unique curved shoe from a contoured last, with an insole designed to match the shape of the human foot. All other shoes at the time were flat inside, which Birkenstock felt made little sense given the natural arched curve of the foot. Birkenstock's innovation was a hit, and he spoke to shoemakers' guilds about the contoured shoe, licensing other shoemakers to produce a similar shoe.

Initially, the shoes were custom-made for individual feet, but with the rise of factory-shoe production at the turn of the century, the market for custom shoes declined. Birkenstock then developed a contoured, flexible arch support in 1902 that could be inserted into factory-made shoes, which became the focus of the Birkenstock operation for the next 50 years, except for during World War I when Birkenstock's factories were used to manufacture **orthopedic shoes** for wounded soldiers.

In 1954, Karl Birkenstock took over the company and shifted focus from orthopedic supports to creating, once again, a shoe designed to provide arch support to the foot. The Madrid, released in 1964, was the first of the modern Birkenstock sandals, based on the trademarked curved "footbed," and it has since led to hundreds of new Birkenstock sandals and shoes, all with the same footbed and comfort. Birkenstock shoes like the Madrid are all built around the ergonomically designed footbed, which today is made of cork (the leftovers from the production of wine bottle stoppers), latex, and jute; the intent is to create a shoe that feels like the wearer is walking in **bare feet** on the sand. This footbed is then attached to **leather** straps to create the sandal. The modern footbed no longer simply supports the arch but includes additional support for the toes and for the heel.

Birkenstocks were not seen in the United States until 1966, when German-American dress maker Margot Fraser, visiting Germany on vacation, purchased a pair of Birkenstocks to help ease her chronic foot pain and **hammer toes**. She then began importing the shoes to the United States, eventually becoming the only distributor for the shoes in the United States.

Birkenstocks are known not only for their comfort but for their appearance, and they are, for many people, linked indelibly with hippies. When Birkenstocks were first introduced to the United States, women's shoes were narrow and designed with fashion, rather than comfort, in mind. Birkenstocks were ridiculed as ugly, and many people have pointed out that they make one's feet look huge. Margot Fraser encountered these comments when trying to market the shoes to the American market, and she ended up turning to the health and fitness industries after shoe retailers told her that women would never wear the shoes. Fraser began selling the shoes to owners of health food stores and other locations that catered to people interested in alternative medicine, food, and lifestyles. She teamed up with one of her first customers, a health food store owner, who provided a loan to help incorporate Birkenstock Footprint Sandals in 1972.

Hippies, academics, and others interested in a more bohemian lifestyle favored Birkenstocks, whose comfort, combined with natural colors and texture, appealed to these groups, and Birkenstocks took off in the 1970s. However, the 1980s saw a decline in their popularity as the natural lifestyle became less popular among Americans. Birkenstock responded by creating new designs and colors to appeal to a wider audience, leading to a resurgence of the brand during the late 1980s and 1990s. Nordstrom became the first department store to carry the shoes in 1988. The company introduced non-leather shoes to appeal to vegetarians and vegans and also released a variety of closed shoes marketed towards nurses and other working people who spend much of their time on their feet. In the new millennium, Birkenstock began working with designers to create new, fashion-inspired designs. For instance, Birkenstock released a new line of shoes called the Architect Collection in 2003, which retailed for $250, and later that year model Heidi Klum designed a new line of fancy Birkenstocks, which sold at high end retailers like Barneys. Still, Birkenstock differs from most big shoe companies in that it does not advertise nationally, does not seek **celebrity endorsements**, and the company only releases a couple of new products per year.

Forty years after Birkenstocks first made their appearance in the United States, they are still thought of as hippy shoes by many American consumers. Unlike other comfortable shoes that are often associated with seniors, Birkenstocks remain linked to their original American consumers: hippies and other members of the counter culture. (Nicknames for Birkenstocks include Jesus sandals, tree huggers, Flintstone feet, and granolas, all of which imply a crunchy, earthy, spiritual lifestyle.) Today, however, with the baby boomers who first made Birkenstocks popular aging, the shoes are experiencing a comeback and a new set of associations: the urban liberal. "Birkenstock liberals" emerged as a supposed voting block in the 2004 presidential elections and were said to favor Democratic presidential candidate Howard Dean. Like "soccer mom," Birkenstock liberal became media shorthand to describe potential voters with a particular political leaning and, more importantly, lifestyle: a white, middle-aged college-educated liberal who enjoys outdoors activities, drives a Volvo, volunteers for charities, and goes to independent movie houses.

Today, there are dozens of Birkenstock knockoffs on the market, yet Birkenstock USA remains a multimillion dollar company with thousands of retail locations selling more than 400 styles and colors of shoes and sandals to a devoted, and still growing, fan base. Unlike the vast majority of shoes sold in the west, Birkenstocks are not made in Asia; they are still made in Germany. Birkenstock USA, with more than $56 million in sales in 2007, remains a privately owned company and, since founder Margot Fraser sold her share of the company to the employees, it remains 100 percent company owned today.

See also: Orthopedic Shoes; Orthotics; Shoemaking

Further Reading Peters, Erika. *The Complete Idiot's Guide to Walking for Health*. Indianapolis: Alpha Books, 2001.

BLAHNIK, MANOLO

Manolo Blahnik is a Spanish fashion designer known for his high-end designer women's shoes. His shoes sell for hundreds to thousands of dollars per pair. Blahnik began as a set designer for theater in Paris in the 1960s, but he was encouraged by American fashion publisher Diana Vreeland to make shoes instead. He began making shoes in the 1970s in London, opening his first shop in 1973. His factory is located

> "Shoes help transform a woman."
>
> MANOLO BLAHNIK

in Parabiago, Italy, and produces, by modern standards, relatively few shoes (about 80 per day), with each shoe undergoing 50 different production processes. Even today, Blahnik designs each and every shoe, makes his own lasts, and carves the molds for his heels by hand.

Blahnik's first shoe was a sling back **pump** in 1971 made for designer Ossie Clark, and over the past three decades he has focused on couture shoes as well as op art shoes, which express his artistic and architectural interests. Many of his shoes were created for designers like John Galliano, Kansei Yamamoto, Christian Dior, and Jean Paul Gaultier.

The majority of Manolo Blahnik shoes, known as Manolos, are **stilettos** and are popular because of their beautiful craftsmanship and unique design elements, such as his signature tapered vamp, which often draw on art and design from other historical periods. They have been seen on the feet of famous women for 30 years. In the 1970s, they were worn by such celebrities as Bianca Jagger and Paloma Picasso, and during the 1980s by Princess Diana and Madonna. Blahnik is often blamed by critics of **high heels** for not only popularizing stilettos but for creating shoes so extreme that they cannot be worn for more than a short period of time by most women.

For many wearers and fans, Manolos are the sexiest of shoes. Joan Rivers is said to have noted, "You just put on your Manolos, and you automatically find yourself saying 'Hi, sailor' to every man that walks by." Blahnik is not unaware of the links between his shoes and sexuality, having once famously said, "The secret of toe cleavage is a very important part of the sexuality of the shoe; you must only show the first two cracks."

In the 1990s, Manolos became a household name to people who would never spend $500 on a pair of shoes through the HBO television show *Sex and the City*. *Sex and the City*'s characters often wore and discussed the shoes, making high-end heels, especially Manolos, one of the running themes through the show. Manolos also appeared in a 1991 episode of *The Simpsons* and were frequently mentioned by Edina and Patsy in the BBC show *Absolutely Fabulous*. Blahnik also designed the shoes for Sofia Coppola's 2006 film, *Marie*

Manolo Blahnik shoes, at the Rodeo Drive Walk of Style Award to honor Manolo Blahnik, September 25, 2008, in Los Angeles. [AP Photo/Shea Walsh]

Antoinette, which won the Academy Award for best costume design. Blahnik won the Council of Fashion Designers of America award three times and numerous other awards over the years, and had an exhibition at the Design Museum in London in 2003.

Today, Manolos can be purchased at one of his boutiques as well as at large department stores, and fans of the shoes often order new shoes without having first seen them.

See also: High Heels; Parker, Sarah Jessica; *Sex and the City*; Stilettos

Further Reading McDowell, Colin. *Manolo Blahnik*. New York: HarperCollins Publishers, 2000; Pedersen, Stephanie. *Shoes: What Every Woman Should Know*. Cincinnati: David & Charles, 2005.

BLISTERS, BUNIONS, CALLUSES, AND CORNS

There are a number of conditions that affect the feet and are caused by irritation to the feet, often by wearing ill-fitting or inappropriate footwear. Blisters are sores on the foot caused by pressure on one area of the foot that result in the formation of a swollen pocket of skin filled with fluid. Blisters are caused by wearing footwear that rubs continuously on one spot, like the toe or the back of the heel, causing irritation and pain, but they can also be caused by a burn or by the feet sweating within the shoes. Wearing new shoes for an extended period of time can cause blisters if the shoes are stiff and rub against the foot, but even worn-in shoes can cause blisters when worn for a very long time, such as running a marathon or taking a long hike.

Preventing blisters involves wearing proper footwear and assuring that footwear is broken in before going on a long walk or run. Wearing **socks** or protective barriers between the feet and the shoes is another way to prevent friction and thus to prevent blisters, as is rubbing petroleum jelly on the area of the foot that is exposed to the pressure. Finally, keeping the feet dry is another way to prevent blisters. Treatment is not really necessary for blisters as they will heal on their own. Doctors do not recommend popping the blister as it could allow infection into the open wound, although many people do pop their blisters in order to relieve the pressure and pain.

Calluses refer to thickened dead skin that accumulates along the sides and bottom of the feet. While not painful, they are a source of discomfort in people (especially women) who want their feet to be soft and smooth. In addition, when severe, calluses can crack, causing pain and the possibility of infection in the feet. Calluses are usually caused by pressure from wearing ill-fitting shoes, high heels, an unusual gait, or carrying excess weight.

Treatment for calluses includes rubbing lotion on the feet, which increases the amount of water in the skin cells and can temporarily relieve the problem or relieve minor calluses. When severe, specially formulated lotions and creams containing urea or salicylic acid will soften calluses. Another treatment method involves soaking the feet in warm water and then scrubbing the calluses with a pumice stone to remove the dead skin. If the callus is caused by flat feet or another type of foot anomaly, an orthotic device or arch support could help by alleviating pressure on one part of the foot. Finally, many people buy callus scrapers, inexpensive devices that combine a sharp blade with a file to scrape and file down the dead skin, although podiatrists discourage their use since they can cut the skin, making the feet even more vulnerable. PedEggs is another popular item, sold on television infomercials, in which a plastic egg opens up to reveal a cheese grater surface that is scraped against the skin, with the callus shavings being caught inside of the egg.

Corns, like calluses, are thickenings of dead skin on the outside of the feet, but they create a more localized hardening, usually shaped like a cone. Unlike calluses, corns are painful because they press on the nerves of the feet, especially when they are irritated by the shoe. Corns are caused by ill-fitting footwear—both shoes that are too tight as well as those that are too loose shoes in which the foot slides forward—and high heels. Wearing better fitting shoes will relieve the pressure of corns, and sometimes orthotics and protective pads will relieve pressure as well and absorb some of the shock from wearing heels. Corns can also be treated through the use of creams containing salicylic acid, and, in severe cases, they can be removed by a doctor. Many podiatrists, however, do not recommend using chemicals to remove corns because they can burn the skin. Diabetics, especially, are cautioned against removing calluses or corns because the risk of ulcers and infections for diabetics is much higher.

Bunions, or *Hallux Valgus*, refer to a condition when the big toe of the foot moves inward towards the smaller toes, often causing a thickening of the tissue around the first toe, and crowding around the other toes. The bunion refers to the bump on the outside of the big toe caused by the bend in the toe. Sometimes bunions can also form on the little toe; these are called bunionettes or Tailor's Bunions. Occasionally, fluid will accumulate in the toe joint, causing bursitis.

Bunions, like corns, are generally found in women who wear shoes that are too narrow for the toes to fit properly. Pointy-toed shoes are the greatest culprit, causing the big toe to get crowded towards the other toes. Men who wear **cowboy boots** are also at risk for bunions. Wearing shoes that are wider in the toes is the best method of prevention and treatment. In addition, there are a number of products available to treat bunions, such as bunion shields, splints, or bandages. Very serious cases require surgery.

See also: Disorders and Injuries; Foot Care Products; Hammer Toe

Further Reading Copeland, Glenn, Stan Solomon, and Mark Myerson. *The Good Foot Book: A Guide For Men, Women, Children, Athletes, Seniors*. Alameda, CA: Hunter House, 2005; Vonhof, John. *Fixing Your Feet: Prevention And Treatments for Athletes*. Berkeley, CA: Wilderness Press, 2006.

''BLUE SUEDE SHOES''

"Blue Suede Shoes" is a rockabilly song first released in 1956 and written and performed by Carl Perkins. The song was said to be influenced by Johnny Cash's suggestion that Perkins write a song about blue suede shoes, a term for the **military shoes** worn in the army when Cash was serving. Evidently, Cash told Perkins about hearing a soldier tell another soldier, "don't step on my blue suede shoes;" later, while Perkins was performing, he heard a young man at one of his performances tell his girlfriend not to step on his "suedes." Perkins wrote much of the song that night after going to bed. Another story claims that Cash told Perkins his story and that Perkins immediately jotted down the lyrics and performed the song that same evening. And Perkins himself evidently said he came up with the idea himself after seeing a boy tell a girl at one of his concerts in Jackson, Mississippi, not to step on his suedes, and he was struck by the fact that the boy valued his shoes over a beautiful girl. In his telling, he couldn't sleep because he was so bothered by the interaction, and he wrote the song late that night on a brown paper bag.

Perkins's original recording of "Blue Suede Shoes" was a number-one hit and sold more than a million copies in the first few months after its release. "Blue Suede Shoes" was covered by at least 10 other artists in 1956 alone and has been covered countless times since then. It is considered to be one of the most influential rock-and-roll songs in history and is referred to in a number of other songs since the 1950s. One of those covers was by Elvis Presley, who released his version soon after Perkins's did in 1956. Perkins and his band were in a serious car accident in March 1956, leaving Perkins in the hospital at the height of his song's fame. Presley began performing the song on television and even showed up on the Steve Allen Show in July 1956 wearing a pair of blue suede shoes, making his own version more popular while Perkins was still convalescing and unable to perform himself. Initially, Elvis's version did not become as popular as the Perkins original, but Presley rerecorded the song in 1960 for his film *G.I. Blues* and gave it another run of popularity. While Perkins's version is the most well known to musical historians and critics, the general public is most familiar with Presley's version.

Blue suede shoes are still associated with rockabilly, and suede Oxfords in a variety of colors were worn in the Teddy scene, a British musical subculture from the 1950s (and revived in the 1970s) that derived its style from both Edwardian fashion and American rockabilly music and style. Teddy boys wore lace-up suede Oxfords, known as creepers, with thick crepe soles. Other groups who wore similar shoes include rockers and followers of ska and psychobilly.

See also: Military Shoes and Boots

Further Reading Kennedy, Rick, Randy McNutt, *Little Labels: Big Sound: Small Record Companies and the Rise of American Music*. Bloomington: Indiana University Press, 1999.

BOOTS

Boots are heeled shoes that cover not only the foot, but the ankle and part of the leg. Boots are an important part of the wardrobe for certain sports, certain professions, and certain climates, but fashion boots have no utilitarian purpose.

Boots were first worn in very cold climates, in terrains that are difficult to negotiate, and among populations who rode horses. The original boots were probably first made in Northern Asia and constructed like a **moccasin**, made of a single piece of hide wrapped around the foot, combined with a separate piece of hide that was wrapped around the leg using hide thongs. The use of fur or grass or other soft substance was probably also used inside of the boot to keep the leg warm, especially because the two-part construction would have allowed cold or dampness in.

The use of boots was first documented among the civilizations of Central Asia, Western Asia, and Eastern Europe. Closed **leather** boots were worn by the nomadic peoples of Eastern Europe and Western Asia while riding their horses, and the soldiers in the **classical civilizations** of **Greece** and **Rome** wore simple open-toed boots made of hides sewn together with thongs. Greek soldiers, for instance, wore half-boots out of leather, which laced up the front with leather laces. Other styles of boots were available as well, including higher boots used for hunting and specialty boots worn in the theatre. Boots are also often found in hot climates in which the terrain is particularly difficult or dangerous, as in parts of the **Middle East**. As the Roman Empire gave way to the Middle Ages in **Europe**, boots became important elements of footwear in Europe as well, worn as protection against the elements, for traveling, and for riding.

European styles included cavalier boots, which extended up the calf and rolled down from the top, and knee-high boots—sometimes called buskins—for the elites, and cockers for peasants. Greek and Roman-style boots, with open toes, were also worn in the Middle Ages until the fifteenth century. Boots made of leather could be waterproofed with linseed oil or other oils, and then heated, but it wasn't until the nineteenth century with the discovery of **vulcanization** that rubber boots were made.

Today, boots are found in every culture with a cold climate, such as among Inuits of the **Arctic region**, native Alaskans, native Siberians, and the residents of Scandinavia. In these cases, boots are traditionally made of animal skins like caribou, polar bear, and seal skin (while today boots can be made of treated canvas or synthetic materials) that protect the feet from cold temperatures. Variants include the *Finnsko* boot that is worn in Lapland and Norway, made of reindeer skin and fur, and the *kamik* or *mukluk*, worn in Greenland and northern Canada, made of seal skin and caribou skin and sometimes dog skin, and lined with fur for warmth. Most boots worn in very cold climates have a separate sole made out of materials like seal skin, which is water resistant.

Special rain boots made of waterproof material like rubber, PVC, or, in traditional societies, seal skin, are also worn in many areas with high levels of rainfall. In addition, some boots, like rain boots or **Wellington boots**, are made without laces or other closures, in order to prevent water, snow, or mud from getting inside. (**Galoshes**, on the other hand, are rubber boots meant to be worn outside of regular shoes to protect the feet from the rain.) Wellingtons (also known as gumboots) are also worn by butchers and slaughterhouse workers to protect the wearers from blood.

Another popular use for boots has been for riding horses, camels, or other animals. Heeled boots were first created to help keep the foot in the stirrup and to protect the leg from contact with the animal. For instance, riders in Central Asian countries like Uzbekistan and Kazakhstan wore boots while riding, as did Mongols, Afghans, Tibetans, and Persians, as well as nomadic tribes like the Scythians. These boots were made of wool, felt, cotton, or leather, and they were highly decorated with embroidery. Many of these boots had upturned toes, like other shoes worn in the Middle East. North African peoples who traditionally rode horses or camels also wore tall leather or wool riding boots, such as among the Berber of Morocco, which were often elaborately decorated with cut outs and embroidery. Sometimes these boots were actually two pieces: a shoe and a boot stocking; after riding, the rider would remove the overshoes and wear the stockings inside. It was the practice of riding boots in these regions that gave way to the wearing of heeled boots in Europe and, later, in North America.

Activities like motorcycle riding, horse riding, hiking, mountaineering, and angling require boots, as do sports like skiing and skating. For instance, waders are high rubber or PVC boots that extend to the chest, which allow anglers to wear them while wading through water. Waders are also used in occupations that involve someone wading in water, sewage, or chemicals. **Cowboy boots** are made of thick leather with a prominent heel designed to hold the foot in the stirrup of the saddle. **Motorcycle boots**, like cowboy boots, are made of thick leather in order to protect the legs of a motorcycle rider from injury during a motorcycle accident. Likewise, hiking boots are made of thick materials that not only protect the feet and legs from potential dangers while hiking, but the soles are rugged, to help with navigating difficult terrain.

Dangerous occupations like firefighting and logging both require protective boots made of thick materials, as do many construction trades, which favor safety or steel-toe boots, with reinforced steel toes to protect the feet from heavy falling objects and from punctures.

The military is another arena that demanded specialized footwear, and, in particular, boots. Soldiers in countries around the world have worn boots for training, fighting, and ceremonial purposes for thousands of years, although the hard leather heeled boot did not develop until the middle of the seventeenth century. Military boots are designed to provide support for the ankle, to allow for the negotiation of a variety of terrains, and to protect the feet from a variety of weather situations. In that sense, military boots share characteristics in common with hiking boots, rain and snow boots, and safety boots in that they are made of sturdy, waterproof materials, have thick soles and heels, and often have reinforced ankles, heels, or toes. Military boots come in a variety of styles and are geared to different weather and environmental conditions.

Boots are not strictly utilitarian items, however. Well-dressed European men have been wearing boots as fashionable footwear for centuries, first for riding horses and later for dress wear. (They picked up the fashion of wearing heeled boots for horses from the nomadic people of Asia.) Elite men wore thigh boots for riding and hunting, and for military use, but boots became popular for regular wear during the seventeenth century, although their popularity waxed and waned with the centuries. Top boots or cavalier boots, made from soft black leather with a cuff at the top, were worn prior to the development of stiff leather boots, and they were worn with the top folded down over long breeches. Because they were so wide, it was difficult to walk in them; the gait of the men who wore them was called the "cavalier swagger."

King Louis XIV's **shoemaker** made a pair of seamless boots for him out of the skin of a calf's leg, an innovation that was not repeated until the eighteenth century. Hessian boots were German military boots, made of hard black polished leather that became popular for regular wear in the eighteenth century and were worn by European men as part of their casual wardrobes. Jack boots, made of "jack" leather that was extra hard, with square toes and thick heels, were popular during the seventeenth and eighteenth centuries, and they replaced the soft cavalier boots. Wellingtons, black leather boots named after the Duke of Wellington, became popular around 1820 and replaced the Hessian as the fashionable boot for men in England. Boots, in fact, became so popular that well-to-do European men wore boots rather than shoes, inside of, rather than outside of, the pants. By the twentieth century, though, boots became unpopular for men.

Until the nineteenth century, elite European women wore boots during riding, but not for regular activities, and, in fact, the boots that women wore were actually men's riding boots. In other cultures, too, women only wore boots when living in very cold climates. The first boots specifically made for women in Europea were said to be a pair designed for Queen Victoria in 1840. These boots set off a trend for fashionable foots among European women in the nineteenth century.

Women's boots during the nineteenth century and into the early twentieth century shared many similarities with women's fashionable shoes at the time with respect to heel height, material, and adornment. They could be high heeled or without a heel, and either laced or buttoned up the leg. Because boots had been associated with masculinity, a very tight fit was created to make them more feminine. In either case, Victorian morality demanded that women's ankles be covered, making boots practical as well as fashionable. At the beginning of the nineteenth century, women's boots were relatively low, but they extended up to mid-calf length by the end of the century. Boots for women became more popular during the first World War, and as skirt lengths shortened, boots and shoes became more ornate. In fact, the twentieth century was the first century in which women's boot styles and ornamentation overcame men's. As the twentieth century progressed, boots became less popular for women, who wanted to show their ankles in their new nylon stockings under shorter skirts and dresses, as they were for men, a situation that reversed itself with the 1960s.

In the 1960s, men began wearing the Chelsea boot, tight ankle boots that were popular among hipsters like mods and were worn by the Rolling Stones. For women, **go go boots** became a trendy choice, popularized by Nancy Sinatra, while the 1970s and 1980s saw the popularization of cowboy boots among both men and women.

Punks, starting in the 1970s, appropriated work boots (especially **Dr. Martens**) and combat boots as part of their own wardrobes, but in general the popularity of boots continues to rise and fall with the decades.

Finally, **stiletto** boots are popular amongst members of the Bondage Discipline Domination Submission (BDSM) community and some foot fetishists. Tight, thigh-high, high-heeled boots, in materials like latex or **patent leather**, are most popular among these groups, as are novelty boots like ballet boots. One notable maker of fetish boots is the Kinky Boot Factory, an English company featured in the 2005 film *Kinky Boots*. The film tells the true story of a family-owned shoe company that turns to manufacturing fetish footwear after meeting a drag queen, in order to save the business and the workers' jobs.

One reason for the popularity of boots in the fetish community has to do with power. Because boots in the feudal and nomadic cultures of Asia and Europe arose with horseback riding and military activities, the wearing of boots in those cultures was always associated with masculine power. Those who had boots were more powerful than those who did not. Today, heeled boots, but especially very tall, very high boots, are still seen as accoutrements of power.

See also: Cowboy Boots; China; Dr. Martens; Europe; Fetishes; Galoshes; Go Go Boots; Jack Boots; *Kinky Boots*; Middle East; Military Shoes and Boots; Motorcycle Boot; Wellington Boot

Further Reading Beard, Tyler. *The Cowboy Boot Book*. Salt Lake City: Peregrine Smith Books, 1992; Edwards, Adam. *A Short History of the Wellington Boot*. London: Hodder & Stoughton, 2006.

BOWLING SHOES

Bowling shoes are shoes that are made to use when bowling. Bowling is a sport played indoors in a bowling alley during which players score points by throwing a bowling ball at a set of plastic-coated wooden pins down a wooden lane.

In order to bowl in the **United States**, players must wear special bowling shoes because players must walk on the lanes, and most street shoes could harm the oiled surface of the lane. While professional bowlers and regular bowlers own their own shoes, casual bowlers rent used (but sanitized) shoes from the bowling alley when they play. Indeed, bowling is one of the only situations in which people will wear shoes that have been worn by thousands of other people before them.

Bowling shoes are made with an upper of cloth, **leather**, or synthetic materials and a rubberized sole. Soles are made of rubber to protect the varnished floor of the lane from scratches and scuffs, and are slick to allow the wearer to slide when throwing the ball. In addition, attached to the sole of the shoe is a suede pad. During bowling, the player strides up the lane and, at the last minute, slides as he or she releases the ball. The slick area of the sole, usually made of microfiber, helps with the slide, while the traction pad, made of higher friction materials like suede or rubber, helps the player to brake. In addition, bowling shoes are designed to help the bowler balance his or her weight when striding down the lane, throwing the ball, and following through after the release.

Bowling shoes are classified as athletic, house, or performance. Athletic bowling shoes are the least expensive and are comfortable, but they do not provide as much support as performance shoes. They often look like sneakers, but the soles are different in that the soles of regular sneakers provide traction, while athletic bowling shoes have a special sliding sole on both shoes.

House shoes refer to the shoes that are available for rent in bowling alleys across the country. They offer more support than the athletic shoes and have, like athletic shoes, a sliding sole on both shoes as well as traction on the heels for braking. Both house and athletic shoes are called universal shoes because they are suited to left- and right-handed bowlers, as well as beginners and more advanced players.

Performance shoes are geared towards helping the bowler increase his or her performance. In performance shoes, one shoe

Shoes like these are rented at bowling alleys across America. [Copyright 2008 Jupiterimages Corporation]

is made for sliding, and one is designed for braking. The shoe made for sliding has a sliding sole and is worn on the side that the bowler does not throw with; the shoe for breaking has instead a traction sole and is worn on the opposite foot. (In other words, a right-handed bowler will wear the breaking sole on the right foot and the sliding sole on the left foot.) Some shoes today come with replaceable sole pads so that the players can keep their shoes and just replace the pads. Some players even adjust the amount of slide that they need for different types of play or floor surface by exchanging the pads.

Bowling shoes today come in a wide variety of colors and styles, and many no longer look like the bowling shoes popularized during the 1950s and are still found in bowling alleys today. While traditional bowling shoes have long been considered ugly, with their black leather uppers (often with stripes), big square toe, and heavy heel, in recent years retro bowling shoes (as well as bowling shirts) have become fashionable among hipsters. In fact, the last few years have seen a rash of thefts of bowling shoes from bowling alleys around the country, as the "so ugly they're hip" look of bowling shoes entered the mainstream.

See also: Athletic Shoes; Sneakers

Further Reading Gideon Bosker, Bianca Lencek-Bosker. *Bowled Over: A Roll Down Memory Lane*. San Francisco: Chronicle Books, 2002.

C

CANDIE'S

Candie's is a brand of footwear, clothing, and accessories. The company is most known for its high-heeled, wood-bottomed slides introduced in 1978. A slide is a simple sandal made with a single wide strap forming the upper, through which the foot "slides" through. The shoes reached their height of success in the mid-1980s, and then sales slumped as fashions changed. In the twenty-first century, however, Candie's has used celebrity-driven advertisements and created new products to make a comeback.

Candie's was developed by Charles Cole, who started his shoe company, El Greco Leather Products, in 1961 and who created the iconic wood and **leather** slide in Italy in the late 1970s. After introducing them in the United States, Candie's were extremely popular in the late 1970s and 1980s, partly due to their appearance in the 1978 movie *Grease*, when Olivia Newton John's character wore them in the final scene as part of her "bad girl" costume. Their popularity also stemmed from their purchase price: just $35 in 1983. Because the shoes were produced in Italy, production costs were low and more people could subsequently afford the shoes. Still, by the 1990s the shoes lost their luster and the brand began to falter.

Cole hired his four children to work in his company, and one son, Kenneth, started Kenneth Cole Productions in 1982, while another son, Neil, opened his own company, New Retail Concepts (NRC) in 1991, now named Iconix. Unlike his family's shoe companies, NRC does not produce shoes but instead purchases brands that have declined in value and revitalizes them through aggressive marketing. NRC licenses the brands to other companies, which are then responsible for making the shoes. In 1991, NRC purchased Candie's for $3 million and went about trying to revamp the brand.

After acquiring Candie's, NRC set out on an aggressive **advertising** campaign intended to bring the brand back to its mid-1980s glory. The new marketing campaign—kicked off by a controversial ad showing Playboy model Jenny McCarthy seated on a toilet wearing nothing but Candie's—marked a radical shift in the approach taken by the senior Cole, who felt that relying on advertising meant that the brand was weak. In addition, the younger Cole expanded the product line to include purses, **hosiery**, and apparel and struck partnerships with leading designers like Betsy Johnson and Vivienne Tam to design new Candie's shoes. The strategy worked, and Candie's became more popular than ever.

Today, Candie's continues to expand its product lines and distribution networks and increasingly relies on celebrity endorsements to sell its products. Not afraid of scandal, a number of Candie's ads have been controversial, including those featuring Alyssa Milano, Carmen Electra and Dennis Rodman, and, most recently, Fergie. The company reliably picks young, popular celebrities to wear its products, from Jenny McCarthy, the Dixie Chicks, and Destiny's Child in the 1990s to Hillary Duff, Fergie, Ashlee Simpson, Kelly Clarkson, and Hayden Panettiere in the current decade. Panettiere, an actress starring in the popular television series *Heroes*, released her first album in 2008, with the first single chosen by Candie's to appear in their upcoming ads.

See also: Advertising; Celebrity Endorsements; Stilettos

Further Reading Cole, Kenneth. *Footnotes: What You Stand For Is More Important Than What You Stand In*. New York: Simon & Schuster, 2003.

CELEBRITY ENDORSEMENTS

Celebrity endorsements are an increasingly important element of shoe **advertising** and, in particular, advertising for **athletic shoes**. Because of the values and strength that they represent, athletes have long been popular choices to promote products. Johnny Weissmuller and Jackie Robinson, for example, were early celebrity endorsers of Wheaties, and Babe Ruth promoted Red Rock Cola in the 1930s.

Today, endorsement contracts are such an important part of an athlete's annual income that many athletes make more money from their endorsement contracts than from their salary or winnings. In return, celebrity athletes and nonathletes are so important to product promotion that companies spend millions of dollars per year on celebrity endorsements alone, choosing celebrities based on their "Q rating," a rating system that ranks celebrities based on popularity and name recognition. Now, when big companies sign a new endorsement deal with a celebrity, they often hold a press conference to announce the partnership, which itself launches the marketing campaign.

The company that would become **Adidas** was the first athletic shoe company to offer free shoes to athletes in order to promote the shoes to the public. Olympic runner Jesse Owens could be considered the first such "celebrity" endorser of shoes, even though he did not promote the shoes in an advertising campaign.

Celebrity shoe endorsements really picked up with **Nike**'s first contract with a big-name athlete, Ilie Nastase in 1972, and for the past three decades, a cornerstone of Nike's advertising has been the use of celebrity athletes, who both allow their names to be used in advertising and show up at sporting events wearing the Nike brand. Perhaps the most important endorsement deal Nike ever signed was with basketball player **Michael Jordan**, who not only became the face of Nike's advertising throughout the 1980s and 1990s, but whose shoe, Air Jordan, first released in 1985, was one of Nike's most successful. (Ironically, Michael Jordan initially preferred both **Converse** and Adidas shoes to Nike and wanted to endorse one of those companies; neither company offered him a contract, however.) Nike now spends almost $500 million per year on celebrity contracts alone to athletes like Tiger Woods, LeBron James, Derek Jeter, and Maria Sharapova.

Candie's is a brand of women's shoes that also relies heavily on celebrities to promote its products. Candie's chooses "It" celebrities to feature in its advertising, from Jenny McCarthy, the Dixie Chicks, and Destiny's Child in the 1990s to Hillary Duff, Fergie, Ashlee Simpson, Kelly Clarkson, and Hayden Panettiere in recent years.

Outside the athletic world, celebrities promote shoes as well, although it is not always so clear to the public that they are doing so. While many celebrities do not sign contracts with shoe manufacturers agreeing to wear or promote their shoes, designer shoe companies provide free shoes to big-name celebrities in the hopes that they will wear them in public, thus increasing the name recognition of the shoes. Having a famous actress, model, or singer wear one's shoes at a high-profile event like the Academy Awards is a guaranteed way to get one's shoes into the public eye and to drive sales. High-end designers like **Manolo Blahnik** and **Jimmy Choo** offer shoes to nominees and attendees at major events like the Academy Awards, the Grammy's, the Emmy's, and the Golden Globes. These giveaways evidently pay off too. A 2004 study showed that 27 percent of women from 20 to 24 got clothing ideas from watching how celebrities dress. Today, it is not uncommon for the agencies that handle Hollywood celebrities to negotiate contracts for them with fashion, footwear, or jewelry designers, through which they not only get to wear designer fashion for free but are paid for it as well.

Sometimes the celebrities chosen to endorse a shoe are an unlikely choice. For example, New Retail Concepts, the company started by Neil Cole, hired Donna Rice, the woman involved in the sex scandal that brought down presidential candidate Gary Hart's campaign in 1987, to promote No Excuses, one of the company's shoe and apparel brands. In 1994, the company hired Paula Jones, the alleged mistress of then President Bill Clinton, to promote the brand as well.

Shoe companies also can get lucky in that their shoes are bought and worn by celebrities without the company's input, which ends up being free advertising to the company. The popularity of **Ugg** boots among celebrities like Pamela Anderson helped turn a relatively no-name shoe into a global phenomenon. Television shoes and movies can act in the same way.

Celebrity endorsements have a downside too. When a celebrity who is associated with a particular brand gets involved in activities that are illegal or scandalous, the brand itself can be harmed. When basketball star Kobe Bryant was put on trial for rape, a crime for which the charges were later dropped, it was just weeks after he signed an endorsement deal with Nike. While Nike did not cancel his contract, Coca Cola and McDonalds, with whom he also had endorsement deals, did. When football star Michael Vick was convicted on charges of running a dog-fighting ring (and killing some of the dogs himself), Nike quickly canceled its contract with Vick, just a day before People for the Ethical Treatment of Animals was scheduled to stage a protest outside of the Nike Town stores. And in 2007, British company **Dr. Martens** released a series of print ads that showed dead rock stars like Kurt Cobain and Johnny Ramone wearing their shoes; the ads were pulled after customers registered their outrage and Cobain's widow, Courtney Love, protested.

See also: Advertising; Adidas; Candie's; Dr. Martens; Jordan, Michael; Nike

Further Reading Mullin, Bernard J., Stephen Hardy, William Anthony Sutton. *Sport Marketing*. Champaign, IL: Human Kinetics, 2007; Thomas, Dana. *Deluxe: How Luxury Lost Its Luster*. New York: Penguin Group, 2007.

CHINA

China has a number of beliefs and practices about feet, especially women's feet, that are expressed in the country's footwear traditions. Like other cultures, the shoes as well as the feet express in China a number of important social features related to the wearer.

Perhaps most famously (or infamously), **foot binding** is most associated with China. Foot binding—in which a young girl's feet were bound in tight bandages in order to deform them, keeping them small—was practiced in China among the Han majority for centuries, only ending in the twentieth century. Having bound feet was a sign of status for Chinese women as it meant that they could not work (given the pain of even standing on bound feet). In addition, in China, to have bound feet meant that a woman was disciplined, virtuous, and that she was brought up correctly. Not only was it popular among elite women but with lower-class women as well as a sign of status and beauty. Because of this intense attention on the feet, bound or "lotus feet" were fetishized, as were the "lotus shoes" made for them.

Chinese Pedestal Shoes. These shoes were worn by elite Manchurian women and date to the nineteenth century. [Photo courtesy of Shoe Icons]

One reason for the interest in tiny feet in China has to do with a Chinese **proverb**, "the woman with the long feet ends up alone in the room." Similar sentiments are found in a number of other cultures as well and refer to the idea that a woman with large feet is a woman who is like a man: she is independent and unable to be controlled, an almost universally despised trait in women. It was often said that a woman with large or unbound feet would not get a good marriage partner. Even after foot binding was banned in 1912, or among groups who did not practice it (like the Manchurians), small feet were still admired, and shoes were still worn that made the feet appear tinier.

Chinese shoes were once known as "foot clothing," and originally there was no distinction in the written Chinese language between **socks** and shoes: both were clothing for the feet. Shoes in China varied depending on the climate and environment, the purpose to which the shoes would be put, whether the shoes were worn by men or women, the young or the old, and whether or not they were worn by royalty. Given the size of China, there were also geographic differences in foot-wear and foot construction as well.

One of the oldest forms of foot coverings in China were made with animal skins secured to the feet with strips of **leather**; later, skin threads threaded through bone needles would be used to sew the shoes together, as was seen on a 4,000-year-old pair of **boots** found by archaeologists. Leather was acquired from the animals available, including sheep, yaks, deer, and even fish, and was most commonly used in the northern and northwest regions of China.

Another ancient type of foot-wear in China was woven straw shoes, made with flax thread and bamboo needles, which date back at least 7,000 years. People living in more extreme northeastern climates would have worn straw or grass boots, while those in the south and southeast wore **sandals**. As shoe technology developed, wooden soles appeared, to which the straw uppers were attached. Woven straw slippers are still worn in China today.

As long as 2,000 years ago, soldiers wore hand-stitched cloth shoes combined with

These beautiful Chinese slippers are open-backed, so they can be easily removed, and are embroidered with silk thread, pearls, and sequins. [2007 Copyright Tan Wei Ming. Image from BigStockPhoto.com]

leather wrapped around the calves for protection; this probably evolved into the military boot of the more modern eras. The boot was worn first in the northern parts of China but spread to the south. By about 200 BCE, at least highly ranked military officers wore leather boots, while solders still wore cloth shoes. Boots were square toed for court appearances or pointy-toed for everyday wear. A few centuries later, however, leather boots were worn by all members of the military, and by the seventeenth century had extended into civilian wear as well, and by about the tenth century had extended to women as well. From the fourteenth to the seventeenth centuries, civilians were prohibited from wearing boots.

Most civilians, however, wore cloth slip-on shoes whose soles are made out of multiple layers of cloth, stitched together, soaked in water, and hammered and dried. Known as "one-thousand-layered shoes," or *Xiuhua* shoes, this technique was developed for boot soles, and the technique is still used in Chinese shoes to-day. Silk shoes were first worn about 3,000 years ago and are still popular today. Whether silk or cotton, it is common for these simple slippers to be embroidered.

The differences in shoe material and construction reflected differences in social status, with shoes made of straw usually being worn by peasants and layered cloth shoes worn by others. Embroidered silk shoes and leather boots, on the other hand, were worn by the upper classes. Boots in general were a sign of wealth in

Imperial China and were typically worn by nobility and military officers. A Chinese proverb said "a man in boots will not speak to a man in shoes." Boots worn by noblemen were often made of silk and were highly embroidered, and elevated.

Elevated wooden-soled shoes were also traditionally worn in China. Historically, Chinese men and women often wore elevated **clogs** with two stilts; these were worn to keep the feet and clothing clean and dry while outdoors or when washing clothes or going to the bathroom. Men's clogs were painted green and women's were red. Another elevated shoe was made of embroidered silk and sat on a concave wooden platform from two to four inches high. Known as "shoes with flower pot soles," they were worn by elite Manchurian women from the seventeenth to the twentieth centuries in order to mimic the lotus shoes that were forbidden to them. The elevated height allowed the wearers to tower over lesser people and created a mincing walk similar to the walk of Chinese women with bound feet, while the heel was used for riding horses. Eventually, as elevated shoes became replaced by regular shoes, wooden shoes became associated with peasants and poverty.

Traditionally, Chinese shoes could be found in five colors: red, blue, black, white, and yellow. Since at least the seventh century, there were strict rules, known as **sumptuary laws**, governing the construction of shoes, the types of materials that could be used, and the wearing of certain colors. For instance, red (or pink) shoes were worn at weddings and other celebrations, and bright yellow shoes could at one time only be worn by the emperor and empress. Only seniors wore black shoes, and white shoes were worn during mourning. Blue shoes (and the related colors green and purple) could be worn at any time, however, although blue was favored among seniors and green and purple among young women. At one time, merchants had to wear one black and one white shoe to distinguish them from other citizens.

Embroidery is the most popular method of adornment in Chinese shoes. The designs are grounded in history and reflect not only Chinese aesthetics but Chinese beliefs as well. Women and girls traditionally embroidered their own shoes, either with readily available patterns or patterns of their own making. Designs reflected the wearer's individual personality and talents as well as the wearer's region. Certain flowers, birds, and animals are considered lucky and are favored in designs, as are scenes and characters from Chinese stories. Patterns were typically embroidered not only on the uppers but on the cotton soles of the shoes as well so that they could be admired when a woman has her feet up. The purpose to which the shoes would be used would be taken into account when choosing the designs, as children would wear very different patterns from adult men or women. Children, for instance, had fierce animals like tigers embroidered on their shoes to bring them protection from evil spirits, and **wedding shoes**, in particular, were adorned with designs intended to bring luck, happiness, and fertility.

Chinese marriages are traditionally arranged by the parents, and the shoes play a role in the wedding and, indeed, in choosing the bride. Girls who are being considered as a bride for a young man would send their prospective mother-in-law a pair of shoes that they made, and this played a role in how the bride was selected.

New brides' feet and shoes were traditionally inspected by the new mother-in-law as the bride arrives for her wedding. It was also customary that every young bride bring four pairs of shoes with her to her new home—one pair for each season—and wealthy girls were expected to have four pairs for each season, as well as her red wedding shoes, often embroidered with lucky designs, and red sleeping **slippers**. (Sleeping slippers were worn at bedtime by women with bound feet because it was improper to go to bed only wearing one's bindings.)

Shoes in China have often been exchanged at important events. Besides weddings, births, engagements, and funerals are occasions in which the symbolic value of shoes plays a role. Longevity shoes, for example, are shoes embroidered with a lotus flower and ladder that are worn by the deceased in order to carry them through to the afterlife. Dead emperors wore jade shoes, and upon death the rest of the emperor's shoes were burned. Today, longevity shoes can be blue, black, or brown for men and bright colors for women.

Some Chinese customs are found in other cultures as well, such as the ancient tradition mandating that people remove their shoes before entering a home. Other rules stipulated that bare feet should not be displayed during worship, but that bare feet were required at banquets. Women did not show bare feet in public.

See also: Beliefs; Class; Foot Binding; Gender; Proverbs; Slippers; Wedding Shoes

Further Reading Hong Fan. *Footbinding, Feminism, and Freedom: The Liberation of Women's Bodies in China*. London: Cass, 1997; Ko, Dorothy. Cinderella's Sisters: A Revisionist History of Footbinding. Berkeley: University of California Press, 2007; Yang, Shaorong. *Traditional Chinese Clothing: Costumes, Adornments & Culture*. San Francisco: Long River Press, 2004; Zamperini, Paola. "A Dream of Butterflies? Shoes in Chinese Culture," in Rielle, Georgio and Peter McNeil, eds. *Shoes: A History From Sandals to Sneakers*. London: Berg Publishers, 2006.

CHOO, JIMMY

Jimmy Choo is a designer of high-end women's shoes and accessories. Based in London, Choo opened his business, Jimmy Choo Ltd. in 1996. Choo was born to a **shoemaker** in Malaysia and, like his father, became a shoemaker, making his first shoe at 11. He later immigrated to London and attended school at the Cordwainers' Technical College where he specialized in **shoemaking**. In 1986, he opened his first workshop in London.

> I don't know who invented high heels, but all women owe him a lot.
> MARILYN MONROE

By 1988, Choo's handmade couture shoes began appearing in magazines, on fashion runways, and on the feet of celebrities like Princess Diana. In 1996, he was approached by Tamara Mellon, who was accessories editor at *Vogue UK*, about starting a ready-to-wear line.

Jimmy Choo shoes are made in Italy and are sold at Jimmy Choo boutiques. After Choo sold his half of the company to Equinox Luxury Holdings in 2001, with Tamara Mellon controlling the other half, Jimmy Choos boutiques expanded from four to 30 within three years. In 2007, the company was purchased by TowerBrook Capital Partners for $364 million. Today, Jimmy Choo Ready-To-Wear shoes and accessories are sold in more than 60 boutiques around the world. Tamara Mellon still serves as president and Sandra Choi, Choo's one-time apprentice and his wife's niece, serves as creative director, and it was under these two women that the Jimmy Choo brand really took off. Jimmy Choo now produces shoes for the Jimmy Choo Couture label, which is a part of Jimmy Choo Ltd.

Jimmy Choo **high heels** are highly sought after by fashion-forward celebrities and non-celebrities, thanks to their impeccable design, quality craftsmanship and luxury materials. Known to aficionados as "Jimmy's," the shoes popularity is rivaled only by **Manolo Blahniks**—and, in fact, in recent years Jimmy's have become more popular than Manolos. Like Manolos, Jimmy Choo shoes were publicized on the HBO television series, *Sex and the City*. Worn by the lead characters and often referred to by name, *Sex and the City*'s publicity, along with the growing ubiquity of Jimmy Choo shoes at Hollywood red carpet events, helped to make Jimmy Choo a household name. Movies like *The Devil Wears Prada* and *In Her Shoes* also featured Jimmy's. On the other hand, because of the limited number of venues in which the shoes are sold (some shoes are sold at department stores, but many designs are not), the shoes retain their luxury cachet.

In 2005, 44 celebrities ranging from Victoria Beckham to Christina Aguilara to Paris Hilton took off their clothes and posed nude, in Jimmy Choo heels, for the photography book *Four Inches*, named after the height of Jimmy Choo heels. The book was sold to raise funds for the Elton John AIDS Foundation.

See also: Blahnik, Manolo; *Sex and the City*; Stilettos

Further Reading Pedersen, Stephanie. *Shoes: What Every Woman Should Know*. Cincinatti: David & Charles, 2005.

CHRISTIANITY

Feet and shoes play a role in the history of Christianity and in the practices of many Christian groups. In the **Classical civilizations** from whence Christianity emerged, it would have been mandatory to remove one's shoes before entering a temple or place of worship or before conducting a sacrifice. The Old Testament, for example, tells both Moses and Joshua to "put off thy shoes from off thy feet, for the place whereon thou standest is holy ground." While most contemporary Christian churches today do not mandate the removal of one's shoes before entering the church (and indeed, it would look extremely odd if one were to do so), some Christian pilgrims elect to go shoeless on their pilgrimage.

Going shoeless, or wearing simple sandals rather than shoes, is a sign of humility and can be found in the Gospels when the Apostles were prohibited from taking with them more than was needed for their journeys. Matthew 10:10 notes to not bring shoes; Mark 6:9 says to wear **sandals**; and Luke 10:4 also says to not wear shoes. This dates back to the Old Testament when servants were expected to serve in **bare feet**.

One of the strongest connections between feet and Christianity, however, is found in the tradition of **foot washing**. The New Testament tells us that Jesus washed his disciples' feet as a way to serve them during the Last Supper. At the time that Jesus lived, servants would have washed their masters' feet, so Jesus's decision to wash the apostles' feet was not about cleanliness. According to the Gospels, during the evening of the Last Supper, the Apostles were fighting over who would have the highest position in the Kingdom of God, demonstrating their pride. The washing of the feet—a humble and menial task normally left to servants—taught the disciples humility. In addition, feet in the Christian tradition often symbolize walking the spiritual path, so feet washing (using water, which often symbolizes the word of God as well as cleansing away false beliefs) can also be construed as Jesus's message to his disciples to continue on the path of righteousness after his death.

Other than the simple sandals worn by pilgrims who want to emulate the behavior of Jesus, shoes do not have great significance within Christianity. However, Catholicism is rich with symbolism related to the clothing and footwear of the hierarchy of the Church. For instance, buskins, or liturgical stockings, are worn by prelates (i.e., bishops, archbishops, cardinals, or the Pope) when they celebrate Mass. They are made of woven (not knitted) silk, heavily embroidered, and are reserved for the Pontifical Mass (i.e., a high mass celebrated only by bishops, cardinals, or the Pope). Buskins are worn over regular **socks**. There are also ordinary prelatial stockings that are less elaborate and are worn for everyday use. The color of the stockings typically matches the color of the cas-

---

Sister Alphonsa

Sister Alphonsa is a newly beatified Roman Catholic Saint. Alphonsa was a nun working in Southern India and is credited with miraculously healing children with club feet. She was born Annakkutty Muttathupadathu in 1910 to very poor parents. After her mother's death, she was raised by her aunt and uncle and went to Catholic school as a child. In 1923, her feet were badly burned when she either fell into a pile of burning chaff, or, as some accounts say, walked on coal in order to escape a forced marriage. In either case, she wanted to devote her life to God, and joined an order of nuns called the Franciscan Clarist Congregation in 1927. She died in 1946, and her grave is a popular location for pilgrims to visit, and is the site of many reported miracles, most involving the curing of club feet.

---

sock, so for the Pope the stockings are white, for the cardinals they are red, and for the bishops they are purple. Buskins extend to the knee and are held up with a garter. The color of the embroidery differs as to the wearer of the stocking—gold for the Pope and the cardinals, while bishops' stockings can only be trimmed in gold. Lesser titles like Abbots have yellow rather than gold trim.

Liturgical sandals are also required at the pontifical mass for the bishops, cardinals, and Pope. These are low-heeled shoes (which resemble **slippers** rather than sandals) with thin **leather** soles and silk uppers, which are tied with silk ribbons on which gold tassels are attached. The color of the sandals must match the robes worn that day. The Pope and the cardinals' sandals may be embroidered with gold or silver.

Outside of the performance of the mass, certain forms of footwear known as ecclesiastical shoes are regularly worn by clerics today. These shoes are based on the style of nineteenth century men's shoes: made of patent leather, with a low heel and a large buckle on the front. Like the buskins and liturgical sandals, stylistic differences in the shoes reflect differences in status among the wearers, with buckles of lower members of the church made of steel while priests and prelates' buckles are silver. Colors are also distinguished among the clerics, with cardinals' shoes being black with red trim. The Pope, on the other hand, wears red cloth, velvet, or silk slippers with a gold cross embroidered on the vamp (which visitors would kiss), although recent Popes have tended to wear more traditional shoes rather than the red slippers, especially when traveling.

Red shoes have a long history in the Catholic Church, long signifying imperial authority within the Church. Legend states that when the Saxon chieftain Odovacar conquered the Roman Empire in 476, he sent the Emperor's red shoes to the Eastern Emperor as a sign of his defeat. Red, too, is the color of blood and thus the red shoes worn by the Pope are often seen as signifying the blood of the Christian martyrs.

Today, Pope Benedict XVI is often seen in red patent leather loafers (allegedly made by Prada) that resemble the ecclesiastical shoes worn by other prelates in the patent leather material and the buckle, but which in color more closely resemble the traditional Pope's red slippers, and some believe it indicates a return to tradition and authority within the church.

See also: Classical Civilizations; Foot Washing; Judaism

Further Reading King, Philip, Lawrence Stager. *Life in Biblical Israel*. Louisville, KY: Westminster John Knox Press, 2001; Nainfa, John Abel. *Costumes of Prelates of the Catholic Church according to Roman Etiquette*. Whitefish, MT: Kessinger Publishing, 2008.

"CINDERELLA"

"Cinderella" is a **fairy tale** popularized by Charles Perrault in 1697 that tells the story of a girl who lives with, and is mistreated by, her stepmother and stepsisters, but is rescued by a prince and lives happily ever after. Cinderella, who is forced to live amongst the ashes of the hearth, is approached by a fairy godmother who grants her wish and allows her to attend a ball. There, she meets the prince and, in her haste to leave before the magic wears off, accidentally leaves behind one of her glass slippers. The prince then brings the **slipper** from house to house in the village to find the woman who wore it. Cinderella wins the hand of the prince in marriage after she is the only woman in the village whose foot is small enough to fit into the shoe.

The basic tale is found in more than 700 variants around the world. Classified by folklorists as Aarne-Thompson (AT) type 510, "the persecuted heroine," these tales involve a heroine who lives in oppressive and unfortunate circumstances and is ultimately rewarded with happiness, love, and marriage. In other words, "Cinderella" is the classic female rags-to-riches tale.

"Cinderella" is specifically classified as AT510A, in which the girl is persecuted by the stepmother (which is classified as AT Motif #S31) or stepsisters; AT510B instead involves the girl being driven from her home by her father and forced to work in someone else's kitchen. Another motif of the "Cinderella" tale is the presence of a magical helper (such as a fairy godmother (F311), magic tree, bird, sheep, or cow) who provides a magical object (D813) and magical clothes (D1050.1). Also common to "Cinderella" tales is the fact that the prince or king, after first seeing Cinderella at the ball (N711.6) must accept Cinderella as his bride in her lowly state (L162) as household maid. (In other words, he must ask for her hand in marriage when she is still a house servant.) Finally, most "Cinderella" tales feature the test of a slipper (H36.1), or sometimes a ring, as the key to the heroine's reward. (It is said that Perrault changed the slipper from a fur slipper to a glass slipper, since fur slippers could be stretched to fit larger feet; not only could glass shoes not stretch, but the prince can clearly see whether or not the foot fits in a clear glass slipper.)

One variant from Scotland, "Rashin Coatie," tells of a girl living with her ill-natured stepmother and stepsisters, whose mother had, before she died, gave her a magical calf who could grant her wishes. Even though the stepmother slaughters the calf, the dead calf still provides her with the means to attend a party at which she meets the prince, and where she leaves behind her satin slipper for the prince to find. When the prince arrives at the girl's home, her stepmother cuts off one of her daughter's toes and heel (AT Motif #J2131.3.1) in order to fit it into the slipper, a deception that is exposed by a bird. Another Scottish variant, "The Princess and the Golden Shoes," includes a magical sheep, and, again, a sister whose toes are cut off to fit into the shoe (from the stepmother: "if the shoe will not fit the foot, make the foot fit the shoe"). Unlike "Cinderella," however, the shoes are golden rather than glass. Like "Cinderella" and the other variants, the dainty size of the heroine's shoes are emphasized, and in this tale the prince was enchanted by the size of the princess's feet and kissed each of her shoes in turn.

The brothers Grimm also had a variant known as "Aschenputtel" in which a wishing tree and a magical bird provide the magic that allows the girl to attend the ball. Like the Scottish tale, the stepsisters try to deceive the prince by cutting off their toes and heels in order to fit into the shoes. (Encouraging her first daughter to fit into the shoe at all cost, the stepmother says "cut the toe off, for when you are queen you will never have to go on foot." Later, when the deception is revealed, she encourages her second daughter by saying "cut the heel off, for when you are queen you will never have to go on foot.") Once again, birds (as well as the blood in the shoe) alert the prince to the trick and, in addition, peck the stepsisters' eyes out as punishment.

Similar tales have been found in Russia, Armenia, Bulgaria, **Greece**, Italy, France, England, Georgia, Ireland, Denmark, Portugal, Norway, Finland, Serbia, Japan, **China**, Vietnam, the Philippines, **India**, the Himalayas, Arabia, Haiti, Chile, Native Canada, and **Native America**. Most involve the evil stepmother,

Next day was proclamation made : "Whereas, a crystal shoe
Has been discovered at the ball, who is the owner—who?
All ladies now must try it on ; the Prince will marry her,
Whoe'er it be, who easily the crystal shoe can wear."
No foot was found to fit the shoe ; they tried throughout the
   town ;
At last they came unto this house, and called the ladies down.
The sisters try to get it on, and pull, and push, and squeeze,
When Cinderella calmly said, "Allow me, if you please."
The sisters scorned her for the thought, and much surprise
   they knew,
When Cinderella from her pocket pulled the fellow shoe.
She tried them on—they fit—and she, no longer kitchen-
   maid,
Stands up to meet the Prince in all her beauty fair arrayed.

Cinderella trying on the glass slipper with the prince kneeling before her. Illustration from 1911 by Walter Crane in Cinderella picture book, New York: Dodd, Mead and Company. [Photo courtesy of Beinecke Rare Book and Manuscript Library, Yale University]

ugly stepsisters, a magical helper (often in the form of a dead animal), and the missing shoe that leads the prince to his beloved, although some tales, such as those found in the Americas, lack the shoe element, and others simply focus on the girl's escape from her tormentors.

No one knows for sure where and when the story first derived. The earliest European version of the tale is most likely "The Hearth Cat," which appeared in print in 1634. In this variant, the girl is not as virtuous as in other versions, killing her stepmother (a feature that is found in many of the **Middle Eastern** versions) and encouraging her father to marry her governess, who turns out to be no better than the first stepmother.

A Chinese version from the mid-ninth century may be the earliest print version of the tale, in which a cave master named Wu marries a woman after his wife dies, leaving his daughter Yeh-hsien to be mistreated by his new wife, who forces her to do all the household chores. After the stepmother kills Yeh-hsien's magical fish, she realizes that the bones of the fish are magic and would grant her wishes. The fish provide her an outfitter of kinfisher feathers and golden shoes, which she wears to a festival, but when her stepmother sees her, she runs off, losing one of the shoes. The gold shoe is eventually sold to the ruler of an island kingdom who declares that he wants to marry the owner of the shoe, and he makes all the women in the kingdom try it on. Alas, Yeh-hsien is the only one with small enough feet to fit into the shoe, and she marries the king, while her stepmother and stepsister are killed by flying rocks. If indeed **China** is the source of "Cinderella," it may have spread from China throughout Asia and then traveled to Europe after the Crusades, starting in the twelfth century.

An even earlier version of the tale was found in ancient **Egypt**, dating to perhaps the first century BCE. Known as "Rhodopis," it involves a Greek slave working in Egypt who is treated harshly by the other servants in the house. She is given a pair of gilded slippers by the master, which finds its way into the hands of the pharoah, who decides that he must marry the girl to whom the slipper fits. Eventually, he finds Rhodopis, who indeed fits the slipper, and she is transformed from slave to the wife of the pharoah. It is said that this first variant, lacking most of the magical elements found in later stories, was based on the true story of the Thracian courtesan Rhodopis.

Whether or not the story originated in China or Egypt, it is clear that the motif of the small slipper only has power in cultures in which large feet are considered unattractive and unfeminine, and where the woman with the tiniest feet must automatically be the most beautiful and well-bred of all (and the stepsisters, with their large feet, are considered grotesque). Certainly that is the case in China, and it may have been the case in the classical world as well. The German variant, "Aschenputtel," also echoes the Chinese emphasis not only on tiny feet, but the belief that even without toes or a heel, a queen will not have to walk on foot, which reflects the pampered nature of an elite Chinese woman with bound feet.

Today, besides the countless books, movies, and other popular cultural forms based on the "Cinderella" story, the larger theme of transformation from poor to rich and low to high remains extremely popular in movies, songs, and literature. For women in particular, the idea that one can be magically transformed into a beautiful woman and can thus win one's true love is a powerful idea.

The fact that it is the shoes that are the key to Cinderella's happiness can be explained by the long historical association between weddings and shoes. If the bride's shoes represent the transfer of a woman from her home to her husband's, and her submission to her husband, then it's not surprising that in "Cinderella" the slipper represents her one hope for love and marriage. (Interestingly, there are a handful of tales that reverse the gender of the hero and heroine and that have a heroine either wearing glass shoes in order to climb a glass mountain to rescue her future husband; or that have a hero wearing glass shoes while rescuing a princess from a sea serpent; the princess takes one of his shoes when he departs, which allows her to find him and marry him.)

See also: China; Dance Shoes; Europe; Fairy Tales; Foot Binding; Wedding Shoes

Further Reading Bettelheim, Bruno. *The Uses of Enchantment: The Meaning and Importance of Fairy Tales*. New York: Vintage Books, 1975; Cox, Marian Roalfe. *Cinderella: Three Hundred and Forty-Five Variants of Cinderella, Catskin and Cap o'Rushes*. London: The Folklore Society, 1893; Dundes, Alan, ed. *Cinderella: A Folklore Casebook*. Madison: University of Wisconsin Press 1982; Opie, Iona and Peter. *The Classic Fairy Tales*. New York: Oxford University Press, 1974; Propp, Vladimir. *Morphology of the Folktale*. Austin: University of Texas, 1968; Tatar, Maria M., ed. *The Classic Fairy Tales*. New York: W. W. Norton, 1999; Thompson, Stith. *The Folktale*. New York: Holt, Rinehart, and Winston, 1946; Zipes, Jack, ed.*The Oxford Companion to Fairy Tales*. Oxford: Oxford University, 2000.

CLASS

In all ranked and stratified societies, one's social position is reflected in the type of clothing and footwear that a person wears. For instance, elites in **Africa**, Asia, and Europe have traditionally worn much more elaborately made and decorated shoes than the masses, with royal family members wearing the most elaborate of all. In general, elites throughout history have tended to wear shoes that are less sensible and comfortable than those worn by the working classes because working people need to wear shoes that allow them to work, while the wealthy wear often choose footwear to signify status. In addition, the foot itself often signifies class position.

For example, small feet have been desirable attributes for women in societies around the world. Large feet are not only seen as unfeminine but they signify peasants and other people who have to work for a living, and thus shoe styles have long been developed to make women's feet appear smaller and daintier. At the same time, those shoes could only be worn by upper-class women because of the discomfort of wearing them and their lack of utility. **Foot binding**, for example, was practiced among the Han in **China** from the tenth century until the twentieth century and was a sign of status in much of the country. Bound feet were desirable partly because a woman with bound feet could not work (and often could not walk), demonstrating her high status and wealth.

In societies around the world, walking with **bare feet** signifies poverty and a lack of opportunity. While footwear was once a luxury in many societies, worn only by the wealthy, it is seen as a necessity today, so those people who do not wear shoes are typically found among the lowest ranks of the underclasses. Throughout much of American and European history, for example, working-class people who did have shoes may have only had two pairs: a regular pair for everyday use and a pair of good shoes for church and special occasions, and shoes were often handed down from parent to child to sibling. For this reason, shoe styles did not really change for working people until after industrialization made owning multiple pairs of shoes, or buying new shoes, possible.

Footwear in the civilizations of **Greece**, **Rome**, and **Egypt** were distinguished by class as well. It may have been customary in Egypt to remove one's shoes when in the presence of a social superior as a sign of respect, a practice also found in some African kingdoms. In addition, only elites in Egypt could wear decorated **sandals** or sandals with upturned toes. In Greece, the only people to go shoeless in public were the poor or ascetics, although Spartan soldiers went barefoot to toughen their feet. While Greece as a whole did not demonstrate intensive class distinctions in their clothing or footwear like Egyptians or Romans did, elites did wear sandals with decorative cutouts and gilded straps, while commoners' sandals were simple in design. Slaves, on the other hand, often wore no shoes, demonstrating their absolute subservience. Roman footwear was also heavily class dependent. Slaves and the poor mostly went barefoot while a free man of status could not be seen outside without foot coverings. For those who did wear shoes and sandals, **sumptuary laws** ensured that certain colors of shoes were worn by certain classes of people, and by law only high-status Roman women could adorn their shoes with gold or jewels.

In the civilizations of the New World, footwear was also distinguished by class. Among the Aztecs, for example, commoners went barefoot while only the nobility could wear sandals in the capital.

Slaves in most cultures went barefoot. In the colonies of the Americas, slaves either went barefoot, or in many cases in North America were issued rough wood and leather shoes once per year. Young slaves, on the other hand, went barefoot until they were old enough to work in the fields. Slave narratives include accounts of the difficulties slaves had in trying to soften these stiff shoes with grease. Sometimes slaves received hand-me-down **boots** from the masters. Field slaves or slaves working in industrial factories found that their shoes wore out quickly.

In Imperial China, one's social position (as well as gender and age) dictated one's footwear choices. Straw shoes were traditionally worn by peasants and embroidered silk shoes by the upper classes. China also had laws that restricted certain types of footwear, colors, or materials to certain classes, with merchants forced to wear one white and one black shoe and the emperor and his wife allowed to wear bright yellow shoes. These customs persisted even after death, as only dead emperors were allowed to wear jade "longevity" shoes.

In Imperial **Japan** we also see class distinctions among footwear, such as the use of special court boots for use by the Imperial family and other nobility, Samurai shoes to be worn by the ruling Samurai from the twelfth to the nineteenth centuries, or tall lacquered *geta*, or wooden shoes, worn by high ranking courtesans. Peasants and other workers generally were required by law to wear straw shoes, while elites could wear cloth shoes or other slip-on shoes imported from China. Because shoes are removed in Japan before entering a building, at one time servants were employed to remove the shoes of the wealthy and to carry them. Handling shoes was considered unclean, so these servants were themselves considered outcasts and, because of their status, were required to only wear straw shoes.

In the **Middle East**, too, class and status were conveyed through footwear. Elites wore finely made leather slippers with beautiful embroidery and jewels on them, and stilted sandals were high wooden clogs worn by high-status women during the Ottomon Empire and beyond.

In **Europe** from the early Middle Ages through today, elites have always worn very different shoes from commoners, and shoes, like clothing, have been a simple way to note one's class status. The materials used to make shoes, from at least the tenth century, were very different for commoners and nobility.For instance, noble men and women wore shoes made from a variety of luxurious fabrics, including silk, velvet, brocade, and soft leather. Embroidery, vegetable dyes, and beading were used to further decorate elite shoes, while peasants and other commoners wore shoes made of leather or other animal skins. **Clogs**, simple footwear made out of a carved block of wood, was also a common form of footwear for peasants and other commoners throughout Europe.

Because elites took part in activities like horseback riding or military service, they also wore beautiful and well-made boots specific to those purposes, while even within the military common soldiers wore simple shoes or boots. Boots, in fact, were markers of nobility in many Middle Eastern and European countries, as only those who could afford to could ride horses.

As shoe styles multiplied in the late Middle Ages and the Renaissance, elites had more styles to choose from while commoners continued to wear simple shoes. *Poulaines*, which were shoes with extremely long toes, became fashionable among the European nobility in the fourteenth century and were confined to elites by legislation that restricted very long toes only to the upper classes; given their unusual shape, they could not have been worn by working people regardless of the laws.

Other extraordinary shoes arose during the Renaissance, such as extravagantly decorated square-toed shoes with toes as wide as eight or nine inches, and *chopines*, high platform mules with soles as high as 20 and 30 inches. Both were only worn by elites, and chopines in particular became a symbol of status, as those women who wore them were obviously not working women and often had to have servants help them to walk or stand. Physical dependency thus became associated with wealth and status, and had become very desirable attributes for upper-class women. **High heels**, which developed in Europe the seventeenth century, were yet another footwear innovation that separated the nobility from working men and women.

As industrialism influenced the manufacture of shoes, they became cheaper to produce and more widely available to members of all classes in Europe and America, reducing the class distinctions of footwear. However, elites continued during the nineteenth century all the way up to the present period to purchase custom-made shoes rather than buy ready-to-wear shoes.

Because of intense competition among shoemakers and the influence of the fashion industry today, styles in footwear change throughout the year, forcing those who want to appear fashionable to buy new shoes often. Today, high fashion shoes and some athletic brands are so expensive that it would appear that only the elite could afford them. Yet, even many poor people today buy expensive brand-name **athletic shoes** in order to achieve the status associated with the brand, and thanks to the proliferation of black market counterfeit shoes and other accessories, many people buy imitation brand-name shoes.

See also: Africa; China; Classical Civilizations; Clogs; Europe; High Heels; India; Japan; Military Shoes and Boots; Sumptuary Laws

Further Reading Dunaway, Wilma A, *The African-American Family in Slavery and Emancipation*. Cambridge: Cambridge University Press, 2003; Rielle, Georgio and Peter McNeil, eds. *Shoes: A History From Sandals to Sneakers*. London: Berg Publishers, 2006.

CLASSICAL CIVILIZATIONS

The term classical civilization refers to the civilizations surrounding the Mediterranean Sea that emerged with the Egyptian culture, continued on through the rise of **Greece**, and ended with the fall of the Roman Empire. This section also includes the cultures of Mesopotamia and the peoples who fell under Roman rule, such as the ancient Hebrews.

Ancient **Egypt** is dated from about 3,000 BCE, and ends with its conquering by **Rome** in the first century BCE. Egyptian footwear reflects both the physical environment in which Egyptian people lived as well as their social and cultural beliefs and practices.

Sandals made of woven vegetable matter like papyrus leaves and palm fibers were probably the earliest type of footwear in Egypt. Sandals had the benefit of keeping the feet cool and protecting feet from the hot desert sand. Later, sandals were most likely made from a combination of animal skin (once tanning was developed), plant fibers, and wood. Indoors, most Egyptians would have gone barefoot.

As far back as 3,000 BCE, Egyptian art shows not only the wearing of sandals— at their most basic, a sole with a thong that attaches between the toes—but the fact that **class** distinctions were already marked on footwear. Pharoahs had the images of enemies painted on the bottoms of their sandals, so they could walk on them, and pharoahs were sometimes buried with sandals fashioned out of gold for the afterlife. Only elite Egyptians wore dyed, adorned, or otherwise decorated sandals, and only the pharoah and members of his court could wear gold or jeweled sandals. Dignitaries could wear pastel colors while red and yellow were worn by the middle class, with the poor and slaves going barefoot. In addition, fashionable sandals with upturned toes could only be worn by elites. Later, simple shoes and **boots** were also developed, with the characteristic pointy, upturned toe found throughout Eastern cultures. While sandals were worn out of doors, shoes were only worn indoors and were carried with a person as they traveled from place to place.

The cultures of ancient Mesopotamia—the Assyrians, Babylonians, and Sumerians who lived in the valley between the Tigris and Euphrates rivers—were farmers and sheep herders. The Sumerians were the oldest of the cultures, dating from 3500 BCE to 2000 BCE. When they wore footwear at all, they wore sandals with **leather** soles, with a toe loop and heel guard, starting in perhaps 2600 BCE. The Assyrians and the Babylonians (2000 BCE–600 BCE) inherited information about tanning and leatherwork from the Sumerians and wore similar sandals (sometimes with upturned toes). Knee high boots were also worn by Assyrians for riding chariots, and soft **moccasin**-like shoes were worn as well. Babylonians also had shoes of wood, felt, and cloth, which they decorated with metal objects.

The ancient Hebrew civilization arose from the Mesopotamian cultures in about 1900 BCE and lived in Egypt and the region in and around present-day Israel, living under Egyptian, Greek, and Roman rule. The ancient Hebrews farmed and raised sheep and wore footwear that was similar to that of other groups in the Middle East. It was common to go barefoot indoors, and like other cultures in this area and at this time sandals were the normative foot covering outdoors; putting on one's sandals was indicative of getting ready to engage in some sort of public activity. Going barefoot outdoors, on the other hand, was a sign of extreme poverty. After the Roman occupation, footwear among the ancient Jews reflected the footwear in use among the Romans. Sandals were made of wood, leather, or palm bark and often included a toe strap. Sandals worn by wealthy women were adorned with applique, shells, or jewels. At least some Hebrews also wore closed shoes, either of leather or linen, and sandals with a cap over the heel were also used.

As in other cultures, the ancient Hebrews removed their shoes when entering a residence, either their own or when visiting another person. Slaves or servants removed the shoes of their masters or of guests when arriving home and were employed as well to put the shoes back on again upon leaving the home. Because of the amount of dust and dirt that feet were exposed to, even when wearing sandals, it was common that one's servants washed one's feet when they arrived home, and washed guests' feet as a sign of hospitality.

Ancient Greek culture begins with the culture of Minoan Crete starting about 3500 BCE and continues through the Mycenaean culture, the rise of classical Greece, and ends with the Roman conquest in the second century BCE. Minoans of the upper classes wore sandals as well as shoes outdoors, but went barefoot indoors, as was customary in so many cultures of this period. The sandals were made of simple soles strapped to the foot with thongs, while the shoes were made of a single piece of leather. Men and women both wore soft boots for traveling, and boots were both of the knee high and calf-high variety. In the winter, men and women both wore fur-lined boots for warmth.

Classical Greek civilization began after the collapse of the Mycenaean culture, after 1150 BCE. The Greeks, like those cultures before them, primarily wore sandals when outdoors and went barefoot indoors. The lower classes went barefoot out of doors as well. The upturned toes found on Egyptian sandals were not popular in Greece, as Greeks generally wore a simpler form of shoes and clothing than their neighbors. There were a variety of shoes available, including slippers, sandals, half and full boots, and both closed and open-toed shoes made for either summer or winter weather.

Sandals or *krepis* were the most common form of footwear, with the simplest sandal made of a leather sole with leather thongs going between the toes and over the instep. Other sandals had a central strap down the middle of the top of the foot, with additional straps coming out of the central strap, and others known as *pedila* had straps that wrapped partway up the calf. The simplest shoes were *karbatinai*, which were made of a single piece of leather wrapped around the foot and tied with leather thongs. *Kothornoi* were tall leather boots worn by actors in the theatre, and *askerai* were winter boots lined with fur. Many women wore *krepis*, leather thong sandals with an ankle strap and an elevated sole made out of cork. Soft leather boots were worn for hunting, for traveling, and by soldiers, and soldiers also wore leather leg protection combined with sandals. While many women and men wore the same styles of shoes, certain styles, when worn by men, could make them appear effeminate and open to ridicule. The Greeks also wore socks called *podeia* made from plant fibers.

While Greek footwear is not as class-specific as either Egyptian or Roman, there were clear differences between upper-class and lower-class Greeks with respect to footwear. For instance, only the poor or slaves went barefoot in public; for everyone else (with the exception of Spartans, who went barefoot in public), shoes were required attire. In fact, shoes were required for participating in the public sphere, which slaves and women were restricted from. Even the gods put on shoes before engaging in any sort of activity. Elites could also decorate their shoes and sandals with decorative cutouts or discs and gilded straps. Sole height and shoe color further distinguished between the wealthy and commoners; for example, having a carved tongue or lingula indicated that the wearer was a citizen. In addition, Greek prostitutes wore platform sandals and were said to advertise their wares on the bottom of their shoes so that the ads could be read in the sand where they'd walked.

It was customary in ancient Greece, as in many other cultures around the world, to remove one's shoes when entering a home (which is still the case today), entering a temple, or performing a sacrifice. On the other hand, shoes were needed upon death to make the transition into the underworld, so shoes were most likely either worn on the dead or included in their burial.

The Etruscans lived in the Tuscany section of Italy from the eighth to the fourth centuries BCE and influenced Roman cultural styles. Initially, the Etruscans did not wear shoes, but they became a status symbol for the wealthy. Eventually, Etruscans wore sandals, lace-up boots, and soft shoes. In the sixth century BCE, shoes with pointed toes emerged, but were replaced with sandals by the fifth century thanks to Greek influence. They wore shoes made with both leather soles and also wooden soles, with elevated wooden *crepida* sandals worn by the wealthy. They also wore *caligae* sandals and *calcei* shoes. While Greek styles influenced the development of Etruscan footwear, the Etruscans elaborated on the designs, and wealthy Greek women purchased Etruscan platform sandals with golden straps for their own use.

Romans borrowed Greek clothing and shoe styles along with cultural, social, and religious elements. As in Greece, appearing barefoot in public was a sign of extreme poverty. Sandals and open-toed shoes and boots were common in Rome as they were in Greece. But Romans had a greater variety of footwear choices, and their shoe styles and practices indicate a much greater degree of differentiation between rich and poor. In general, shoes were a status symbol for wealthy Romans.

Sandals, called *solae*, could range from simple and practical to highly adorned with gold and other precious materials. Generally, they were made with a sole of leather attached to the foot either with a simple toe strap (over the second toe; unlike the Greeks who wore the toe strap over the big toe) or a number of leather straps. One common Roman sandal was the *gallicae*, a sandal with solid leather sides but an open toe area. They were especially worn by farmers and by runners. Men's and women's sandals began to differ about the third century, with women's sandals becoming narrower with pointed toes and men's became broader with blunt toes.

Crepida were borrowed from the Greek Krepis and also referred to sandals. These were thick-soled shoes covering just the heel and sides of the foot, and lacing up the ankle, and usually leaving the toes open. The sides were created by a network of cutouts that was done in a variety of patterns. Another shoe worn by Romans was a **clog** called the *sculponae*. Like a modern **Dr. Scholl's** slide, it had a wooden sole with a simple leather strap serving as the upper.

A variety of closed shoes and boots were also worn when outdoors. One of the earliest Roman shoes was the *carbatina*, simple one-piece shoes made of hide, similar to **moccasins**. The carbatina evolved into the *calcei*, soft leather shoes worn by free men with their togas. (It was inappropriate to wear sandals with the toga.) Sometimes calcei had solid sides and sometimes the sides had decorative cutouts. Roman law dictated the type and color of shoe that could be worn by the classes; free men wore pale colors, senators wore black and sometimes red, while emperors wore red shoes and boots encrusted with precious stones. Women also wore calcei as well as ankle or calf-high boots, often in white and often decorated with precious stones and tied with straps or with silk.

Soldiers wore thick-soled, open-toed, lace-up boots known as buskins or *caligae* with hobnails nailed into the soles, which allowed them to march for weeks at a time. They were cut from a single piece of leather, like the carbatina, and the leg portions were made up of a network of straps or laces. Later, the *campagus militaris* became the official military boot. This was a more substantial shoe boot for soldiers and officers. Roman soldiers also wore cloth or wool leggings, borrowed from Eastern cultures, and after conquering Gaul, borrowed the Gaulish style of leather boot with carved wooden soles. Knee-high boots were special boots that tended to be limited to horsemen, hunters, and government officials, and were often featured in artwork as being worn by the gods. They may have been worn by officials during parades, and the elaborate versions had a cat head on them.

Cothurni, also borrowed from the Greeks, were knee-high hunting boots that laced up the front. The term also describes the boots worn by actors with three to five inch high soles. Actors also wore the *soccus*, a thin **slipper** or **sock**. Off-stage, women wore the soccus in their homes. (Other forms of socks were boot and sandal linings with a notch between the toes for the toe straps.)

Romans initially wore shoes outdoors, rather than sandals, although sandals became acceptable shoes for outdoor use during the late second century, and like Greeks, Romans removed their shoes before entering a private home or temple. Upper-class visitors would remove their shoes when entering a visitor's home and put on a pair of indoor sandals that would have been carried by their slaves. Even while indoors, however, sandals were removed when reclining on furniture. Asking a slave for one's sandals or shoes meant that one was preparing to leave.

Like in so many other ancient civilizations, shoes and sandals were removed when entering a Roman temple. On the other hand, special sandals that were not otherwise worn on regular ground could be worn in a temple. In fact, Greeks, Romans, and Egyptians all had special, non-leather sandals that could be worn in sacred temples.

See also: Boots; Class; Sandals

Further Reading Blundell, Sue. "Beneath Their Shining Feet: Shoes and Sandals in Classical Greece," in Rielle, Georgio and Peter McNeil, eds. *Shoes: A History From Sandals to Sneakers*. London: Berg Publishers, 2006; Golden, Mark, Peter Toohey. *Sex and Difference in Ancient Greece and Rome*. Edingburgh: Edinburgh University Press, 2003; Sebesta, Judith Lynn, Larissa Bonfante. *The World of Roman Costume*. Madison: University of Wisconsin Press, 1994.Sumner, Graham, Raffiello, Amato. *Roman Military Clothing*. Oxford: Osprey, 2005.

CLEATS AND SPIKES

Cleats are **athletic shoes** with rubber, plastic, or sometimes metal studs, or cleats, on the outer soles, while spikes are athletic shoes with metal spikes inserted into the outer soles. Both cleats and spikes are worn in order to provide the athlete with better traction on a soft surface, usually grass or dirt. Cleats are worn for baseball, soccer, and football, while spikes are worn for golf and certain sports in track and field. They generally are worn under the ball and heel of the shoe but could cover the entire outer sole.

Soccer, or association football, developed in **Europe** perhaps as far back as the Middle Ages but became formalized in the nineteenth century. Shoes worn when playing soccer are known as football boots. The earliest football boots would have been made of **leather**, and because they were **boots**, provided support for the ankle. The first official record of the use of cleats was in 1891, referring to the insertion of rounded leather studs into the soles of the boots to provide better grip and traction. Prior to that time, players may have instead fashioned some sort of gripping mechanism out of strips of leather attached to the bottom of the boots. Other forms of cleats would have been metal spikes or tacks. With the use of cleats, football boots became heavier because additional layers of leather were used in the sole to allow for the insertion of the studs. Players rubbed grease onto their boots to soften them. In addition, in warmer climates in southern Europe and South America, players began wearing football boots that did not cover the ankle; modern football boots now uniformly resemble these warm weather variants, which look more like baseball shoes.

The first modern football boots were made by **Adidas** in 1954. They were lighter, had a non-leather sole, an upper made of kangaroo skin, and included replaceable rubber or plastic studs, which could be screwed in at different lengths for different surface conditions. In the 1990s, Adidas introduced another innovation in the form of rubber blades instead of studs, which faced different directions and allowed for better grip. Also in the 1990s, **Nike** introduced non-leather football boots, which are lighter and more flexible than their predecessors. Today, football boots have different cleats for different types of surface: replaceable aluminum cleats which are worn in wet dirt, firm plastic cleats for regular surfaces, and short, plastic, or rubber cleats for very hard surfaces. Different shoes are also worn in indoor conditions as well as for Astroturf.

These soccer, or football, shoes have molded plastic cleats on the bottom. [Copyright 2008 Jupiterimages Corporation]

American football developed in the **United States** in the late nineteenth century and grew out of soccer and rugby. Football players today wear football cleats. The first shoes worn for football were leather boots, derived from European, or association football, boots. The boots had leather cleats on them to allow for better grip of the field, but they had to be changed by a cobbler when wet weather approached. In 1927, former football coach John Riddell invented replaceable cleats, which he marketed to teams and schools through his company, the Riddell Corporation.

Like soccer, American football cleats require different types of cleats for different surfaces and weather conditions. Football players can play in sunny weather, rain, or snow, and on natural grass or Astroturf. When playing on natural grass, players will wear molded bottom shoes with the cleats molded into the sole of the shoe, or shoes with replaceable cleats that can be switched as weather conditions change. Cleats range from one-half inch to one inch in length to account for conditions ranging from very wet to very hard and dry to very hard and icy. Players who play on Astroturf, on the other hand, will wear shoes with Astroturf treads.

Baseball is an American sport that became popular during the mid-nineteenth century in the United States, but which evolved out of earlier games played in Great Britain as early as the eighteenth century. Baseball players originally wore leather shoes, but in the early twentieth century they began adding detachable spikes to their shoes to help grip the field. Spikes were banned in 1976, however, because of the damage they caused to the grass on the field and were replaced by plastic cleats in the 1980s.

Spikes are made of metal and are screwed into the sole of a shoe, or into a spike plate affixed to the sole of the shoe. The oldest spiked shoes are probably **golf shoes**. At least as far back as the mid-nineteenth century, golfers wore heavy leather Oxford shoes into which they inserted metal spikes into the soles to help them grip the turf. In 1906, Spalding began selling saddle shoes, a form of Oxford with a saddle-shaped piece of leather on the upper, which served to reinforce the shoe during athletic moves. The shoes were designed to be worn for tennis and squash, but they were adopted by golfers in the 1920s once the company began putting spikes on them. By this time, though, controversy had already emerged about the damage done to turfs and clubhouse floors by metal spikes. In the 1990s, golf courses in the United States began to ban the use of metal spikes, leading to the use of rubber knobs called Soft Spikes instead of metal spikes.

Spiked athletic shoes were another early development. In 1893, spiked running shoes were developed by the first sports shoe company in the world, J. W. Foster and Sons (later to become known as **Reebok**), and by the end of the century, the Spalding Company. These shoes were made entirely out of leather, but with metal spikes on the bottom. This technology was taken a step further in 1925 by Adi Dassler of Adidas, who created running shoes featuring a different distribution of spikes for long or short distance running.

Today, while joggers do not wear spiked shoes, competitive runners and other athletes who perform in track and field events continue to wear spiked shoes. Modern track and field shoes are very light and do not have many of the features such as heels, support, and cushioning found in **jogging shoes**. Instead, they have spikes in their soles to increase traction when sprinting, jumping, or throwing. Sprinters, distance runners, jumpers, and other field athletes all wear different shoes, based on their sport's needs. Most spiked shoes have no spikes in the heel, with the exception of those worn by high jumpers or javelin throwers. Most spikes are about one-fourth of an inch high (but can range from three-sixteenths of an inch to half an inch) and can be narrow and sharp, conical and tapered, or conical and terraced in shape, all of which help the athlete increase speed or traction.

Finally, modern **snow shoes** are also made with spikes to grip the snow and keep the wearer from sinking into the snow. Mountaineers also wear spiked shoes to help them to grip the ice when climbing.

See also: Athletic Shoes; Adidas; Reebok; Golf Shoes; Snow Shoes

Further Reading Baker, William. *Sports in the Western World*. Totowa, NJ: Rowman & Littlefield, 1982; McComb, David. *Sports in World History*. New York: Routledge, 2004.

CLOGS

Clogs are carved wooden shoes, sometimes with separate uppers formed out of cloth or **leather**. They have been worn in cultures around the world. Clogs were often worn by peasants working in the fields to keep their feet from getting dirty or muddy, by industrial workers working in factories, or by elites who wore them outdoors to, again, protect the feet and clothing from dirt, mud, or water. In many cultures, clogs are the traditional footwear of the poor, as the shoes are simple to make, long lasting, and can withstand a great deal of hard use.

Many clogs were made from a single piece of wood, including the French *sabot*, the Geman *klomp*, the Korean *namakshin*, and the Dutch *klomp*. These are the traditional Northern European clogs. Birch, sycamore, willow, and alder are some of the woods used for construction. To make a carved wooden clog, the clogger or clogmaker uses a piece of log cut with an axe to the approximate size of the person's foot, and would, after drying it out, shape it with a stock knife or clogger's knife, and carve out the interior with hollowing tools. Clogmakers could be found in villages throughout **Europe** through the early years of the twentieth century, and they often worked as itinerant cloggers, traveling from place to place, cutting rough clogs from wood, and selling them to clogmakers or clogmaking factories.

Other cultures, on the other hand, made clogs from a carved piece of wood attached to a separate upper made of cloth or leather. Sometimes the upper is simply a strap or even a thong, as in the Japanese *geta*, while other times the upper is a fully enclosed shoe, as in the Venetian *chopine* or the Chinese flower pot shoe.

Clogs were worn throughout Europe starting in about the twelfth century, primarily by peasants. Because they rarely wore out, they were passed down from parent to child, and people in Norway, Belgium, and Holland had fancier clogs, known as Sunday clogs, which were painted, to wear to church and for special occasions. Since leather shoes were not affordable for many, clogs were sometimes decorated to appear to have stitching and buttons. French clogs, or *sabots*, occupy an interesting place in history because French textile workers during the nineteenth century were said to have thrown their shoes into the mills during a strike in order to disrupt the work, which is said to be the origin of the term "**sabotage**."

By the fourteenth century, European elites began to wear a different type of clog as an overshoe in order to protect their shoes from dirt and mud. For instance, as far back as the thirteenth century, men and women in Spain were wearing *galochas* (also known as *zuecos*)

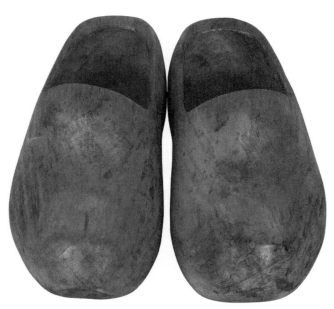

These clogs from Northern Europe are made the traditional way, carved out of a single piece of wood. [Copyright 2008 Jupiterimages Corporation]

or **galoshes**, which were elevated overshoes made of wood (sometimes with two or three stilts) with a strap of leather across the vamp. They probably arose thanks to the Arab conquest of Spain and are most likely related to the Middle Eastern stilted sandal or *kabkab*. This trend may have spread to Italy, with the *chopines*, elevated clogs worn by elite women that were covered in velvet, to wear over shoes, and which were often designed to match the shoes they were worn with. The higher the elevation (they eventually reached 30 inches in height), the higher the status of the wearer, as women wearing high chopines needed their servants to assist them while walking. Prostitutes wore clogs called *tappini* (tappinare means a sex act performed by a prostitute), while high-price courtesans wore very high chopines. Another type of European clog was the patten, which, like the chopine and the galosh, was an overshoe worn to keep shoes clean and dry. Chopines, made of cork or wood, were worn primarily in Italy and Spain, but the more utilitarian wooden or metal pattern was worn throughout Europe by anyone who wanted to protect their fine shoes and nice clothing from the elements outdoors.

The peasants of many Asian countries wore clogs as well. Filipinos, prior to the arrival of the Spanish, once wore clogs called *bakya*, made of a thick piece of wood, cut into the shape of a foot, and adorned on the sides with painted designs. Uppers were made of a wide leather or cloth strap. Today, uppers are often made of plastic or rubber. They have largely been replaced by simple slippers or rubber sandals for everyday use, but are still worn with traditional dress at cultural events and are purchased by tourists visiting the Philippines.

Another wooden shoe is the Korean *namakshin*, a carved wooden clog with two heels or stilts. Similar to the other clogs discussed here, the namakshin was originally developed to protect the feet and clothing from mud and dirt, but unlike those shoes it was still worn into the twentieth century. Like other Korean shoes, women's namakshins had pointed toes. The history of the namakshin comes not from Asia, however, but from Holland. In 1651, a Dutch merchant ship shipwrecked off the shore of **Korea**, and the sailors who were left behind began making traditional Dutch clogs to sell to local people.

The Chinese traditionally wore clogs as well. Historically, **China** had both elevated clogs with two stilts, which were worn to keep the feet and clothing clean and dry while outdoors, and pedestal shoes, known as flower pot shoes, slippers of embroidered silk that sat on a concave wooden platform, from two to four inches high, which were worn by elite Manchurians. The elevated height allowed the wearers to tower over lesser people and created a mincing walk similar to the walk of Chinese women with bound feet, while the heel was used for riding horses. They were called flower pot shoes because it appeared as though the shoe was resting on a flower pot. The Chinese also had clogs that resemble the Korean namakshin.

The *geta* is the Japanese version of the clog, a wooden sandal with a cloth thong, which stands on one to three stilts or "teeth." Geta can be quite high, and the height serves both to protect the feet and the kimono from dirt, mud, or water and, in addition, once served as a marker of status. The geta were worn originally by the elites, with special geta for use by emperors and priests, and became quite fashionable for city dwellers starting in the seventeenth century. As with the

Italian chopine, Japanese courtesans wore a special geta called the *oiran geta*, which was a very tall, lacquered geta that made the wearer walk with a sensual gait. Other traditional geta include *takaba geta*, with very high teeth to wear in the rain.

Stilted sandals, known as *kabkabs*, were elevated wooden sandals worn by high-status women during the Ottomon Empire throughout the Middle East. The stilted sandals stood on two stilts and were often extremely high. The uppers were made of leather, silk, or velvet and were often intricately decorated with embroidery, inlaid wood, mother of pearl, and other precious materials. Designed to keep a woman's feet clean and dry while outdoors or in the bath house, they became items of status among the wealthy women who wore them. Like wooden clogs found in other cultures, these shoes were known for the distinctive sound that they made while walking and from which the name is derived.

Many Central Asian countries had wooden shoes as well, which were carved with upturned toes, similar to the shoes worn in those countries. There were both plain clogs, to be worn while working, and fancy clogs, carved and inlaid, to be worn on special occasions. These clogs had four stilts with metal studs on the bottom, to aid in traversing mountainous terrain.

India also has a shoe that is related to the clog known as the *paduka*, a toe-knob sandal with an elevated sole, to protect the feet from the hot ground. The paduka varies on the basis of material and the height of the sole, which can range from a flat sandal to a 10 inch high elevated platform, made of two stilts. The difference in paduka materials and adornment reflect the status difference of their wearers, with padukas made of ivory, silver, precious woods, or bronze being worn by members of the highest castes. India also has another traditional wooden shoe that is carved entirely out of wood to resemble a regular shoe known as a *juttee*, and which sits on two stilts.

Both clogs and toe-knob sandals were worn in **Africa**, but they are not indigenous to sub-Saharan Africa. Instead, they were introduced from India and perhaps the Arab world. Elevated clogs were often worn by kings such as among the Yoruba of Nigeria, in order to elevate him above the commoners.

In Europe, as working people could begin to afford leather shoes, especially after the industry was mechanized in the nineteenth century, clogs were largely displaced by shoes. During World War II, however, with leather and other materials used to make shoes being rationed, many European governments tried to encourage their citizens to begin wearing clogs again, although many people found it difficult to begin wearing shoes that had long been associated with poverty.

Since the 1970s, when clogs enjoyed a resurgence in popularity in the West, clogs are now worn by many people as a simple, comfortable shoe. For example, chefs often wear padded clogs while they cook, to protect their feet from food. **Crocs**, a waterproof plastic shoe made for boating and popularized in the 2000s, is the latest incarnation of the clog.

Clogs are also associated with a folk dance known as clogging, which involves using wooden-soled shoes to stomp on the ground to the downbeat of the music.

Practiced throughout Northern Europe from the eighteenth to the twentieth centuries, clogging was said to have been started by factory workers who tapped their wooden clogs on the floor while working and is practiced in the Appalachian region of the United States as well. Today, cloggers wear leather shoes with taps on the soles of the feet, similar to tap dancing shoes. Tap dancing is derived from clogging.

See also: China; Crocs; India; Japan; Europe; Dance Shoes; Sabotage

Further Reading Atkinson, Jeremy. *Clogs and Clog Making.* Shire Publications, 2009; Green, Harvey. *Wood: Craft, Culture, History.* New York: Penguin, 2007; Jenkins, J. Geraint, *Exploring Country Crafts.* Wakefield: EP Publishing, 1977.

CLUB FOOT

A club foot, or *talipes equinovarus*, is a birth defect that causes excessive supination, or under pronation, in which the ankles roll outward and the foot then rotates inward. In extreme cases, the foot is turned almost entirely on its side, making a person with untreated club foot walk on the outside of the foot, rather than on the bottom of the foot.

Club foot can be a genetic condition, often associated with other diseases such as Edwards Syndrome, or it can be caused by problems during gestation or the birthing process. In the case of postural club foot, it is caused by the position of the fetus in the womb and can either occur in one foot or both feet. It is a birth defect in which the tendons and ligaments of the foot are formed incorrectly, and children born with this condition have small, stiff feet that cannot be placed into a normal position. About one-tenth of one percent of all births have some form of this disorder. Without treatment, the condition will worsen and the bones and other structures of the feet will become malformed as well.

Club foot can be treated with braces, splits, or plaster casts that force the foot into a flatter position. The Ponseti method refers to manipulating the foot, followed by the application of a full foot and leg cast, to maintain the position of the foot. This process begins very early, during infancy, and the casts are replaced every few days over a period of weeks or months in order to continue stretching the foot into a normal position. During the last phase of the process, doctors often recommend clipping the **Achilles** tendon to keep the feet realigned, a procedure known as an Achilles Tenotomy. In addition, leg braces, which attach to special **orthopedic shoes** and keep the feet positioned normally, are then worn for a period of years to continue to provide support and control for the foot. Finally, some doctors recommend surgery that involves cutting and repairing a number of the tendons and the ligaments in the foot.

Because of the pain, lack of mobility, and social stigma associated with club foot, a number of medical charities provide treatment for children with club foot in Third World countries whose families would otherwise not have access to treatment.

See also: Disorders and Injuries; Orthotics

Further Reading Hay, William, Anthony Hayward, Myron J. Levin, Judith M. Sondheimer. *Current Pediatric Diagnosis & Treatment.* New York: McGraw-Hill Professional, 2002; Moore, Keith L., and T. V. N. Persaud. *Before We Are Born: Essentials of Embryology and Birth Defects.* Philadelphia: Saunders, 1998.

COBBLER. *See* Shoemakers.

COLE, KENNETH

Kenneth Cole is an American shoe designer and founder of Kenneth Cole Productions, which makes shoes, accessories, perfume, and clothing. The company is known for its involvement in a number of social issues and for its humorous and sometimes controversial **advertising** campaigns.

Kenneth Cole got his start in the shoe business while working for his father, Charles Cole, whose shoe company, El Greco Leather Products, originally released the **Candie's** brand of shoes. Cole hired his four children to work in his company, and Kenneth began working in 1976, designing many of the company's shoes. In 1982, he started Kenneth Cole, Inc. in order to sell his own shoes. He started the company with a relatively small budget, had his shoes made in Italy, and debuted his first collection in 1982. Because he wanted to show his shoes in Manhattan but didn't want to pay for renting a hotel room or showroom, he instead borrowed a 40 foot semitrailer and planned to park it in midtown Manhattan. But because the city only granted truck parking permits for a limited number of reasons, Cole changed the name of his company to Kenneth Cole Productions and was granted a permit to shoot a film. He called it "The Birth of a Shoe Company" and used the production in order to show and sell shoes; at the end of the three day "shoot," he sold his entire collection of 40,000 shoes.

Since the earliest days of the company, Kenneth Cole Productions has been involved in charitable work, through corporate donations to organizations such as the American Foundation for AIDS Research, Rock the Vote, and Riverkeeper. The company also uses its advertising to promote causes that are important to the Cole family, including AIDS awareness, gun control, voting, and homelessness. In fact, the print ads in the early years of the company did not feature the company's products; instead they were just used to promote awareness of a variety of issues, beginning with AIDS in 1984. Even today when shoes or other products are included, the company's ads still include a Kenneth Cole quote about a social issue. Many of the messages have been controversial, such as those arguing for gun control, safe sex, reproductive freedom, gay rights, and Democratic politics. Others have been less so, such as the 1998 (repeated in 2003) campaign inviting customers to bring in shoes for the homeless, in exchange for a 20 percent discount on Kenneth Cole shoes.

In 2008, the company began the "We all walk in different shoes" campaign, which includes non-normative models who are featured because of the unusual ways their lives turned out, thanks to severe injury, disease, transgender status, or other "difference."

The company went public in 1994 in order to attract enough capital to expand. Today, Kenneth Cole products are sold in more than 7,500 locations, including department stores, specialty stores, via catalog, Web site, and through 80 Kenneth Cole stores. The company sells its shoes under a number of brands: Kenneth Cole New York, the most expensive brand, Kenneth Cole Reaction, and Unlisted, the least expensive brand. The company also offers additional products under the names Tribeca and Gentle Souls, and since 2003, Bongo. It also began licensing its name to apparel manufacturers such as Liz Claiborne in the late 1990s to produce Kenneth Cole-branded clothing.

In 2007, Kenneth Cole started the Awareness Fund, a 501c3 organization dedicated to providing funds to support charities like the American Foundation for AIDS Research and Help USA. Cole's work to support causes important to him have only helped the company's bottom line, as many customers support a company because, in part, of the causes that they are associated with. Kenneth Cole has won a number of awards for design, advertising, and for his charitable projects, including the Humanitarian Leadership Award given by the Council of Fashion Designers of America. In 2008, Kenneth Cole stepped down as CEO but remains as chairman and chief creative officer of the company. The company had profits of $536 million in 2006.

See also: Advertising; Candie's

Further Reading Cole, Kenneth. *Footnotes: What You Stand For Is More Important Than What You Stand In*. New York: Simon & Schuster, 2003.

CONCEALMENT SHOES

Concealment shoes are shoes that are concealed in houses in order to bring luck or ward off bad spirits. The tradition is found primarily in England (although concealment shoes have been found in other European countries as well) and was imported to Canada and the **United States** during the colonial period. Shoes have been found that were concealed as early as the fourteenth century and as late as the 1930s. In North America, shoes are most commonly found in nineteenth century homes.

Shoes were either inserted into the foundations or walls of houses during construction or were often concealed in walls while the house was standing. The most commonly found shoes are old, worn children's shoes. Families would never have buried a new pair of shoes; first, because new shoes were too expensive to dispose of this way, and also because older shoes carry the essence or spirit of the person who wore them, and it's the connection to the person that is central to warding off the spirits. New shoes would have been spiritually "empty." And children are thought to have stronger spirits than older people.

Shoes were thought to be able to ward off evil spirits, perhaps because the spirit would encounter the shoe and think it was encountering a real person. They may also ward off evil spirits because spirits are said to dislike **leather**. Sometimes the shoe was stitched close to hold bad spirits within them, acting as a spirit trap. (An early case of such an activity was when a fourteenth century English priest named John Schorn supposedly trapped the devil in a boot.) Concealed shoes were most often placed into entryways like doorways, chimneys, or windows, since those are the areas of the house that are most vulnerable to spirits entering.

Shoes are often used in sympathetic magic because the shoe retains the shape of its wearer, and thus carries a more direct linkage to that person than, say, an item of clothing. So, a worn shoe would continue to retain a connection to the wearer long after the wearer's death. In addition, shoes are historically thought to signify luck, perhaps because for much of history only the wealthy were able to wear shoes. Because the shoes of the dead carry the spirit of the wearer with them, they can both bring bad luck, but can also help to ward off other spirits from the home. While there's no way to know how many concealment shoes were worn-out shoes of the living or shoes from a dead family member, it is probably the case that at least some of the shoes were from a dead person. Another idea behind concealment shoes is that people could not bear to throw away the shoes of their dead relatives because they were so personal to them.

Today, the largest collection of concealment shoes in the world is found at the Northampton Museum and Art Gallery, which not only has more than 200 concealment shoes (included in its collection of 12,000 shoes) but maintains the Concealed Shoe Index, a database with more than 2,000 shoes from around the world.

See also: Bata Shoe Museum; Beliefs; Europe; United States

Further Reading Davies, Owen, Willem de Blecourt. *Beyond the Witch Trials*. Manchester: Manchester University Press, 2004; Easton, Timothy. "Spiritual Middens" *Encyclopedia of vernacular architecture of the world* v.1, Cambridge University Press, 1997; Eastop, Diana. "Garments deliberately concealed in buildings," in: Wallis, R and Lymer K. (eds.) 2001. *A Permeability of Boundaries? New approaches to the Archaeology of Art, Religion and Folklore*. BAR International Series S936. Oxford: British Archaeological Reports, 79–84; Swann, June. "Shoes concealed in buildings," *Costume: Journal of the Costume Society* No. 30 (1996), pp. 56–99.

CONVERSE

Converse is one of the oldest American makers of **athletic shoes** in the United States and was at one time the biggest producer of athletic shoes in the country. Known especially for its signature basketball shoe, the Converse All Star, the black and white canvas shoe is now the iconic American **sneaker**, beloved by skateboarders, basketball players, punks, rebels, and teenagers everywhere. It is the best-selling shoe in the world. Converse is now owned by **Nike**.

The Converse Rubber Company was founded in 1908 by Marquis Mills Converse, a shoe store and department store manager. The company's first shoes included rubber **boots**, and they began making canvas tennis shoes with rubber soles in 1915. In 1917, Converse released one of the first basketball shoes, the Converse All Star, a black and white canvas high top sneaker with a star in a patch on the ankle.

As basketball grew in popularity in the United States, the All Star grew alongside of it. All Stars were worn, for example, by the Harlem Renaissance basketball team starting in 1923; the team won the first World Championship in 1939 wearing All Stars. Also in 1939, the first NCAA game was played and both teams wore All Stars. By the 1950s, Converse shoes were worn by virtually all professional and college basketball players. The Pro Leather was released in 1976 and quickly became dominant in pro basketball.

Converse's two biggest-selling shoes are the direct result of two athletes from the first part of the twentieth century, Chuck Taylor and Jack Purcell. Chuck Taylor, a basketball player who played for the Buffalo Germans and the Akron Firestones, wore his first pair of All Stars in 1918, while still in high school. The former player joined Converse in 1921 as a salesman and played a major role in the future of All Star shoes. Taylor traveled around the country, teaching basketball clinics and selling shoes, and in

Jack Boys, the new CEO of Converse Inc, holds up a giant-sized Chuck Taylor All Star shoe at the company headquarters in North Reading, Massachusetts, June 12, 2001. For more than half of the last century, Converse's Chuck Taylor All-Star sneakers ruled every schoolyard, high school, and pro basketball court in America. Earlier in 2009 the company went bankrupt, but under a management team there are hopes of turning the brand name around. [AP Photo/Charles Krupa]

1923 the company added his name to the shoe's ankle patch, and people began calling All Stars shoes Chuck Taylors, or Chucks. In the 1930s, Taylor's signature was added to the All Star shoe design, making Taylor the first player-endorser of an athletic shoe and making the Chuck Taylor All Star the first celebrity athlete shoe. Chucks were extremely profitable and comprised half of the American basketball shoe market until the mid-1970s.

In 1935, Jack Purcell, a Canadian badminton player, teamed with the B. F. Goodrich Rubber Company and designed a low top sneaker known as the Jack Purcell shoe, or simply as "Jacks." In 1972, Converse purchased Goodrich's footwear line and began producing the shoes, which are still extremely popular today.

During World War II, Converse made military boots and other equipment for the U.S. Army, and American soldiers also wore All Stars for training. During the 1950s and 1960s, the company expanded, opening factories and buying other companies, including those that manufactured sporting equipment, footwear, and industrial equipment.

Converse struggled through the 1970s due to foreign competition, poor business decisions, and lack of funds and sold off many of its affiliated lines and products, although the All Star remained extremely popular during this period. The company was purchased and sold multiple times throughout the 1970s and 1980s and experienced two bankruptcy proceedings, but by 1994 was spun off into its own company again. With the rise of Nike in the 1980s, Converse faced steep competition again and began diversifying its footwear, making running shoes, tennis shoes, and shoes geared toward other sports and markets. In 1995, Converse also began making clothing, which put the company further into debt.

Shoes Hanging Over Power Lines

Since the 1980s a phenomenon has arose in most cities and many suburbs in the United States in which old sneakers (and sometimes boots) are found tied together by the laces and hung over power lines (sometimes known as "shoefiti"). The most commonly given explanation is that shoes on power lines indicate drug activity in the area and are a form of advertising, although at least one police department has challenged that claim, saying that there is no correlation between sneaker locations and crime, drug-related or not. On the other hand, many people simply feel that young people sometimes throw their shoes over power lines to celebrate the end of school or simply as a fun form of benign vandalism or as a way to taunt a weak kid. Others point to the tradition in the military of throwing military boots over a power line when leaving the service or just leaving one's post as a possible origin for this practice. Given the large numbers of shoe sightings around the country, chances are good that there are many different reasons for the shoes being there, with the simplest being perhaps the best explanation: when someone gets a new pair of shoes, they dispose of their old pair by tossing them over the wire.

Shoefiti.   [Copyright 2007 Wally Stemberger. Image from BigStockPhoto.com]

Converse has used other athletic endorsers over the years, but none have had the impact of Chuck Taylor or Jack Purcell. Magic Johnson, for example, signed on in 1979, a relationship that lasted until 1992 and included the release of the Magic Johnson shoe and apparel line. Johnson eventually canceled his contract, saying he was dissatisfied with the company's old fashioned marketing and a corporate image that continued to be associated with Chuck Taylor. Larry Bird was another celebrity endorser who was featured in a series of popular commercials in which Bird, dressed as his grandmother, dominated on the court in her Converse shoes.

Even with the release of new shoes in the 1980s, the company continued to be known for its basketball shoes, and in particular, the All Stars. Converse became the first shoe company to officially represent the Olympic Games in 1984, and in 1985 Converse was named the official shoe of the NBA, a title which the company lost in the 1990s. In 1997, the company released the All Star 2000, a leather version of the All Star with a classic Chuck Taylor patch (or "chuck patch"). Other designs based on new athletes were less successful, and the company continued to struggle through the 1990s. The company filed again for bankruptcy in 2001, and when it restructured after yet another purchase, closed its last American factory.

All Converse production now takes place in **China**, Vietnam, and Indonesia. In 2003, Converse was purchased by Nike, to the dismay of longtime Converse fans.

While the classic All Star has changed over the years (the company released a low cut version in 1962, added new colors in 1966, and began adding new materials like suede, denim, and hemp), it has also remained largely the same, which is important to the brand's loyal wearers. In fact, the iconic black and white classic All Star remains extremely popular today, and with the rise of retro fashion in the 1990s, the All Star is more popular with nonathletes and collectors than ever today. Because of this, Converse not only continues to sell the classic All Star but has also re-released numerous early models with new twists.

Converse shoes have been associated with a number of subcultures, including the greasers of the 1950s, punk in the 1970s, and the grunge movement of the 1980s. All Stars were worn by the cast of *West Side Story*, James Dean wore Converse shoes, Danny Zuko wore them in *Grease*, and Rocky Balboa wore them in *Rocky*, helping to make them the shoe of choice for disaffected urban teenagers and rebels. Kurt Cobain's devotion to Converse One Stars (and his death in 1994 wearing a pair) propelled the brand to greater popularity among young fans of the grunge scene. In 2008, Converse, with the cooperation of Cobain's widow Courtney Love, released new Chuck Taylor and One Star models, both with Cobain's signature and the phrase "punk rock means freedom" inside the shoe. Pop punker Avril Lavigne, Felicity of the TV show *Felicity*, and the heroine of *Juno* also wore All Stars. For 50 years, All Stars have been associated with youth culture in the United States, and in particular, with outsider culture.

Fans of All Stars have been modifying their shoes for years. Starting in the 1970s, kids began writing on the white rubber side of the outer sole, and today, customers can "design" their own pair of custom All Stars, Jack Purcells, or other shoes via the company's Web site. All Stars remain a symbol of coolness today, although the fact that the company is now owned by Nike and the shoes are now produced overseas has cut into its popularity among youth somewhat.

See also: Nike; Skateboarding Shoes; Sneakers

Further Reading Aamidor, Abraham. *Chuck Taylor, Converse All Star: The True Story Behind the Man Behind the Most Famous Athletic Shoe in History*. Bloomington: Indiana University Press.

CORDWAINER. *See* Shoemakers.

COWBOY BOOTS

Cowboy boots are **leather** heeled **boots** worn traditionally by American cowboys, and which today are associated with country-western music and fashion. Cowboy boots are, for many, the iconic footwear associated with the United States.

Boots have long been worn by people who rode horses. Boots with heels were created to help keep the foot in the stirrup and to protect the leg from contact with the animal. For instance, riders in Central Asian countries like Uzbekistan and Kazakhstan wore boots while riding, as did Mongols, Afghans, Tibetans, and

Cowboy boots are perhaps the most iconic footwear of the United States and embody America to the rest of the world. [Copyright 2008 Jupiterimages Corporation]

Persians. This practice moved into Europe during the Middle Ages, and European gentlemen began wearing tall leather riding boots with stacked heels when riding horses. By the nineteenth century, these boots had evolved into Hessian boots, worn for both sport riding and mounted combat during war. In the 1840s, the Duke of Wellington began wearing a lower boot that was more closely fitted to the leg. These boots, known as Wellingtons, were worn by officers in wars throughout the nineteenth century, including the American Civil War, and were worn home by the soldiers after the war, including those who returned to Texas. Many of these boots were made by the Quartermaster Corporation, and, after the war, they were known as Coffeyville boots, based on the pattern of a bootmaker named John Cubine out of Coffeyville, Kansas. One version of the cowboy boot's history places the boots' origins in these Civil War boots.

The alternative story is that the American cowboy boot came originally from the footwear of the Spanish conquistadors, who wore tall leather riding boots while conquering Central and South America on horseback. These boots evolved into the boots worn by Mexican *vaqueros* who ran cattle and sheep in northern Mexico, and were later coopted by Texas cowboys.

In either case, the cowboy boot was first worn in the United States starting in the mid-1860s. From the 1860s to 1890, when the train line was completed from Texas to Kansas, cowboys on horseback drove cattle from Texas to the stockyards in Kansas, and wore boots crafted by Kansas bootmakers specifically for their journeys. During the 1880s, new styles began to emerge, including decorative inlays and stitch patterns, the stovepipe top, and different heel heights.

Cowboy boots have a number of distinctive features made specifically for horseback riding, many borrowed from boots made hundreds of years ago: the toes are narrow in order to easily slip into the stirrups; the curved, underslung Cuban heel keeps the feet in the stirrups; the sole is smooth to allow the foot to easily slip out of the stirrups; and the reinforced arch braces the feet. Cowboy boots also have sharp metal spurs attached to the heel in order to motivate the horse to gallop. The thick leather shaft extends most of the way up the calf in order to protect the rider from both contact with the horse as well as from high brush and cactus.

The cowboy boot industry is still centered in Texas, and the best custom bootmakers are still in Texas as well. People who still make cowboy boots by hand often make them alone. One person measures the foot, makes the last, cuts the pattern, cuts the leather, and fits the leather to the last. In other shops, different craftsmen work, each specializing in a different task: stitching, stretching, and so forth.

Cowboy boots are constructed in four pieces, like the original **Wellington boot**: the top (in two pieces), vamp, and bottom. The shaft, or top, of the boot is made of two pieces, extends about 12 inches, and is the part of the boot that protects the leg. It is also the focus for much of the design, including top stitching, piping, inlays, and overlays. The vamp is produced from one piece of leather and makes up the upper of the shoe. This is the piece that is stretched over the last and sewn to the top, with the reinforced toe box inserted inside. Cowboy boots have small leather or canvas loops, or pulls, sewn inside of the tops, in order to pull the boot on. Toes can be pointy, round, or boxed, depending on fashion, although pointy toes are traditional. The bottom includes the insole and outsole, which are both stitched to the vamp while still on the last. And finally, the heel, usually about one and a half inches high, is made of stacked leather or wood. Since the first part of the twentieth century, the toe wrinkle, or decorative stitching on the top of the foot, emerged, and is now a distinctive part of cowboy boot style.

Cowboy boots remained the footwear of cowboys for years. They were originally popularized in this country through the westerns of the 1930s and 1940s, with actor/singers like Gene Autry, Dale Evans, and Roy Rogers wearing them to great effect. It was also Hollywood that created much of the decorative styles that we know today. Prior to this time, boots were primarily utilitarian, although they did have some decoration. But they started to be made with different colors, different kinds of leather, and exotic skins like ostrich, alligator, python, and stingray, and lots of embossing and inlays. Known as the Hollywood or Tejas style of boot, these boots included floral and abstract designs, images of horses, cactuses, and cattle, as well as brands, the Star of Texas, and curlicues. The biggest cowboy boot makers of today all have roots in this period as well, including Tony Lama, Justin, Nocona, Hyer, and Acme.

Cowboy boots have long been popular among country western singers, and in certain regions of the country like New Mexico, where men wear them with jeans and women wear them with a long prairie skirt and turquoise jewelry. They became popular in other areas of the country after John Travolta wore them in the 1980 movie, *Urban Cowboy*, and other movies like *Top Gun* featured them. Their popularity was further bolstered by the rise of crossover country western artists like Shania Twain in the 1990s.

Many people collect cowboy boots now, and vintage boots from the 1920s through the 1950s are especially popular among collectors. Mass-produced boots start at less than $100 but can still cost a few hundred dollars. Custom cowboy boot makers make customized boots that are works of art. Custom boots can sell for thousands and even tens of thousands of dollars per pair.

Cowboy boots now represent the classic American man: independent, hard working, self-reliant and strong. Former Presidents George Bush and Ronald Reagan wore them during public appearances and on their ranches in Texas and California, bringing them onto the international stage.

See also: Boots; Shoemaking; United States; Wellington Boot

Further Reading Beard, Tyler. *The Cowboy Boot Book*. Salt Lake City: Peregrine Smith Books, 1992; Beard, Tyler, Jim Arndt. *Cowboy Boots*. Layton, UT: Gibbs Smith, 2004; June, Jennifer, Dwight Yoakam, Marty Snortum. *Cowboy Boots: The Art and Sole*. New York: Universe Publishing, 2007.

CROCS

Crocs are a brand of comfortable **clogs** first developed to wear for boating, but which became a footwear sensation in the early years of the twenty-first century. Originally known as "amphibious comfort clogs," they are made of a resin called Croslite and feature a slip-resistant sole, molded arch support, and a molded heel cup for comfort.

Crocs were developed by George Boedecker, Scott Seamans, and Lyndon Hanson, three friends who took a boating trip in Mexico in 2002. Seamans brought along a pair of molded resin clogs made by a Canadian company called Foam Creations. The men were impressed by the shoes and realized they were perfect for boaters and others who wanted a shoe that was slip resistant and also would not smell when wet. They made a deal with Foam Creations and began selling the shoes, which they called Crocs, at boat shows.

Since their first boat show in November 2002, people who wanted comfortable, easy-to-clean, slip-resistant, and resilient shoes began purchasing them, including chefs, nurses, food service workers, and gardeners. The shoe's comfort derives from Croslite, which is said by the company to mold itself to the wearer's feet. Because they come in bright colors, they also appealed to children, and their "ventilation system," which is a series of holes in the upper, make them

An array of Crocs clogs sit in a storefront display in Boulder, Colorado, on October 3, 2006. [AP Photo/David Zalubowski]

useful for watersport activities. The shoes were originally sold in boating stores and surf shops, but they are now sold in health food stores and comfort shoe stores, as well as thousands of other retail markets around the country.

After Crocs took off, the company purchased Foam Creations in 2004 in order to assure that competitors like Holey Soles could not use Croslite for their Crocs-knock offs, but it later sold the manufacturer in 2008 in order to cut costs and refocus on the Crocs line of shoes.

Today, Crocs are worn by anyone who wants a comfortable shoe in bright colors. While many hospitals have now prohibited the wearing of traditional Crocs (because the holes provide a safety concern), the company now makes them without holes specifically for nurses and other health care professionals. They also remain popular among children and teenagers, who decorate the shoes by inserting plastic decorative buttons called "jibbitz" into the shoe's holes. (Crocs bought the company that makes the accessories, called Jibbitz, in 2006.) Celebrities began wearing Crocs in 2005, and their fad appeal exploded.

In the few years since the company has been in business, Crocs has expanded its product line, adding new products like Crocs with synthetic fur lining, **sandals**, **boots**, and dress shoes, most of which do not have any of the distinctive Crocs features but which are made at least in part with Croslite. The Crocs that are lined with synthetic fur are being called Cruggs by a number of observers, who refer to the shoes as the offspring of Crocs and **Uggs**, the most notoriously trendy yet ugly shoes of the new millennium. (Crocs, too, are criticized for being ugly and anti-fashion.) Crocs even makes a boot called the Nadia Winter boot, which is a marriage of the Crocs bottom and a synthetic suede Uggs upper. In 2007, the company also released a new line of products called "You by Crocs," including shoes made of **leather** and suede.

In 2007, Crocs began opening its first retail stores, even though sales of the shoes had been declining throughout the year. Facing tougher economic times, competition from knockoffs, and the inevitable end of the fad, Crocs began losing money in 2007, and since then have had to close factories and lay off staff.

Crocs have as many detractors as they have fans, mostly due to their ugly appearance. On the other hand, their ugliness is part of their charm, as their wearers can assert that they are not slaves to fashion.

See also: Orthopedic Shoes; Birkenstocks

Further Reading Langer, Paul. *Great Feet for Life: Foot Care and Footwear for Healthy Aging.* Minneapolis: Fairview Press, 2007.

CRUSH VIDEOS

Crush videos are videos in which a woman is shown crushing small animals to death, usually while wearing **stiletto** heels.

Those who watch crush videos (also known as "squish videos") are said to have a crush **fetish**, in which they derive sexual pleasure from watching the crushing of such animals. Some crush fetishists evidently enjoy seeing inanimate objects such as grapes or toothpaste tubes being crushed (generally by women with very large feet), but the term is generally reserved for those who watch animals being killed in this fashion. This type of fetish is known as hard crush. Hard crush videos range from those involving large and small insects and worms to those involving the deaths of mammals such as guinea pigs, rabbits, kittens, and puppies. Many videos showcase the torture of these animals, where it can take up to 30 minutes or longer for the animal to die.

In the **United States**, creating, distributing, or possessing crush videos has been illegal since 1999, and many other countries also have banned them.

Some crush fetishists enjoy seeing women in high heels crush inanimate objects, such as cigarettes. [Copyright 2008 Anneke Schram. Image from BigStockPhoto.com]

Nevertheless, they are widely available on the Internet. In the last couple of years, Chinese videos have circulated featuring the deaths of cats, dogs, rabbits, and toads. Known there as GTS (which stands for "great women, small men"), the videos may not be illegal in **China** although public sentiment in China is widely against them.

Crush fetishists are a subset of foot fetishists, and while there are no known statistics on the number of crush fetishists, it is thought that this subculture is in the low thousands.

Besides the videos, magazines like *The American Journal of the Crush Freaks*, distributed by crush filmmaker Jeff Vilencia, *Squish!*, and *In Step*, at one time catered to this community.

The impulse behind crush videos is, for many, similar to the impulse behind Bondage Discipline Domination Submission (BDSM): adherents enjoy fantasizing about themselves being crushed and experience that vicariously through watching a woman crush inanimate objects or animals.

See also: Fetishes; Stilettos

Further Reading Roberts, Adam. "Crush Videos," in Stallwood, Kim, ed. *A Primer on Animal Rights: Leading Experts Write about Animal Cruelty and Exploitation.* New York: Lantern Books, 2002.

D

DANCE SHOES

Dance shoes are shoes made to be worn while dancing. There are many different kinds of dance shoes, all geared to different kinds of dance, including tap shoes, clogging shoes, ballet **slippers**, and swing shoes. Dance shoes are different from street shoes in that they tend to be more flexible, often have padding to protect the feet, and have different kinds of soles and heels to allow for spinning, sliding, gripping, or tapping. Dance shoes need to fit well, be flexible, and be comfortable; to that end, they have padding that other kinds of shoes don't have.

The earliest specialty dance shoes in Europe were probably the heelless slippers worn by ballet dancers in the early eighteenth century. Prior to that time, dancers in **Europe** wore the same heeled shoes that were worn by both men and women. The dance slippers worn by ballet dancers starting in the 1830s later became popular ballroom slippers, worn by wealthy women in the late 1800s when they went to fancy balls and parties. Because of the different requirements of different forms of dance, dance shoes today are made especially for each type of dance.

Ballet is one of the earliest European dance forms, emerging out of courtly dance in the seventeenth century. While originally ballet dancers wore regular heeled shoes, by the early eighteenth century dancers began to wear flat slippers. Today, **ballet shoes** are worn by female ballet dancers who are not dancing pointe. They are flat slippers made of canvas or **leather**, covered in satin, with a leather sole reinforced with padding under both the ball and the heel of the foot. They are constructed to allow a dancer full extension in pointing her toes, but they are not worn while dancing *en pointe* and don't have the hard shank or reinforced toe box of pointe shoes. Pointe shoes, on the other hand, are worn by female pointe dancers and are made with a leather, cardboard, or plastic shank that supports the arch of the foot, and a stiff box, or toe, made with alternating layers of cloth, paper, and paste that are formed into a flat platform. Male ballet dancers wear slippers or ballet boots.

Ballroom dancing as a specific dance form evolved out of the courtly balls attended by European nobility in the sixteenth to the nineteenth centuries. Men and women of the European courts learned to dance at a young age, and all important social and political events were marked by dancing. Dancers wore fashionable shoes of the time rather than special dance shoes. By the mid-seventeenth century, professional dancers emerged and began dancing alongside of noble men and women, and members of the public began attending theatrical performances that included professional dancers, such as in the emerging ballet.

Many women's and girls' tap shoes are in the style of Mary Janes. They have metal taps screwed into the heel and toe region of the sole. [2005 copyright Eileen Meyer. Image from BigStockPhoto.com]

Today, ballroom dancing includes standard dances like the waltz and tango, Latin dances like the samba and paso doble, and various forms of nightclub dance such as salsa, swing, lindy hop, and merengue.

The waltz is one of the most widely known European dances and emerged from the Austrian court in the seventeenth century, but it evolved out of peasant dances from Germany and Austria. The tango was probably a folk dance from Spain that was imported to Argentina, and then found its way back to Europe and the **United States** in the early twentieth century, where it became a standard ballroom dance.

Latin dance styles like the samba, cha cha, and rumba originated in Latin American, on the other hand, and emerged as a fusion of dance forms from Europeans, African slaves, and indigenous South Americans and Carib Indians. In many cases, European dance forms arrived in the Americas and were adapted by slaves, while in other cases, such as in the Cuban rumba, Haitian mambo, or Brazilian samba, the dances evolved out of African dance forms. The paso doble, on the other hand, while known as a Latin dance, began as a Spanish folk dance based on the bullfight, which became popular among elites only in the twentieth century.

For the most part, both male and female ballroom dancers wear heeled shoes with suede soles, which allow for gripping and sliding along the floor. **Men's shoes** are made of **patent leather**, lace up, and have either one-inch heels or, for Latin dancing, higher "Cuban" heels. Women wear two to three inch high-heeled **sandals** or open-side **pumps** with ankle straps. These shoes are made of fabric or leather and tend to be higher for Latin dances and lower for European ballroom dances. When dancing Latin, a female dancer's shoes are designed to make her dance more on her toes. Cuban heels are relatively wide heels and can be found on both men's and women's dance shoes. Men's Cuban heels are usually one and a half inches high.

Nightclub dances like the swing, jive, and lindy hop are also popular ballroom dances today. The jive evolved out of slave dances in the southern United States, while the foxtrot, the lindy hop, the jitterbug, and the charleston emerged out of African-American jazz in the 1920s. The term "swing" today is often used to refer to these nightclub dances, although today swing is known as either east coast swing or west coast swing.

Swing shoes were once primarily wing tip shoes with rubber bottoms, which allow for spinning. For swing dancing, shoes need to have soles that enable both spinning and sliding. **Athletic shoes** won't work because the rubber soles are too soft and will not allow for spinning and sliding; the soles will stick to the floor instead of allowing movement. Sole choices are suede, hard leather, hard rubber, or plastic. Suede grips the dance floor at first, but as it wears it gets slicker, although dancers can rough up the suede to make it grip better.

Some swing dancers also use regular shoes and have them "chromed," which means covering the outsole with suede or hard leather, which can be done at a shoe repair store. Another thing that dancers do is "tape" street shoes to make them work for swing dancing. Taping involves applying masking tape to the soles to make them slide, but it is a short-term solution, as the tape will wear off after a short period of dancing.

Clogging is a European and American folk dance. Practiced throughout Northern Europe from the eighteenth to the twentieth centuries, clogging was said to have been started by factory workers who tapped their wooden **clogs** on the floor while working, and it is practiced in the Appalachian region of the United States as well. Cloggers traditionally wore wooden-soled clogs to stomp on the ground to the downbeat of the music. Today, cloggers wear leather shoes with taps on the soles of the feet, similar to tap dancing shoes.

Tap dancing emerged from the dances of African-American slaves in the seventeenth and eighteenth centuries, which were translated by blackface minstrel dancers in the nineteenth century and which were also danced by African-American minstrels. It was also heavily influenced by European clogging. While the slaves danced barefoot, early tappers wore leather shoes with wooden soles and heels, which allowed for the loud percussive sounds associated with tap dancing.

By the early twentieth century, tappers began attaching thin metal plates underneath the toes and heels of their shoes, as tapping evolved into a dance involving both toe and heel steps. Modern tap shoes today still are made this way. Men's tap shoes are modeled after traditional men's Oxfords, but with taps attached, while women's tap shoes are low- or—in the style of Broadway or the Radio City Rockettes—high-heeled shoes with, again, taps attached under the toes and heels. Girls' tap shoes are modeled after the patent leather tap shoes popularized by Shirley Temple in the 1930s, with big bows in the front.

Another American dance form is country-western dancing, which emerged in the nineteenth century as a form of entertainment for cowboys in the western states and which drew from the folk dances popular among the European and Mexican immigrants of the region. It was practiced in bars, at barn dances, and other locations where ranchers, farmers, and others congregated at night or on the weekends, and it involves both dancers and a caller who calls out the steps for the dancers to follow. The square dance, polka, two step, and line dance are examples of country-western dances that emerged during this period, all of which were influenced by the life and traditions of cowboys. Male country-western dancers either wear **cowboy boots** or men's ballroom shoes. Women sometimes wear cowboy boots, but more commonly they wear high- or low-heeled dance shoes.

Jazz dancing is another American dance form. It is linked to jazz music, created by African Americans in the south and Midwest at the turn of the century. While jazz music influenced a number of different dance forms such as swing and tap, jazz dancing arose in the 1950s as a performance art that became standardized in Broadway musicals into what is now known as modern jazz and is primarily seen in musical theatre. Male and female jazz dancers wear soft, flexible, lace-up leather shoes with very low heels and soles made of suede to allow for traction.

Finally, foot thongs are elastic and cloth foot coverings that are worn over the ball of the foot, and attach between the toes. They are worn by dancers who are dancing barefoot in order to give the foot protection and padding.

See also: Ballet Shoes; Clogs; Cowboy Boots; Europe

Further Reading Clarke, Mary, Clement Crisp. *The History of Dance*. New York: Crown Publishers, 1981; Kassing, Gayle: *History of Dance: An Interactive Arts Approach*. Champaign, IL: Human Kinetics, 2007.

DIABETES

Diabetes is a condition caused by a lack of insulin production in the body. Diabetes affects 171 million people around the world and 23.6 million in the United States. There are two types of diabetes: type 1 diabetes and type 2 diabetes. Type 1 diabetes is a condition in which a person cannot produce insulin. It was once known as juvenile diabetes because it affects primarily otherwise healthy children and may be genetically based. Type 2 diabetes, also known as adult onset diabetes, on the other hand, is a condition that develops when the body either doesn't produce enough insulin or is resistant to insulin and may be caused by obesity. When insulin is either not produced or is not used by the body, glucose can accumulate in the blood, causing blood sugar levels to rise to dangerous levels, producing hyperglycemia. Without insulin, the person will eventually go into a diabetic coma.

People with diabetes need to test their blood sugar levels to ensure that their blood sugar remains in a healthy range. While diabetes cannot be cured, it can be managed. Treatment includes insulin injections for Type 1 diabetics, and oral medications combined with dietary changes and healthy weight maintenance for Type 2 diabetics.

The symptoms of diabetes include lowered energy levels, excessive urination and thirst, and increased appetite, and the disease can ultimately result in hypoglycemia, kidney failure, blindness, nerve damage or neuropathy, heart disease, and stroke. In addition, diabetics can experience a variety of problems with their feet because nerve damage often leaves them with a loss of feeling in their feet, known as neuropathy. In addition, diabetes causes the blood vessels of the legs to harden, resulting in a lack of blood flow to the feet. This can make it difficult for the body to heal wounds normally, which can cause additional foot problems. This problem is made worse by smoking.

Neuropathy results in a loss of sensation in the feet and can result in injuries, infections, and ulcers, especially when combined with poor blood flow. When infections and ulcers are undetected because of the loss of sensation, they can lead to gangrene, one of the most severe conditions, which can lead to the **amputation** of toes, part of the foot, or the entire foot. Even without serious infection, neuropathy can change the shape of a diabetic's feet, making it difficult for a patient to find comfortable shoes to wear.

Because of the loss of blood flow, diabetics often experience dry and cracked skin on the feet. Calluses are another common condition, and calluses, when left untreated, can turn into ulcers as well. Ulcers can also be caused by poorly fitting shoes, which often lead to blisters, and can lead to serious infections and amputation if untreated. Another problem related to the loss of blood flow to the feet is that diabetics' feet often feel cold.

Diabetes is the largest single cause of foot amputation in the world, with 5 percent of all adult diabetics losing either toes or feet to the disease. In order to prevent amputation, and the infections that lead to it, diabetics are counseled to take a number of steps to preserve their feet, including regular foot washing, keeping them moisturized but dry, inspecting them for injuries, calluses, blisters, signs of **athlete's foot** or other conditions, carefully tending toenails to reduce the chance of **ingrown toenails**, and wearing diabetic **socks** and **orthopedic shoes**. Special diabetic foot lotion is recommended to keep feet moisturized, and diabetic foot powder is often used to help keep feet dry.

Wearing socks is important for diabetics. When feet are cold because of loss of blood flow, wearing warm socks is a way to keep the feet warm and avoid injuries that could result from using heating pads or other forms of heat. In addition, clean socks can keep the feet dry and comfortable and can protect the feet from pressure. Special compression socks and stockings are also worn by many diabetics. They provide pressure to the legs and can increase blood flow, which in turn decreases foot swelling. Other socks worn by diabetics include seamless socks and socks made with material that wicks moisture from the foot.

Because it is so critical for diabetics to wear shoes that fit well, are comfortable, and do not cause any additional pressure or rubbing, many diabetics wear orthopedic shoes made for diabetics, known as diabetic shoes.

Diabetic shoes are designed without seams inside, which can cause blisters or other injuries, and they are often lined with extra soft material to further protect the feet. Diabetic shoes also have additional ankle, heel, and arch support to avoid pressure points that can cause blisters or calluses and are made of special materials to allow the feet to breathe and to keep the feet dry. They are made in a variety of widths to provide extra room in the toes. Diabetic shoes are also designed to reduce stress on the bottoms or sides of the foot and to accommodate disorders such as **hammer toes** or amputated toes. Some diabetic shoes (such as wound care shoes, worn immediately after major surgery) are only available with a prescription by a podiatrist; if a diabetic patient has severe foot deformities, custom-made shoes are also an option.

Diabetics have a wide variety of shoe options to choose from today. There are now specially made diabetic **sandals**, which have wider straps than regular sandals and which also cover the toes to prevent injuries like stubbed toes. Diabetic sandals are also seamless on the inside to prevent friction. **Flip flops** and other sandals with toe straps are not recommended for diabetics because of the possibility of damage to the tissue between the toes, nor are open-toed sandals.

See also: Amputation; Disorders and Injuries; Blisters, Bunions, Calluses and Corns; Orthopedic Shoes

Further Reading Veves, Aristidis, ed. *The Diabetic Foot*. New York: Humana Press, 2006.

DISORDERS AND INJURIES

There are a number of conditions and diseases that affect the foot, causing pain or discomfort, as well as a number of injuries that are commonly found associated with feet. Some of these are genetic conditions, some are caused by the wearing of inappropriate footwear, and some are caused by injuries. While women's footwear is to blame for a large number of foot problems, senior men are more likely to have problems with their feet than other groups.

Relatively minor conditions that affect the feet include **blisters, bunions, calluses, and corns**, **hammer toes**, **ingrown toenails**, **plantar warts**, "burning feet," and **athlete's foot**.

Blisters can cause pain and swelling to the toes, heel, or any area of the foot that has experienced pressure or rubbing from footwear. Blister pads can be worn over blisters to prevent additional rubbing and to prevent blisters from being formed in the first place, heel hugs can be worn inside the back of the heel, and blister prevention patches are bandage-like patches that can be worn anywhere that the shoes rub against the foot.

Bunions refer to a condition when the big toe of the foot moves inward towards the smaller toes, often causing a thickening of the tissue around the first toe and crowding around the other toes. Bunions can cause localized pain at a particular area of the foot and are generally caused by wearing tight shoes or high heels, which cause the toes to push against each other. Arch supports can be worn to distribute body weight, and bunion pads and slings can relieve the pressure and pain, while toe spacers can place the toes back into a normal position.

Calluses refer to thickened dead skin that accumulates along the sides and bottom of the feet. Calluses are usually caused by pressure from wearing ill-fitting shoes, high heels, an unusual gait, or carrying excess weight. Corns, like calluses, are thickenings of dead skin on the outside of the feet, but they create a more localized hardening, usually shaped like a cone. Corns are caused by ill-fitting footwear and high heels. Callus and corn pads as well as bunion pads can be worn to relieve discomfort.

Hammer toes are similar to bunions in that they involve changes in the toes resulting from ill-fitting footwear. Hammer toes are permanently bent, but they can be alleviated by wearing wide shoes or doing foot exercises. Toe straighteners and hammer toe cushions are worn to relieve pressure, to straighten the toes, and to relieve the pain. **Orthotic** insoles are also used to redistribute weight inside the shoe.

Athlete's foot is a fungal infection that causes itching, redness, and scaly skin, usually between the toes but often on other parts of the feet as well. Preventing athlete's foot involves wearing sandals or other foot protection when in public places, especially pools and locker rooms, washing and drying feet carefully, and at other times wearing natural material socks and shoes that allow the feet to breathe.

Ingrown toenails refers to a condition in which the side of a toenail grows into the toe bed, which can cause pain and infection. As with other disorders of the foot, ingrown toenails are often caused by tight or high-heeled shoes. In addition, ingrown toenails can be caused by an injury to the toe or trimming the toenails into a rounded shape, and it is found most commonly in people with curved toenails. Treatment typically involves soaking the feet in warm water, wearing loose fitting shoes, elevating the nail from the toe, and keeping the area clean and dry.

Some people are afflicted by a condition known as "burning feet," in which they feel a burning or pins-and-needles sensation in their feet. This could result from sensitivity to particular shoes or socks, athlete's foot, obesity, or being on one's feet all day long, which in some people means that bodily fluids collect in the feet, resulting in swollen and burning feet. The most common cause of burning feet, however, is nerve damage or neuropathy, which is common among diabetics. Treatment would vary based on what kind of condition is causing the feelings.

Plantar warts are warts caused by the HPV virus and are found on the bottoms of the feet. The infection, which is relatively harmless, is picked up most commonly in public areas like swimming pools and locker rooms. Some plantar warts disappear on their own, but if they do not the typical treatment is to have the warts frozen or burnt off of the feet.

Other conditions that afflict the feet include high arches and**fallen arches**, excessive pronation or supination, **neuromas** and metarsalgia, heel spurs, and plantar fasciitis.

People who walk with excessive pronation or under pronation, also known as supination, often have fallen arches and arch pain. Excessive pronation is a condition where the ankles roll inward when one walks or runs; supination refers to the ankles rolling outward when walking. Being excessively pronated is often referred to as having knock knees because the knees angle towards each other and sometimes hit each other. It is relatively easy to detect whether one walks with too much pronation or supination by the wear on one's shoes; if the wear is primarily on the inside, then super pronation is the problem; if the wear is primarily on the outside of the shoe, then the problem is supination. Pronation or supination can be aided with the use of orthotic arch supports or orthopedic shoes that are designed to control for motion and provide extra stability.

People with pain under the ball of the foot, caused by metatarsalgia or neuromas, can treat the pain by wearing cushioned insoles, metatarsal pads, or dancer pads. Metatarsalgia is a condition in which the long bones of the feet become stressed, causing pain in the ball of the foot. Neuromas are bundles of pinched nerves that occur between the third and fourth toes, which also cause pain in the ball of the foot. Metatarsal pads help this condition, as do arch supports, which take the weight off the ball of the foot.

Heel pain can be caused by heel spurs, in which a piece of bone forms on the heel bone, and plantar fasciitis, which is inflammation of the tissue forming the arch of the foot. Heel cups and heel cushions can help solve this problem, and arch supports can relieve the pain associated with heel spurs as well. Heel spur pain can be alleviated with orthotics. Plastic arch supports and arch cradles that can be placed into the shoe, cushioning insoles, and arch bandages can all alleviate this pain. Another cause of heel pain is the Haglund's deformity, or pump bump, which is a growth of bone at the back of the heel. It is caused by friction with shoes, like blisters, and can be treated with heel hugs, heel sleeves, and other types of padding that cover and protect the heel.

High and low or fallen arches can also cause foot problems. High arches, known as cavus foot, is a condition in which a person has unusually high arches, which places extra weight on the balls and heels of the feet. It often leads to hammer toes and calluses and causes pain and instability. It is generally caused by another condition such as polio or cerebral palsy and can be genetic in origin. Orthotic devices can be worn in the shoe to provide stability and comfort, taking the pressure off of the other parts of the foot, and when the condition is severe, braces can also be worn. In severe cases, surgery can be used. Fallen arches, or flat feet, on the other hand, is a more common condition and does not cause substantial problems in the majority of people affected by it. On the other hand, some people with flat feet do experience pain, and flat feet can contribute to other problems like plantar fasciitis and problems with the **Achilles** tendon. Flat feet can be caused by obesity, arthritis, or too much exercise, and pain associated with flat feet can be alleviated with orthotic devices.

More serious conditions include those caused by diseases such as arthritis and **diabetes**. Arthritis, for example, is an inflammation of joints, generally caused by age, injury, or infection. It especially affects the feet, both because of the number of joints in the foot and the fact that the feet bear the body's weight. Arthritis in the foot causes pain, swelling, and stiffness and is exacerbated when the patient is overweight. Arthritis can be controlled through drugs and physical therapy, and feet problems can be alleviated with orthotic devices, orthopedic shoes, or even braces.

Diabetes, too, can cause severe problems for patients' feet. Nerve damage often results in a loss of sensation in the feet and it causes the blood vessels of the legs to harden, resulting in a lack of blood flow to the feet. For both of these reasons, injuries can both go undetected for long periods of time and can take longer than usual to heal. The result is often infection, ulcers, and sometimes gangrene, which can lead to **amputation**. Besides normal treatment for diabetes, diabetics can also care for their feet with special diabetic powders and lotions and they can wear diabetic socks and **orthopedic shoes**, which can alleviate pressure, accommodate orthotics, and provide the extra cushioning that diabetics need.

Finally, injuries to the foot include turf toe, stress fractures, sprained ankles, broken bones, dislocations, and problems with the Achilles tendon. Many of these injuries are caused during sports and may result from overuse, inadequately cushioned shoes, or running on hard surfaces. Because the foot is composed of so many bones, joints, and tendons and because it bears the weight of the entire body, it's not surprising that injuries to the feet are so common, especially among athletes.

Turf toe is a condition in which the big toe becomes sprained due to dancing or other activities in which the toe is hyper-extended. It results in a stiff, swollen, and painful toe and can be treated with dancer pads.

Ankle sprains, in which the ligaments of the ankle are injured, are common injuries and are generally caused by a fall or sudden twist of the ankle. It results in swelling and pain and may also cause fractured toes. Untreated, an ankle sprain can lead to chronically weak ankles.

Stress fractures are caused by repeated impact on the feet, such as through long distance running or walking, and cause increasing levels of pain until they are diagnosed and treated. Stress fractures most commonly occur along the toe bones, or metatarsals.

Athletes like snowboarders and windsurfers often fracture their TMT joint, a condition first documented among soldiers whose feet got caught in their stirrups, resulting in the fracture.

Physical therapy is often prescribed for injuries of the foot and ankle, combined with rest, anti-inflammatory drugs, elevation, compression bandages, and ice. In addition, orthopedic inserts such as arch supports or heel inserts or orthopedic shoes may be prescribed during the healing period. Some conditions, such as turf toe, demand taping the toe into one position to promote healing and to control movement, while other conditions, such as sprained ankles, involve immobilizing the entire foot to prevent movement. Occasionally, surgery is warranted.

See also: Blisters, Bunions, Calluses and Corns; Diabetes; Flat Feet and Fallen Arches; Foot Care Products; Hammer Toe; Ingrown Toenails; Neuroma; Orthotics; Orthopedic Shoes

Further Reading Jahss, Melvin. *Disorders of the Foot and Ankle: Medical and Surgical Management*. Philadelphia: Saunders, 1991; Lorimer, Donald, Donald Neale. *Neale's Disorders of the Foot*. New York: Elsevier Churchill Livingstone, 2006.

DR. MARTENS

Dr. Martens, known as Doc Martens or Docs, are heavy **boots** and shoes favored by punks, working men, and rebels of all kinds.

Doc Martens were developed by Klaus Maertens, a German military doctor who broke his leg while skiing on leave in 1945. Because the German Army boots were too uncomfortable to wear while his leg was healing, he created his own boot, modeled on the Army boot and using rubber from truck tires for the soles. Because the shoes were still not comfortable enough to walk in, Maertens enlisted the help of an old army friend, an engineer named Herbert Funck. Funck used molded PVC in such a way that air was captured in pockets in the rubber.

Funck's invention was then attached to a shoe using a process by which one sole was sewn onto the shoe, and a second sole was heat-sealed to the first layer. Maertens and Funck began selling the shoes under the name Dr. Maertens, after the war in 1947. The initial customers were German soldiers who had been injured in the war, followed by housewives, and in 1952 the partners opened a factory in Munich to serve their growing German market.

In the 1950s, the partners opened a factory in Northamptonshire, England. In 1959, they began placing advertisements in trade magazines seeking to widen their distribution, and eventually they were contacted by a Northamptonshire shoe manufacturer named R. Griggs & Company, which purchased the rights to the sole and began manufacturing a variety of shoes. (Griggs once made the bull-dog shoes worn by the British Army.) The first pair to be released by Griggs was called the 1460, because the first shoe was produced on April 1, 1960. Griggs changed the name from Dr. Maertens to Dr. Martens. The 1460 is the iconic Doc Marten; a red or black **leather** ankle boot with yellow stitching around the rubber sole.

A pair of Dr. Martens 1460 workboots are part of an exhibition of Dr. Martens boots, April 23, 2003, in New York. The boot, manufactured since 1960, has a history of individuals customizing it to suit their own style. [AP Photo/Joe Kohen]

By the 1960s, English punks and skinheads began wearing the boots, favoring the clunky military appearance of the black 1460 boots. English mods, on the other hand, wore the red boots. Soon, Doc Martens were worn by many of the most famous musicians of the era like Sid Vicious, Billy Bragg, Joe Strummer, Morrissey, Pete Townsend, the members of Madness, the Who, the Clash, and the Buzzcocks, and later, Sinead O'Connor, Cyndi Lauper, and Kurt Cobain. Because of their link to skin-heads, a lot of people associate Doc Martens with violence, rebellion, and anarchy, although police officers, factory workers, and postal workers began favoring them as well. Even Pope John Paul II wore white Doc Martens.

During the 1980s, Doc Martens spread from the punk scene into New Wave, then into the grunge scene and from there into mainstream culture. They were widely worn by young people, men and women, especially in the United States, and they were one of the first unisex shoes of the 1980s. They also became popular with many lesbians. By the 1990s, new colors and styles had been added to the Doc Martens line, including floral prints, polka dots, and neon colors. Customers can also customize their boots through the company's Web site.

The company exploited its association with musicians by releasing a compilation CD in 1995 featuring songs by New Order, Suede, and Blur. Further albums followed, and the company sponsored musical events like Lollapolooza through-out the 1990s. In 1999, Doc Martens released a special 1460 boot with the logo of ska band Madness on it.

Doc Martens are still produced by Griggs and are now marketed solely through Griggs' subsidiary, AirWare. The company closed its English factory in 2003, out-sourcing production to **China** and Thailand. Today, Dr. Martens are made in a variety of styles, including **sneakers**, **pumps**, and knee high boots, but the 1460 still accounts for half of the company's sales. While they remain the ubiquitous youth boot, having influenced the development of other boots like Timberlands, Doc Martens have never regained the popularity that they achieved from the 1960s to the 1990s.

See also: Boots; Military Shoes and Boots

Further Reading Wardlow, Daniel. *Gays, Lesbians and Consumer Behavior: Theories, Practice and Research Issues in Marketing*. New York: Harrington Park Press, 1996.

DR. SCHOLL'S

Dr. Scholl's is a brand of **foot care products**, **orthotics**, and shoes. The brand is owned by SSL International, and the American rights to the Dr. Scholl's brand are held by Schering-Plough Corporation, a pharmaceutical company. The Dr. Scholl's brand of shoes has been produced by Brown Shoe Company since 1991, which licenses the name Dr. Scholl's from Schering-Plough.

Dr. Scholl's was founded by William Scholl, an apprentice for a **shoemaker** in Indiana at 16 who began selling specialty comfort shoes and inserts in 1899 in Chicago. He enrolled in medical school in order to study foot problems and became a podiatrist in 1904.

While still in medical school, he invented an arch support called the Foot-eazer, which he began selling during his part-time job as a shoe salesman. He then founded the Scholl Manufacturing Company in 1906, selling foot care products to the public. The company, which opened a factory in Chicago in 1909, began producing arch supports, plasters, and a variety of pads and powders to relieve a variety of foot conditions. In 1911, Scholl opened the Dr. Scholl's Foot Comfort Shop in London, followed by his first American store in 1928. Eventually, Scholl's opened more than 500 stores around the world, including the Middle East, Europe, and Australia. Scholl's stores were successful because his brother, who joined the company in 1908, devised eye-catching dis-plays geared to show the customer all the problems facing feet, along with Dr. Scholl's solutions.

Scholl invented a number of products for both the feet and the legs, including compression **hosiery**, corn pads, and a variety of arch supports, cushions, and insoles. Scholl is also known for his successful 1905 campaign to convince shoe-makers to create shoes in standardized sizes and to create shoes in a variety of widths to fit different widths of feet. Scholl also pioneered the practice of selling shoes in different sizes to customers whose feet were different. He also taught a correspondence course for "shoe fitters." He hosted walking contests in the

United States and sold "pedometers" to participants and sponsored a Cinderella Foot Contest that aimed to measure "foot imbalance" in participants.

In 1912, he founded the Illinois College of Chiropody and Orthopedics. The school is now known as the Scholl College of Podiatric Medicine. In 1947, Scholl established the Dr. Scholl Foundation, a grant-making institution providing funds for children, the developmentally disabled, and seniors as well as for educational, religious, and environmental programs.

Scholl began selling shoes in 1933, but it wasn't until 1968, with the release of the Scholl Exercise **Sandal** (designed by Scholl's son), that the iconic Dr. Scholl's shoe was created. The shoes were simple wooden slides with a **leather** strap and buckle that were devised to provide exercise as the wearer walks because the toes had to grip a raised toe crest in order to stay in the shoe. Dr. Scholl's sandals became extremely popular throughout the 1970s, partly because they were sold through drug stores, alongside other foot care products. Today, Scholl's footwear includes the original Exercise Sandal (now available in hand-painted designs), cork Bioprint shoes, and gel Gelactive shoes—all designed to relieve foot and back pain.

Throughout the decades, Dr. Scholl's has continued to develop new products, including compression socks for use while flying, gel cushion insoles, and

Dr. Scholl's foot products are seen at a small company store at Schering-Plough Corp., headquarters in Kenilworth, New Jersey, September 6, 2006, that displays some of the products owned by the Schering-Plough Corporation. Fred Hassan, the chief executive, calls it the toughest job he's ever had: taking a drug company in critical condition, treating all its worst ills simultaneously, and restoring it to health. But within 3 1/2 years, Hassan has managed to put Schering-Plough back in the black, nudge up its depressed stock price, and cure most of the problems he inherited from the prior management. [AP Photo/Mel Evans]

customized orthotics. Dr. Scholl's products include pads, gels, creams, powders, and chemical treatments for **blisters, bunions, calluses, and corns**, **athlete's foot**, **plantar warts**, **foot odor**; insoles, pads, heel cups, arch supports, and orthotics for **flat feet and fallen arches**, **neuromas**, plantar fasciitis and heel pain; insoles and orthotics for excessive pronation; medications for **ingrown toenails** and toenail fungus; and gel inserts and other insoles for burning and aching feet.

After William Scholl's death in 1968, his family incorporated Scholl Inc. and split it into a U.S. division and an international division. Schering-Plough Corporation bought the company in 1978, and in 1987 it sold the international portion to European Home Products, which became Scholl PLC and merged with Seton Health Care Group in 1998, ultimately becoming SSL International, the company that still owns the international rights to the Scholl's brand.

See also: Athlete's Foot; Blisters, Bunions, Calluses, and Corns; Disorders and Injuries; Foot Care Products; Foot Odor; Flat Feet and Fallen Arches; Ingrown Toenails; Neuroma; Plantar Warts

Further Reading Copeland, Glenn. *The Foot Book: Relief for Overused, Abused and Ailing Feet.* New York: Wiley, 1992; Tourles, Stephanie. *Natural Foot Care.* Pownal, VT: Storey, 1999.

EARTH SHOES

Earth Shoes is a brand of shoes that was popular in the 1970s and that was rereleased in 2001. Today, the company Earth Shoes makes a variety of shoes, all with the company's innovation, the "negative heel."

Earth Shoes are known for having a heel that sits lower than the rest of the foot, and no other shoe had this feature when they debuted in 1970. Like **Birkenstocks**, another shoe popular in this era, Earth Shoes also have a cushioned, contoured foot bed. According to the company, the lowered heel, which was created to make wearers feel like they are walking on sand, is supposed to create a more natural way of walking. It is said to facilitate better breathing, better posture, and toner calf and thigh muscles, and some people report that their back pain disappears when wearing Earth Shoes. In addition, the company says that wearing Earth Shoes is like working out and that they "burn more calories with every step" because the leg muscles must work harder with the heel depressed.

Earth Shoes were originally conceived by a Danish yoga instructor named Anne Kalso in 1957, who thought that shoes with a raised heel are unhealthy since the heel bears most of the weight of the body. Wearing shoes with a negative heel (or simply standing barefoot and flexing the toes), on the other hand, mimics a yoga pose known as the mountain. Kalso felt that mimicking this pose would realign the posture into a more natural alignment. Working with a Portuguese **shoemaker**, Kalso designed and tested the original shoes over a period of years and sold them (called Kalso Minus Heel Shoes) in Copenhagen. American tourists Raymond and Eleanor Jacobs discovered them while traveling and signed a deal with Kalso to distribute the shoes in the **United States**. They began to sell the shoes (after first giving away a number of pairs), renamed Earth Shoes after the first Earth Day celebration, in 1970 in New York City.

The Jacobs incorporated their company as Earth Inc. and sold their shoes largely via word of mouth. In 1972, they opened a factory in Massachusetts and sold franchises for new stores throughout the United States, primarily in college towns. By 1974, when the company began advertising, the shoes were being talked about in newspaper and magazine articles and on television talk shows, increasing their popularity further. By 1975, at the peak of the the company's success, retail locations had expanded to 135 and the company began creating accessories. But Earth went bankrupt in 1977 after a number of store owners filed lawsuits against the company, saying they could not keep up with customer demand.

In 1994, shoe designer and manufacturer Michel Meynard acquired the rights to the Earth Shoe name and concept and reintroduced the shoes in 2001, at the Earth Day celebration in Boston. The new company, Earth Footwear, is run by Meynard's family and produces shoes and accessories. It now manufactures the shoes in **China**, but the company considers itself environmentally and socially responsible.

Earth Shoes in the 1970s resembled, as they do today, another famously "healthy" shoe, the Birkenstock. Wide (especially in the toes), boxy, and, to many consumers, unattractive, the Earth Shoe appeals to consumers who don't have fashion at the top of their list when choosing shoes. Earth Shoes come in a variety of styles, including sandals, shoes, and boots, and a variety of colors and fabrics, including non-leather shoes, and they sell at retailers like J. Jill. In 2004, Earth Shoes received the **American Podiatric Medical Association**'s seal of acceptance.

See also: Birkenstocks; Orthopedic Shoes

Further Reading Langer, Paul. *Great Feet for Life: Foot Care and Footwear for Healthy Aging.* Minneapolis: Fairview Press, 2007.

EGYPT. *See* Classical Civilizations.

THE ELVES AND THE SHOEMAKER

"The Elves and the Shoemaker" is a Grimm **fairy tale** classified as AT Type 503, "the helpful elves," first published in the Grimm collection of tales in 1812. This type of tale has been found in variants in many different cultures, such as the English tale "Hob Thrust," or "The Fairies and the Humpbacks" from Scotland. It is related to the tales "The Sorcerer's Apprentice" (AT Type 325) and "Rumpelstiltskin" (AT Type 500) in its use of magical assistants.

In the Grimm version, a hardworking but poor **shoemaker** finds that elves start making his shoes for him in the middle of the night, rescuing his failing business and bringing him and his wife success. But when he and his wife make the brownies (or elves, fairies, or dwarves) a set of clothes and shoes (because they are naked), the elves spirit away, never to return. In some variants of the tale, the elves leave because these creatures see clothes and shoes as a way to enslave them and not as a gift. A gift of clothing and shoes is also seen as payment for labor, and they do not want to see themselves as workers. In other variants, however, they are thrilled with their gift and leave the shoemaker, saying "now we are boys so fine to see, why should we longer cobblers be?" (A similar motif is found in the Harry Potter books, where the house elves can be freed of their labors with the gift of an item of clothing.) In this tale, shoes are symbolic of freedom and opportunity, in the sense that the elves are now free to leave because they have clothes and shoes, with these items representing freedom of opportunity and the chance for mobility.

But perhaps more important is the notion of shoemaking as work. The shoemaker himself is hardworking but on his own he cannot earn enough to care for his family; it's only with the magical labor of the elves that he finds some success. But because of the gift of the clothes and shoes, the elves leave, either no longer wishing to be cobblers—which was not an exalted occupation—or not wanting to be bound to the job. While the Grimm tale ends happily, with the shoemaker continuing to prosper even after the departure of his helpers, many scholars note that the dream of being saved from constant labor is a common dream among workers around the world.

See also: Fairy Tales; Shoemakers

Further Reading Bettelheim, Bruno. *The Uses of Enchantment: The Meaning and Importance of Fairy Tales*. New York: Vintage Books, 1975; Grimm, Jacob and Wilhelm. *Household Tales*, Margaret Hunt, translator. London: George Bell, 1884, 1892; Opie, Iona and Peter. *The Classic Fairy Tales*. New York: Oxford University Press, 1974; Propp, Vladimir. *Morphology of the Folktale*. Austin: University of Texas, 1968; Tatar, Maria M., ed. *The Classic Fairy Tales*. New York: W. W. Norton, 1999; Thompson, Stith. *The Folktale*. New York: Holt, Rinehart, and Winston, 1946; Zipes, Jack, ed.*The Oxford Companion to Fairy Tales*. Oxford: Oxford University, 2000.

EROTICISM

Feet and shoes have been the objects of erotic attention throughout history. There are different theories that try to account for why certain historical periods and certain cultures tend to sexualize the feet and, in particular, the female foot. One theory suggests that rises in sexually transmitted diseases correlate to an increased sexual focus on the foot as a form of safe sex. Gonorrhea and syphilis epidemics in **Europe**, for example, can be correlated to a rise in poetry and literature about the female foot, the popularity of sexualized shoes like the *poulaine* in the fourteenth century or the *chopine* in the sixteenth century, as well as a whole host of ideas and practices surrounding the foot in the nineteenth century, such as the valorization of the small female foot, the rise of brothels specializing in sexual acts involving feet, and the exclusion of female feet from photographs during that period. In recent years, since the rise of AIDS in the 1980s and 1990s, **fetishes** of the foot have exploded on the Internet. Another explanation for the historical appearances of foot or shoe fetishism is that the foot becomes more erotically charged during times and places when it is kept literally and figuratively under wraps. So during Victorian Europe when women's feet were covered in shoes and concealed under long layers of clothing, they were subsequently more eroticized by fetishists, and the sight of an unclothed foot or ankle was arousing for many men.

Different cultures consider different types of feet attractive. For instance, small feet were eroticized in **China** and Victorian England, while narrow feet with high arches and long toes were preferred in Medieval Europe. The Roman ideal foot had a longer first toe, while the ideal Greek foot had a longer second toe. In general, women's feet tend to be eroticized, while men's feet do not.

Foot fetishists are people whose sexual arousal centers around the foot—stroking, caressing, and kissing the feet, or sometimes using the foot or toes as part of lovemaking. While foot fetishists make up a surprising number of paraphiliacs, they still account for a relatively small amount of the general population. On the other hand, as we have noted, there have been times historically when the treatment of feet as sexual objects was far more pervasive.

Red High Heels. These shoes, with Lucite platform soles and spindle-shaped heels, are classic stripper shoes. [2006 copyright Mark Winfrey. Image from BigStockPhoto.com]

For instance, **foot binding** was practiced in China from the tenth century until the twentieth century. Like many other markers of beauty that are associated with the wealthy, bound feet were considered beautiful partly because a woman with bound feet could not work (and often could not walk), demonstrating her high status and wealth. In addition, small feet were associated with femininity and vulnerability, while large feet were associated with masculinity. Because of this intense attention on the feet, bound or "lotus feet" were fetishized, as were the shoes made for them, and evidently many Chinese men, known as "lotus lovers," fondled and licked the bound feet of their wives or lovers and used them in sexual practices. For a brief period during the eighteenth century, French courtesans began binding their feet as well, thanks to the influence of Chinese style on European fashion and a new interest in small feet in Europe.

Shoe fetishists find shoes to be sexually arousing. Fetishists will sometimes caress or lick shoes; other times the fetish involves being stepped on by the shoes, or watching someone in high heels step on someone or something else, as in a crush fetish. Sometimes the smell of the shoe is what is arousing. The types of shoes found arousing are often very **high heels** (the erect ankle and arched foot and leg is considered a sign of sexual availability in many animals), very tight **boots**, or boots that are laced up like corsets. Heels that are so high that the woman cannot walk—or not walk easily—are also arousing because of the constraints to mobility that it causes. Tightly laced boots or shoes are sexual for fetishists because of the idea of constraints and the pain and submission involved in being tightly constrained. The process of lacing itself is arousing, as is the process of unlacing because of the possibility of release. Shiny materials like **patent leather** or pleather are arousing, as are soft materials like satin or fur. Other types of erotic shoes are those with toe cleavage or with partial coverage, like slingbacks and mules—which are "naked" in the back—or open-toed shoes. Deep-throated heels that reveal much of the upper foot is also sexually arousing for some.

While it has been most common throughout history that women's feet and shoes were sexualized, there have been cases where men's shoes were eroticized as well. The *poulaine*, a men's shoe with a pointed toe as long as 24 inches, was popular in Medieval Europe among wealthy men while reviled by the Catholic Church, which considered its phallic connotations degenerate. The toes of the poulaine had to be stuffed with wool and horse hair in order to keep the toes erect. It is said that men stood on street corners and waved their toes while women walked by. Another men's shoe that had sexual connotations was the duckbill or bearpaw, a flat shoe with an extremely wide (as wide as eight inches) toe. The toes of these shoes were slashed to reveal the brightly colored lining or fur inside the shoes, suggesting the shape and color of a vagina. Typically, however, it is women's feet, and women's shoes, that are eroticized.

High heels are arousing not only to shoe fetishists, but have been seen as sexy since at least the seventeenth century. One reason that high heels are seen as sexual is because of what they do to the posture and gait of the woman wearing them. With very high heels, the spine curves, the hips and buttocks are thrust out, the breasts are thrust forward, the legs are elongated, and the gait changes. The pelvis also shifts so that it appears that she's ready for sex. Extraordinarily high shoes like the chopine and other towering platforms also cause the woman to walk delicately, or with help, making her vulnerable and sexy. Some also point to the phallic nature of the high heel itself. Finally, high heels make the feet appear smaller, which in itself has been valued and sexualized around the world.

Because of the sexual nature of women's feet and shoes, prostitutes throughout history have often worn highly sexualized footwear. For instance, in China prostitutes and concubines bound their feet in order to make themselves more beautiful and sexually attractive. Today, Western prostitutes routinely wear high heels and shoes that reveal much of the foot, such as the clear Lucite heels favored by many prostitutes and strippers, or the elevated sandals once worn by Greek and Roman prostitutes. It is said that both Egyptian and Greek prostitutes advertised their wares on the soles of their sandals so that men could read their advertisements in the sand while they walked. Venetian courtesans wore platform shoes called *chopines* with 30 inch heels, and Japanese courtesans wore special lacquered *geta*. Even nineteenth century Italian criminologist Cesare Lombroso made an association between high heels and prostitutes in his writings about female criminals and prostitutes. Even during periods when high heels were unfashionable among "respectable" women, they remained popular for sex workers and have been associated in popular culture with either prostitutes or bad girls ever since.

See also: China; Europe; Fetishes; Foot Binding; High Heels; *Kinky Boots*; Stilettos; Transgender Shoes

Further Reading Davidson, Hilary. "Sex and Sin: The Magic of Red Shoes," in Rielle, Georgio and Peter McNeil, eds. *Shoes: A History From Sandals to Sneakers*. London: Berg Publishers, 2006; Steele, Valerie. *Fashion and Eroticism: Ideals of Feminine Beauty from the Victorian Era to the Jazz Age*. New York: Oxford University Press, 1995; Steele, Valerie. *Fetish: Fashion, Sex and Power*. New York: Oxford University Press, 1996; Steele, Valerie. "Shoes and the Erotic Imagination," in Rielle, Georgio and Peter McNeil, eds. *Shoes: A History From Sandals to Sneakers*. London: Berg Publishers, 2006; Vianello, Andrea. "Courtly Lady or Courtesan? The Venetian Chopine in the Renaissance," in Rielle, Georgio and Peter McNeil, eds. *Shoes: A History From Sandals to Sneakers*. London: Berg Publishers, 2006; Walford, Jonathan. *The Seductive Shoe: Four Centuries of Fashion Footwear*. New York: Stewart, Tabori and Chang, 2007.

ESPADRILLE

Espadrilles are **sandals** made with braided jute soles and a fabric upper and often include fabric laces that tie around the ankle. The upper is traditionally made in two pieces, with the toe and the heel sewn separately to the jute sole.

The term *espadrille* is French and comes from the esparto grass that was once used to make the shoes. The shoes derive from the Catalonian region of Spain where they have been made since at least the thirteenth century. They are still made in Spain today, although espadrilles can be made in any other country and are often made in Bangladesh today, where most of the world's jute comes from.

Espadrilles were once the Spanish version of the natural fiber shoe, worn by peasants in farming communities around the world. Both men and women once wore flat espadrilles while working in the fields of the Pyrrenese mountains, between France and Spain. Other groups who wore them were priests, soldiers, and miners. Espadrilles were worn in Spain for at least 4,000 years, based on archaeological evidence: a pair of espadrilles in the Archaeological Museum of Granada has been dated to 2000 BCE.

Traditional espadrille making involves two primary jobs: one person makes the soles, and a seamstress makes the fabric upper and sews it to the soles. The sole is made from jute that has been spun into a rope and coiled to form the sole. The sole is placed into a mold to be shaped, and then sewn to keep its shape. Separately, the two canvas or cotton pieces that make up the upper are then cut and are sewn to a separate jute braid. The braid is then fastened to the sole. Finally, the sole is treated to make it more long lasting; traditionally that was done by coating it with tar, while today it is vulcanized with rubber. Traditional colors included black and white (for Sunday wear).

Espadrilles became fashionable in Europe and the United States in the 1970s, but they were the inspiration for the platform shoe in the 1930s, when **Salvatore Ferragamo** borrowed the wedge shape of the espadrille, but made his platform shoes with cork. Today espadrilles are made primarily for women and can be either in the form of flats or wedge platforms, with or without the ankle tie. Modern espadrilles often have rubber outer soles, beneath the jute. They are summer shoes and tend to be popular during periods when bohemian or gypsy looks are fashionable rather than more refined styles.

See also: Ferragamo, Salvatore; Platform Shoes; Sandals

Further Reading Veillon, Dominique. *Fashion Under the Occupation*. New York: Berg, 2002.

EUROPE

Europe is important to an understanding of footwear primarily because the modern **fashion industry**, which for centuries has shaped shoe styles and design, has its roots in Europe. The earliest shoes worn in Europe would have been similar to shoes worn around the world prior to the Iron Age: simple animal skins used to wrap around the foot, held together by skin laces, or, in southern regions, **sandals** with a sole of animal hide attached to an upper made of woven plant fibers. As much of Europe came under Roman rule starting in about the first century, Roman styles of dress were adopted by Europeans in the Middle Ages, including the wearing of tunics with hose, which evolved from the Roman **sock**.

By the end of the Roman Empire in the fifth century, Roman shoemaking techniques had been lost and shoes in Europe were relatively simple. While peasants largely went unshod or wore the simple shoes of wrapped animal skin tied with thongs, new shoe construction techniques were introduced to the region by the early Middle Ages. For example, turnshoes—shoes made with a separate upper and sole, sewn together inside-out and turned right-side

15th century poulaines. These shoes scandalized the Catholic church as well as secular authorities. [Copyright © 2009 Bata Shoe Museum, Toronto (Photo: Brian Hillier)]

out with the seams hidden inside—appear to have been introduced into Europe by the eighth century. Also, the technique of sewing the uppers with thread rather than animal skin thongs was introduced by the eleventh century, although shoes were still secured along the upper with thongs.

Early Medieval shoes were similar in construction to **moccasins** and were either of the ankle boot or slipper variety (still known as *carbatines*, from the Greek term), made of cloth, **leather**, or velvet; soles were flat, without heels. Finally, because of the rise of **Christianity** in Europe, it became important to cover the feet, leading to the prevalence of shoes over sandals even in the warmer climates of Southern Europe. During this period, men wore hose sewn from pieces of woolen fabric, which were either attached to the underwear or, later, the tunic.

Throughout the Middle Ages and the Renaissance, shoes remained a privilege of the wealthy. Starting in the twelfth century, peasants began wearing wooden **clogs**, and these were passed down from parent to child. It wasn't until the eighteenth century that commoners began regularly wearing shoes other than clogs. These clogs evolved into pattens, which were elevated wooden soles, sometimes on wood or metal stilts, with leather straps to fit over the feet. These were worn as **overshoes** to protect the shoes of the wealthy from becoming soiled.

Noblemen wore, from about the thirteenth to the seventeenth centuries, soft leather **boots** that extended to the knee and rolled down from the top, known as cavalier boots. Roman-style buskins, which protected the legs but left the toes open, were also worn in the Middle Ages until the fifteenth century, primarily by hunters.

Chopines. These elevated clogs were worn by both prostitutes and high-status women in southern Europe from the fifteenth to the eighteenth century. [Copyright 2009 © Bata Shoe Museum, Toronto]

In the late Middle Ages, from about the tenth to the twelfth centuries, European shoes were influenced by the fashions of the East, thanks to the information and goods brought back from the Holy Land by the Crusaders and the influence of the Byzantine Empire. Pointed toe shoes, which were inspired by shoes worn in the **Middle East**, became fashionable among the European nobility starting in the twelfth century and reached their height of popularity in the fourteenth and fifteenth centuries. Made of new fabrics brought back from the Middle East, with the toes shaped by whalebone and stuffed with moss, hair, or wool, these fell out of fashion in the thirteenth century, but experienced a resurgence in popularity as *poulaines*, introduced in the fourteenth century. Poulaines, also known as *krakows*, were shoes with toes a third or more longer than the foot; some had toes as long as 24 inches.

Peasants who could afford to wear shoes continued to wear simple leather foot coverings or clogs, while other moderately long-toed shoes became popular among commoners who could afford them, like merchants. **Sumptuary laws** were issued in 1363 that restricted very long toes only to the upper classes, allowing lower classes to wear shoes with shorter toes. In some ways, this legislation was somewhat redundant, as very long-toed shoes simply could not be worn by working men. The Catholic Church took a strong stand against the implied sexuality and extravagance of the poulaines, leading to their eventual replacement with wide-toed shoes.

The twelfth century also saw the development of **shoemakers' guilds** and the professionalization of the craft of shoemaking, with shoes being made of smaller pieces put together using more sophisticated patterns. Also at the end of the Middle Ages, shoe technology changed, with turn shoe construction being replaced by welt shoe construction, in which shoes are made on a wooden last, with the upper sewn to three layers of sole. Because welted shoes don't have to be turned inside out, the sole can be made of thicker leather, making the shoes more durable and also allowing for the development of the heel.

The High Renaissance, from the mid-fifteenth to the mid-sixteenth centuries, saw new shifts in shoe fashion partly as the result of new technologies in shoemaking, such as the development of the last, which allowed shoemakers to shape shoes to a wooden model of the foot. Low-cut slippers with very wide, square toes, known as duckbills or bearpaws, became popular in the sixteenth century for elite men, replacing the pointy-toed shoes of the late Middle Ages, which, due to the extremes of their length, were inconvenient even for elites, who waddled while wearing them. It is said that these wide-toed shoes were created because Charles VIII had six toes and could not fit into the more narrow shoes. The width of the shoes also paralleled the width of the men's clothing at this time, which emphasized a man's chest and shoulders. The toes of these shoes were, like the clothing of the time, slashed to reveal the brightly colored lining or fur

These mules date from the late Baroque period, from 1690 to 1720. [Photo courtesy of Shoe Icons]

inside the shoes. Again, sumptuary laws were enacted to restrict the width of the toes (they got as wide as eight inches by mid-sixteenth century, necessitating a law restricting them to six inches), and Mary I eventually outlawed them in order to appease the Catholic Church. They were replaced by slightly slimmer shoes known as *eschapins*, which were also slashed. In addition, noblemen at this time began to wear leather boots with hard leather soles, heels, and soft leather tops for riding.

Hose were still worn by men in the Renaissance and extended from the waist to just above the knee, and they were worn over hose extensions that were worn below the knee. With the development of the knitting machine, stockings became more form fitting.

Women during this period wore soft **slippers** made of fancy materials like silk and brocade. Because the fabrics of these shoes were so delicate, a woman who went outside needed protection from the elements. Pattens were worn outside of shoes to protect them from dirt and mud.

Fashion during this period wasn't limited only to elites; European middle-class men and women also began wearing styles of clothing and shoes influenced by the courts.

Chopines or *pianelle*, wooden or cork soled, open-backed platform clogs originating among Venetian courtesans, became popular during the fifteenth century and were initially worn by wealthy women when they went outside to protect their feet and clothing from dirt and mud. (Initially, the chopines served like pattens and were worn over shoes; eventually they were worn as standalone shoes.) With platforms that eventually ranged from six to 30 inches in height, chopines became a symbol of status, as those women who wore them were obviously not working women and often had to have servants help them to walk or stand. Because of the connections to courtesans, the wearing of chopines was erotically charged, and art from the period often shows women wearing chopines in the bedroom, awaiting a lover. Not only did courtesans and upper class women wear them, but lower-class prostitutes as well.

The platforms were made of cork or wood and were generally covered with velvet or other fancy material to match one's clothing. While sumptuary laws restricted the height of the platforms after a number of miscarriages caused by pregnant women falling off of their shoes, women flouted the law and wore them anyway. On the other hand, the church approved of even the very high chopines because their height restricted dancing and other sinful activities. *Zoccolos* were a version of chopine with two stilts, rather than a single platform, underneath the sole. While chopines were no longer worn in most Italian cities by the seventeenth century, they remained popular in Venice until the eighteenth century.

High heels arose in Europe in the late sixteenth century and became popular for men and women throughout the seventeenth century. The derivation of high heels is debated, with one story telling of Catherine de Medici who brought high heels (probably derived from *chopines*) to Paris to make herself seem taller in the mid-sixteenth century, and another pointing towards Louis XIV who wore high heels to make himself seem taller a century later. Men were already wearing heeled riding boots by this time, which probably came from the Mongols and other Eastern invaders starting in the thirteenth century, and the heels from the boots entered men's dress shoes by the turn of the seventeenth century. Made from stacked leather, the heels ranged from two to five inches in height.

> Red heels, a status symbol in 17th and 18th Century Europe were worn only by the privileged classes, hence the term "well heeled."
>
> LINDA O'KEEFE

Shoes during the seventeenth century were made from leather and, for women, fancy materials, and were square-toed (although not wide like the duckbilled shoes of the sixteenth century) fastened with buckles or bows. Cavalier boots were popular for regular wear during the seventeenth century, thanks to the fashion set by Charles I. Boots were worn with boot hose held up with garters. **Galoshes**, which began as Spanish **overshoes**, evolved into boots to be worn over shoes during this century.

By the end of the seventeenth century, Paris became the center of European fashion, centering around the court of Louis XIV, and the French silk-weaving industry. From this time onward, the styles worn by the French and other European courts became the source for new fashion styles in clothing and footwear for centuries. At this time, those styles included high wooden heels, often red, for men's shoes (following a trend set by King Louis XIV who wore five inch high red heels) and buckles, rosettes, and ribbons to fasten and decorate shoes.

Elites through the sixteenth century onward continued to distance themselves from commoners and the poor through their extravagant fashions in clothing and footwear. High-heeled shoes made of silks, brocades, and other sumptuous materials, like the long-toed shoes from before, separated the nobility from working men and women, allowing their status to be visible at all times. Buckles, worn on men's shoes from the end of the seventeenth century, were expensive and were only worn by elites. In addition, high-heeled shoes for women made women's feet seem smaller, an important attribute emphasized in women's shoes through the eighteenth and nineteenth centuries.

During the first wave of European colonization, from the fifteenth to the nineteenth centuries, European fashions in both clothing and footwear influenced the clothing and shoe styles in the colonies. **Shoemakers** arrived in the American colonies (French and English) as early as 1628, who outfitted the colonists' feet according to the European styles of the time. But American elites continued to wear shoes shipped from England and France for centuries, maintaining European style in the colonies.

Women in Venice during the seventeenth century continued to wear chopines of embroidered silk, velvet, or other fancy materials, which were often designed to match the woman's dress. The heels on women's shoes during this period were often curved (known as the Louis heel after Louis XIV), and the toes, at the beginning of the century, were pointed upwards. Women's shoes were highly decorated with buckles and embroidered braids, which could be removed from one pair of shoes and added to another.

The soft, wide boots popular among elite men from the fourteenth to the seventeenth centuries were replaced in the eighteenth century with stiff leather boots. Known as **jack boots**, these were often cut away behind the knee, to allow the knee to bend. Men, however, like women, continued to wear heeled shoes, usually black, with large buckles and fancy embroidery. Men's heels began to be made of wood during this century and dropped to about one inch in height, and toes went from the seventeenth century style of square to pointy in the eighteenth century.

As the public spaces in Europe's cities became more civilized, with parks and sidewalks and other spaces created for walking, elites spent more time outdoors and thus their footwear changed. Wearing pattens or other types of overshoes was no longer as necessary in the eighteenth century because there were safe places to walk outdoors, and men's shoes became more practical, less effeminate and adorned. On the other hand, even as elite men could venture out into public spaces, elite women were still largely confined to the domestic realm, so their shoes continued to be constructed with appearance, rather than functionality, in mind.

By the beginning of the nineteenth century, and after the French and American revolutions at the end of the previous century, heels became less popular for both men's and women's shoes, as did some of the opulence of previous eras. In general, wealthy men and women began to distance themselves sartorially from the extravagance of previous eras. Women began to wear narrow (because tininess in women's feet was highly valued), low-heeled or flat slippers in the fashion of ballet slippers, with satin laces that tied around the ankles.

Men's shoes also became more conservative and stayed that way for the rest of European history. **Wellington boots**, black leather boots named after the Duke of Wellington, became popular and replaced the Hessian, or German military boot, as the fashionable boot for men. Boots, in fact, became so popular that well-to-do European men wore boots rather than shoes for everyday wear, although some men still wore shoes with low heels or no heels at all, and with laces (or elasticized cloth panels known as a gore) rather than a buckle.

Materials in the nineteenth century became less lavish, with leather replacing highly adorned silks, velvets, and brocades for many. For the first time, women's shoes were made out of leather, rather than exquisite cloth, and dark shoes became worn not only for mourning, but for regular wear, leading to the rise of black as the most popular shoe color for women. Also at this time, as pants were becoming popular in Europe, men's stockings were replaced by socks to be worn under pants. With the death of Queen Victoria's husband Albert, dark socks became popular for men, just as black shoes became popular for women.

With industrialism in the mid-nineteenth century, shoes became cheaper to produce and more widely available to members of all classes. Newer styles were also developed more rapidly, and thus shoe fashions began to change more rapidly than ever. Heels came back into fashion for women's shoes, for example. Lace-up or elastic-sided ankle boots became popular for men, replacing the high boots from the eighteenth century. The first boots specifically made for women were said to be a pair designed for Queen Victoria in 1840, which created a new trend for women's boots. Women's boots, in fact, became a necessity at this time as women's skirts grew larger, supported by large wire frames and, when walking, exposing women's feet and ankles. High-heeled ankle boots, which laced or buttoned up the side, were a way of covering a woman's vulnerable feet and ankles from display and became normative by the end of the century.

The nineteenth century included other technological innovations as well, such as synthetic dyes and the sewing machine, all of which reduced the amount of labor going into shoes and allowed for easier and cheaper production. Also during the early decades of the nineteenth century, left- and right-footed lasts were first created by shoemakers in Philadelphia, allowing, for the first time, different shoes to be worn on left and right feet. (Prior to this time, it was through wearing a shoe on either the right or the left foot that allowed it to be shaped to the foot.) While machine-made shoes allowed for shoe consumption among all the classes, elites continued to purchase custom-made shoes. Shoes for a variety of different purposes were developed during this century as well, such as dress shoes, walking shoes, dancing shoes, riding boots, opera boots, and rubber-soled **athletic shoes**, which were developed at the end of the nineteenth century.

As the twentieth century arrived, social and economic changes throughout European and world society impacted the fashion industry and shoe styles throughout the world. At the turn of the century, Victorian morality continued to shape women's fashion, and women's ankles were covered with long skirts and ankle boots, as well as silk stockings in dark colors. As the century progressed and women's skirts became shorter and moral standards loosened, women began to wear showier shoes again. Tiny feet were in high demand, so women's shoes were very small during the 1910s. Strappy women's shoes emerged in the 1920s and in the 1930s, and platform heels became popular, as did sandals, which had not been popular since the fall of **Rome**.

See also: Boots; Classical Civilizations; Concealment Shoes; Fashion Industry; High Heels; Middle East; Military Shoes and Boots; United States

Further Reading David, Alison Matthews. "War Wellingtons: Military Footwear in the Age of Empire," in Rielle, Georgio and Peter McNeil, eds. *Shoes: A History From Sandals to Sneakers*. London: Berg Publishers, 2006; Grew, Francis and Margrethe de Neergaard. *Shoes and Pattens*. Woodbridge: Boydell, 2006; McNeil, Peter, Giorgio Riello. "Walking the Streets of London and Paris in the Enlightenment," in Rielle, Georgio and Peter McNeil, eds. *Shoes: A History From Sandals to Sneakers*. London: Berg Publishers, 2006; Muzzarelli, Maria Giuseppina. "Sumptuous Shoes: Making and Wearing in Medieval Italy," in Rielle, Georgio and Peter McNeil, eds. *Shoes: A History From Sandals to Sneakers*. London: Berg Publishers, 2006; O'Keeffe, Linda. *Shoes: A Celebration of Pumps, Sandals, Slippers & More*. New York: Workman Publishing, 1996; Steele, Valerie. Encyclopedia of Clothing and Fashion. Farmington Hills, MI: Charles Scribner's Sons, 2005; Vianello, Andrea. "Courtly Lady or Courtesan? The Venetian Chopine in the Renaissance," in Rielle, Georgio and Peter McNeil, eds. *Shoes: A History From Sandals to Sneakers*. London: Berg Publishers, 2006.

Khrushchev's Shoe

Nikita Khrushchev was the leader of the Community Party and, after Stalin's death, he became the Premier of the Soviet Union during the Cold War until his ouster in 1964. He was infamous for disrupting United Nations proceedings, which culminated in October 1960 when Khrushchev expressed his anger at the Philippine delegate by calling him names and allegedly banging his shoe on his desk. The event made worldwide news and succeeded in making Khrushchev look uncivilized and uneducated. In addition, it became a symbol of the Cold War, which was largely a war of words and threats. Some reporters now feel that while Khrushchev did remove and wave his shoe, he did not in fact bang it on his desk, and one UN employee said that he never intentionally removed his shoe (which was actually a sandal), but that it fell off. In any case, there are no photos of the shoe-banging incident, even though photographers were in the room. Whether or not Krushchev waved or banged his shoe, however, the incident still served to create an image in many people's minds that the Soviet Union was unstable, uncivilized, and out of control and that its leader was a caricature, not worthy of respect.

FAIRY TALES

There are a number of fairy tales that feature either shoes or feet as important motifs. This is because both feet and shoes are often used in folklore and myth to represent travel, adventure, luck, and marriage.

Shoes have been found in the mythologies of many people. Greek and Roman mythology tells of gods who wore winged footwear, representing the gods' power of flight or their ability to travel. Certainly, shoes in general symbolize travel and freedom, as in the *Wizard of Oz*, where the ruby **slippers** allow Dorothy to travel to a magical world, or in "Winkin, Blinkin and Nod," where the characters sail off in a wooden shoe.

"**Cinderella**" tells the story of a girl who lives with, and is mistreated by, her stepmother and stepsisters, but after being granted a wish by a fairy godmother, meets a prince who rescues her from her life of misery. Key to the story is a pair of glass slippers that Cinderella wears when meeting the prince and which she accidently leaves behind. In "Cinderella," the glass slippers signify escape from a life of boredom and abuse. In addition, the shoes are tiny, and Cinderella's own feet are impossibly tiny, the tiniest in all the land, because in **Europe** and **China** where the tale was popular, tiny feet signified beauty, femininity, and good upbringing, traits that women with larger feet do not possess. Finally, the shoes provide the heroine with the means to achieve a fairy tale wedding. If a bride's shoes often represent the transfer of a woman from her home to her husband's, then it's not surprising that in "Cinderella," the slipper represents her one hope for love and marriage.

In "**The Shoes That Were Danced to Pieces**," another Grimm tale, the shoes represent, again, travel and escape to a magical place. The story tells of 12 princesses who are under a spell that makes them go out dancing every night, ruining their **dance shoes** in the process. In this tale, because the princesses are confined to their bedroom by the king, a magical spell and their dancing shoes allow them to leave their room and journey to an otherworldly place where they dance the night away. But unlike in "Cinderella," where the shoes are the vehicle to the happily ever after, in this tale the shoes do not represent future happiness. In fact, once the hero solves the puzzle of where the princesses have been going, he marries the princess of his choice, but she will not, presumably, be going out dancing anymore.

In "**The Red Shoes**," a Danish tale, the shoes signify something much darker. In this Hans Christian Andersen tale, Karen is bought a pair of red shoes, which she cannot stop thinking about, and wears everywhere, ultimately neglecting her mother and everything that is important to her. Here, shiny red shoes signify pride, vanity, and lust, and when Karen falls under their spell, devastation awaits her, including the death of her adopted mother, abject poverty, and even the loss of her own feet, replaced by wooden feet. Andersen, himself the son of a shoe-maker whose father was once shamed by a woman who insulted the fancy shoes he made for her daughter, wrote another tale involving shoes and pride. In "The Girl Who Trod on a Loaf," a proud little girl wears fancy shoes and clothes to visit her poor family, but is so concerned about keeping her shoes clean that she stepped on the loaf of bread that she was bringing to her mother, rather than step in a mud puddle. As with "The Red Shoes," Inge, the little girl, was severely pun-ished for the sin of pride.

In all of the above cases, the shoes symbolize high status, as Cinderella's tiny feet that fit into the glass slipper indicate that she is of good breeding (even when working as a maid), and the 12 princesses are able to afford new dancing slippers every night. In "The Red Shoes," however, Karen comes from a poor background, so the fact that she is wearing red shoes that were made for a princess is an indica-tion that she has stepped above her station in life, and for that she must be punished.

On the other hand, the shoes in "The Red Shoes" and "The Shoes That Were Danced to Pieces" both allow the wearer to dance and to escape a humdrum life. Unfortunately for Karen, she cannot stop dancing once she begins and must re-treat after her feet are cut off to the most humdrum life of all, working as a maid. No prince and fairy tale marriage await this antiheroine.

The "Goloshes of Fortune" is another tale by Hans Christian Andersen, which echoes some of the themes from the other tales. This tale is about two fairies who bring a pair of magical **galoshes** to a party. One of the fairies says that, upon placing the galoshes on one's feet, "every wish is fulfilled at the moment it is expressed, so that for once mankind have the chance of being happy," but the sec-ond fairy replies that "whoever puts on those goloshes will be very unhappy, and bless the moment in which he can get rid of them." The tale then tells of five men who wear the galoshes, and each in turn are transported to another time or place in which they thought that they would be happier, but in which they are, in fact, more miserable. It is only when the **boots** are removed that the wearers gratefully are returned to their original position. After the fifth man ends up dead thanks to the trip he took with the galoshes, the fairies remove the boots, reviving the man, and take the galoshes with them. Here, the galoshes provide for an escape to a more exciting time, but as with Andersen's other tales, there is a dark side to this fantasy, and the interesting life provided by the galoshes ends up being dangerous indeed. Like *The Wizard of Oz*, another story featuring a magical pair of shoes, one lesson to be learned is that one should not wish for a different life than one has and should be thankful for what one already has.

While shoes in the above tales can offer the hope of escape from a humdrum life, in the classic fairy tales like "Cinderella," this hope comes often in the form of marriage for the heroine. In tales in which men are the heroes, however, instead of allowing a man or boy to escape from a dull or abusive life, shoes—or more commonly boots, as they represent outdoors and activity—allow the wearer to accomplish magical feats. In particular, tales like "Jack the Giant Killer" or "Hop o' My Thumb" feature the motif of the seven league boots (AT Motif D1521.1) in which the hero is given a gift of magical boots that allow the wearer to travel great distances in one stride. But the hero does not escape a life of drudgery—he uses the boots and his travels to accomplish an important task. Boots that allow the wearers to quickly travel long distances are also found in modern role-playing games like Dungeons & Dragons. A happy ending is very different, then, for men and for women in fairy tales.

Shoes are important elements in other fairy tales like the Grimm brothers' version of "Snow White" in which, at the end of the story, the evil witch attends the wedding of Snow White and the prince and is forced to dance in a pair of iron shoes that have been heated to a red-hot glow until she dies, a fate not unlike that suffered by Karen in "The Red Shoes." "Puss in Boots" also features a character wearing boots, but in the case of this story they are simply an item of apparel (which are not found in all variants of the tale) and do not appear to have much symbolic meaning other than the fact that they make Puss a character of some status.

Another Grimm tale, "**The Elves and the Shoemaker**," tells of a pair of naked elves

> ### Urban Legends
>
> Shoes are a frequent subject of urban legends, with Nike occupying the greatest number of legends. Popular beliefs about Nike include a rumor that if you mail Nike your worn out shoes, you will get a new pair for free, and an alleged Nike ad featuring a bloodied shoe at the site of a suicide bombing and a caption that reads: "you may not survive the blast but your shoes will." Puma was also the subject of two hoax ads, featuring couples having sex wearing their Pumas. Adidas was the target of a rumor that said that the name Adidas came from the words "All day I dream about sex." Vans were the subject of an ugly rumor in the 1990s that alleged that the design —interlocking six-sided stars—are there because Vans hates Jews and wants their customers to walk on Jews. These rumors are all false.

who magically help a shoemaker to make shoes. In this story, the shoes are symbolic only in the sense that the elves are now free to leave the shoemaker because they have clothes and shoes, since these items represent freedom of opportunity. But perhaps more important is the notion of shoemaking as work. The shoemaker himself is hardworking, but on his own he cannot earn enough to care for his family; it's only with the magical labor of the elves that he finds some success, with success equaling shoes, the classic embodiment of wealth. Because they were given the gift of the clothes and shoes, however, the elves leave, either no longer wishing to be cobblers—which was not an exalted occupation—or not wanting to be bound to the job.

"**The Old Woman Who Lived in a Shoe**" is an unusual case. A nursery rhyme rather than a fairy tale, it is both a form of entertainment and education for children and a forum for conveying social commentary. In this rhyme, the shoe can represent Great Britain's attempts to control her colonies in the nineteenth century; it could be a morality tale about the dangers of unwed pregnancy; or the shoe could represent fertility and marriage, or its lack, as in the case of the woman in the shoe. It also signifies poverty, and while usually the lack of shoes signifies poverty, in this case the shoe could be metonymic of the woman's general lack of resources.

See also: "Cinderella"; "The Old Woman Who Lived in a Shoe"; "The Red Shoes"; "The Shoes That Were Danced to Pieces"

Further Reading Bettelheim, Bruno. *The Uses of Enchantment: The Meaning and Importance of Fairy Tales*. New York: Vintage Books, 1975; Grimm, Jacob and Wilhelm. *Household Tales*. Margaret Hunt, translator. London: George Bell, 1884, 1892. Opie, Iona and Peter. *The Classic Fairy Tales*. New York: Oxford University Press, 1974; Propp, Vladimir. *Morphology of the Folktale*. Austin: University of Texas, 1968; Tatar, Maria M., ed. *The Classic Fairy Tales*. New York: W. W. Norton, 1999; Thompson, Stith. *The Folktale*. New York: Holt, Rinehart, and Winston, 1946; Zipes, Jack, ed. *The Oxford Companion to Fairy Tales*. Oxford: Oxford University, 2000.

FASHION INDUSTRY

The fashion industry as we know it today emerged from the styles popularized by the French court in the seventeenth and eighteenth centuries. Today, while Paris remains a center of the international fashion industry, a handful of other cities such as New York, Milan, London, and Tokyo are also centers for fashion production and design.

> "If God had wanted us to wear flat shoes, he wouldn't have invented Manolo Blahnik."
>
> ALEXANDRA SHULMAN, EDITOR OF VOGUE

During the Middle Ages in **Europe**, professional tailors emerged for the first time, making clothing for the wealthy. Prior to this time, clothes were made in the home, by women and servants, which remained the case for the poor throughout much of European history. Dress became more elaborate for the wealthy, while it remained functional for commoners. Until 1675, wealthy men and women had their clothes made by tailors. After 1675, however, dress designers emerged and began making clothes for members of the European courts as well as forming their own guilds.

The beginnings of the fashion industry can be dated to the middle to late seventeenth century, when Louis XIV helped make France a political and cultural powerhouse in Europe. Prior to that time, Florence, Venice, Rome, and Flanders were all independent centers of fashion. In the fifteenth century, for instance, Burgundy (a duchy controlling Flanders and much of France) was the European fashion leader, followed by Italy in the sixteenth century, then Germany and Belgium, followed by Spain. With the coronation of Louis XIV in 1643, the center of fashion shifted to France.

France's influence extended through the realms of fashion, politics, and culture. Under King Louis XIV, French fashion came to be the standard for fashionable men and women throughout Europe, and as European influence extended throughout the world, French fashion did as well. In addition, the king threw his weight behind the development of a silk-weaving industry in Lyon, France, which eventually became the largest producer of luxury silks in Europe. Individual silk designers became known for their work, and the dressmakers who made the clothing and shoes worn by members of the royal court became well known in their own right. Besides textiles, France dominated other fashionable industries, such as wig making, tailoring, and hat making.

Mass media played a role in the dissemination of French styles as the production of engravings, handbills, and other media illustrated the styles of clothing being worn to a wider audience. Mannequins were also sent to other courts, dressed in the style of the French court, further advertising and spreading these styles. Costume plates drawn by well-known European artists were another way of disseminating fashion throughout Europe. Fashion during this period began to change quickly because as middle class people began wearing the styles of the courts, elites needed to quickly develop new styles to stay ahead of them.

In 1693, the first fashion magazine emerged and began to replace mannequins as the primary way that fashion information spread through Europe. By the mid-seventeenth century, fashion magazines were the primary source of fashion information throughout Europe. By the eighteenth century, wealthy American colonists, too, were influenced by European fashion, as mannequins and other information about fashion traveled to the New World. Prior to the American Revolution, American fashions were most heavily influenced by England, but after the Revolution France replaced England as America's inspiration for fashion.

After the French revolution, England once again began to dominate fashion for much of the nineteenth century. One reason was the Industrial Revolution, which occurred in England and changed how clothing was made. With the development of the sewing machine in 1846 and the introduction of patterns for clothing, clothing was made cheaper and easier, and more ready-to-wear clothing was available for the first time. Before the development of ready-to-wear clothing, both garments and shoes were created for individual clients and to their exact measurements; with ready-to-wear clothing, clothing was created with patterns and could be purchased "off the rack." The postrevolutionary era also saw the first ready-to-wear salons open as well as the first department store, located in Paris.

Another change in fashion after the demise of the French court in the nineteenth century was the rise of independent fashion designers, beginning with Charles Frederick Worth, and the emergence of haute couture. Haute couture refers to custom-made fashion made by designers like Worth, who opened his own fashion house, catering to wealthy French women in Paris in 1858. Worth showed his designs on models at his shop, and wealthy customers chose the design they liked in the fabric of their choice, and Worth then made the clothing for the customers. Worth was the first designer to produce seasonal collections and to use live models, and he dressed wealthy women from France, Germany, England, Russia, and the **United States**. Another reason for the rise of haute couture was that the emerging middle class and the availability of ready-to-wear clothing forced European elites to develop more inaccessible fashions in order to distinguish themselves from the middle class. Prior to this time, dressmakers, whether or not they worked for the court, dressed wealthy customers according to the fashions of the time and in accordance to the wishes of the customer. With the rise of couture, designers created their own fashions, influencing both royal and non-royal alike. So even as the middle class gained access to ready-to-wear clothing, wealthy customers continued to buy custom designs.

With respect to both clothing and shoes, the fashion industry involves more than the design and production of fashion; it is also the major force behind what is considered fashionable (i.e., what clothes or shoes are stylish at a given time). Prior to the development of the fashion industry, clothing and shoe styles did not change very rapidly, and even among elites, footwear and clothing styles might remain relatively constant for decades (and in some cultures, centuries), and when changes did occur they were often because of the diffusion of styles from other cultures, as with the French *poulaine*, which came from the **Middle East**. This changed in the mid-fourteenth century, as the shape of elite men and women's clothing and shoes began to change more rapidly.

Today, on the other hand, the designers, producers, and marketers of the fashion industry create and promote new fashions as often as four times a year. Fashion, and the designers of fashion, now drive both production and consumption. These artificial "seasons" dictate the production and purchase of clothing and footwear, and because neither clothing nor footwear needs to be purchased that often, the industry uses perceived obsolescence to make consumers feel that their clothing is out of fashion, creating the space for new collections to emerge with every season.

One result of the emergence of the fashion industry, and in particular the French-centered fashion industry, was a decline, starting in about the seventeenth century, in national fashions that had once been indicative of specific cultures. Another change that began to occur in European fashion starting in the sixteenth century was that fashionable clothes, shoes, jewelry, and other elements of style became more accessible to well-to-do merchants and craftsmen rather than simply the nobility. As commoners began to purchase and wear fashionable clothing or shoes, **sumptuary laws** began to be enacted in order to control the wearing of luxury items by non-elites.

With mass production after the Industrial Revolution at the end of the nineteenth century, custom clothing and bespoke shoes gave way to mechanized production of clothing and shoes for the masses. Elites continued to wear custom-made items for a while, but today even the wealthy wear clothing and shoes that were made at least in part by machine. What distinguishes ready-to-wear clothing from haute couture, for example, is that the former is mass produced in standard sizes to be worn off the rack while the latter refers to custom-fitted clothing to a customer's specifications.

The 1930s saw the rise of American designers, as European fashion took a backseat to the war and the French fashion houses shut down. American designers emerged to fill the gap and provide fashions to Americans. The twentieth century also saw the rise of British designers during the 1960s, and in the 1980s

Milan and Tokyo became centers of fashion. Also during this time, fashion magazines and fashion shows began to play a larger role in the spread of fashion and heavily influenced and driove the rapidly changing nature of fashion.

In terms of footwear, while most people today buy mass-produced shoes from department stores, **shoe stores**, or big-box retailers, the wealthy can buy high-end shoes directly from designer shoemakers like **Jimmy Choo** or **Manolo Blahnik**. The shoes are not custom-made for the wearer, and most are produced at least in part by machine today, but they are produced in limited numbers to ensure their exclusivity.

In both fashion and footwear today, the brand name is most important to elites, with the quality and exclusivity that it implies. The masses, on the other hand, are able to wear clothing and shoes with design elements borrowed directly from high-end fashion, blurring the line between high-end and low-end fashion and, in terms of footwear, designer shoemakers and mass-produced shoes.

See also: Europe

Further Reading Barwick, Sandra *A Century of Style*, London, Allen & Unwin, 1984; Cosgrave, Bronwyn. *The Complete History of Costume and Fashion: From Ancient Egypt to the Present Day*. New York: Checkmark Books, 2000; Steele, Valerie.*Paris Fashion: A Cultural History*. New York: Oxford University Press, 1998; Steele, Valerie. *Encyclopedia of Clothing and Fashion*. Farmington Hills, MI: Charles Scribner's Sons, 2005; White, Nicola, Ian Griffiths. *The Fashion Business: Theory, Practice, Image*. London: Berg Publishers, 2000.

FERRAGAMO, SALVATORE

Salvatore Ferragamo was an Italian shoe designer who was known as the **shoemaker** to the stars because of his work in Hollywood in the 1920s. He pioneered a number of innovations in footwear, such as the platform heel and the **stiletto** heel, and he is known for his novel use of materials as well as his artistic designs.

Ferragamo was born in 1898 in Italy, and he made his first pair of shoes at the age of nine. His parents were too poor to afford to buy shoes for his sisters' communion, so he made the shoes himself rather than see them go to church wearing the traditional **clogs** worn by the rural poor. He then went to Naples to train as a shoemaker and opened his first shop in his parents' home at the age of 14.

When he was 16, he moved to the **United States** and worked in a **boot** factory in Boston that one of his brothers worked at. From there, he moved to Santa Barbara and opened his first shop, offering shoe repair and custom-made shoes. He began getting clients from the film industry and began making shoes for actresses and actors to wear both in film and outside of films. When the film industry moved to Hollywood in 1923, Ferragamo followed and opened his first shop there, known as the Hollywood Boot Shop. His Hollywood clients from that era included Gloria Swanson, Joan Crawford, Greta Garbo, and Bette Davis, and he famously had lasts made for each celebrity client.

Ferragamo also studied anatomy at the University of Southern California because he wanted to learn how to make shoes that were not only beautiful but

Ferragamo. These stilettos have an upper made of Tavarnel lace, decorated with paillettes. They date from the 1950s. [Photo courtesy of Shoe Icons and Ferragamo Creations]

felt good to wear. Because of what he learned about the distribution of the body's weight over the arch of the foot, he perfected a steel arch to support the instep in heels, making stylish women's shoes more comfortable.

Ferragamo wanted to expand in the United States, but he did not feel he could open a factory in the United States without craftsmen trained to make the shoes by hand. He returned to Italy in 1927 and chose Florence as the location to open his first factory, hiring craftsmen to carve the lasts and make the uppers. While Italy did not at that time have a reputation for producing footwear, and indeed Americans thought of Italy as a place to buy inexpensive leather goods, Florence was known as a cultural and artistic center. With Ferragamo's presence, both Florence and Italy would become famous for its designer footwear, and Ferragamo's reputation as a creative designer of custom-made, high-quality footwear would be assured.

Through the 1920s and 1930s, Ferragamo expanded his business in Italy and designed shoes for many of the wealthiest women of the world. He also developed many of his most well-known innovations and experimental designs during this period, such as the metal arch support, which meant that heeled shoes no longer needed toe caps to hold the feet in the shoes. This innovation allowed for the creation of high-heeled **sandals**.

During World War II, Italy was isolated from much of the world, and Ferragamo, like other Italian designers, had to cope with restrictions on the use of materials such as steel and **leather**. Starting in 1935 when Italy was subject to a trade embargo thanks to its invasion of Ethiopia, he began experimenting with new materials like felt, hemp, raffia, and cloth, creating radical new designs out of necessity. In 1936, Ferragamo created the wedge heel out of Sardinian cork, and in 1938 he resurrected the platform heel. These inventions came about both due to a paucity of traditional materials as well as a desire to create a stable and comfortable shoe. He was said to be inspired by the Spanish **espadrille** and originally the cork heels were made by sewing together wine bottle corks. They became incredibly popular during the late 1930s and entered the United States in 1941, but fell out of fashion after the war. Since then, platforms and wedges have been popular in the 1970s, 1990s, and 2000s.

After World War II, Ferragamo's company continued to thrive, hiring new craftsmen and continuing to produce handmade shoes as well as, by the end of the 1940s, handbags. Because of the country's isolation in the war, a fashion industry developed in Italy that rivaled that of Paris and began to thrive during the 1950s. In 1951, the first fashion runway show in Italy was held in Florence, showcasing Italian designers and including Ferragamo's shoes. By the end of the decade, Italian luxury goods were being exported in record numbers to the United States and other countries, including Ferragamo's shoes, handbags, and scarves, and the first New York City retail outlet opened in 1948 on Park Avenue. Hollywood celebrities continued to buy Ferragamos, including Katherine Hepburn, Sofia Loren, Audrey Hepburn, Rita Hayworth, Marilyn Monroe, and Ava Gardner. Ferragamo also opened up a factory in England to make ready-made shoes in order to compete with other shoe companies. In 1955, Ferragamo is credited by many with inventing another critical shoe development, the **stiletto** heel, a heel made out of steel that allowed for shoes to sit on very high, very thin heels.

Ferragamo was inspired by a variety of sources, including art, architecture, and tribal design. He was inspired by archaeological discoveries like ancient Egyptian sandals and the uncovering of the ruins of Pompeii, and his shoes reflected these inspirations in their use of color, sculptural shapes, and decoration. Some of his most innovative designs included the invisible heel in 1947, a high-heeled wedge sandal with an upper made from one long piece of nylon, and the cage heel, a high-heeled sandal made with an open heel like a cage. In 1978, his daughter Fiamma designed the Vara **pump**, a low -heeled red pump, which has been the company's most popular design. During his lifetime, Ferragamo took out more than 350 patents on materials, inventions, and processes, including leather substitutes, heels made of Bakelite, wooden soles, and uppers made of materials like raffia or jersey. Ultimately, he designed more than 20,000 shoe models. Ferragamo won a number of awards during his lifetime and since his death, including the Neiman Marcus award in 1947, the Guggenheim First Prize for Industry and Culture in 1999, and the Rodeo Drive Walk of Style Award in 2006.

In the 1960s, the company, under the management of Ferragamo's widow Wanda, expanded further, making thousands of pairs of shoes per day. For the first time, she also changed the production process and introduced mechanization, although much of Ferragamo's production techniques remain, such as the creation of dozens of sizes, including six widths, for each model, in order to assure the most "made to measure" fit. During the 1980s, the company continued to expand, opening its first Asian store in Hong Kong and adding fragrance to a growing list of products that by this time included men's shoes, accessories, handbags, and scarves. In the 1990s, the company began licensing eyewear as well.

After Ferragamo's death in 1960, his wife took over the company as chair, and the company continues to be family owned today, with his children and other relatives playing, at various times, important roles in the company. Today, Salvatore Ferragamo operates stores throughout Europe, the United States, Mexico, South America, and throughout Asia, and in 2008 the company released a special line of shoes under the label Ferragamo Creations. This label sells classic Ferragamo shoes that were originally made in the 1940s and 1950s in very limited numbers, including shoes that were never before offered to the public, like the shoes Marilyn Monroe wore in *Some Like It Hot*.

In 1995, the family opened the Salvatore Ferragamo Museum in the company's headquarters, the Palazzo Spini Feroni in Florence. The museum houses 10,000 pairs of Ferragamo shoes as well as the designer's designs, drawings, tools, and other artifacts, like the signed lasts for each celebrity client.

See also: Fashion Industry; High heels; Platform Shoes; Sandals; Stilettos; United States

Further Reading Ricci, Stafnia. "Made in Italy: Ferragamo and Twentieth-Century Fashion," in Rielle, Georgio and Peter McNeil, eds. *Shoes: A History From Sandals to Sneakers*. London: Berg Publishers, 2006; Ricci, Stefania; Glanz Margo, Mercedes Iturbe. *Walking Dreams: Salvatore Ferragamo, 1898–1960*. Spain: Editorial RM, 2006.

FETISHES

A fetish is a sexual attraction to an object, body part, or nonperson (such as an animal) and is considered a paraphilia by the American Psychiatric Association when it causes the person emotional stress, hampers their relationships, or puts them into harm's way.

Fetishes are thought to derive either from a form of conditioning by which an object becomes associated with sexual arousal, or they could arise thanks to a traumatic experience early in life. A third possibility is that they are a result of a hormonal imbalance or problem with the structure of the brain. There are other theories as well; for instance, one theory states that most people are attracted to certain features of the body over other features, and that fetishists simply have an overabundance of this form of attraction, while other theorists posit that some individuals may continue to value "transitional objects" such as stuffed animals (which were used by the child to cope with the withdrawal of the mother) long into adulthood. If patients seek treatment for their fetish, the usual forms of treatment include psychoanalysis and cognitive therapies such as aversive conditioning. On the other hand, many scientists who study sexuality don't consider fetishism to be a paraphilia at all, but instead regard it as another form of sexual expression. It is only when the attachment to the object (such as a foot) becomes more important than an emotional or sexual connection with another adult that fetishism becomes pathological.

> Your ladyship is nearer to heaven than when I saw you last, by the altitude of the chopine.
>
> WILLIAM SHAKESPEARE

While there are both male and female fetishists, the majority of the documentation on fetishists, including foot and shoe fetishists, is on men, and the most fetishized feet and footwear belong to women.

Foot and footwear fetishes are the most commonly documented form of fetish and involve a sexual interest in feet or footwear, and sometimes both. A foot fetishist's sexual arousal centers around the foot—stroking, caressing, and kissing the feet, or sometimes using the foot or toes as part of lovemaking. Foot fetishists will typically find certain features of the foot, or of particular feet, to be arousing, such as **foot odor**, long toes, high arches, or painted toenails. Small female feet have been highly valued in many cultures and represent femininity and vulnerability, most famously expressed through the Chinese practice of **foot binding**. In this case, tiny feet (and the lotus shoes worn over them) were both objects of erotic desire and signs of status and wealth. On the other hand, some find very large feet in women to be arousing. Shoe fetishists find shoes to be sexually arousing. Fetishists will sometimes caress or lick shoes or will ejaculate into them; other times the fetish involves being stepped on by the shoes or watching someone in high heels step on someone or something else, as in a crush fetish. On the other hand, sometimes the smell of the shoe is arousing.

Some theorists postulate that foot fetishism becomes more popular as sexually transmitted diseases rise; using the feet for sexual release becomes a form of safe sex. Another theory suggests that periods of high morality when feet—in particular, female feet—are kept from public sight are also correlated with increases in foot fetishes. So during the Victorian era when women's feet were covered in shoes and concealed under long layers of clothing, they were subsequently more eroticized by fetishists (during the mid-nineteenth century there was a busy underground market in foot fetish pornography and accessories), signifying perhaps other body parts that were also hidden. In fact, foot and shoe fetishism were first defined as a sexual issue in nineteenth century England,

Kinky Shoes. These platform stilettos with Lucite heels could satisfy a shoe fetishist's needs. [2008 copyright Eimantas Buzas. Image from BigStockPhoto.com]

and it may be that these developments were rooted directly in the Victorian morality of the time. Freud, for example, thought that shoes are fetishized because little boys see shoes when trying to look up their mother's long skirt.

Fetishes involving shoes or feet are among the most common fetishes today, based on academic studies and simple Web searches; an Internet search for fetish, for example, will return more entries for feet than for other fetishes, and the most commonly searched fetish term is feet. During the rise of fetishism in the nineteenth century, high heels were second only to corsets as objects of fetishistic worship and play.

The types of shoes valued by shoe fetishists are often very **high heels** (because of the way they impact a woman's back, hips, buttocks, and breasts), very tight, thigh-high **boots**, or boots that are laced up like corsets. Tightly laced boots or shoes are erotically charged for fetishists because of the idea of constraints and the pain and submission involved in being tightly constrained. The process of lacing itself is arousing, as is the process of unlacing because of the possibility of release.

Other types of erotic shoes are those with toe cleavage or with partial coverage like mules or deep throated heels, which reveal much of the upper foot. Shiny materials like **patent leather** or pleather are arousing, as are soft materials like satin or fur. Heels that are so high (up to eight inches) that the woman cannot walk, or cannot walk easily, are also arousing because of the constraints to mobility that it causes.

Extreme **stilletto** heels and tightly laced boots are popular among the Bondage Discipline Domination Submission (BDSM) subculture. Here, the focus is on sexual behaviors that include the use of consensual pain, submission, or dominance. A dominant person enjoys controlling his or her sexual partner. A submissive person is one who seeks out a partner to dominate him or her. Extreme heels and tightly laced boots and shoes play a similar role in BDSM as do corsets, an item of clothing worn to constrict the torso. The lacing and unlacing of the boots is erotic, as is the lack of mobility that is achieved through the wearing of extremely high heels, which causes the wearer to hobble. Often the submissive partner will be the partner who is encumbered, and hardware like locks are often worn on the shoes and boots of the submissive. On the other hand, often the dominant partner wears the extreme high heels. A woman in extreme heels is both hyper feminine and hyper masculine, a combination that many men (fetishists and non-fetishists alike) find very arousing. Stilettos, too, are both fragile looking and very dangerous, a combination that comes into play in the crush fetish.

Shoe fetishes and BDSM practices are also related through the crush fetish, in which an individual derives sexual pleasure from watching a woman's stillettoed foot crush objects or small animals, generally in videos called crush videos. The feet shown in crush videos are often large. The impulse behind a crush fetish is, for many, similar to the impulse behind BDSM: adherents enjoy fantasizing about themselves being crushed and experience that vicariously through watching a woman in very high heels crush inanimate objects or animals. Even fetishists without a specific crush fetish often fantasize about or enjoy having a woman in high heels walk on them, causing them both pain and humiliation and making them feel insignificant.

In general, high heels are fetish items not simply because they are sexy and change the wearer's body in ways that are sexually arousing. High heels also represent aggression, power, and domination and is a required part of the dominatrix's outfit. Men who want to be dominated, even when they have no shoe or foot fetish, choose to be dominated by a woman in high stilleto heels. High heels are often used within BDSM sex play to scratch, stab, or penetrate one of the partners. Fetish porn, too, emphasizes strong, dangerous women in dangerously high heels.

Foot and shoe fetishists have countless Web sites that promote their interest, and 1960s magazines like *High Heels, Boot Lovers' Digest, Bizarre Life, Women Who Administer Punishment (WHAP)*, and *Bitches in Boots* featured shoe fetish photos and articles regularly. Today, most fetish material is available online. Photos and videos of women (usually) engaged in sexual activities with their feet ("foot jobs" being the most prevalent), licking and sucking feet, using their feet or heels to walk on or dominate a man, or having their feet ejaculated upon are extremely prevalent on the Internet, as are photos and videos of feet being bound, whipped, or otherwise tortured.

See also: Boots; Crush Videos; Eroticism; Frederick's of Hollywood; High Heels; Stilettos

Further Reading Steele, Valerie. *Fashion and Eroticism: Ideals of Feminine Beauty from the Victorian Era to the Jazz Age*. New York: Oxford University Press, 1995; Steele, Valerie. *Fetish: Fashion, Sex and Power*. New York: Oxford University Press, 1996; Steele, Valerie. "Shoes and the Erotic Imagination," in Rielle, Georgio and Peter McNeil, eds. *Shoes: A History From Sandals to Sneakers*. London: Berg Publishers, 2006

FLAT FEET AND FALLEN ARCHES

Fallen arches, *pes planus* or flat feet, is a common condition of the feet. It refers to a condition in which the arch of the foot has failed to develop normally, a process that normally occurs during the first few years of a child's life, causing the feet to lie flat on the ground. Flat feet can also develop later in life in a person who had normal arches, due to either injury (such as to the tendons of the ankle) or to another condition, such as super pronation, obesity, arthritis, or excessive exercise.

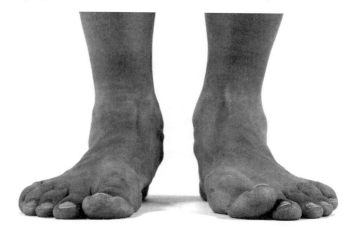

Flat feet can be flexible, which means that the arch returns when the foot is flexed, or rigid, which refers to a total lack of an arch. People with the second condition generally have foot pain and experience a lack of support for the body's weight, which can cause calf, knee, hip, back, and shoulder pain. In addition, flat feet can contribute to other problems like plantar fasciitis and problems with the **Achilles** tendon.

Fallen Arches, Flat Feet. This person's feet have fallen arches. [2008 Copyright Suzanne Tucker. Image from BigStockPhoto.com]

Treatment for flat feet used to include **orthopedic shoes**, which hold the feet in a normal position. Today, treatment includes stretching, toe curls, arch taping, and wearing comfortable shoes combined with **orthotic** arch supports. Children who may be developing flat feet are encouraged to spend time walking barefoot as a way to exercise the muscles of the feet. In addition, if the patient is overweight, the condition can be alleviated through weight loss, and if it is caused by exercise, switching to low-impact activities or exercising on soft surfaces will also help. Severe cases can be treated with surgery, in which a titanium implant can be inserted into the foot to simulate an arch. The majority of those with flat feet have flexible flat feet; they do not experience pain or other symptoms and generally don't require treatment at all. If superpronation is the problem, treatment can include orthotic arch supports and orthopedic shoes.

See also: Disorders and Injuries; Orthotics; Orthopedic Shoes

Further Reading Jahss, Melvin. *Disorders of the Foot and Ankle: Medical and Surgical Management.* Philadelphia: Saunders, 1991; Lorimer, Donald, Donald Neale. *Neale's Disorders of the Foot.* New York: Elsevier Churchill Livingstone, 2006.

FLIP FLOPS

Flip flop is a 1960s term that refers to casual thong **sandals**. Popular today among beachgoers, gym goers, soldiers (who wear them in the shower), and vacationers, thong sandals are one of the earliest forms of footwear in the world.

Thong sandals, or flip flops, are made of just two pieces: a sole, made of **leather**, foam, rubber, wood, or other material, connected to a strap made of fabric, plant fiber, or leather, which attaches to the sole on both sides of the foot and in between the first and second toes. The sandals stay on the feet because the toes grip the toe strap when a person walks.

Flip flops were worn in **Egypt**, **Rome** and **Greece**, sub-Saharan **Africa**, **India**, **China**, **Korea**, and **Japan**, as well as in many Latin American cultures. They are common in regions with hot weather, where footwear is designed to protect the bottom of the foot yet keep the foot cool. African versions have been made of wood, leather, recycled rubber, and palm leaf and could be very simple or could be elaborately decorated, and some are even made in the shape of animals like crocodiles. **Middle Eastern** versions are known as *niaal* and are often made of camel hide. Flip flops are also popular in countries where shoes are to be removed when entering a building, which is why they are so popular in Asia. In Japan, both the *zori* and the *geta* are flip flops. *Geta* are elevated flip flops with a high wooden sole and fabric thongs, while *zori* are made of woven straw, again with a fabric thong. Flip flops were also worn by ancient Greeks and Romans, but the Greeks wore the toe strap between the first and second toes, while the Romans wore the strap between the second and third toes. It was also worn in Mesopotamia, and here, the strap was worn between the third and fourth toe. Thong sandals were also worn in Central and South America, although not always in the flip flop style. In India, a related sandal is the toe knob sandal; this shoe has no straps at all; just a knob which sits between the first and second toes.

Flip flops like these are popular shoes for beachgoers. [Copyright 2008 Jupiterimages Corporation]

Flip flops were first introduced into the **United States** after World War II, when American soldiers brought zoris back from Japan. Soldiers again played a role in the flip flop's popularity when they brought **Korean** flip flops to the United States in the late 1950s. Their greatest boost in popularity, however, came when California surfers and beachgoers began to wear them in the 1960s. Flip flops became firmly associated with the California beach lifestyle, an association that remains today.

Today, flip flops come in a huge variety of styles and are made of a variety of materials, including rubber, foam, plastic, leather, suede, and fabric. They now come in heeled varieties (generally kitten heels) and are adorned with everything from embroidery to beads to crystals. There are also now sports flip flops, which have the support of an athletic shoe but the thong between the toes.

While most people wear flip flops with casual wear like jeans, shorts, bathing suits, or sun dresses, some people have taken to wearing flip flops for dressier occasions. A flip flop controversy erupted in 2005 when members of a college women's lacrosse team wore flip flops to the White House to meet President Bush. The news media devoted dozens of stories to not just what happened, but whether it signaled a fundamental change in American culture. While many young people claim that flip flops are more dressy now and thus can be worn in a variety of social contexts, many people still feel that to wear them at a formal occasion signifies laziness and comfort over style.

Part of the popularity of flip flops has to do with the low cost. Flip flops can be purchased in drug stores and other low-end retailers as well as department stores and shoe stores, and prices can start as low as $5 per pair in the United States; costs are lower in other parts of the world.

With millions of flip flops sold per year, podiatrists worry about the impact on wearers' feet, especially as flip flops move from beach or vacation wear to everyday wear. Recently, doctors have released warnings about the long-term effects of wearing flip flops. Wearers will alter their gait when walking in flip flops, taking shorter, lighter steps, which could cause foot, leg and back pain. In addition, because of the lack of arch and ankle support, they can cause injury with long-term use, resulting, for example, in excessive pronation, tendinitis, and sprained ankles. The **American Podiatric Medical Association** discourages walking in flip flops for long distances or wearing them while engaged in sports or strenuous activities, and it encourages the wearing of flip flops that have the organization's Seal of Acceptance, thanks to features like a contoured foot bed or toe straps that are less likely to cause injury.

See also: Classical Civilizations; China; India; Japan; Sandals

Further Reading Steele, Valerie. *Encyclopedia of Clothing and Fashion*. Farmington Hills, MI: Charles Scribner's Sons, 2005

FLORSHEIM

The Florsheim Group is an American footwear company that has been producing shoes since 1892. The company is known for making good quality dress shoes for men. The company was founded by Milton Florsheim and his shoemaker father Sigmund in 1892 in Chicago. The Florsheims quickly decided that they did not want to sell their shoes wholesale to retailers who would put their own companies' names on their products. Instead, they set up a model that allowed for individuals to set up retail locations to sell Florsheim-branded shoes to the public.

Early on, the company tried to marry the concepts of mass production with quality construction and materials, which, when combined with their network of dealers, made the company a huge success and made their shoes, and the Florsheim brand, well known in small towns throughout the east. By encouraging entrepreneurs to open up Florsheim shops, Florsheim was one of the first companies to come up with the idea of franchising its product. In addition, by placing the brand name on the shoe (on the pull strap inside of every shoe), Florsheim was one of the first companies to formally brand its product. The Florsheims continued their innovative distribution in the 1980s when they created a computerized system that allowed customers in Florsheim stores to directly order shoes from inventory at the company's warehouse.

At the turn of the century, Florsheim began to expand distribution to large cities, selling to retailers in those locations, and the company opened up its own **shoe stores**, with the first storefront opening in Chicago in 1892. The company also made boots for American soldiers during the Spanish-American War, World War I, and World War II. As early as 1930, the company was selling shoes made by five Chicago-area factories in thousands of retail locations around the country. By the late 1950s, Florsheim, which had been purchased by International Shoe Company in 1952, controlled more than 70 percent of the men's dress shoe market in the **United States**. (In 1931, Florsheim began making women's shoes, but it discontinued the women's line in the 1970s.)

In the late 1970s and 1980s, Florsheim, like other American shoe companies, saw sales fall thanks to competition from inexpensive imports. Because of competition, the company closed some stores, but it saw profits go up in the remaining locations, thanks in part to the introduction of casual shoes and comfort shoes and the use of former football coach John Madden as a company pitchman. The company also followed industry trends and began to move manufacturing facilities outside of the United States. (Today, the shoes are primarily made in **India** and **China**.) Thanks to struggles with the parent company, Florsheim also cut back on production costs, making its once high-quality shoes with lower-quality materials, a move that hurt the business further.

In 1990, Florsheim began opening specialty boutiques in Sears stores, replacing the men's shoe departments in those stores and increasing profits for both companies. The International Shoe Company filed for bankruptcy in 1991 and spun off its two footwear divisions, Florsheim and **Converse**, into separate companies.

Throughout the 1990s, the company renovated its image and tried to reach out to a younger demographic, many of whom saw Florsheim shoes as stodgy old men's shoes, through revamping its product lines, creating new **advertising** campaigns, and redecorating its stores. The company brought in less expensive shoes and also created new lines for the original demographic, such as Frogs golf shoes. Still, the company still struggled throughout the 1990s, closing dozens of store locations, even while they began selling shoes in J. C. Penney in 1998. Florsheim also has a licensing agreement to make John Deere work boots and Joseph Aboud dress shoes, and in the late 1990s, it began selling other shoes in its outlets, such as **Dr. Martens**.

In 2002, Florsheim was purchased by Weyco Group (formerly the Weyenberg Shoe Manufacturing Company), which included key members of the Florsheim family who went to work at Weyco starting in the 1960s. This purchase put the company back into family hands for the first time in 50 years. The Weyco Group now manufactures and distributes Florsheim shoes, as well as Stacy Adams apparel and Nunn Bush comfort shoes. Florsheim today operates 39 retail locations in the United States, down from hundreds in the company's heyday, and sells the majority of its shoes in specialty stores and department stores. (The company stopped selling shoes in Sears in 2002.) The company's profits are up, in part because of the nostalgia among many Americans for old-fashioned American brands like Converse, **Dr. Scholl's**, **Hush Puppies** and Florsheim, and in part because of a restyling of the product line to make the shoes more contemporary.

See also: Men's Shoes; Shoe Stores

FOOT AND SHOE ADORNMENT

Adorning the foot with makeup and jewelry has been practiced by women for thousands of years in cultures around the world. Foot adornment is most common in cultures where women either go barefoot or wear **sandals** for much of the time. Adorning shoes is another way that both men and women have set themselves apart from others, and is often indicative of **class** or status.

Henna is one of the oldest forms of foot decoration. Known as *mehndi*, in **India**, Pakistan, and Bangladesh, as well as other Muslim and North **African** countries, it is a temporary vegetable dye applied to the hands, feet, fingernails, and hair. Because women in the cultures in which henna is most popular typically do not show any parts of their body in public besides the hands and the feet, these highly adorned regions become an important part of the costume of women. Traditional Indian henna designs are quite intricate and are often painted on brides' hands before their weddings, a process that can take hours. Muslims also use henna as decoration, and designs are equally intricate.

People who want a permanent design on their feet can choose to get their feet tattooed. Tattoos on the foot are relatively rare around the world. But some tattoo traditions did include the feet, such as in some **Native American** cultures, some East Indian tribes, and among Polynesian and Micronesian cultures. For instance, tattooing the feet was common in Borneo, and the tattoos were used to protect the wearer from harmful spirits, illness, and harm. In contemporary culture, many people do get their feet tattooed, but many tattooists will not tattoo a customer's feet because feet are both very painful areas to get tattooed, because they often do not heal as well as other parts of the body, and are generally harder to maintain than areas of the body that are not constantly being rubbed by the presence of shoes or socks.

Another **Middle Eastern** and Indian tradition is the use of foot jewelry, including toe rings, anklets, and "barefoot sandals." Made of silver, gold, brass, and often precious or semiprecious gem stones, these pieces are traditionally worn with bare feet as a form of decoration, and often include bells. Toe rings are the simplest form of decoration and can be worn on any toe. Anklets are bracelets to be worn around the ankle, and barefoot sandals, or foot thongs, are items of jewelry that combine the toe ring along and anklet, connecting them with additional decorative chains that create the appearance of a sandal.

The final area for foot adornment is toenail polish. Confined primarily to women, wearing toenail polish is one of the most common ways in which women decorate their feet. Nails can be simply painted at home with drugstore purchased nail polish or can be more elaborately decorated, either at home or at a nail salon, with decorative effects such as painted designs, stickers, or glue-on jewels and charms. The rise of toenail polish can be traced to the popularity of **high-heeled sandals** in the **United States**, which began in the 1930s.

Shoes have also been the focus for adornment throughout history. **Moccasins**, for instance, simple shoes made of one or two pieces of hide or tanned **leather**, were and are worn by most Native American tribes in North America and often are elaborately decorated with colored dyes, beads, porcupine quills, embroidery, and fringe.

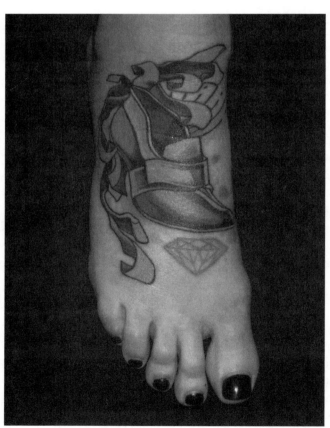

This tattoo of a Victorian shoe was tattooed on a foot by Jeff Hayes of Rival Tattoo Studios in Albuquerque, New Mexico. [Photo courtesy of Jeff Hayes]

Sandals, another very early form of footwear, have also been adorned since at least as far back as the ancient civilizations of the **Middle East**, with Greek, Roman, and Egyptian men and women of the upper classes wearing sandals adorned with painted designs, beads, and precious jewels. African sandals and shoes worn by chiefs and their families were also elaborate, with a variety of animal skins, furs and feathers, dyes, embroidery, and carvings used to decorate them.

Clogs, or basic wooden shoes, have been worn in cultures around the world and were often highly adorned through carving and painting designs on the wood soles. Shoes worn throughout Asia and the Middle East by wealthy people were decorated as well, through embroidery, beadwork, silver bells, and, again, a variety of dyes and materials.

Both upper-class men's and women's shoes throughout Medieval Europe but especially into the Renaissance were heavily decorated, with lavish fabrics, buttons, buckles, bows, beads, and jewels. Duckbill shoes were popular for noblemen starting in the sixteenth century and featured slashed leather uppers that revealed the underlying silk or fur in bright colors. Latchets, which evolved as a way to close men's and women's **pumps** at the end of the sixteenth century, allowed for ribbons to be used for the first time on European shoes, which resulted in huge ribboned bows, sometimes made of lace or in the shape of roses, on the tops of both men's and women's shoes.

While **shoe fasteners** such as buttons and buckles were partly functional, shoe buckles, which first became popular during the reign of Louis XIV in the seventeenth century, were worn primarily by noblemen and were often highly lavish, made of precious metals and adorned with jewels and a variety of decorative motifs, and often combined with ribbon bows. Buckles continued to get larger and more elaborate throughout the eighteenth century, and by the 1770s both men's and women's shoes featured such large buckles that they became a source of social satire in the media. Buckles, like decorative braiding and other decorations, could be removed from shoes and worn on other pairs. Shoe buckles gradually got smaller and were eventually replaced by shoe laces after the French and American Revolutions at the end of the eighteenth century.

Certain shoes are particular focuses for decoration, including the penny loafer, in which a penny is inserted into a small pocket over the instep, the **cowboy boot**, which incorporates decoration over the entire shaft and often includes spurs as well, and the moccasin.

Today, probably the most elaborately decorated shoe is the woman's **high-heeled** evening sandal. Made with uppers of satin, silk, leather, and other fabrics and decorated with beading, jewels, rhinestones, chains, or glass, these shoes signal the status of the wearer and her social aspirations. For those without the funds to purchase such shoes themselves, there are companies that offer detachable shoe clips that can be worn to add pizzazz to women's shoes in the form of rhinestone rosettes, bows, flowers, or butterflies.

In addition, certain types of shoes have been decorated by their wearers; in particular, kids have been drawing on their canvas **sneakers** for years. Since the rise of **Crocs** in the early 2000s, another form of decoration has arisen. Jibbitz are small plastic buttons that are made to insert into the holes in one's Crocs. Another similar invention are CoolZips, beaded zipper pulls that were created to attach to zippers, such as on backpacks or clothing, but are sometimes worn on shoes as well.

See also: Classical Civilizations; Crocs; Henna; India; Middle East

Further Reading O'Keeffe, Linda. Shoes: A Celebration of Pumps, Sandals, Slippers & More. New York: Workman Publishing, 1996; Yue, Charlotte and David. Shoes: Their History in Words and Pictures. Boston: Houghton Mifflin, 1997.

FOOT BINDING

Foot binding is the practice of binding a young girl's feet with cloth in order to restrict their size and control their appearance. Foot binding was practiced in

China by the Han ethnic majority from the tenth century until the twentieth century.

Foot binding began in the tenth century when dancers in the Imperial court wore very tight shoes. The practice then developed into foot binding and spread from the courts into elite households, particularly in north China, but by the twelfth century it had become popular among women of all social classes, including the poor.

Like many other markers of beauty that are associated with the wealthy, bound feet were considered beautiful partly because a woman with bound feet could not work (and often could not walk), demonstrating her high status and wealth. In addition, in China, to have bound feet meant that a woman was disciplined and virtuous and that she was brought up correctly. Women with bound feet would also have to take tiny steps when walking, which demonstrates grace. Women with bound feet were also considered beautiful, and thus marriageable, because small feet meant that they were feminine; large feet are associated with masculinity, authority, and control, none of which are characteristics sought in a wife. Parents looking for brides for their sons would find all of these traits attractive, so bound feet would not only be a sign of status but a marker of marriageability. The fact that a girl with bound feet could not walk also most likely meant that she was a virgin, making her even more attractive.

Girls' feet were typically bound at the age of five or six, with tightly wound strips of cloth. Often the big toe was left unbound, but the other toes were folded down under the sole of the foot. Over a period of months and years, the bandages would be removed and the foot rewrapped. The result was that the bones in the feet would break and become more deformed as the girl reached adulthood; the result was that the foot would remain bent over, and thus tiny. Many girls walked on their heels because the pain in the toes was so severe, leading to very hard heels. (Once the years-long process was over, however, and the bones had healed into their new position, the pain was no longer a problem.) Other results of foot binding included infection, paralysis, and muscular atrophy. Different sized feet were called different names, such as the silver lotus (which measured four inches) and the gold lotus (three inches), which was the most sought-after size.

Lotus shoes like these were worn by women with bound feet and were elaborately decorated. [Photo courtesy of Shoe Icons]

Because of the intense attention on the feet, bound or "lotus feet" were fetishized, as were the lotus shoes made for them. Chinese shoemakers made the shoes themselves, but women embroidered and decorated their own lotus shoes with colors and imagery appropriate to their status in life (with black being worn by older women), season of year (peonies indicating springtime), or for bedroom wear. There are questions today as to whether men were sexually aroused by the sight, touch, or smell of the feet. Some reports indicate that men fondled and licked the feet, while others indicate that the somewhat rotten smell had to be masked by perfume and that men would never see a woman's feet at all, since women wore special **slippers** over their bindings to bed at night. In either case, prostitutes (both male and female) and concubines adopted the practice to make themselves more beautiful and sexually attractive.

A small-footed Chinese lady. Starting as early as the tenth century, foot binding became a common practice in high society in China and was not discontinued until the early 1900s. Photo taken in 1905. [Photo courtesy of the Library of Congress Prints and Photographs Division]

Foot binding was prohibited in China in 1912 but continued in isolated regions well into the 1940s; it was banned again in 1949 when the Communists came into power. When the Revolutionary Party found women in villages with bound feet, they forced them to unbind them, which caused almost as much pain as the initial binding. Unbound feet were known as "liberated feet," and some grew as much as an inch after unbinding. In 1998, the last factory to manufacture shoes for women with bound feet ended production. Some effects of foot binding are permanent: some elderly Chinese women today suffer from disabilities related to bound feet.

See also: Beliefs; China; Class; Gender; Proverbs

Further Reading Hong Fan. *Footbinding, Feminism, and Freedom: The Liberation of Women's Bodies in China*. London: Cass, 1997; Jeffreys, Sheila. *Beauty and Misogyny: Harmful Cultural Practices in the West*. New York: Routledge, 2005; Ko, Dorothy. *Cinderella's Sisters: A Revisionist History of Footbinding*. Berkeley: University of California Press, 2007; Kunzle, David. *Fashion and Fetishism: A Social History of the Corset, Tight-Lacing and Other Forms of Body Sculpture in the West*. New York: Rowman & Littlefield, 1982.

FOOT CARE PRODUCTS

Since the late nineteenth century, a variety of foot care products have been marketed to treat a number of foot disorders, injuries, and conditions. The leading maker of foot care products in the **United States** is **Dr. Scholl's**. Products include powders, creams, sprays, as well as insoles, pads, and wraps.

Pads are commonly used for treating **blisters, bunions, calluses, and corns**. Blister pads can be worn over blisters to prevent additional rubbing and to prevent blisters from being formed in the first place. Heel hugs can be worn inside the back of the heel and blister prevention patches are bandage-like patches that can be worn anywhere that the shoes rub against the foot. Callus and corn pads as well as bunion pads can be worn to relieve discomfort with bunions or corns. Toe caps are also devices that can be worn to protect the toes from rubbing and to combat corns, blisters, and calluses.

Another type of pad, the metatarsal pad, is worn underneath the ball of the feet and is used by people with pain under the ball of the foot, caused by metatarsalgia or **neuromas**. Also known as dancer pads, these are commonly worn by dancers to alleviate ball-of-foot pain and can help with pain caused by turf toe as well.

Toe spacers are foam devices that are worn between the toes to keep the toes in a normal position. They are often worn to combat bunions or **hammer toe**.

Creams and powders are used for a variety of conditions, including bacterial infections, calluses, foot odor, and **athlete's foot**. For instance, athlete's foot is a fungal infection that causes itching, redness, and scaly skin, usually between the toes but often on other parts of the feet as well, and is treated with antifungal creams, powders, or sprays. **Plantar warts**, caused by the HPV virus, can be treated with over-the-counter wart medications. Calluses are often treated with creams and lotions, usually with urea, and foot odor is often treated with medicated foot powders and sprays that absorb moisture and keep feet dry.

Arch supports and other insoles are worn by people with conditions ranging from excessive pronation to supination, to neuromas and metatarsalgia, to heel spurs. Arch supports are also worn by people with fallen arches and can alleviate foot, leg, hip, and back pain.

Heel cups, hugs, sleeves, and cushions are products that are designed to combat heel pain or to protect the heel from pressure. Heel pain can be caused by heel spurs, the Hagland's deformity, or plantar fasciitis.

See also: Athlete's Foot; Blisters, Bunions, Calluses and Corns; Disorders and Injuries; Dr. Scholl's; Foot Odor; Hammer Toe; Ingrown Toenails

Further Reading Jahss, Melvin. *Disorders of the Foot and Ankle: Medical and Surgical Management*. Philadelphia: Saunders, 1991; Lorimer, Donald, Donald Neale. *Neale's Disorders of the Foot*. New York: Elsevier Churchill Livingstone, 2006.

FOOT MASSAGE

Foot massage is the manipulation of the feet for therapeutic purposes. Massage therapists are trained in a variety of massage techniques, but anyone can give a massage. Techniques include acupressure, Shiatsu, Swedish massage, **reflexology** and Thai massage. Many **pedicures** also include a foot massage.

Because feet carry the weight of the body, foot massages are a very popular way to relax and to relieve some of the pressure associated with standing and walking. Foot massage can also be used as a form of foreplay prior to sexual activity between partners. Here, massage is less therapeutic and is instead focused on physical pleasure. Foot fetishists often massage and fondle feet as a form of sexual play or as a prelude to other forms of sexual contact involving the feet.

Massaging the foot involves stroking and rubbing the foot, including the toes, the top of the foot, the sole, the heel, and ankle. Some people use scented oils when massaging. Techniques include applying different levels of pressure to the feet, kneading the surface of the foot, making circular motions with the fingers, and rotating the foot, including all of the toes, to stretch out and relax the muscles and tendons.

One type of foot massage is Chinese foot massage, an ancient Chinese practice that borrows from **acupuncture** and is related to reflexology. It assumes that there are pressure points in the feet that correspond to the rest of the body; by stimulating those pressure points via massage, energy flow can be unblocked, and the person will feel better. The foot has almost three dozen points that correspond to a variety of pathways that themselves are associated with organs in the body. Applying pressure to those points brings the body back into balance.

Foot massages can be relaxing, therapeutic, or sexually arousing. [Copyright 2008 Jupiterimages Corporation]

Thai foot massage, which derives from **China** via Thailand, borrows from Shiatsu, Chinese massage, and reflexology. It is based on the principle that applying pressure to areas of the feet will stimulate internal organs and cause healing in the body.

Reflexology is a more specialized form of foot massage, which involves placing pressure on the feet and hands in order to reduce stress and diagnose and treat illness. It is based on the belief that the body is broken into zones that correspond to specific areas of the hands and feet. By placing pressure onto specific areas of the feet, this will affect the corresponding body parts and result in better blood flow to the affected regions.

See also: Acupuncture; Eroticism; Pedicure; Reflexology

Further Reading Atkinson, Mary. *Hand and Foot Massage: Massage Taken to the Extremes*. London: Carlton, 2001; Dougans, Inge. *The Complete Illustrated Guide to Reflexology: Therapeutic Foot Massage for Health and Well Being*. Boston: Element, 1996; Vonhof, John. *Fixing Your Feet: Prevention And Treatments for Athletes*. Berkeley, CA: Wilderness Press, 2006.

FOOT ODOR

Foot odor is a common hygiene problem found when people's feet give off an odor, generally due to excessive sweating of the feet. Feet have more sweat glands per inch than any other area of the body, so the fact that feet sweat is normal and to be expected. Excessive sweating, however, can cause foot odor. Having smelly feet is embarrassing for most people and can cause a significant amount of shame. Many people with foot odor, for example, do not feel comfortable removing their shoes or socks when other people are present, and thus do not, for example, get **pedicures**. There are, however, foot fetishists who find foot odor sexually arousing.

Foot odor can be caused from poor hygiene, wearing shoes or **socks** that do not breathe, or wearing shoes and/or socks for too long without changing them. Other conditions that can exacerbate smelly feet include hair on the feet and **athlete's foot**. Foot odor can also be caused by bacteria that live in warm, dark, and moist areas and that often give out a strong odor.

Foot odor can also be a side effect of hyperhidrosis, a condition in which the body sweats excessively, either all over, or, in this case, on the feet, as in plantar hyperhidrosis. This condition can be treated through prescription antiperspirants, Botox injections into the affected areas, oral medications, or even surgery to sever the nerves that cause sweating or to remove the sweat glands.

People with foot odor are often advised to wear socks made of natural materials because synthetic materials do not allow for much ventilation, causing the feet to sweat more. Similarly, wearing open-toed shoes or shoes made of fabrics that can breathe is another way to control foot odor. When possible, shoes should be washed, especially in the case of **athletic shoes**, which are often made of materials that can be washed and which are more likely to be worn when the feet are sweating. In general, keeping shoes dry, aired out, and rotating them between wearings are all good ways to keep odor down.

Washing and drying the feet regularly is a good way to control foot odor, and many doctors recommend using antibacterial or deodorant soaps for this purpose. In fact, some people just use deodorant or antiperspirant made for the armpits on the bottom of the feet, to prevent excessive sweating. Soaking feet in a salt water solution is another method, as the salt in the water will dry out the feet.

Perfumed powders are another treatment for foot odor, although this may not eliminate, nor prevent, odor, but will simply mask it. On the other hand, specially made foot powders containing aluminum chloride hexahydrate can keep the feet from sweating, which will prevent foot odor. Foot powder, baby powder, or even cornstarch can also be sprinkled directly into shoes, both to reduce odor and to absorb moisture.

Odor Eaters is the brand name of a line of products that treat foot odor, including foot powder, spray, and insoles. The original product is an insole that absorbs moisture and odors. Discovered in England in 1970 by Mary Elizabeth Combe of Combe Incorporated, a manufacturer of personal care products, Fresh Sox were paper insoles with activated charcoal. Combe brought the product to Herbert Lapidus, a researcher at the company, who borrowed the idea, creating a latex insole using activated charcoal. He purportedly tested the product on his wife, who had smelly feet. Odor Eaters were released in 1974, and have been popular items ever since. The company has hosted a Rotten **Sneaker** Contest every year since 1974, which awards cash prizes to children and teenagers with the rottenest sneakers. Contestants must first be chosen as a finalist in one of eight regional contests and are judged on the basis of the condition and odor of their shoes.

See also: Athlete's Foot; Disorders and Injuries; Foot Care Products; Dr. Scholl's

Further Reading Copeland, Glenn, Stan Solomon, and Mark Myerson. *The Good Foot Book: A Guide For Men, Women, Children, Athletes, Seniors*. Alameda, CA: Hunter House, 2005; Vonhof, John. *Fixing Your Feet: Prevention And Treatments for Athletes*. Berkeley, CA: Wilderness Press, 2006.

FOOT STRUCTURE

Humans share a number of anatomical features with other mammals, including the structure of our feet. Humans are terrestrial vertebrates, which move using legs and feet, as opposed to invertebrates or vertebrates like snakes, which slink. Like most terrestrial vertebrates, humans have five digits, or toes, on the feet. Humans are distinguished from other terrestrial vertebrates by the type of feet that we have; human feet are known as plantigrade, which means that we walk on the flats of our feet as opposed to, for example, dogs, who walk on their toes, or horses, who walk on their hooves. Other differences include the way that our toes are used and the way that our feet meet the ground. For instance, humans and other primates do not have pads on the bottoms of our feet, like dogs; instead, we have sensitive toe prints. In addition, primates have nails rather than claws at the end of our toes.

Humans are bipedal, which changes the structure of the plantigrade foot considerably. Because we walk on two feet rather than four, our feet need to support the entire weight of our bodies, necessitating the development of an arch. In addition, because humans are primates, our feet, in our pre-bipedal past, were once prehensile, with long grasping toes and an opposable big toe. As our ancestors became bipedal, the big toe eventually moved in line with the other toes, and our toes shortened, losing the ability to grab objects.

Human feet are divided into three parts: the forefoot, the midfoot, and the hindfoot, with 26 bones in all. The hindfoot, or heel region, includes the talus bone or ankle and the heel bone or calcaneus. The midfoot has five bones that form the arch of the foot, and the forefoot includes the bones that make up the toes, or phalanges, and the longer bones, or metatarsals, that connect the toes to the forefoot. The phalanges are broken into three smaller bones, while the big toe is broken into two smaller bones. The toe bones both bear weight and also provide for locomotion.

All of the bones are connected with 33 separate joints and dozens of ligaments, which connect the bones together. The plantar fascia is one of the ligaments and allows for the longitudinal arch in the foot. (Humans also have a secondary arch called a transverse arch, which is lower and runs perpendicular to the longitudinal arch.)

In addition, the foot has 20 muscles that are connected to the bones by tendons. The **Achilles** tendon, for example, connects the calf muscle to the heel bone. The muscles allow the foot to hold its shape, while flexing and extending the muscles allows the foot to move. The muscles within the foot are known as intrinsic muscles, and those that are outside of the foot, but which play a role in the movement of the foot such as the calf muscle, are extrinsic muscles.

Because of the number of muscles, bones, joints, ligaments, and tendons in the foot, and the enormous amount of pressure and stress that these features experience, it is not surprising that there are a number of **disorders and injuries** that frequently occur to the foot. For instance, supination and pronation refer to conditions where the ankles roll inward or outward when one walks or runs. Another problem is metatarsalgia, a condition in which the long bones of the feet become stressed, causing pain in the ball of the foot. Heel pain can be caused by plantar fasciitis, which is inflammation of the tissue forming the arch of the foot. High and low or fallen arches can also cause foot problems, placing extra weight on the balls and heels of the feet. Finally, injuries to the foot include stress fractures, sprained ankles, broken bones, and problems with the Achilles tendon. Many of these injuries are caused during sports and may result from overuse, inadequately cushioned shoes, or running on hard surfaces.

Foot problems are exacerbated by obesity. In fact, recent studies have shown that children with obesity not only experience more problems of the feet, but that the structure of their feet often change due to their weight. Severely overweight children are found to have feet that have grown in length and width and to experience problems with instability when walking or standing.

See also: Animal Feet; Disorders and Injuries

Further Reading Amato, Joseph Anthony. *On Foot: A History of Walking.* New York: NYU Press, 2004; Sarrafian, Shahan. Anatomy of the Foot and Ankle: Descriptive, Topographic, Functional. Philadelphia: Lippincott, 1993.

FOOT WASHING

Foot washing is an important part of many religious traditions and is related to purity and humility. Muslims traditionally wash their feet before praying (a practice called *wudhu*) as well as their hands, hair, and face. Feet must be washed three times. The reason for wudhu in **Islam** is that without purifying one's body, one's mind cannot be purified. Because Muslims pray five times a day, and thus must pray when at work, at school, and in public spaces, foot baths are common sites in predominantly Muslim countries, and a few communities with large numbers of Muslims have installed foot baths in public places so that Muslims would no longer have to wash their feet in public sinks.

In India, traditionally the parents of a bride wash the feet of their daughter's groom as a way of showing respect to the man who will take care of their daughter. In Buddhism, water for foot washing is one of the eight offerings traditionally made to Buddha, which allows the believer to purify one's negative karma and achieve the body of a Buddha.

In **Christianity**, on the other hand, foot washing has a slightly different meaning. The New Testament tells us that Jesus washed his disciples' feet as a way to serve them during the Last Supper. At the time that Jesus lived, servants would have washed their masters' feet, so Jesus's decision to wash the apostles' feet was a way of teaching humility.

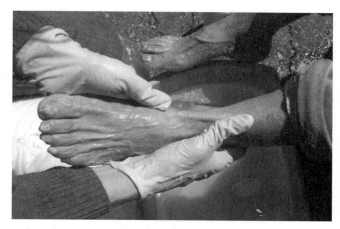

A homeless woman has her feet washed on Good Friday, March 25, 2005, at the downtown Los Angeles Mission. The foot washing is a Christian tradition memorializing Jesus's washing the feet of his disciples. [AP Photo/ Nick Ut]

According to the Gospels, during the evening of the Last Supper the Apostles were fighting over who would have the highest position in the Kingdom of God, demonstrating their pride. The washing of the feet—a humble and menial task normally left to servants—taught the disciples humility. In addition, feet in the Christian tradition often symbolize walking the spiritual path, so feet washing (using water, which often symbolizes the word of God as well as the cleansing away of false beliefs) can also be construed as Jesus's message to his disciples to continue on the path of righteousness after his death. The Gospels tell us that Peter refused to let Jesus wash his feet, but Jesus tells him that without having his feet bathed by him, he will "have no inheritance with me." In addition, Jesus said that the disciples should wash each other's feet as he had done.

Another important foot washing reference from the New Testament refers to the scene in which a follower of Jesus, prior to his crucifixion, weeps on Jesus's feet, kisses them, dries them with her tears, and anoints them with ointment. The woman was referred to in the Gospel of Luke as a "sinner;" the Church later identified her as Mary Magdalene, Jesus's first female disciple, and began the tradition of calling Mary Magdalene a prostitute. Whether or not it was Mary Magdalene, because of her actions Jesus forgave the woman her sins and scolded his host for not having provided water to wash his feet, nor a kiss, nor oil to anoint his head.

Today, some Christian groups continue to practice foot washing, following in the teachings of Jesus. In the Catholic Church, the priest or prelate will wash the feet of 12 poor men, who represent the apostles, during Holy Week. Other churches practice foot washing as a regular part of their services. Mormons include feet washing as one of their ordinances, which are rituals that convey particular blessings onto the faithful who practice them. Mormons consider foot washing, baptism, and the Lord's Supper (known as the Eucharist in other traditions) to be prescribed by the New Testament. For Mormons, foot washing appears to be less about service and more about spiritual cleansing and is reserved for those who keep the covenants and keep themselves pure.

For Christians who practice foot washing today, it is intended to bring them closer to Jesus and to fill them with a sense of humility and service, concepts that are expected to be reinforced through other aspects of service to community.

Foot washing was used in a new way in 2006, when South African former Security Minister Adriaan Vlok apologized for his crimes as part of the apartheid regime by washing the feet of Reverand Frank Chikane, an antiapartheid activist who Vlok attempted to assassinate in 1989. The use of foot washing here was an attempt by Vlok, reviled throughout the country for his part in the terrors inflicted by apartheid, to atone for his sins and to demonstrate humility.

See also: Beliefs; Christianity; Islam

Further Reading Thomas, John Christopher. *Footwashing in John 13 and the Johannine Community*. Sheffield: JSOT Press, 1991; Vaughn, R. L. *The Doctrine of Foot Washing*. Mount Enterprise, TX: Waymark Publications, 2006.

FREDERICK'S OF HOLLYWOOD

Frederick's of Hollywood is a retailer of sexy apparel and footwear based in Los Angeles that is also known as a purveyor of sexy and fetish footwear.

Frederick Mellinger, the Hungarian-American son of a tailor who worked for a mail order supplier of women's underwear, suggested that the company sell black underwear rather than just the standard white, a suggestion for which he was fired. Later stationed in Europe during World War II, Mellinger was inspired by the sexy lingerie that he saw in France and by his fellow soldiers' pinups featuring sexy women wearing racy undergarments. Upon his return after the war Mellinger opened a store called Frederick's of Fifth Avenue in New York, where he sold the kind of underwear that he thought men wanted women to wear. His best customers were Broadway dancers. In 1947, Mellinger moved the business to California and changed the name to Frederick's of Hollywood. For the next 40 years, the company specialized in racy lingerie and sleepwear, fetish wear, wigs, and footwear. Hollywood starlets and models made up one of the company's earliest consumer groups, but housewives eager to look sexy for their husbands were also major buyers. One of Mellinger's first items, and among the raciest, was a bikini that he first saw in France and began selling in California.

Mellinger was interested in creating what he thought of as the ideal female form. In 1948, Mellinger used his knowledge of anatomy to design a push-up bra, the world's first. From there, he began specializing in lingerie designed to change a woman's figure, including fanny pads, corsets, girdles, and other foundation garments. He also developed both an inflatable bra as well as a water bra. He also expanded the product line to include other types of sexy accessories, including long wigs, false eyelashes, and, later, sexual aids, clothes, and shoes. His products, while worn by women, were primarily geared towards men, since Mellinger believed that women should dress to please men.

In 1947, Mellinger established the company's headquarters on Hollywood Boulevard, and beginning in 1952 began to open retail stores, primarily in malls, until his company had 200 stores across the country. (In 2005, the original store closed and reopened a few blocks away, at Hollywood and Highland Avenue.)

Frederick's began selling shoes in 1960, designed by footwear designer Norman Kaplan. These shoes were known for their four-to-five inch heels and very sexy shapes. **Stilleto** heels in **patent leather**, leopard-print, and satin, four inch high patent stiletto **boots**, and **high-heeled**, open-backed mules are iconic Frederick's shoes. Today, Kaplan's son Michael continues to design Frederick's of Hollywood shoes, as well as a variety of high-heeled shoes, including Lucite heels, **fetish** shoes and thigh-high boots.

The 1970s was the decade of Frederick's peak popularity. As the United States became more sexually conservative in the 1980s, the company's profits began to fall, leading to a restructuring in 1985 that brought a new CEO and a new plan to "de-sleazify" the company's product line and image. Retail stores were redecorated in a more conservative design and the flagship store, known as the Purple Palace, was redecorated as well and included a gray paint job over the iconic purple exterior. Wigs, sexual aids, and other items were dropped from the catalog, which was also redesigned to promote a classier image. By the early 1990s, sales had improved, although not to their 1970s-era highs.

In 1997, the company was sold to Knightsbridge Capital Corporation and then in 2000 to Wilshire Partners, but it continued to struggle and continued to clean up the company's image, trying to appeal to new customers. The company filed for bankruptcy in 2000, in part due to competition from Victoria's Secret, and after three years of restructuring that included closing 40 retail stores the company came back under a new ownership. This time, the new management decided to return to the company's roots and refocus on its "naughty" image as a way of differentiating itself from Victoria's Secret and attracting a newer, younger audience. Stores were once again redesigned, but this time with bold fabrics like red velvet and leopard print.

In 1989, Frederick's opened the Lingerie Museum at the store's original location at 6608 Hollywood Boulevard to celebrate the history of lingerie and the company's own beginnings. The museum, which once housed famous undergarments worn by Hollywood celebrities, closed in 2005 when the company moved its headquarters down the street.

In early 2008, Frederick's merged with Movie Star Inc., a wholesale manufacturer, and now sells its products to other retailers as well as direct to customers through the company's own 130 retail stores, Web site, and catalog.

See also: Eroticism; Fetishes; High Heels; Stilettos

Further Reading Gottwald, Laura. *Frederick's of Hollywood, 1947–1973: 26 Years of Mail Order Seduction*. New York: Drake Publishers, 1973.

G

GALOSHES

Galoshes are rubber boots worn over shoes in inclement weather to protect one's shoes. They derive from other forms of **overshoes** popularized in **Europe**, such as pattens, which were worn to protect shoes from water, mud, or dirt.

Known as *galochas*, galoshes date to Medieval Europe and were originally a form of patten, made of carved wood, with a simple upper strap, and later, a fully formed but open-backed upper made of fabric or leather. They probably arose thanks to the Arab conquest of Spain in the eighth century, and derive from the Middle Eastern stilted sandal. The wooden overshoe of Medieval Europe became less critical as European public spaces became more pedestrian-friendly in the eighteenth century with the construction of paved streets and poured sidewalks, and pattens eventually disappeared in Europe.

Boots were also worn in the Middle Ages, from the Roman buckskin to the cavalier boot to the **jack boot** and the **Wellington boot**, but boots at this time were worn primarily for riding and for military wear and not as a form of protection from the weather. While leather could be waterproofed using linseed oil, boots at this time were not truly waterproof.

The modern galosh's roots can be traced to the technology of **vulcanization** developed by Charles Goodyear, which not only allowed for the development of rubber-soled shoes like sneakers, but rubber boots like galoshes. With the ability to mold rubber into a flexible, durable substance that could be used in virtually any climate, and the development of rubberized elastic webbing (which was inserted into boots to allow them to easily be pulled on and off), the modern galosh was created. First produced by L. L. Bean in 1911, this boot was made with a waterproofed leather upper combined with a rubber bottom, but other galoshes are made entirely out of rubber. Another innovation was the invention of PVC in 1928, which also later led to the use of vinyl-based latex for waterproofing boots.

Today, galoshes and other rubber shoes are made from synthetic rubber and are either made from pieces cut from sheet rubber, which are combined on a last, or are made via slush molding in which liquid rubber is poured into a mold placed over a last, creating the galosh form. Some galoshes today are made with rubber outsoles combined with waterproofed nylon or other fabrics on the upper.

Some galoshes are lined with fabric, and while most galoshes slip over the feet and legs, thanks to the elastic webbing, some also have fasteners at the ankle to make the fit tighter. Because galoshes are not intended to be worn all day, but instead are designed to be worn over shoes while outdoors in bad weather, some galoshes are light enough to be folded up and carried in a bag or placed in a drawer when not warn. Others, however, are made of heavier material and are not suitable for folded storage.

See also: Boots; Overshoes; Vulcanization

Further Reading Haven, Kendall. *100 Greatest Science Inventions of All Time*. Westport, CT: Libraries Unlimited, 2006.

GENDER

Gender assumptions, stereotypes, and roles play a major role in the treatment of feet in cultures around the world as well as in the types of shoes worn by men and women. Shoes serve to cover and protect the feet and to allow humans to journey long distances and through difficult climates and terrains. However, the types of shoes worn by men and women in cultures around the world do not equally provide for mobility. Men, as it has often been noted by feminists, are often defined by what they do and what they have achieved, while women are defined by how they look.

> Give a girl great footwear and she can conquer the world.
>
> BETTE MIDLER

While it is typical for men's shoes (especially working men) to be functional and comfortable, allowing them to move easily from place to place and to do a variety of things, it is often just as typical for women's shoes to be created and worn primarily for aesthetic reasons. Women are generally defined by how they look as well as their reproductive abilities. Women's shoes—from **high heels** to **platform shoes** to tight-fitting shoes—are made to adorn the female body, but not to allow her mobility; in fact, many of the most popular women's shoes impede women's mobility, and thus impede women's opportunities.

Ironically, this was not always the case. In many cultures, at least with respect to elites, men's shoes were as highly adorned and impractical, if not more so, than women's. For instance, noblemen in Imperial **Japan** and **China**, in much of the **Middle East**, and in Medieval Europe wore shoes that were more elaborate than women's. In Europe, it wasn't until the eighteenth century that men's fashion, including their footwear, became less ornamental and women's became more so. Ornamentation is reserved for women's shoes today.

Where women's footwear impedes women's mobility, however, it also enhances their beauty, femininity, and, in many cultures, their marriageability. In addition, many women's shoes, both today and historically, are not only worn to make a woman more beautiful but ensure that her feet conform to normative standards. Women's feet, in most cultures, for instance, must be small, so women's shoes are often made to be smaller than her feet, and **foot binding** is a practice that is only endured by women in order to make them beautiful (thus marriageable) and keep them controlled. Of course, more than any other foot practice or form of footwear, foot binding was not only done to women to enhance their beauty, but also to restrict their mobility and freedom.

Comparing a man's workboot with a woman's **stiletto** heel perhaps brings this contrast into relief. Work boots are made to be worn during working and protect the foot from weather, falling items, uneven terrain, or dangerous surroundings. Until very recently in history, **boots** were almost always worn by men (with the exception of riding boots), because of their association with being outdoors and being active. Women's shoes, on the other hand, have long been associated with indoor living and inactivity, and thus **slippers** and shoes made out of delicate fabrics have long been common.

Stilettos are worn when a woman attends a leisure event, but they are also often worn during the workday. They are neither functional nor sensible; they are designed to make the feet and legs look sexier, and indeed, to make the body appear sexier because a woman's role in society is to be sexually attractive and sexually ready for a man. At the same time, they will cause a woman's feet to hurt by the end of the day, and, with long-term use, will cause bunions, corns, **neuromas**, and any number of other conditions. (Women, in fact, have four times the number of foot disorders as men, most of which can be traced to high heels and tight shoes.)

Women must spend far more money on their shoes than men. They are expected to own multiple pairs of shoes in order to have shoes for different outfits and different looks—the average American woman today owns 30 pairs of shoes. Men, on the other hand, can often get away with a pair of athletic shoes, dress shoes, and perhaps a pair of work shoes. Because women's shoes are much more deeply embedded in the world of fashion than men's are, women must buy new shoes every season in order to remain fashionable and to not look out of date. This costs an enormous amount of money and also serves to make women seem materialistic and trivial.

Because shoes have always been markers of **class** and status, women's shoes historically marked their status vis-a-is their husband's (or father's) worth. Wealthy women in Venice wore *chopines* to give them physical height and social status, but, as with today's high heels, they were so impractical as to radically impede a woman's mobility and even health. The Japanese *geta*, the Manchurian elevated shoe, and the Chinese lotus shoe all served the same purpose. By making it difficult for women to walk unassisted, these shoes reinforced the notion that women are weak and dependent, a perception that really only could apply to women of wealth. As poor and working-class women could not afford to wear such impractical footwear, their femininity was also maligned.

As women's role in Western society began to change in the twentieth century, footwear became more practical for many women. Flat shoes or shoes with low heels, and **athletic shoes** became popular for women, allowing them to move their bodies in ways that women had never done before. Today, women can use their shoes to signal their own financial independence, demonstrating that they are equal to, and not dependent upon, men. Yet women are still constrained, both by the uncomfortable and impractical shoes that they wear and their enslavement to fashion.

See also: Class; Foot Binding; Eroticism; High Heels; Men's Shoes

Further Reading Breward, Christopher. "Fashioning Masculinity: Men's Footwear and Modernity," in Rielle, Georgio and Peter McNeil, eds. *Shoes: A History From Sandals to Sneakers*. London: Berg Publishers, 2006; Jeffreys, Sheila. *Beauty and Misogyny: Harmful Cultural Practices in the West*. New York: Routledge, 2005; Ko, Dorothy. *Cinderella's Sisters: A Revisionist History of Footbinding*. Berkeley: University of California Press, 2007; Kunzle, David. *Fashion and Fetishism: A Social History of the Corset, Tight-Lacing and Other Forms of Body Sculpture in the West*. New York: Rowman & Littlefield, 1982; McNeil, Peter, Giorgio Riello. "The Male Cinderella: Shoes, Genius and Fantasy," in Rielle, Georgio and Peter McNeil, eds. *Shoes: A History From Sandals to Sneakers*. London: Berg Publishers, 2006; Rexford, Nancy. "The Perils of Choice: Women's Footwear in Nineteenth-Century America," in Rielle, Georgio and Peter McNeil, eds. *Shoes: A History From Sandals to Sneakers*. London: Berg Publishers, 2006.

GO GO BOOTS

Go go boots refer to tight calf-high or knee-high **boots** worn in the 1960s, made out of **patent leather** or pleather, with low heels. For most of European and American history, women did not wear boots, as boots were primarily made for outdoor activities, which women did not, for the most part, participate in. European noblewomen wore riding boots for riding, but it wasn't until the mid-nineteenth century that women began wearing boots as indoor footwear. Boots during the nineteenth and early twentieth century were either ankle or calf boots, with heels of varying heights, and were very tight, fastened with laces or buttons. They were intended to be feminine but also to hide women's ankles during the Victorian era. At the end of this period in the 1920s, as women's skirts and dresses became shorter and public morality relaxed, boots were largely replaced by heels for women.

However, in the 1960s a form of boot became popular for women again, when low-heeled, form-fitting boots were first introduced. As hemlines shortened throughout this decade, high boots became fashionable and, because of the low heels, the boots were comfortable for dancing and were soon seen on women dancing in clubs throughout Europe and the United States. French designer André Courreges designed a calf-high white vinyl boot with cutouts on the side for his 1964 collection. Courreges's boots were designed to look space-age and fit perfectly into the desire for self-expression and creativity felt by many women in the 1960s. Combined with the miniskirt, introduced by London designer Mary Quant in 1961, this look came to symbolize the 1960s.

For much of the 1960s, tight boots made of patent leather or, more commonly, vinyl or other synthetic materials (thanks to a shortage of leather) in a range of colors became the rage for young women in America and Britain. Heels were generally low, with higher heels only emerging in boots in the 1970s. The most common closure was a front- or side-zippered closure, although boots were also released with lacing up the front at the end of the decade. Toes could be pointed, round, or squared, and typically reflected the toe shape popular at the time.

Because of their sexiness and the ease with which one could dance in them, go go boots became associated with go go dancers—dancers who danced on pedestals or in cages in discos and bars. They were further popularized by Nancy Sinatra's song, "**These Boots Are Made For Walkin**," and by the character Emma Peel in the British spy show, "The Avengers." In both cases, the boots symbolized sexuality but also independence, women's liberation, and freedom.

Go go boots fell out of fashion by the late 1960s as more women were wearing pants and as miniskirts turned into maxi skirts. They were largely replaced by the **platform shoe** as the primary footwear for the young and hip, although the Dallas Cowboy Cheerleaders began wearing go go boots with their uniforms in 1972 and wore them until 1989, when they were replaced with **cowboy boots**.

See also: Boots; These Boots Are Made For Walkin

Go go boots like these have experienced a resurgence in popularity in recent years. [Copyright 2008 Jupiterimages Corporation]

Further Reading Rielly, Edward J. *The 1960s*. Westport, CT: Greenwood Press, 2003.

GOLF SHOES

Golf shoes are shoes that are worn while playing golf. Golf is a game in which players hit a small ball with a golf club across a grassed course; the goal is to get the ball into 18 holes in as few strokes as possible. Games like golf were played in Medieval Europe, but modern golf originated in Scotland in either the fifteenth or seventeenth century.

At least as far back as the mid-nineteenth century, golfers wore heavy **leather** shoes into which they inserted metal hobnails or **spikes** into the soles to help them grip the turf. The first specialized golf shoes, however, were not released until the 1890s in England. At that time, golfers could choose from spikeless golf shoes, **boots** made with rubber knobs, **overshoes** with spikes that were worn over regular shoes in 1891, and rubber overshoes that were released in 1895.

The first spiked golf shoes were made from wing-tip Oxford shoes. In 1906, Spalding began selling saddle shoes, a form of Oxford with a saddle-shaped piece of leather on the upper, which served to reinforce the shoe during activity.

The shoes were designed to be worn for tennis and squash, but were adopted by golfers in the 1920s once the company began putting spikes on them. Today, the Oxfords popularized in the first half of the century remain the defining style on the golf course.

These golf shoes, based on the traditional Oxford design, still have metal pleats, which are banned on many golf courses today. [Copyright 2008 Jupiterimages Corporation]

The Field and Flint Company of Massachusetts began making golf shoes in 1910 and introduced the FootJoy line of golf shoes in the 1920s, which was popularized by the American Ryder Cup golf team that wore the shoes starting in 1927. By the 1920s, specialized golf shoes were worn by well-dressed golfers, but many golfers still played golf in regular street shoes or rubber-soled sneakers. In the 1940s, a salesman with Field and Flint named Ernie Sabayrac convinced golf clubs to begin selling spiked shoes in their shops, which they had not done before. Prior to this time, many golfers bought shoes in retail shops and added their own spikes. After the 1940s, most golfers wore specialized golf shoes made with spikes.

New innovations in golf shoes were introduced in the 1980s, when shoe companies began considering foot support in their design and shoes were made that could accommodate **orthotics**. In addition, because golfers often must walk and stand on wet grass for hours, waterproof materials like Goretex and waterproofed leather were added to shoes by Ectonics, one of the major golf shoe makers.

The other major innovation had to do with the spikes. By the 1920s, controversy had already emerged about the damage done to golf course turf and clubhouse floors by metal spikes. In the 1990s, golf courses in the United States began to ban the use of metal spikes. Spikeless shoes that used rubber knobs instead of metal spikes, known as Soft Spikes, were then introduced in 1993. In addition, removable cleats were introduced.

Because women did not play golf in any great numbers until the twentieth century, when women did play golf, they wore regular women's shoes. The 1940s saw the first golf shoes for women, which were simply smaller versions of men's spiked leather Oxfords.

Today, the newest type of golf shoe are golf **sandals**. They are based on **sport sandals** like Tevas but are equipped with rubber spikes. Some golfers also wear golf **boots** in the winter, and golf **moccasins** are also available, although some courses prohibit the wearing of nonstandard golf shoes. Some beginning players simply wear tennis shoes.

Golf shoes today provide cushioning, are lighter and more comfortable than the shoes of old, and still provide traction and grip. While there are still metal-studded golf shoes on the market, which many golfers prefer because of the additional grip, most golf courses prohibit the use of metal spikes, and most players on the PGA wear rubber-studded shoes. Golf shoes are traditionally worn with golf hose, a knee-high, colorful wool **sock**, usually with a plaid design.

See also: Athletic Shoes; Cleats and Spikes

Further Reading Schoeffler, O. E., Gale, William. *Esquire's Encyclopedia of 20th Century Men's Fashions*. New York: McGraw-Hill, 1973; St. Pierre, Denise. *Golf Fundamentals*. Champaign, IL: Human Kinetics, 2004.

GRAUMAN'S CHINESE THEATRE

Grauman's Chinese Theatre is one of the most famous movie theaters in the world. Located on Hollywood Boulevard, it derives its fame from its forecourt with footprints (as well as handprints and autographs) of Hollywood stars immortalized in cement. It was declared a historical landmark in 1968 and was renamed Mann's Chinese Theatre after theatre chain owner Ted Mann purchased it in 1973.

Opened in 1927 with a showing of Cecil B. DeMille's *King of Kings*, Grauman's was designed by the architectural firm Meyer and Holler with the Chinese Chippendale style in mind. It resembles an opulent Chinese pagoda, and many of the architectural features in the construction, like the temple bells, pagodas, and the Ming Dynasty Heaven Dogs, were imported from **China**, while other elements, such as the 30 foot high dragon, were carved in the United States. The cost to build the theatre was $2 million.

Almost 200 celebrity foot and handprints adorn the walk in front of Grauman's Chinese Theater in Hollywood, California. [Photo courtesy of Shutterstock]

The forecourt, open to the public, has been used since 1927 to immortalize Hollywood actors (starting with Mary Pickford and Douglas Fairbanks) who are invited to press their feet and hands into the cement. Celebrities of Hollywood's golden era like Marilyn Monroe, Bette Davis, Jean Harlow, John Wayne, Elizabeth Taylor, and Shirley Temple are represented in the forecourt, and in more recent years, Harrison Ford, Eddie Murphy, Sylvester Stallone, and Mel Gibson have been included, totaling about 200 prints, including three horses (Roy Rogers's Trigger, Tony Mix's Tony, and Gene Autry's Champion). There are one or two ceremonies per year when new prints are added.

Grauman's is visited by millions of tourists per year, most of whom can't seem to resist placing their own feet in the prints of their favorite stars. Because shoes are thought to be personally connected to their wearers, footprints, for many people, leave more than just a print. They leave a personal emanation behind, one that remains long after the person is gone. Therefore, tourists who place their feet into the prints left by stars like Marilyn Monroe (whose prints, like most left by female celebrities, are of high-heeled shoes) can feel that they are connecting, in some small way, with the celebrity.

Many tourists mistake the footprints at Grauman's with the Hollywood Walk of Fame, also located on Hollywood Boulevard, in which celebrities are immortalized by having a star placed in the sidewalk in their honor.

See also: Australopithecus Footprints

Further Reading Endres, Stacey, Robert Cushman. *Hollywood at Your Feet: The Story of the World Famous Chinese Theatre*. Los Angeles: Pomegranate Press, 1992.

GREECE. *See* Classical Civilizations.

H

HAMMER TOE

Hammer toe is a condition in which one or more of the toes are bent into a hammer shape. It usually affects the second, third, and fourth toes rather than the big toe and is generally caused by wearing ill-fitting shoes. Tight women's shoes and women's **high heels** are often the cause. When wearing tight shoes for long periods of time, the toes will be squeezed together, causing the muscles to tighten. If the condition goes untreated, the toe will be permanently bent.

Other conditions associated with hammer toes are **blisters, bunions, calluses, and corns**, all of which can be formed because of the toe rubbing against the too-small shoe. But because the toe is bent, the corns or calluses may grow in the middle joint of the toe rather than on the top of the toe. Hammer toes, with or without other conditions, causes pain and can cause permanent deformities of the foot, making it difficult to find shoes that fit.

Hammer toes can be alleviated through wearing wide shoes (as well as shoes that are a bit longer than one's foot) or doing toe exercises to stretch the tightened muscles. High heels should be avoided, as should narrow shoes. Toe straighteners and hammer toe cushions, as well as corn pads, are worn to relieve pressure, to straighten the toes, and to relieve the pain. **Orthotic** insoles are also used to redistribute weight inside the shoe. If these measures don't improve the condition, surgery can be used as well to correct the shape of the toes.

See also: Blisters, Bunions, Calluses and Corns; Disorders and Injuries; High Heels

Further Reading Copeland, Glenn, Stan Solomon, and Mark Myerson. *The Good Foot Book: A Guide For Men, Women, Children, Athletes, Seniors*. Alameda, CA: Hunter House, 2005; Jeffreys, Sheila. *Beauty and Misogyny: Harmful Cultural Practices in the West*. New York: Routledge, 2005.

HANES

Hanes is an American **hosiery** and underwear brand owned by Hanes Brand Inc., a consumer goods company that produces Hanes as well as other underwear and stocking brands, including **L'eggs**, Just My Size, Champion, Playtex, Bali, and Wonderbra.

Hosiery has been worn in the West as far back as the Middle Ages, when both men and women wore woven or knitted hose under their clothes. Prior to that time, in the classical world, men and women had bare legs, although **socks** were sometimes worn with shoes or sandals.

With the invention of the knitting machine in 1589, wool and silk stockings were made more easily and became better fitting, and by the eighteenth century, cotton stockings were being made as well. At the end of the eighteenth century, men began wearing pants and short socks rather than stockings, but women continued to wear machine-made stockings. Nylon stockings emerged in 1940 and, after World War II, replaced the use of silk stockings. Then in the 1960s, nylon panty hose replaced stockings made with separate legs. Today, socks are worn by both men and women, with women also wearing a variety of panty hose, stockings, and tights.

Hanes was founded by John Wesley Hanes, who began making men's socks and underwear in 1901 under the name Shamrock Mills. His brother Pleasant Hanes opened the P. H. Hanes Knitting Company in 1902 and introduced two-piece men's underwear. In 1910, Shamrock Mills was renamed Hanes Hosiery Mill and began making women's stockings in 1918. By the 1920s, the company had expanded its line to include underwear and sleepwear. When nylon was invented in 1938, Hanes began using it in its products and developed both seamless stockings and panty hose in the 1960s. In 1965, P. H. Hanes Knitting Company and Hanes Hosiery Mill merged to become Hanes Corporation.

In the 1970s, Hanes Corporation began acquiring other underwear, bra, and hosiery brands, including Bali. Hanes created the L'eggs brand in 1972, which eventually spun off into its own company.

In the 1970s, millions of American women were entering the job market, and Hanes took advantage of this demand by introducing a line of panty hose packaged in a white plastic egg in 1969. During the 1970s and 1980s, L'eggs was the biggest brand of panty hose in the **United States**, thanks to the way that Hanes marketed the product. Besides introducing the innovative egg packaging, Hanes was the first big-name company to sell panty hose in supermarkets, drugstores, and convenience stores, making the product and the brand a household name and wiping out the old-fashioned stockings and garters. L'eggs were displayed in their own special display unit, separating them from the other brands of hosiery then in the stores at the time. L'eggs remains the biggest selling panty hose brand in the world today and sells panty hose, tights, and shapewear.

During the 1980s, Hanes continued to create new brands, including Just My Size for full-figured women and Hanes Her Way, and the company also acquired Champion. In the 1990s, Hanes launched the Barely There brand and purchased Playtex.

Hanes Corporation was purchased by Consolidated Foods Corporation (later named Sara Lee) in a hostile takeover in 1979. Until that time, the company was still owned by the Hanes family. Sara Lee let Hanes go in 2006 as part of a larger restructuring in which the parent company sold or spun off much of the company's brands. After the restructuring, Hanes was left with much of Sara Lee's debt, and from 2006 to 2008 Hanes was forced to cut jobs and close manufacturing plants. In 2008, the company cut 8,100 workers and shifted its production facilities from the final plants in the United States and Latin America to Asia.

Hanes Brand remains the largest producer of underwear, socks, and stockings in the United States, with its products bought by eight out of 10 American households, according to a company survey. Hanes employs 50,000 people, with most located outside of the United States, and reported sales of $544 million in 2007.

See also: Europe; Hosiery; L'eggs

Further Reading Grass, Milton. *The History of Hosiery, from the Piloi of Ancient Greece to the Nylons of Modern America.* New York: Fairchild Publications, 1955.

HENNA

Henna refers to a dye made from the leaves of the henna plant that is used to color skin and hair. It is often used to decorate the feet. The leaves of the henna plant, *lawsonia inermis*, when ground up and mixed with water, coffee, or tea and made into a paste and applied to the skin for 30 minutes, are used by cultures around the world to dye the skin and the hair. Henna is known as *mehndi*, in **India**, Pakistan, and Bangladesh as well as other Muslim and North African countries. Sometimes it is also used to stain the fingernails, as was practiced by women in **Egypt**, Minoa, Mycenea, and Medieval Spain as well as in Muslim countries and through parts of South Asia. Henna has also been used medicinally in India, the **Middle East**, and North Africa. Henna has most likely been used since the late Neolithic period in North Africa, South Asia, and the Middle East—the locations in which henna naturally grows.

It is said that Mohammad once said "there is no plant dearer to Allah than henna."

When henna is used to decorate the skin, it is usually worn on the hands and feet, where the designs will last the longest, thanks to the thick skin. After creating the paste, it is drawn on the skin with a stick or other implement, sometimes based on a pattern and sometimes drawn freehand. Because women in the cultures in which henna is most popular typically do not show any parts of their body in public besides the hands and the feet, these highly adorned regions become an important part of the costume of women.

Traditional Indian henna designs are quite intricate and are often painted on brides' hands before their weddings, a process that can take hours. Muslims also use henna as decoration, and designs are equally intricate and generally represent fertility and marital happiness. Sometimes the groom's name is included among the designs. Henna is used for weddings in Muslim countries as well, and women will stay up late at night applying henna to each other's hands. In this sense, henna is both a form of body and hair decoration and also a form of social bonding.

This woman's foot has been painted with henna. [2007 copyright Michael Pettigrew. Image from BigStockPhoto.com]

The Fulani of West Africa also use henna on the hands, forearms, feet, and shins for special occasions like weddings and baptisms. Moroccan women will wear henna on many special occasions, such as to commemorate religious holidays, circumcisions, and marriages, and will use it as well during pregnancy and after childbirth to counteract evil spirits. Using henna on one's fingernails and toenails prior to giving birth is a common practice in many cultures. In Morocco, the "Night of the Henna" was a traditional celebration held the night before a wedding in which the bride, groom, and members of the wedding party would have henna applied to their hands and feet. Sudanese women also wear henna for weddings and other occasions.

Henna's popularity during special events in the Middle East and India is tied to not only its ability to decorate the body, but ideas about the power of henna. Henna is thought to be able to dispel the evil eye when applied in specific magical designs, making it serve as a protective amulet for the wearer. Among the Berbers of North Africa, for example, feet are thought to be especially vulnerable to evil forces, so henna is applied to the feet to protect them.

See also: Africa; Foot and Shoe Adornment; India; Islam; Middle East

Further Reading Monger, George. *Marriage Customs of the World: From Henna to Honeymoons*. Santa Barbara: ABC-CLIO, 2004; Van den Beukel, Dorine. *Traditional Mehndi Designs: A Treasury of Henna Body Art*. Berkeley, CA: Shambhala Publications, 2000.

HIGH HEELS

High heels are iconic women's shoes today and date, in one form or another, back to the classical world. However, the modern high heel was first introduced into western culture in the sixteenth century, and, at that time, was worn exclusively by men. Today, high heels are the ultimate symbol of femininity.

High platform **sandals** and **boots** were worn by actors in both ancient **Greece** and **Rome** to indicate different characters and their social status. The *cothornus*, for example, a high platform boot, was worn by Roman actors as far back as the third century BCE. Boys may have worn elevated sandals in order to impersonate women on the stage. Etruscan women also wore high platform sandals, a practice which was borrowed by Greek women. Platform sandals may have also been worn in ancient **Egypt**.

But high heels in the West did not derive from the footwear of Rome. Instead, the heel came from the horseback-riding peoples of Central and Eastern Asia, such as the Persians and the Mongols, both of who wore stacked leather heeled boots while riding. Their footwear may have entered **Europe** through the Mongol invasions of Central Europe in the thirteenth century and could also have come through the Crusades. Mongolian horseback riders were members of the upper **class**, and heeled shoes, then, were associated with wealth.

The use of heeled boots while riding and the association of high heels with wealth both were passed onto Europeans. Until heels arrived in Europe, pointed toe shoes kept noblemen's feet from slipping out of the stirrups. But at the beginning of the sixteenth century, short (approximately one to one-and-a-half inch), canted, stacked leather heels were placed on shoes in order to hold the shoes in the stirrups when riding. Heels moved from the riding boot to men's court shoes in France after that, and became taller and narrower, and by the late seventeenth century, noblemen's heels had risen to four inches. Louis XIV wore five inch red heels during his reign, from the mid-seventeenth to early eighteenth centuries. The women of the French court began wearing them after Catherine de Medici, the Duchess of Orleans, wore them at her wedding in 1533 to appear taller, and from there they spread throughout European courts.

These high-heeled ankle strap sandals were made possible by the invention of the steel arch by Ferragamo. [Copyright 2008 Jupiterimages Corporation]

High platforms had been worn for centuries in many cultures by the time the true heeled shoe developed in the west. The *chopine* was a high platform clog worn by wealthy Venetians in the sixteenth century, and stilted wooden sandals were worn in the **Middle East**, **India**, and Japan. In fact, Catherine de Medici, who was originally from Florence, had her heels adapted from chopines, but instead of having a shoe on top of a single platform, her shoes were made in the modern fashion, with an elevated heel and lowered toe.

Through the seventeenth and eighteenth centuries, wealthy men and women throughout Europe were wearing high-heeled shoes, and heels themselves came to signify wealth, as the term "well-heeled" demonstrates. It goes without saying that high heels were not only unaffordable but also impractical for working people. (It's not surprising, then, that very high heels today are known as "limousine shoes," for women who don't actually have to walk.) High heels were also impractical when going outdoors in the centuries before European streets were cleaned up and sidewalks were available for walking. Many men and women wore pattens, a form of **overshoe**, to protect their shoes during this time. **Sumptuary laws** were passed in France during the seventeenth century that restricted the wearing of red heels to members of the court, and one English law from 1670 prohibited women from wearing heels to deceive men about their height.

By the mid-eighteenth century, women were wearing high, curved "pompadour" heels (named after Madame de Pompadour, the mistress of Louis XV) or "Louis" heels (after Louis XV) as well as binding their feet to make them appear narrower. In fact, one benefit of high heels for women was that they made women's feet appear smaller, and through the Victorian era tiny feet were highly valued in European women, partly thanks to stylistic influences from **China**. Even middle-class women with money began wearing heels, albeit low ones, during the eighteenth century.

Heels went out of fashion after the revolutionary era at the end of the eighteenth century; low-heeled shoes were worn even by elites during the nineteenth century as high heels were associated with the aristocracy, which was considered frivolous after the French and American revolutions.

The high heel became fashionable again at the end of the nineteenth century, although only among women, with men's shoes retaining heel heights of about one inch and women's starting at around two inches in height. With only women wearing heels, they became firmly associated with femininity and with frivolity, an association that remains to this day.

Since mechanized shoe production began in the late nineteenth century with the first high-heeled factory opening in the **United States** in 1888 (but especially since the 1970s when offshore production allowed for the production of very inexpensive shoes) high heels have not been exclusively worn by the wealthy and have been worn by every social class, finally losing their association with status and wealth.

With the twentieth century, heel heights began to rise again, even as women's opportunities in the world increased. As women acquired the right to vote and became more active in the modern world, they did so wearing heels (even when playing sports), demonstrating that women's rights did not necessarily mean a loss of femininity. As skirt lengths became shortened in the 1920s and shoes were for the first time shown, heels became more elaborately decorated as well.

In the 1920s, Italian shoe designer **Salvatore Ferragamo** was working in Hollywood and invented the metal arch support, which provided enough support for high-heeled shoes that the shoes no longer needed to be closed (the closed toe held the feet in the shoes), leading to the first true high-heeled **sandals**.

A new form of high heels, based in part on the high **clogs** of the sixteenth century, was developed in the 1930s, also by Ferragamo. Because steel, leather, and other materials were not available to Ferragamo, who had relocated to Italy, during World War II, he began experimenting with new materials. Ferragamo invented the modern **platform shoe**, using non-rationed materials like cork to substitute for the stacked leather of traditional heels. In addition, he began using a wedge shape rather than the separate heel in order to provide more structure to the shoes. Platforms became popular in the United States in the 1930s, but went out of style immediately after the end of the war, although they had a resurgence in popularity in the 1970s and again in the 1990s. The 1970s, in fact, also ushered in the first period since the eighteenth century when men wore heels higher than an inch, as many men wore platform shoes during the disco era.

The next major innovation in high heels was the **stiletto** heel. Stiletto heels are made of steel and allow for very thin, very high heels. They were developed in the 1950s and allowed for shoes that are much higher than previous heels. They quickly became popular in America and Europe and are now associated with femininity and sexuality. Kitten heels (also known as Sabrina heels), which are low stiletto heels, also emerged in the 1950s and are experiencing a resurgence in popularity today. Other famous heel inventions of the 1950s include Roger Vivier's "comma heel" and Andre Perugia's corkscrew heel.

Since the 1970s, heels change height and size with almost every season, going from chunky to narrow and from high to low. But high and narrow heels remain the most feminine of all the heels. Today it is not uncommon to see celebrities and the very wealthy wearing heels as high as five inches, bringing back the notion that the higher the heel, the higher the status of the wearer.

High heels retain their allure for women today due to a combination of factors. Many women feel empowered in high heels because they make the wearer appear taller, and thus more powerful. It is no surprise that women who are CEOs and occupy other powerful positions routinely wear high heels. On the other hand, because of the pain that they cause and the way that they impede mobility, high heels make women at the same time more vulnerable and less powerful.

High heels are certainly popular due to the way that they arch the foot, lengthen and accentuate the legs, arch the back, and cause the hips and chest to jut outward, creating a more sexualized gait. High heels are an iconic feature of pornography and are worn by prostitutes and strippers the world over (with certain types of heels, like clear Lucite heels known as "hooker heels," favored by prostitutes and strippers), with extremely high heels being more associated with sexuality than low heels.

High heels cause a variety of foot problems because of the way that the foot is positioned on a slant, with the toes bent and supporting the weight of the body. In fact, women have four times more foot disorders than do men, and the majority of those are caused by high heels. Problems stemming from the increased weight on the ball of the foot include calluses and neuromas, a thickening of the tissue in the ball of the feet. Women who wear high heels often find that their **Achilles** tendon becomes shortened because of the permanently arched position of the foot. Another problem that stems from both high heels and, as is the case with many high-heeled shoes, narrow-toed shoes is that the toes get pushed together, causing blisters, corns, **hammer toes**, and bunions. In addition, habitual high heel wearers can find that they have increased pressure on their knee joints, causing pain and osteoarthritis, and their spines can fall out of alignment.

To counteract these problems, podiatrists encourage women to wear high heels for no longer than 12 hours a day and to wear flat shoes or supportive shoes as much as possible.

See also: China; Disorders and Injuries; Europe; Ferragamo, Salvatore; Gender; India; Japan; Middle East; Platform Shoes; Stilettos; Sumptuary Laws

Further Reading Semmelhack, Elizabeth. "A Delicate Balance: Women, Power and High Heels," in Rielle, Georgio and Peter McNeil, eds. *Shoes: A History From Sandals to Sneakers*. London: Berg Publishers, 2006; Steele, Valerie. *Fashion and Eroticism: Ideals of Feminine Beauty from the Victorian Era to the Jazz Age*. New York: Oxford University Press, 1995; Steele, Valerie. *Fetish: Fashion, Sex and Power*. New York: Oxford University Press, 1996; Walford, Jonathan. *The Seductive Shoe: Four Centuries of Fashion Footwear*. New York: Stewart, Tabori and Chang, 2007.

HOSIERY

Hosiery refers to coverings for the legs and feet. It includes panty hose, which are knitted hose that cover legs, feet, and torso, **socks**, which cover the feet, ankles, and often lower legs, and stockings, which cover individual feet and legs and are held up with garters.

Leg coverings have been worn in a variety of contexts, for both functional reasons—to protect the feet and legs in cold weather—as well as decorative reasons. For instance, in the **Arctic Region**, socks of woven grass or fur are worn underneath the boots to keep the feet warm. The ancient Greeks wore socks of matted animal fur for warmth, and the Romans often wore socks, called *soccus*, with their **sandals**, or indoors over their bare feet. But for the most part, their legs were bare under their togas. At the same time, European "Barbarians" wore animal skin leggings secured at the waist by a leather belt. And cotton and silk socks have been worn in **China** and **Japan** for centuries, partly because shoes are removed while indoors in those cultures, so socks were worn in part to keep the feet clean.

As much of **Europe** came under Roman rule, Roman styles of dress were adopted by Europeans in the Middle Ages, including the wearing of tunics and cloaks, for centuries. In fact, pants did not develop until the eighteenth century in Europe, so for centuries men covered their legs under their tunics with hose, which evolved from the Roman sock.

During the Middle Ages, wealthy men wore brightly colored, tight hose generally made of wool, which were initially cut and sewn together. As men's tunics became shorter in the fourteenth century, the need for well-fitting hose became more pronounced, so the hose were better made and better fitted, extended from the upper thigh to the feet, and were cut from four rather than two sections of cloth. Called *chausses*, each leg had its own hose that covered the foot and that were secured to their tunic by straps tied to a belt, which attached to the braies, a form of underpants. Also at this time, codpieces were worn to cover the crotch. By the end of the fourteenth century, the chausses were secured to the doublet or undertunic, with laces (known as points) all around the undertunic. The hose worn by noblemen was embroidered or made of luxurious fabrics like velvet or silk, was often a different color for each leg, and was sewn to fit a specific man. By the fifteenth century, the hose became still better fitting and could have separate soles sewn on for indoor wear.

Women in the Middle Ages wore long undergarments underneath their clothes, so it is difficult to tell from paintings whether they wore leg coverings as well. But at least by the fourteenth century it appears that women did wear stockings made of woven cloth that were most likely held up by some form of garter, which would have tied around the leg above the knee. In fact, because women's skirts went to the floor through the early twentieth century, women's stockings remained short until that time.

William Lee invented a knitting machine in 1589, which allowed for the rapid production of wool and silk stockings. While the technology was not immediately embraced, when it was, after Lee's death, stockings became more popular and better fitting. By the eighteenth century, new technological advances allowed for the knitting of cotton stockings by machine. During cold weather, those who could afford it often wore multiple pairs of stockings at once, and men who wore **boots** often wore boot hose over their stockings to protect the stockings from wear and damage.

Hose at this period separated into two items, breeches, which were worn on the upper legs and torso, and stockings, which were worn on the lower legs. By the eighteenth century, men and women were both wearing stockings, with silk being used for the wealthy and wool and cotton for commoners.

By the end of the eighteenth century, as pants were becoming popular in Europe, replacing breeches, men's stockings were replaced by socks to be worn under pants. Until the development of elastic, socks still had to be held up with garters on the calves. With the death of Queen Victoria's husband Albert, dark socks became popular for men, just as black shoes became popular for women. At this same time, more women were wearing machine-made stockings of cotton or silk. At the end of the nineteenth century, a circular sock machine was invented, allowing for socks to be machine-knit as a whole garment rather than sewn together from pieces.

In the twentieth century, silk stockings continued to be worn by women, but with skirt and dress hemlines rising in the 1920s, stockings became, for the first time, long enough to cover most of the leg and were held up by garters around the upper thigh. (Prior to this time, women's stockings covered only the calf.) Nylon was invented in 1938, and after World War II silk stockings were replaced by nylon stockings, which were made flat, in the shape of a leg, and were originally shaped by dropping stitches (as a sweater is knit). (Socks, too, began to be made with nylon.) Like silk stockings, nylon stockings were still made in one flat piece and sewn together, resulting in the characteristic (and erotic) seam down the back. In the 1950s stockings were for the first time sewn in one piece on the new circular knitting machine, which meant that the rear seam disappeared. The stockings were now shaped by tightening the stitches.

Panty hose, a one-piece garment made up of nylon legs combined with a built-in panty, were invented in 1959 but were not widely worn until the mid-1960s, when they replaced stockings and garters. This invention came in time for the miniskirt, which ushered in new opaque and brightly colored tights. Control top panty hose were introduced in the 1960s and included a reinforced panel in the front to hold in the stomach. By the 1970s, panty hose were made with spandex or other elastic material mixed with nylon, making the panty hose fit better.

The 1970s and early 1980s saw the greatest jump in panty hose sales, as companies like **L'eggs** began heavily marketing panty hose in the **United States**, selling the products in the cute plastic eggs in supermarkets, drug stores, and convenience stores. The introduction of "ethnic" panty hose and plus-size panty hose in the 1980s and 1990s increased sales further by expanding into new markets.

Since the mid-1980s, many women no longer wear panty hose, preferring to wear dresses and skirts over bare legs, except in situations where the dress code or conservative politics demand it. (Panty hose are also worn to conceal leg hair stubble, scars, and varicose veins.) Many women now find panty hose to be confining and don't like to wear them with open-toed shoes and sandals. Because of this, panty hose sales have been steadily declining in the United States since the mid-1980s, although new products and niche products have been filling the gap in sales. These include opaque tights that are worn under short skirts, fishnet or patterned stockings, body shaper products like Spanx, and leggings, which are footless tights worn under tunics and short skirts. There are even panty hose marketed to combat cellulite and compression hose to be worn to improve one's circulation. Spanx, for example, makes footless, body shaping hose to be worn under pants and capris and which can be worn with open-toed sandals.

See also: Hanes; L'eggs

Further Reading Grass, Milton. *The History of Hosiery, from the Piloi of Ancient Greece to the Nylons of Modern America.* New York: Fairchild Publications, 1955.

HUARACHE

Huaraches are Mexican **sandals** made with a recycled tire outsole, a **leather** insole, and a woven leather upper. They have long been worn in much of Central and South America and are extremely long-lasting sandals. The word *huarache* is from the Tarascan language, an indigenous language spoken in the Michoacan state of Mexico.

Sandals are thought to be the earliest form of foot covering. Made with a sole of woven plant fiber or hide, with simple straps made of hide or grass, they were and are worn by peoples around the world to protect the feet from hot or rocky earth. They were probably first worn by peoples in warm regions where it was important to keep the bottom of the foot protected but the top of the foot cool.

Huaraches were most likely first worn by peasants in Mexico hundreds of years ago and derive from the sandals worn by Native Americans of the region. Mayans, for instance, wore sandals made of untanned hides and laces made of plant fiber, which laced up the leg. Aztec peasants often went barefoot, but nobles wore sandals made of leather and woven plant fiber straps, often decorated, while in South America the Incas wore sandals made of woven fiber soles and uppers made of either fiber or llama skin. The **Southwest Indians** of the **United States** once wore simple yucaa fiber sandals as well until those were replaced by the **moccasins** worn by other Native peoples of North America.

Huaraches were originally made entirely of leather, but the 1930s saw the first use of tire treads as soles in Mexico. They were handmade by *huaracheros*, and even today, handmade huaraches remain popular, although they can also be machine-made.

Traditional huaraches are constructed from a hand-cut piece of rubber, which is stitched to a hand-cut piece of leather, which is then stitched on a last to the upper, which is handwoven from a single piece of wet leather. Today, huaraches are still made in Mexico in the traditional slip-on, open-toed style, but they can also be purchased as closed shoes, sandals with buckles, and other varieties of sandals.

North Americans began wearing huaraches in the 1960s as **Birkenstocks** and other comfortable sandals became popular. Jack Keroac wore them in *On The Road*, helping to popularize them among hippies and other members of the counterculture in the United States.

Some American runners have taken to running in traditional huaraches, or sometimes barefoot, inspired by the Tarahumara runners of Northern Mexico, who run extreme distance races wearing sandals made with tire soles and plant fiber or leather uppers. In the early 1990s, **Nike** created a line of shoes called Air Huaraches, inspired by traditional huaraches. While Air Huaraches were discontinued, Nike will be unveiling a new Air Huarache in 2009.

See also: Sandals; Southwest Indians

Further Reading Adams, Richard. *Prehistoric Mesoamerica*. Norman, OK: Universit of Oklahoma Press, 1991.

HUSH PUPPIES

Hush Puppies is a brand of casual family footwear owned by Wolverine World Wide Inc. Hush Puppies account for one-third of Wolverine's shoe sales, with 19 million pairs sold in 2006 alone.

Hush Puppies have their origins in **shoemaker** G. A. Krause, who along with his uncle Fred Hirth founded the Hirth-Krause Company in 1883, which sold shoe accessories, purchased finished shoes, and then sold them to the public. Krause opened, with his son Otto, his first shoe factory in 1903, called Michigan Shoe Makers, and in 1908 created the Wolverine Tanning Company with his son Victor to supply **leather** to his shoe factory; in 1921, both companies combined to form the Wolverine Shoe and Tanning Corporation.

Wolverine initially made **boots** out of cow leather, but in 1914 began making boots as well as gloves out of the less expensive horse hide. During World War II, Wolverine made gloves for the military, which requested that they try pigskin as a new material. After the war, Victor Krause developed a new method for tanning pigskin, leading to a brushed pigskin that was softer than either the horse or cow leather that they had been using. Because the pigskin was not sturdy enough for the company's Wolverine boots (known as "thousand mile shoes"), Victor designed a casual pair of **men's shoes** using the new material. He treated the pigskin with Scotchgard to protect the material and combined the pigskin upper with a soft rubber-crepe sole. Released in 1958, this was the first Hush Puppy.

Hush Puppies were marketed as an alternative to dressier, but less comfortable shoes and the much more casual **athletic shoes**. Hush Puppies were the first non-athletic casual shoe and filled an important market niche as Americans began working in offices more than factories. Hush Puppies got its name from the southern fried food that was traditionally fed to barking dogs to keep them quiet; in addition, "barking dogs" also meant sore feet; Hush Puppies, because of their comfort, could then quiet those barking feet. The basset hound was soon chosen as the product's mascot, and the shoes took off in popularity through the 1950s and 1960s. By 1963, one in 10 American adults was said to own a pair of Hush Puppies, including members of the Rat Pack. Prince Phillip famously wore them during a visit to the **United States**ce in 1959.

The Wolverine Shoe and Tanning Company was renamed Wolverine World Wide in 1964 and continues to produce Hush Puppies as well as other Wolverine brands like Bates and Merrell. The shoes are no longer produced in the United States and instead are manufactured in **China**, Vietnam, and Brazil. Hush Puppies were first sold internationally in 1959 when Canada licensed the shoes, followed by England, South Africa, Australia, and **Japan**. Hush Puppies are now sold in 140 countries.

Hush Puppies lost much of their popularity in the 1970s and 1980s, as they had to compete with the growing athletic shoe market as well as inexpensive imported shoes. The company responded by closing most of its U.S. factories and many of their retail outlets. Today, only 5 percent of Wolverine's shoes are made in the United States, following another restructuring in the early 2000s that included layoffs and factory closures.

The company regained much of their popularity in the 1990s, thanks in part to the shoe's retro appeal and the company's restructuring in favor of its flagship brand. Because so many young people wanted to wear the original 1950s Hush Puppies, the company reissued them and encouraged fashion designers to use the older models in their runway shows. Their resurgence can also be traced to a documentary about American fashion designer Isaac Mizrahi that was released in 1995; in the film, Mizrahi was wearing a pair of Hush Puppies and also used the shoes in his runway show. This appearance led to a trend of gay men wearing Hush Puppies. Sales went from 30,000 shoes in 1994 to 430,000 in 1995. While Hush Puppies were once associated with seniors who favor comfortable shoes, to-day many young people wear Hush Puppies, especially after designers like Anna Sui used them in their collections and after the company reissued the original model in new colors like Day-Glo orange, green, and purple. In addition, casual Fridays and an overall trend towards more casual work apparel has helped the brand further.

While Hush Puppies don't have the celebrity clients of women's brands like **Jimmy Choo** or **Manolo Blahnik**, they are favored by a number of famous men. Tom Hanks's character wore Hush Puppies in the film *Forrest Gump*, and Mike Meyers wore them in *Austin Powers*. They were worn by Kevin Spacey and Nicho-las Cage at the Academy Awards, and they were also worn by Sylvester Stallone, Jim Carrey, Forrest Whitaker, and Mikhail Gorbachev, who invited the company to be the first American company to do business in the Soviet Union. Jimmy Buffet famously wore them and released a song in 1974 called "Come Monday" that fea-tured the line, "I've got my Hush Puppies on." And perhaps most famously, Roll-ing Stones guitarist Keith Richards was wearing a pair of Hush Puppies during a concert in 1965 when he was accidentally electrocuted; it is said that the shoes he was wearing prevented him from sustaining worse injury.

Styles today range from the traditional Oxford to Mary Janes, boots, and even **sneakers**, and the company owns the Brooks brand of athletic shoes as well as

Merrell outdoor shoes. The company also produces shoes under the name of Harley-Davidson and Caterpiller, and in 2006 it acquired the license for Patagonia Footwear. Hush Puppies also licenses its logo and name to other companies who make clothes, luggage, and accessories. In 1995, the Council of Fashion Designers of America named Hush Puppies Fashion Accessory of the Year.

See also: Leather; Men's Shoes; Shoe Stores

Further Reading Vejlgaard, Henrik. *Anatomy of a Trend.* New York: McGraw Hill, 2008.

INDIA

Indian culture includes a great many beliefs and traditions surrounding feet and shoes, which center around notions of purity and impurity, important concepts to Buddhists and Hindus alike. Feet have important significance to many Indians and are highly venerated. For example, touching the feet of elders or social superiors is an important Indian tradition, demonstrating respect and submission. Indians are expected to do this at special ritual occasions and when first seeing a person after a separation; the elder is expected to then bless the person in response by touching his or her head. If an Indian has harmed someone else and seeks forgiveness, one way to do that is to stroke or kiss the victim's feet.

Respect, love, and submission also come into play with the tradition by which Indians will kiss or wash the bare feet of a guru or religious teacher or sprinkle water that has bathed a holy man's feet onto one's own head. The feet of holy men are themselves holy in part because the feet of the gods are holy; in fact, according to Hinduism, the gods use their feet to create and influence the world. Therefore, adherents venerate the feet of holy men and worship the feet, footprints, and shoes of the gods.

For example, the god Vishnu's footprints are represented on sacred items and amulets, and a symbol of Vishnu's foot is placed

Paduka. These traditional Indian toe knob sandals are decorated with Ivory inlay and date from the nineteenth century. [Photo courtesy of Shoe Icons]

on a devotee's head as a blessing. Buddha, too, is often represented by his footprints, which are worshipped by Buddhists. During the Festival of Lights holiday known as Diwaili, Indian homes are decorated with the footprints of the goddess Lakshmi, and to celebrate Krishna's birthday homes are adorned with footprints of Krishna.

Being barefoot is also a way to demonstrate humility, as is illustrated by the custom of walking barefoot around and near the monument of Gandhi in India, or the practice of Hindu ascetics going barefoot. In fact, the three major religions of India—Hinduism, Buddhism, and Jainism—are all rooted in a tradition in which adherents go barefoot as a way of foregoing the pleasures of the world.

Indian Slippers. These beautiful slippers are made of leather and are covered with metallic thread fabric. The slightly upturned toe comes from the Middle East. [2008 copyright Ken Durden. Image from BigStockPhoto.com]

In addition, some Hindus will walk on nails as penance during certain spiritual occasions.

Like many cultures, it is customary in India (especially in the south) to remove one's shoes before entering a home or a temple because shoes represent pollution. This is most common in high caste families' homes. On the other hand, feet can be impure as well, and hygiene is very important to Indians. In the past, Indians went to bathing houses to bathe; today women in particular bathe and scrub their feet religiously and massage them with scented oils.

Adorning the feet is also very important. **Henna** is used to stain and decorate the feet in India. Traditional Indian henna designs are quite intricate and are often painted on brides' feet before their weddings, a process that can take hours, and which can last for weeks. Feet are also adorned with toe rings, toe chains, and jingling anklets made of silver or brass; gold jewelry is traditionally reserved for elites.

Feet in India, as in many other cultures, also have a strong erotic connotation. Men often kiss and caress their lovers' feet, and having a woman's foot touch her lover's head means that she loves him.

North Indian shoe. This shoe dates from the nineteenth century, has the characteristic Eastern turned up toe, and is decorated with beads. [Photo courtesy of Shoe Icons]

Because most of India is a hot country, shoes have not always been worn by the majority of the population. Simple **sandals** of woven grass or wood are the original form of footwear in India. (The colder regions of the subcontinent like Bhutan and Nepal have other types of footwear, including heavy **leather** boots to protect the feet against the cold.) *Kapula*, for example, refers to simple sandals made of woven grasses that are still worn today in the Himalyan region. But for much of the history of India, many people simply went barefoot. Because of this, shoes have always been markers of high status and caste. In addition, shoes throughout India vary on the basis of region, religion, and **gender**. Because the cow is sacred to Hindus, wearing leather shoes is still relatively uncommon for most Indians. For that reason, shoes are often made of wood, plant fibers, and metals.

One of the oldest forms of footwear still being worn in India is the *paduka*, which literally means small foot. At its most simple, it is a simple thong sandal made with a wooden sole and a knob on a post between the big toe and second toe. The paduka keeps the foot cool yet protects it from the hot ground. This sandal goes back perhaps five thousand years, and was worn, and is still worn, by holy men, although fancier versions of it were also worn by elites as a sign of status. The paduka is also a traditional **wedding shoe**.

The paduka varies on the basis of material and the height of the sole, which can range from a flat sandal to a multi-inch high elevated platform made of two stilts. (The stilts are said to be a reflection of the Jain desire to refrain from stepping on insects.) The difference in paduka materials and adornment reflect the status difference of their wearers, with padukas made of ivory, silver, precious woods, or bronze being worn by members of the highest castes. Other fancy padukas would be worn for special occasions only, such as weddings, and brides entered their marriages with fancy padukas as part of their dowry. Toe knob sandals like padukas are found in **Africa** today, thanks to trade with India, and are worn by Hindus in Indonesia as well.

Other simple wooden sandals were worn at least as far back as the second century BCE. With the development of Buddhism in India in the third century, Indians began wearing wooden sandals with straps, and royals wore sandals adorned with jewels, and by at least the fourth century some Indians were wearing sandals made with leather or animal skins. Known as *chappals*, they are composed of a leather sole in the shape of a foot with a strap across the foot and a toe ring to support the foot. They are still worn in India today by people of all castes.

In the eleventh century, India was conquered by Mahmud of Ghazna, who brought **Islam** to the subcontinent as well as stylistic influences from the **Middle East**. Turned-up toes were introduced into Indian footwear, and adornment styles from the Middle East became popular as well, including gold and silver embroidery. Finally, slip-on shoes like *babouches* became popular to allow for easy removal when entering a mosque.

With the arrival of Mughals from Central Asia in the sixteenth century, Indian cultural forms became more sophisticated, at least for the elites, who began to wear extremely luxurious clothing and footwear. By the seventeenth century, *mojaris*, or camel skin slippers with upturned toes, were being worn by the nobility. Often encrusted with jewels and decorated with lavish embroidery, they demonstrated the wearer's high status and style. Known as *juttees* today, these often heavily embroidered slippers are still worn in India today (although without the upturned toe) and are the traditional shoe of Rajasthan. Other **slippers** and open-backed mules were made of felt, cloth, velvet, and silk. Juttees or mojaris are still the most common shoe worn by Indian brides at their weddings. In addition, there are wooden shoes that sit on stilts that are carved to resemble juttees.

Even though Hindus, who make up the vast majority of India's population, revere cows, leather has been used for making sandals and shoes in India for hundreds of years. While Hinduism prohibits eating beef or slaughtering cattle, cows who die a "natural" death and cows slaughtered by Muslims are permitted to be used for leather. Since only untouchables (those who occupy the lowest rung in the Indian caste system) are allowed to handle dead animals, the task of butchering the animals and tanning, cutting, and preparing the leather falls to the members of the lowest caste. While shoemakers, known as *mochis*, have a higher status than those who work with leather, they are still untouchable.

Even Gandhi, himself a Hindu, promoted the use of leather shoes as a way to encourage Indian self-sufficiency and made his own *chappals* himself as a way to challenge the existing caste inequality in India. Since the nineteenth century, European shoes have become more commonly worn in India. This is one reason that Gandhi encouraged the wearing of traditional Indian shoes.

See also: Class; Foot and Shoe Adornment; Henna; Islam; Leather; Middle East; Sandals

Further Reading Tarlo, Emma. *Clothing Matters: Dress and Adornment in India*. Chicago: University of Chicago Press, 1996.

INGROWN TOENAILS

Ingrown toenails (known as onychocryptosis) refers to a condition in which the side of a toenail grows into the toe bed, which can cause pain and infection. As with other disorders of the foot, ingrown toenails are often caused by shoes worn by women; in particular **high heels** and tight shoes, both of which cause the toes to be compressed together in the shoe. In addition, ingrown toenails can be caused by an injury to the toe or trimming the toenails into a rounded shape, which causes the side of the nail to push into the skin. Most commonly, however, the condition is linked to the shape of a person's toenails. People with curved toenails are more prone to ingrown toenails because their nails can easily curve down and penetrate the skin around the nail.

With an ingrown toenail, the skin will grow around the nail, causing inflammation, redness, pain, discharge, and, when left untreated, an infection. People with **diabetes** are at greater risk for infection because, due to impaired blood flow in the legs, they often cannot feel that they have a problem, nor can the body heal itself well.

Treatment typically involves soaking the feet in warm water, wearing loose-fitting shoes, elevating the nail from the toe, and keeping the area clean and dry. When the condition is severe, the nail, or part of the nail, may need to be surgically removed, and for persistent conditions the nail cells must be destroyed to keep the nail from growing back.

See also: Diabetes; Disorders and Injuries; Toenails

Further Reading Copeland, Glenn, Stan Solomon, and Mark Myerson. *The Good Foot Book: A Guide For Men, Women, Children, Athletes, Seniors*. Alameda, CA: Hunter House, 2005.

IN HER SHOES

In Her Shoes is a 2002 novel by Jennifer Weiner and a 2005 movie of the same name starring Cameron Diaz and Toni Collette.

The book and the movie tell the story of two sisters, Rose and Maggie. Rose, played by Toni Collette in the film, is an average-looking, responsible attorney who reads romance novels, fantasizes about being swept off her feet by a handsome man, and compulsively buys expensive and beautiful shoes. Maggie is her younger, more beautiful, and irresponsible sister, played by Cameron Diaz, who can't get her life together, and gets drunk and sleeps around. Maggie journeys to Florida to meet the grandmother both sisters thought was dead, played in the film by Shirley MacLaine. It is there that Maggie grows as a person, learns to read, and takes responsibility for herself.

The title, *In Her Shoes*, refers to both the way that the sisters learn to walk in each other's shoes, eventually growing to understand each other, and also the fact that they both have the same size feet (8 ½), and thus can wear each other's shoes. Shoes are important in both the novel and the film primarily because Maggie resents Rose for her large collection of expensive high-heeled shoes. After Maggie leaves a note telling Rose not to touch her shoes, Rose tries them on anyway, and Weiner writes, "It wasn't fair, she thought, stalking into the kitchen in the Pradas. Where was Rose going to wear a pair of shoes like these, anyhow? What was the point?" Clearly, Rose, the flashy, outgoing, and beautiful sister, feels that she should be the one to have the beautiful shoes, as Rose, dowdy and dull, doesn't have the wardrobe or the lifestyle to do justice to them. Yet Maggie, because she can't hold down a job, can't afford them. In another scene, Maggie ruins Rose's favorite pair of shoes, which is a metaphor for all of the other ways that Maggie has ruined Rose's life—trashing her apartment, sleeping with the man she loves, and generally using her.

The book and the movie end with the usual "chick lit" and "chick film" happily-ever-after ending: marriage. Because shoes were a major theme in the movie, the shoes that Rose wears to her wedding are significant as well—a gift from her grandmother Ella that she wore to her own wedding. This ending draws not only from "**Cinderella**" and countless other fairy tales where the happy ending must end, for the woman, with a marriage, but also draws on Cinderella's connection between shoes and the fairy tale wedding. The fact that Ella gives Rose a pair of shoes to wear to her wedding is also drawn from the practices of countless cultures where the bride wears a special pair of **wedding shoes** at her own wedding, symbolizing the bride's new future and marital bliss.

See also: Gender; High Heels

Further Reading Weiner, Jennifer. *In Her Shoes*. New York: Atria Books, 2002.

ISLAM

Religious and cultural beliefs about feet and shoes in Islam often revolve around the idea of purity and impurity. In Muslim tradition, as in other religions like

Hinduism and Buddhism, shoes must be removed before entering a Mosque; in addition, Muslims remove their shoes before praying, whether in a Mosque, at home, or anywhere else. While this is not found in the Koran, it has become customary in Muslim countries and apparently stems from Mohammad's command to remove any dirt off of one's shoes before saying prayers.

Removing one's shoes before entering a holy place or engaging in a holy practice is both a sign of respect and humility in Islam as well as in other religions. It is also a very practical matter in that shoes touch the dirt, and keeping dirt out of sacred spaces is a common practice. In addition, Muslims must wash their feet as well as their hands, hair, and face before praying, a practice called *wudhu*. Feet must be washed three times. The reason for wudhu is that without purifying one's body, one's mind cannot be purified. Because Muslims pray five times a day, and thus must pray when at work, at school, and in public spaces, foot baths are a common sight throughout countries with large Muslim populations. Even in the **United States**, a few communities with large numbers of Muslims have installed

Maharaja Slippers. These leather slippers are worn by both men and women in much of the Muslim world. [2007 Copyright Ashwin Kharidehal Abhirama. Image from BigStockPhoto.com]

foot baths in public places so that Muslims would no longer have to wash their feet in public sinks. These foot baths have caused controversy in those communities among non-Muslims.

For many Muslims, feet are also considered to be the lowest part of the body and thus the most unclean. In some North African and Middle Eastern countries, for example, showing the soles of one's feet (or shoes) to others is not acceptable. Westerners traveling in Middle Eastern countries are often warned to sit with their shoes on the floor so that the soles of their feet are not pointed at other people. On the other hand, there is nothing written in the Koran about this, and these beliefs and practices vary from country to country, even when those countries are predominantly Muslim. In fact, beliefs about the impurity of feet may simply stem from cultures in which people's feet got dirty from either going barefoot or wearing **sandals**.

On the other hand, there is ample evidence of the fact that shoes may in fact be impure in many countries with a Muslim majority. Throwing shoes at Muslims is often seen as a grave offense, and in Iraq after the fall of Saddam Hussein, media accounts showed countless images of Iraqis hitting statues and portraits of

Hussein with their shoes as a way of insulting and degrading his memory. And in 2008, just before President Bush left office, an Iraqi journalist threw his own shoes at Bush as a way of protesting the Iraqi war. If shoes are in contact with the ground, which is dirty, and if shoes have to be removed before entering a holy space, then hitting someone with one's shoe is a way of directing symbolic and literal pollution at one's enemy. (This is also seen in ancient royal footstools decorated with images of the king's enemy on them.) But again, the Koran says nothing about the impurity of shoes, and the tradition of hitting someone with shoes extends into India as well, implying that these practices are not grounded in religion but are perhaps based on cultural norms that have more to do with hygiene than with the sacred.

Because shoes are removed before entering a mosque as well as private homes, there are a great variety of shoes available in the Muslim world that are easy to slip on and off, such as mules. *Khussas*, for example, are traditional **slippers** worn by both men and women throughout the Middle East. Originally made of wood, but today made of leather or cloth and often highly decorated with embroidery and beading, khussas are most popular in rural regions.

See also: India; Middle East; Slippers

Further Reading Gulevich, Tanya. *Understanding Islam And Muslim Traditions: An Introduction to the Religious Practices, Celebrations, Festivals, Observances, Beliefs, Folklore, Customs, and Calendar Systems of the World's Muslim Communities, Including an Overview of Islamic History and Geography*. Detroit: Omnigraphics, 2004; Stillman, Yedida Kalfon. *Arab Dress from the Dawn of Islam to Modern Times*. Leiden: Brill, 2003.

J

JACK BOOTS

Jack boots are tall **boots** made of hard **leather**, which were popular in **Europe** in the seventeenth and eighteenth centuries and which were also worn by soldiers in a number of armies in the twentieth century. Jack boots were originally tall, shiny, very hard boots with chunky heels and wide, square toes. They took their name from jack leather, the type of leather that was used to construct them, which was made from waxed leather that is coated with tar or pitch. Jack leather was also used to make beer tankards and other waterproof vessels.

Jack boots, also known as great boots, became popular after 1660 when European nobility began to wear the boots for riding. They were originally designed to be worn over regular shoes so that the wearer could remove his boots after coming indoors and still have on his dress shoes. The inside of the boots were often lined with pockets to store valuables.

Because jack boots were so stiff, they had to be pulled off with a "boot jack," a tool for

Jack boots. Boots like these were worn in the American Civil War. [Copyright 2008 Jupiterimages Corporation]

removing boots, which is another source for the name jack boot. In addition, while the boots were knee high, they were cut away behind the knee to allow the knee to bend over the hard leather.

Jack boots were replaced by Hessian boots, another tall, stiff boot, often decorated with a tassel, in the nineteenth century. Hessians then evolved into **Wellington boots**, popular in Great Britain throughout the nineteenth century. But tall, stiff riding boots were still worn by soldiers and officers on horseback in most of the

European armies from the eighteenth to twentieth centuries. In particular, jack boots (which were no longer worn over shoes) were worn in the French and German armies until the twentieth century. They were also worn by soldiers in the Soviet army and are still worn in the Russian army for dress purposes.

Today, jack boots refer to the tall, pull-up combat boot worn by German soldiers in both world wars. The soles of modern jack boots have hobnails nailed into them in order to make the boot more durable. Today, jack boots are associated almost entirely with the Nazi regime, thanks to film footage of Nazi soldiers "goosetepping" in their jack boots, and with their skinhead neo-Nazi followers who continue to wear them. The term jack boot now is often used to refer to fascism or threats of authoritarianism, as in "jack booted thug."

See also: Boots; Military Shoes and Boots

Further Reading David, Alison Matthews. "War Wellingtons: Military Footwear in the Age of Empire," in Rielle, Georgio and Peter McNeil, eds. *Shoes: A History From Sandals to Sneakers*. London: Berg Publishers, 2006; United States War Department. *Handbook on German Military Forces*. Baton Rouge: Louisiana State University Press, 1990.

JAPAN

Japan has a wide variety of traditional footwear, some of which is still being worn today. For the most part, however, Japanese men and women now wear Western-designed shoes, although Tokyo has become a source of fashion in its own right for both Japan and the Western world.

Traditional Japanese shoes reflect both the climate and environmental features of Japan, the resources available (predominantly rice straw from growing rice), and cultural beliefs and reflect important **class** and status distinctions among the Japanese. For example, it was once mandatory in Japan to remove one's shoes when in front of a social superior as a sign of respect, and the wealthy employed servants to remove their shoes for them when entering a building. In addition, because it is customary in Japan to remove one's shoes before entering a building (both to keep the home clean and also to protect the traditional tatami floor mats), traditional Japanese footwear is designed to be easily slipped on and off.

These modern wooden geta have two low stilts and velvet thongs. [Copyright 2008 Jupiterimages Corporation]

Until the fourth century, the Japanese lived by hunting and gathering, and either went barefoot or wore simple **sandals** of woven plant matter or animal skin. After rice farming was introduced into Japan in the third century, rice farmers began to wear large wooden sled-like sandals called *ta-geta* to keep their feet from sinking into the mud in the rice fields. These are functionally related to the *geta* of today and to **snow shoes**.

The oldest shoes still worn in Japan are sandals made of rice straw, twisted into ropes and plaited to form the sandal's sole, with the ropes acting as straps. Known as *waraji*, these were traditionally worn by peasants and were probably introduced from **China** in the eighth century. Japanese nobles most likely wore Chinese-style closed shoes during this period, like court **boots** made of fabrics like silk brocade or **leather** boots for military officers. **Sumptuary laws** ensured that only elites could wear cloth shoes, while peasants had to wear straw shoes. Starting in the twelfth century, soldiers began wearing a form of waraji known as *ashinaka*, which were easy to run in, and waraji became worn by travelers of all kinds. In fact, waraji are still found at the borders of villages and at roadside shrines. Today, they are still sometimes worn by Buddhist monks.

Another form of plant fiber footwear are the straw snow

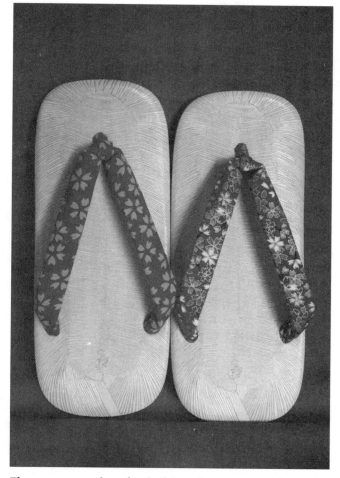

These are examples of colorful modern zori, which are the origins of the modern western flip flop. [Copyright 2008 Jupiterimages Corporation]

boots worn in the mountainous regions of Japan. Made of rice straw, bamboo sheaths, and other materials, they are known as *fukagutsu* and are still worn today. In addition, snow shoes called *kanjiki* are worn in the snowy regions of Japan.

At the end of the eighth century, trade between China and Japan ceased and new forms of footwear developed in Japan. The *zori* is a straw **sandal**, traditionally made with plaited tatami straw soles with a straw rope thong between the toes and originally worn by the upper classes. Zori can also be made of other materials like plaited vinyl, and zori made with silk are worn for special occasions, with one type of zori, the *nikai zori*, given by a man to his fiance as an engagement gift. The zori is the origin of the western **flip flop**.

Another shoe that developed at the end of the eighth century is the *geta*, a wooden platform sandal with a cloth thong, generally with one to three stilts or "teeth" underneath. Geta can be quite high, and the height serves both to protect the feet and the kimono from dirt, mud, or water, and to serve as a marker of status. In this sense, they are functionally related to two kinds of European **clogs**: the patten, worn over shoes to protect footwear and clothing from dirt, and the *chopine*, originally worn for the same reason as the patten, but which evolved into a sign of status for wealthy European women. The geta were worn originally by the elites, with special geta for use by emperors and priests, and became quite fashionable for city dwellers starting in the seventeenth century. Originally, families in Japan made their own shoes, but starting in the fourteenth century craftsmen began making zori and geta for wealthy customers.

During the Edo period (the seventeenth through the nineteenth centuries), Japanese courtesans wore a special geta called the *oiran geta*, which was a very tall, lacquered geta, sometimes with three teeth, which created a more sensual walk. The feet of courtesans were highly sexualized, and the women encouraged this by whitening their feet and painting their toenails. As with the Venetian chopines, sumptuary laws were eventually passed during that time that prohibited the wearing of lacquered geta because of their ostentatious nature.

After industrialization in the nineteenth century, geta became less expensive to produce, making them more accessible to the masses. Geta remained the normative shoe for Japanese citizens until the mid-twentieth century, when many Japanese began wearing closed shoes. Geta are rarely worn today (and many Japanese miss the distinctive "click clack" sound that they made when worn) but are still worn by sumo wrestlers, sushi chefs, and for special occasions.

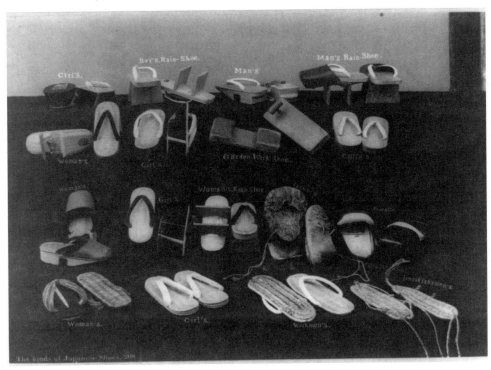

This photo, taken in 1900, shows a number of different traditional Japanese shoes, including a variety of geta and zori. [Photo courtesy of the Library of Congress Prints and Photographs Division]

One special form of geta was the *chakkiri-geta*, which had three teeth and was worn to cut tea leaves. Other traditional geta include *takaba geta*, with very high teeth to wear in the rain (these can be worn with toe caps), heavy iron geta known as *kurogane geta* that are worn during training for jujitsu masters, children's geta that are lower and broader than adult geta, and *pokkuri geta*, which are high hollow-soled geta with one large platform with bells included inside. They are worn by girls on special occasions and make a sound like "pokkuri" when worn.

"Sanbashi no onna." Woodcut of young woman wearing geta by Utagawa Kuniyoshi, 1844–1850. [Photo courtesy of the Library of Congress Prints and Photographs Division]

Because the Japanese remove their shoes before entering homes, a special **sock** evolved to be worn in the house to keep the feet clean. *Tabi* are cotton socks with a separation between the big toe and the rest of the toes and are designed to be worn with thonged zori or geta and, when in a building, to be worn alone. Special tabi known as *jika-tabi* have a rubber sole and can be worn outdoors and are typically worn by construction workers today. At one time, elites only wore their tabi once and handed the used pairs down to their servants.

While most Japanese people wear western-style shoes today, they still retain the tradition of removing shoes before entering the home (and public places like restaurants and the theatre). The shoe cupboard where shoes are stored in a home's entryway (the only place where a visitor can stand in a home wearing shoes) is called a *getabako* or geta box.

Today, the Japanese, especially Japanese youth, are trendsetters when it comes to popular culture and fashion, often leading the way in terms of what others around the world will be wearing. At the end of the twentieth century, for example, young Japanese women began wearing very high **platform shoes** known as *atsuzoko*, which were not only popular but dangerous thanks to their height.

See also: China; Class; Clogs; Flip Flops; Europe; Sandals

Further Reading Chaiklin, Martha. "Purity, Pollution and Place in Traditional Japanese Footwear," in Rielle, Georgio and Peter McNeil, eds. *Shoes: A History From Sandals to Sneakers.* London: Berg Publishers, 2006; Deal, William. *Handbook to Life in Medieval and Early Modern Japan.* New York: Oxford University Press, 2007; Perkins, Dorothy. *Encyclopedia of Japan: Japanese History and Culture, from Abacus to Zori.* New York: Facts on File, 1991.

JOGGING SHOE

Jogging shoes are **athletic shoes** worn while jogging. They became popular during the rise of jogging and other fitness activities during the 1970s. Exercise and physical fitness became important concepts to Americans during the 1970s, leading to the development of a nationwide fitness boom in which exercise, led by jogging, became a major pastime for many Americans. This led to a change in the concept of health and beauty both in the **United States** and beyond as well as a boom in the athletic shoe industry.

Jogging exploded in the 1970s, with millions of people buying special athletic shoes known as jogging shoes. Joggers ran in city and suburban neighborhoods, in parks, on school tracks, in wilderness areas, and in 5 kilometer, 10 kilometer, and even marathon races. Jogging, which is distinct from competitive running, was and is touted as an activity that can increase one's cardiovascular health, build muscles, and make a person look and feel better. The rise of jogging also coincided with the rise of the self-help and personal growth movements in the United States, and jogging's focus on individual achievement fit nicely with the focus of the decade. Jogging is also a democratic sport in that it is available to anyone at any time and doesn't require a gym membership or fancy equipment, aside from a good pair of jogging shoes (and for women, a jog bra). Women, in fact, embraced jogging and became more involved in physical fitness at this time than ever before.

These shoes are specially designed to be worn while jogging. [Copyright 2008 Jupiterimages Corporation]

Like most athletic shoes, jogging shoes are made out of breathable fabric combined with **leather** on the upper, with a rubber sole. The forerunners to modern jogging shoes were the first rubber-soled shoes, called sandshoes or plimsolls, which were first made in the late nineteenth century based on the technology of **vulcanization**, which allowed for rubber to be fused with fabric, and 1917 saw the first rubber-soled shoes sold in the United States under the name of **Keds**. While shoes for specialized sports such as baseball, basketball, tennis, and bicycling were all released during this period, jogging shoes did not emerge until the 1970s. **Reebok** had been making spiked leather shoes for runners since the late nineteenth century, and **Adidas** developed the idea further in the 1920s, creating a line of running shoes in which the number and distribution of **spikes** indicated whether the shoe was for long- or short-distance running. But until the 1970s, these shoes were worn by an elite group of competitors since most normal people had never tried running. Even then, many competitive runners who could not afford spiked running shoes wore simple, flat, rubber-soled sneakers.

Jogging shoes depended on both the rise of the fitness and jogging movements and on the developments in athletic shoe technology, originally pioneered by Nike. Founded in 1964 by a former University of Oregon runner and track and field coach, Phil Knight and Bill Bowerman wanted to create a better running shoe, which they accomplished via innovations like waffle soles, breathable nylon uppers, and cushioning in both the mid-sole and the heel. Nike developed new technologies like foam, air, and gel cushioning in the heels, allowing for much greater shock absorbency when jogging.

Today, joggers have a wide variety of shoes available to them, including those that emphasize cushioning, very lightweight shoes for short distance, shoes that control for pronation and supination, those that emphasize stability, and shoes for running off-road. They are far lighter than the spiked, all-leather shoes of the nineteenth century and early twentieth century and are designed for maximum shock absorbency and comfort.

Today, most Americans own a pair of jogging shoes, although it is thought that less than a quarter of jogging shoes are worn for jogging.

See also: Adidas; Athletic Shoes; Nike; Reebok

Further Reading Fixx, James F. *The Complete Book of Running*. New York: Random House, 1977; Haven, Kendall. *100 Greatest Science Inventions of All Time*. Westport, CT: Libraries Unlimited, 2006; Luciano, Lynne. "A Culture of Narcissism." In *Looking Good: Male Body Image in Modern America*. New York: Hill and Wang, 2001.

JOHN, ELTON

Elton John is a singer, musician, and songwriter who has sold more than 200 million records, has had more than 50 top 40 hits, and has won five Grammy awards. He was knighted by Queen Elizabeth in 1998 and is known for his work on behalf of AIDS charities. He is also known for the extravagant footwear he wore during much of the 1970s.

Elton John's fashions, especially during the 1970s, were incredibly flamboyant and included furs, jumpsuits, and huge sunglasses. He also wore enormous hats and wigs and favored foot-tall, extravagantly decorated **platform shoes**. In fact, he was one of a number of male celebrities who popularized platform shoes and boots for men, a trend that did not survive the decade, however.

Over the years, some of John's most famous shoes have been donated to charity, and one pair of platform books resides in the **Bata Shoe Museum** in Ontario.

See also: Bata Shoe Museum; Platform Shoes

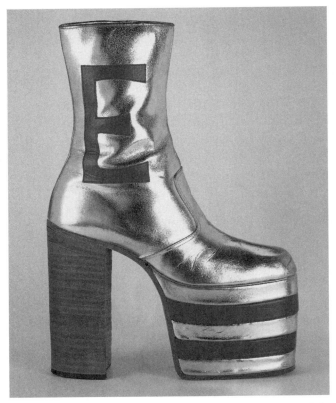

Singer/songwriter Elton John often wore platform boots while performing on stage. [Copyright © 2009 Bata Shoe Museum, Toronto (Photo: Hal Roth)]

Further Reading Schmidt, Mark Ray. *The 1970s.* San Diego: Greenhaven Press, 2000; Sims, Josh, Mal Peachey. *Rock Fashion.* London: Omnibus, 1999.

JORDAN, MICHAEL

Michael Jordan was a professional basketball player from 1984 to 1999 and is known as one of the greatest basketball players of all time, having won the NBA championship six times as well as five MVP awards and a number of other honors. He played for the Chicago Bulls until his second retirement in 1999, but returned to basketball to play for the Washington Wizards for two seasons until permanently retiring in 2003. Michael Jordan is also well known for his extensive product endorsement deals and, in particular, for the Air Jordan shoe created for **Nike**.

In 1984, Nike approached Michael Jordan, who was then in his first year with the Chicago Bulls, as a way to revitalize the company's sales after the decline of jogging's popularity in the 1980s. While Jordan was a new player who already had endorsement deals with other companies, Nike thought that his appeal —he had a charismatic personality on top of being a star athlete—could help create a new market for Nike products, widening their audience from joggers to other sports.

Jordan, however, did not yet wear Nikes and instead was wearing **Converse** and **Adidas** basketball shoes. But Converse did not offer him a lucrative contract, and Adidas did not offer Jordan a deal at all. Jordan ended up signing with Nike, albeit reluctantly, and agreed to have a shoe created in his name. The initial five-year deal was worth $2.5 million to Jordan, but much more to Nike. After the Air Jordan I was released in 1985, the shoe revolutionized the athletic shoe industry. Basketball shoes at that time were white, but the Air Jordans were black and red and were banned by the NBA, although Jordan wore them anyway, paying thousands of dollars in fines. The result was that millions of kids purchased the shoes, wanting to emulate Jordan's athletic excellence and style. The second shoe in the Air Jordan line, the Air Jordan II, came out in 1987 but was less successful than Air Jordan I, and there was a chance that Air Jordan III would not be released. However, Nike invited Jordan to provide input on the new line of shoes, leading to a new design as well as a full line of clothing.

Since the original Air Jordan's release in 1985, there have been 22 incarnations, all based in part on Jordan's input, with the last shoe due to be the Air Jordan XXIII, in 2008. Air Jordan became a sub-brand of Nike known as Jordan Brand in 1997 with the release of Air Jordan XIII; today, Air Jordans do not feature the Nike name or logo. The Jordan Brand releases a new shoe every year and reintroduces an old style for one day each year in order to satisfy collectors.

Michael Jordan's role in the promotion of the Air Jordan was unlike any promotion deal that the **athletic shoe** industry had seen up until that time. Jordan did not simply wear the shoes. He was featured in countless commercials during the 1980s and 1990s, including commercials featuring director and actor Spike Lee. In the commercials, Lee played his character from his 1986 film *She's Gotta Have It* who, in the original film, did not even remove his Air Jordans when having sex. Another commercial drawing from the film featured Lee's character, when trying to figure out why his beloved Nola favored Jordan over him, saying "it's gotta be the shoes," which became a popular tagline. In fact, Spike Lee has collaborated with Jordan and Nike on a number of Air Jordan shoe models, offering the names of some of his characters to the shoes and featured the shoes in many of his movies, like *Do The Right Thing*. He also directed a number of Nike commercials, some featuring Jordan, throughout the 1980s and 1990s.

Nike's success with Michael Jordan goes beyond increasing the company's visibility in other sports like basketball. Michael Jordan, because of his athletic excellence, his personal charisma, and his sense of style, was a perfect person to sell Nikes to new audiences—both kids and adults who play basketball, but also millions of young people, primarily African American, who viewed Jordan as a role model and who idolized him and his lifestyle. The Michael Jordan/Nike commercials not only promised viewers the ability to "be like Mike" (from the Gatorade commercial) in an

---

Killing for Shoes

During the 1980s and 1990s, there was a spate of murders and muggings in urban areas in the United States in which teenagers were killed or injured for their expensive athletic shoes. The shoes were most often identified as Nikes, and in particular, Air Jordans. Social observers blamed the killings (which also used sportswear as the motivation) on the aggressive advertising of companies like Nike that promoted expensive, brand-name shoes to inner city kids who lacked the resources to purchase them. As celebrity-endorsed shoes like Air Jordans became status items for inner city kids, self-esteem and self-worth became linked to the ownership of such shoes, even though their means to purchase them are often limited. While Nike was certainly not directly responsible for the crimes, it did (and still does) spend billions of dollars targeting African-American, inner-city youth with the newest shoe model and its promise of status. And consumers respond. Gang members in particular want their shoes to be in pristine condition and will toss out a pair once they get scuffed or worn. Michael Jordan himself, when confronted with media stories of the killings, expressed regret that the shoes that he thought would help kids to try to achieve great heights instead caused them to kill each other. In June 2008, Nike pulled a line of shoes known as Air Stabs from British retailers after a spate of stabbings in that country, which were unrelated to the shoes.

athletic sense, but they also promised the sort of upward mobility that inner-city kids desire and often try to achieve via athletic performance. Yet the truth is that few kids do achieve financial success through a career in sports, and the enormous hype created by Nike through the marketing of Air Jordans led to a rash of muggings and killings in the 1980s and 1990s, when kids began stealing other people's Air Jordans, often killing to get these valuable and expensive status symbols.

Air Jordans remain popular today, and older versions are highly sought after by collectors.

See also: Advertising; Athletic Shoes; Celebrity Endorsements; Nike

Further Reading Garcia, Bobbito. *Where'd You Get Those?: New York City's Sneaker Culture: 1960–1987*. New York: Testify Books, 2003; Mullin, Bernard J., Stephen Hardy, William Anthony Sutton. *Sport Marketing*. Champaign, IL: Human Kinetics, 2007; Papson, Stephen, Robert Goldman. *Nike Culture: The Sign of the Swoosh*. London: Sage Publications, 1998; Vanderbilt, Tom. *The Sneaker Book: Anatomy of an Industry and an Icon*. New York: The New Press, 1998.

JUDAISM

Judaism is the religion of the Jewish people and dates back 4,000 years. The foundation for Judaism is the Torah, or Old Testament, which is also the first book of the Christian Bible. The beliefs and practices associated with feet and footwear among many Jews today derive from Biblical passages.

Ancient Jews lived in and around what is now the modern state of Israel. Traditionally, the people were farmers and sheep herders. The ancient Hebrews, like other early civilizations of the Middle East, primarily wore **sandals**. After the Roman occupation, footwear among the ancient Jews reflected the footwear in use among the Romans. It was common to go barefoot indoors and, as with other cultures in this area and at this time, sandals were the normative foot covering outdoors; putting on one's sandals was indicative of getting ready to engage in some sort of public activity. Going barefoot outdoors was a sign of extreme poverty, and both captives and slaves were barefoot.

Sandals were made with a thick **leather**, wooden, or palm bark sole and a leather thong attached to the foot (sometimes as a toe strap). Sandals worn by wealthy women were adorned with applique, shells, or jewels. At least some wealthier people also wore closed shoes, either of leather or linen, and sandals with a cap over the heel were also used. Elite women also wore closed shoes, and soldiers wore **boots** that laced up the legs similar to Roman boots.

As in other cultures, the ancient Hebrews removed their shoes when entering a residence, either their own or when visiting another person. Slaves or servants removed the shoes of their masters or of guests when arriving home and were employed as well to put the shoes back on again upon leaving the home. Because of the amount of dust and dirt that feet were exposed to, even when wearing sandals, it was common that one's servants washed one's feet when they arrived home and washed guests' feet as a sign of hospitality.

Entering the temple or engaging in a holy activity also mandated bare feet, and the priests officiated at the temple without shoes. This stems from the Biblical passages in Exodus 3:5 and Joshua 5:15 when God said "put off thy shoes from off they feet, for the place whereon thou standest is holy." In addition, some Hasidic sects remove shoes when approaching the grave of a holy man because it is holy space. Today, Jews do not remove their shoes before entering a synagogue, although the rabbi still removes his or her shoes when conducting the priestly blessing.

Shoes and death are connected in Jewish tradition. Ancient Israelis went barefoot, both indoors and outdoors, during the seven-day mourning period known as sitting Shiva, according to God's instruction in Isaiah 20:2. This is still observed today among many Jews, who refrain from wearing leather shoes during this period. (When shoes, and in particular leather shoes, must be worn, it is customary to place a pebble in one's shoes to remind oneself that they are mourning.) In addition, observant Jews do not wear shoes on Tisha b'Av, the ninth day of

"Victim's Shoes" by photographer Michael Keena, is part of his exhibit, "Impossible to Forget: The Nazi Camps Fifty Years After," that ran through March 23, 2003, at Houston's Holocaust Museum. The images, from 30 Nazi concentration camps, were taken over a dozen years beginning in the early 1980s. [AP Photo/Michael Keena]

Hungarians light candles with torches at the memorial of shoes remembering the Holocaust victims on the bank of the River Danube during a commemoration of the Hungarian Holocaust Day in downtown Budapest, Hungary, April 16, 2008. It is the official memorial day for the more then 600,000 victims of the Hungarian Holocaust, marking the day when members of the World War II Hungarian Nazi party shot Jews into the water at this spot of the River Danube in 1944. [AP Photo/Bela Szandelszky]

mourning when Jews remember the destruction of the first and second Temple of Jerusalem, and on Yom Kippur, the day of atonement. Finally, Jews should not be buried in leather shoes.

Another ancient Jewish tradition is to put the right shoe on first, but to remove the left shoe first and to tie the left shoe first because the right shoe is more important than the left and should not remain uncovered.

Shoes were an important part of making a legal transaction for ancient Jews. The Hebrew term for latchet, or **shoe fastener**, is also the term for binding in general and relates to the concept that shoes were used to bind legal contracts. Taking off one's shoe (or unlacing one's sandal) and giving it to someone else was indicative of making an agreement with them. According to Ruth 4:7–8, "a man plucked off his shoe and gave it to his neighbor: and this was a testimony in Israel." Removing the shoe was also a way of transferring rights of ownership or responsibility and occurs during marriage rituals and other partnerships.

In the ancient Jewish tradition, a widow who is expected to marry her brother-in-law can remove a *halitzah* shoe, a **moccasin**-like shoe made from the skin of a kosher animal, from his foot, releasing him from the obligation, so that she may marry another man. On the other hand, if the man refused to marry her as he is obligated, the woman or an elder can remove his shoe, spit on it or him, and shame him by saying he is a man "whose shoe has been loosed." It is thought that the European and American tradition of throwing a shoe after a bride or newly-wed couple (or tying shoes onto the car of the newlyweds) comes from the ancient idea of the shoe as a symbol of sending someone away.

Shoes often have a different symbolic association for many Jews today. After the end of World War II, photos and collections of shoes left behind at concentration camps after their Jewish owners were murdered have become a potent symbol of the horrors of the Holocaust. Indeed, since the Holocaust piles of shoes are often used to represent other mass slaughters and genocides, and memorials of all kinds often use shoes to represent the masses of dead.

See also: Beliefs; Class; Classical Civilizations; Middle East

Further Reading de Vaux, Roland. *Ancient Israel: Its Life and Institutions*. New York: McGraw Hill, 1961; Nahshon, Edna, ed. *Jews and Shoes*. New York: Berg Publishers, 2008.

KEDS

Keds is the brand name of the first **athletic shoes** ever released in the **United States**, and they are still sold today. Today, the Keds brand is owned by Stride Rite Corporation, a manufacturer of children's shoes.

Keds were originally produced by the U.S. Rubber Company, which was one of a number of rubber companies to emerge in the 1890s after the discovery of **vulcanization**, which allowed for the creation of durable and flexible rubber products. In terms of footwear, it also allowed for the shoe upper to be fused with the sole while the rubber is still liquid, making the bond much more durable. One of the first products to be created with the new technology were rubber-soled shoes, known as sandshoes or plimsolls. The U.S. Rubber Company was the first American company to license the technology of vulcanization and to sell shoes with rubber soles.

For the first few decades of the company's existence, from 1892 to 1913, U.S. Rubber sold shoes under 30 different brand names, which in 1916 were consolidated under one name: Keds. The company wanted to call their shoes "peds," but that name was already taken so they settled upon Keds instead. The first Keds were sold in 1917 and were dubbed "**sneakers**" by the advertising agency hired by Keds because the shoes were so quiet that one could sneak up on someone in them.

In 1926, Keds released the Triumph, the iconic Keds shoe, made with a canvas upper, cotton lacing, and a flat rubber sole. By the 1920s, leading tennis players were wearing Keds, and in the 1930s the company began developing new technologies to make their shoes more comfortable, including a simple cushioning system for the arch. By this time, Keds and **Converse** were the primary brands of athletic shoes in the United States. In 1938, Keds introduced the Kedette, a woman's heeled canvas shoe. While Kedettes no longer have heels, these shoes are a good example of Keds' movement into the casual and even dress shoe markets. At the same time the company was moving its shoes into everyday wear, it was also developing shoes for the more serious athlete. In 1949, the ProKeds basketball shoe was released, and over the years ProKeds shoes have been worn by some of the biggest professional and college basketball players, like Kareem Abdul Jabar.

In the 1950s, U.S. Rubber actively marketed to kids with characters like Kedso the Clown and Kolonel Keds, who starred in Keds television commercials during daytime cartoons and children's shows. Kedso the Clown sang in his commercials, "if you want shoes with lots of pep, get Keds, kids' Keds. For bounce and zoom and in every step, get Keds, kids' Keds."

The U.S. Rubber Company changed its name to Uniroyal in the 1960s and turned much of its efforts towards manufacturing and selling tires, although it continued to sell Keds as well. Stride Rite, founded in 1919 as the Green Shoe Manufacturing Company, bought Keds from Uniroyal in 1979 for $18 million.

Keds began to lose favor with the public in the 1970s as new companies like **Nike** emerged to take over the athletic shoe market. Because of many of Nike's innovations, like the waffle heel or air and gel cushioning, athletic shoes became more performance oriented. Because most Keds were not designed with real athletic performance in mind, they began to feel old fashioned compared to the new technologies, although young women and kids continued to wear them in great numbers.

Keds became popular again in the 1980s with the endorsement of Sugar Ray Leonard and the popularity of Keds among young girls who enjoyed their classic retro style, although for the next two decades the company's fortunes rose and fell. Because of Keds's association with a "simpler" time in America, Keds have always had a foothold in popular culture, worn by Baby in *Dirty Dancing*, Joanie in *Happy Days*, Kelly in *Saved by the Bell*, and cheerleaders everywhere. But to many, by the 1990s Keds seemed hopelessly out of date.

In the last few years, the company rallied again, bringing in designers like Lily Pulitzer, Todd Oldham, Max Azria, and Nanette Lepore to design new lines and hiring actress Mischa Barton as the new face of the company in 2005. The company has also been trading on the shoe's retro appeal by reintroducing, in 2004, the classic Triumph sneaker as well as other classics like the Champion. ProKeds, too, has reintroduced in the last couple of years classics like the Royal Canvas and Royal Master shoe. The company also has dozens of other styles of shoes, including **sandals** and wedge heels, demonstrating the brand's continued popularity among young women.

Keds also offers custom-sneaker design, where customers can choose fabrics and colors and customize the shoe with their own design. It is clear that Keds's approach is to regain and solidify its hold on the lifestyle market while leaving the athletic market to companies like Nike and Adidas. Finally, Keds has been capitalizing on the use of ProKeds among the hip hop community by signing a licensing agreement with hip hop mogul Damon Dash in 2004, although Stride Rite bought back the name in 2008 in the midst of a new rebranding effort.

See also: Advertising; Athletic Shoes; Celebrity Endorsements

Further Reading Haven, Kendall. *100 Greatest Science Inventions of All Time*. Westport, CT: Libraries Unlimited, 2006.

KINKY BOOTS

Kinky Boots is a 2005 film about a family-owned shoe company in England that had to turn to making **fetish** footwear in order to save the business and the workers' jobs. After the company became known for the new footwear, they became known as the Kinky Boot Factory. The term kinky boots also refers to fetish **boots**.

Based on a true story, the film tells the story of Charles Price, the son of a Northamptonshire **shoemaker**, who is forced to take over his father's business after his death, only to find that the company is failing. After meeting a drag queen named Lola who complains about the difficulty of finding good shoes, Price decides to begin making men's drag and fetish footwear, hiring Lola as the company's new designer.

The film was based on the story of W. J. Brookes & Company, which had been making men's shoes and boots for 115 years in Northampton, the center of traditional **shoemaking** in England. Current owner Steve Pateman took the company over after his father died. While Patemen did not actually meet a drag queen named Lola, he did begin making fetish footwear for both men and women after being contacted by a fetish shop named Laces, which was looking for a new supplier. The Kinky Boot Factory is the nickname for the company today, after the popularity of the film.

Kinky shoes, boots, accessories, and clothing are now sold under the name Divine and are still made in Northamptonshire and sold to fetish shops throughout England and abroad. While the original employees of Brookes no longer make the shoes (instead, they are made by another family company), Divine now sells its own shoes as well as shoes purchased from American manufacturers that sell to American exotic dancers. Divine's men's shoes are created on a men's last (rather than just a large women's last) so that they fit men's feet better, although most of the shoes are still purchased and worn by women.

Kinky boots also refers more generally to fetish boots. Fetish boots are boots with extraordinarily high **stiletto** heels, are typically made from **patent leather** or shiny synthetics like pleather or vinyl, and are usually thigh high. Kinky boots are worn by dominatrixes and members of the Bondage Discipline Submission Masochism (BDSM) community and can be worn by both men and women, although they are more commonly worn by women.

"Kinky Boots" is also the name of a 1964 song sung by Patrick Macnee and Honor Blackman, the two stars of the

These shiny black stiletto boots are popular among dominatrixes and others in the fetish community. [2006 copyright Robert Hammer. Image from BigStockPhoto.com]

British spy show, *The Avengers*. Both Blackman and Diana Rigg, who starred in the show after Blackman left, wore tight **leather** clothing (catsuits in particular) and boots in the show. It was at this time that fetish wear like catsuits and thigh-high boots from the fetish world moved into mainstream fashion, in part via *The Avengers* and also when **go go boots** were first introduced in England and the **United States**. Go go boots are similar to kinky boots in that both are tight boots made of shiny material. But while kinky boots are generally knee high to thigh high, with stiletto heels, go go boots, in their original incarnation in the 1960s, were mid-calf to knee high and had very low heels.

See also: Boots; Go Go Boots; Eroticism; Fetishes

Further Reading Rogers, Dave. *The Complete Avengers: Everything You Ever Wanted to Know about The Avengers and The New Avengers*. New York: MacMillan, 1989; Steele, Valerie. *Fetish: Fashion, Sex and Power*. New York: Oxford University Press, 1996; Steele, Valerie. "Shoes and the Erotic Imagination," in Rielle, Georgio and Peter McNeil, eds. *Shoes: A History From Sandals to Sneakers*. London: Berg Publishers, 2006.

KOREA

Koreans share many customs related to feet and footwear with **China**, with whom they share a border, and **Japan**. For example, Koreans remove their shoes before entering a home, temple, and many restaurants. Most shoes in Korea are thus designed to be easily slipped on and off and have no laces or straps, and most homes have shelves or cubbyholes in the entryway to store shoes of the residents and guests.

On the other hand, it is not customary to display bare feet in front of people in Korea, so, like the Japanese, Koreans wear **socks** indoors. The traditional indoor sock is known as *poson*, *bushon*, or *beoseon*, and are tight-fitting cotton socks with upturned toes (padded for winter), which have been worn since the Joseon period (fourteenth through nineteenth centuries) by both men and women.

Namakshin. These Korean clogs derive from Dutch sailors who were stranded in Korea in the seventeenth century. [Copyright © 2009 Bata Shoe Museum, Toronto (Photo: Brian Hillier)]

One of the oldest forms of shoe in Korea is the *chipshin*, a canoe-shaped straw shoe with open toes worn by peasants, which has largely been replaced by white leather shoes today. The most common shoe worn traditionally in Korea is a flat **slipper** with slightly upturned toes, also in the shape of a canoe, known as a *kajukjin*. Worn by both men and women (although women's are narrower and made with more delicate fabrics), these shoes have been modernized with a heel today and still retain the upturned toe. These shoes are traditionally made with leather, cotton, felt, or silk and come in a wide variety of colors; *kkotsin* are embroidered with a floral pattern. Today, men and women who have traditional Korean weddings still wear these distinctive boat-shaped shoes.

Gomooshin are traditional shoes, once made of leather and introduced by Japan but now made of rubber. Shaped like most Korean shoes in the shape of a canoe, these shoes were worn by Korean farmers when working outside to protect the feet from water and mud.

Another traditional Korean shoe is the *namakshin*, a carved wooden **clog** with two stilts. Similar to the Italian *chopine*, the Indian *paduka*, the Japanese *geta*, and the Middle Eastern *stilted sandal*, the namakshin was originally developed to protect the feet and clothing from mud and dirt, but unlike many stilted shoes, it was still worn into the twentieth century. Like other Korean shoes, women's namakshins had pointed toes. The history of the namakshin comes not from Asia, but from

The kajukjin is the most common form of traditional Korean shoe today. Worn by both men and women, the men's version has a more bulbous toe than the women's. [2008 copyright Lora Morier. Image from BigStockPhoto.com]

These straw shoes, or chipshin, are open at the fronts and sides like a sandal. [2008 copyright Jupiterimages Corporation]

Holland. In 1651, a Dutch merchant ship shipwrecked off the shore of Korea and the sailors who were left behind began making traditional Dutch clogs to sell to local people.

Another form of wooden shoes are *mokhwa*, wooden semi-**boots** covered with leather, with legs made of cloth and covered in fur, felt, silk, or leather. These were worn by officials during the Joseon period for ceremonial purposes, and are still worn today by grooms in traditional weddings.

Like other cultures, in Korea, the shoes as well as the feet express a number of important social features related to the wearer. **Sumptuary laws** restricted the wearing of certain colors to the wealthy, while commoners could only wear white and pale colors.

See also: China; Clogs; Europe; India; Japan; Middle East

Further Reading Pratt, Keith, Richard Rutt, James Hoare. *Korea: A Historical and Cultural Dictionary*. Surrey: Curzon Press, 1999.

LEATHER

Leather is the tanned skin of animals and usually refers to the skin of cows. Leather is one of the oldest and most common material used in the construction of footwear. Tanned leather is the most commonly used leather in footwear and is made from the middle layer of the animal's skin. Tanning preserves animal skin and also makes it both durable and flexible.

Rawhide refers to leather that is not tanned. Instead, the skin is removed from an animal during butchering, the flesh is scraped away, and the skin is soaked in a solution of water and lime or lye, and then stretched and dried, and sometimes also smoked. Sometimes the hair is left on and sometimes it is removed during this process. In societies where the technology of tanning was not developed, or in cases where a tougher leather is desired, rawhide has also been used in the making of shoes, especially for the soles. Animal skin that has not been treated at all will quickly decompose, rendering it useless for footwear or anything else. Animal skins that are treated but that still have the fur or hair on the outside are known as deer skin, seal skin, bear skin, sheep skin, and so forth. Untanned, but treated, skins from animals with fur are known as pelts.

Tanning was first developed in the Neolithic period, about 7,000 years ago in South Asia, and later in a variety of locations through the **Middle East** and Near East. By the first millennium, tanning was practiced in all of the ancient and **classical civilizations** of the old world.

Tanning in ancient times involved soaking the skins in water, scraping away the flesh, and eliminating the hair by using urine or lime. The skin was further softened by soaking it in animal brains (usually, the animal's own brains) or by rubbing and soaking the skin in animal dung and water. The actual tanning process involved using the chemicals derived from plant tannins, such as tree bark, to make the skin elastic and strong.

Because of the filthy and smelly nature of the work, tanning was done outside of towns by the poorest of citizens. On the other hand, because of the amount of work involved in tanning leather, leather was expensive, which is one reason why shoes were primarily worn by the wealthy prior to modern times.

Tanners were and still are in many places drawn from the lowest classes. In **India**, where working with the skins of dead animals, especially cows, is considered to be unclean, tanners are known as "untouchables," and in **Japan** in the nineteenth century, people who worked with animal skins were called the "greatly defiled." In both cases, they were outcasts from society.

The Roman methods of tanning were lost during the Middle Ages, so European shoes were initially made from untanned, but treated, rawhide. Tanning was reintroduced into **Europe** by Arabs, who had continued to keep the technology alive and brought it with them when they conquered Spain in the eighth century.

Today, tanning uses modern chemicals to treat the skin, after first curing the skin with salt to prevent decomposition, removing the flesh with a fleshing machine, and soaking the skin in brine. The skins are soaked in water to which lime is added to remove the hair, along with a variety of toxic chemicals. After deliming the skin, it is treated with enzymes, salt, and sulfuric acid, after which it is soaked in water and biocides and is ready to be tanned, during which the skin is stretched and soaked in a concentration of either vegetable tannin, chromium sulfate, formaldehyde, or synthetic polymers for eight to 12 hours. It is this final stage of the process that transforms the skin into leather. It wasn't until the end of the nineteenth century that tanning chemicals other than plant products were first used, such as chromium sulfate.

Tanning is dangerous to the workers who work with it. Chromium is a known carcinogen that can cause convulsions, liver and kidney damage, ulcers, and even lung cancer. The chemicals used in leather production affect nearly everyone in the supply chain, with tannery workers and leather workers at risk of a variety of cancers from leather dust, chromium, and other chemicals. Even **shoemakers** are at increased risk for cancer. In Third World countries that slaughter cattle and produce leather for the international market, tanning is even more dangerous and is primarily carried out amongst the poor. Indeed, production of hides and skins has shifted to developing countries like **China** and India, which now produce most of the world's leather. These countries have lower labor costs and more lenient environmental regulations.

Because of the toxins used to prevent skins from rotting, tanning causes environmental destruction and ensures that the skins will take decades to biodegrade. For example, the tanning of buffalo hides during the great buffalo extermination of the nineteenth century was a primary factor in the destruction of many forests and pollution of many rivers on the eastern seaboard in the **United States**. For every pound of leather, a pound of waste is produced, which can contaminate air, water, and the ground and spread to humans. In China, where much of today's leather is produced, rivers have been poisoned by the waste produced by tanning, and local people can no longer swim in them or drink from them.

The leather used in shoes includes full-grain leather, which refers to leather that has been tanned, but not otherwise sanded, corrected-grain leather that has had any imperfections sanded or removed, and split leather, which is what is left of the animal's skin after the top-grain leather has been removed. Split leather is used to create fuzzy suede because it does not have the top or skin on it. **Patent leather**, developed in the nineteenth century, is leather that has been coated with plastic to make it shiny. Today, shoe soles are commonly made out of synthetic materials, with leather being reserved for use in the uppers.

Other animal skins used in shoes include deer skin, which is the most popular material for making Native American **moccasins**, and seal skin, which is waterproof and is thus used for boots worn in northern climates like **Alaska** and the **Arctic Region**. Other animals used in traditional shoes include caribou, bison, and elk. Exotic leathers are used in high-end shoes today and are taken from animals like ostrich, alligator, and snake, and kangaroo skin is used in soccer shoes today. Some of these animals have been hunted to near extinction thanks to their use in the shoe trade.

Because many people will not wear leather or leather from certain types of animals because of moral or religious reasons, the identity of the animal must be noted on any leather product in a number of countries. In India, for instance, where Hindus consider the cow to be sacred, leather made from cows is not regularly used, while Muslims do not use products made from the skin of pigs.

Leather, or the skin of animals in general, is often prohibited during holy times, or in sacred spaces, perhaps because leather is derived from dead animals. For instance, Greeks, Romans, and Egyptians all had special, non-leather **sandals** that could be worn in sacred temples because leather was not allowed. Nor is leather allowed in Hindu temples. In addition, Jews both today and in Biblical times refrained from wearing leather shoes during mourning, on Tisha b'Av, the ninth day of mourning, and on Yom Kippur, the day of atonement. Jews also should not be buried in leather shoes. In **Europe**, it was believed that leather shoes had a protective quality, in part because spirits fear leather.

Finally, vegetarians, vegans, and animal advocates generally shun leather because of the animal suffering that is involved in making it. Leather is a byproduct of the meat industry in most countries, but in India, where much of today's leather comes from, it comes from spent dairy cows who are trucked out of India to be slaughtered with methods that were long ago made illegal in the United States. In the United States, too, animal protection organizations have long documented the mistreatment of cattle who are awaiting slaughter

> ### *Werner Herzog Eats His Shoe*
>
> Werner Herzog is a German film director who makes complicated and artistic films, including *Fitzcarraldo*, *Grizzly Man*, and *Aguirre, Wrath of God*. In 1980, Les Blank, a documentary filmmaker, directed a film called *Werner Herzog Eats His Shoe*, in which Herzog eats his own shoe to fulfill a promise that he made to fellow filmmaker Errol Morris. Morris had been filming a documentary called *Gates of Heaven*, about pet cemeteries, when Herzog challenged him to a bet, agreeing to eat his own shoe if Morris ever completed the movie and showed it in a public theatre. (*Gates of Heaven* was released in 1978 to wide critical acclaim.) In *Werner Herzog Eats His Shoe*, Herzog boils a leather shoe at gourmet restaurant Chez Panisse and eats the upper in front of the UC Theater in Berkeley, where *Gates of Heaven* was playing.

and the suffering of those raised for both meat and leather in this country. Because of ethical concerns about leather, there is now a wide variety of vegan or non-leather shoes on the market, made with materials like microfiber, pleather, vinyl, and canvas. These range from low-end shoes that are purchased from retailers like **Payless Shoe Source** to high-end shoes created by designers like Stella McCartney and Marc Bouwer.

See also: Classical Civilizations; China; Europe; India; Islam; Japan; Judaism; Middle East; Vegan Shoes

Further Reading Thorstensen, Thomas C. *Practical Leather Technology*. Huntington, NY: Robert E. Krieger Publishing Co., 1976; Welsh, Peter C. *Tanning in the United States to 1850*. Washington, DC: United States National Museum, 1964.

L'EGGS

L'eggs is a brand of panty hose produced by **hosiery** manufacturer **Hanes**. Hanes Hosiery, established in 1901 as Shamrock Mills, led the way in making nylon stockings in the 1940s, seamless stockings in the 1950s, and panty hose in the 1960s. In 1979, Sara Lee Corporation engineered a hostile takeover of Hanes, but Hanes split off from Sara Lee in 2006.

Women have worn stockings since the Middle Ages, when they wore hose made of woven cloth and held up by a garter tied around the leg. The production of stockings became easier in the sixteenth century with the invention of the knitting machine, allowing for knit wool stockings and for the wealthy, silk stockings. Later, cotton stockings were made as well. It wasn't until the twentieth century that women's stockings were first worn above the knee, as women's skirts until the 1920s covered most of their legs. Now silk stockings, followed by nylon stockings, worn with a garter belt or an elastic garter around the thigh became mandatory dress for women, followed by the emergence of the panty hose in the 1960s, which eventually replaced the separate stocking and garter and liberated many women from the discomfort of these garments.

There were not many companies making panty hose at this time, and with millions of American women entering the job market in the 1970s, there was a great demand. Hanes was one of the first companies to take advantage of this demand by introducing in 1969 a line of panty hose packaged in a white plastic egg, called L'eggs. During the 1970s and 1980s, L'eggs was the biggest panty hose brand in the **United States**, thanks to clever marketing strategies. Besides introducing the innovative egg packaging, Hanes was the first big-name company to sell panty hose in supermarkets, drug stores, and convenience stores (on top of department stores), making the product and the brand a household name and wiping out the old-fashioned stockings and garters. L'eggs were displayed in their own special display unit, separating them from the other brands of hosiery then in the stores at the time.

The company's flagship product, Sheer Energy, was released in 1973. L'eggs also made a variety of control-top panty hose and created one of the first lines aimed at African Americans, called Brown Sugar, as well as one of the first plus-size panty hose lines, Just My Size.

In 1991, L'eggs discontinued the use of the plastic egg and started selling the panty hose in a cardboard box with an ovoid peak in order to save costs. The plastic was costly and created extra costs for transportation and storage. In addition, the company cited the environmental benefits of switching to cardboard when announcing the change. L'eggs was also responding to a decade-long downturn in panty hose sales since the mid-1980s, when sales were at their highest. Sales in the industry had been declining as their increased durability meant less replacement purchases and as bare legs became acceptable in the workplace.

L'eggs remains the biggest-selling panty hose brand in the world today, and the company sells panty hose, tights, and shapewear.

See also: Hosiery; Hanes

Further Reading Grass, Milton. *The History of Hosiery, from the Piloi of Ancient Greece to the Nylons of Modern America*. New York: Fairchild Publications, 1955.

LIFTS

Lifts refer to inserts placed inside of shoes to make the wearer appear taller. Lift shoes, also known as elevator shoes, are shoes that are built with such an insert inside it. Lifts are worn by men who are worried that they are too short as well as by people with irregular leg lengths.

High heels were first worn by European men in the sixteenth century and were part of a fashionable man's wardrobe for almost 300 years. At the end of the eighteenth century, men's heels dropped and, with the exception of the 1970s when high **platform shoes** were popular for men, and a handful of heeled shoes such as Cuban heels and **cowboy boots**, men have not worn high heels since.

The end of high heels for men is bad news to shorter-than-average men, since tall men are valued in cultures around the world. In fact, studies indicate that women are drawn to men who are taller than they are, leading scientists to posit that height in men is a sign of good genes. In addition, recent research has shown that taller men father more children than shorter men, indicating that height really may be an indicator of good genes and reproductive fitness. Another recent study demonstrates that shorter men have a harder time getting hired than taller men and, on average, make less money. Perhaps for this reason, many short men lie about their height, and many men use artificial means to elevate themselves and to decrease the social and business handicaps that often accompany short men.

It has long been rumored that Hollywood celebrities like Sylvester Stallone, Russell Crowe, and Tom Cruise fudge their height by wearing lifts in their shoes, or custom-made elevator shoes. Actors in particular are at a disadvantage if they are short because studios will be less likely to hire them as action stars or as romantic leads against tall actresses.

For men who only want to appear an inch or so taller, a one-inch lift can fit into a regular shoe. For men who want to appear taller than that, however, custom-made shoes or **orthopedic shoes** designed to be extra deep have to be worn, in order to accommodate a taller lift. It is said that the shoes worn by celebrities today can't be distinguished from an ordinary shoe, especially since they are generally covered by trousers.

Lifts, elevator shoes, and orthopedic shoes are sold through a variety of Web sites and mail-order companies, with a great deal more variety in men's shoes than women's since men are the primary customer. Elevator shoes can add between two and four inches to one's height.

See also: Gender; High Heels; Men's Shoes; Orthopedic Shoes

Further Reading Munzenberg, K. Joachim. *The Orthopedic Shoe: Indications and Prescription.* Weinheim, Germany: VCH, 1985.

MARCOS, IMELDA

Imelda Marcos was the first lady of the Philippines from 1965 to 1986, and, after her husband, Ferdinand Marcos, declared martial law in 1972, she also took on a number of posts in her husband's government. After the 1986 revolution that resulted in her husband losing his post, the Marcoses left the Philippines and much of the world found out about her extravagant lifestyle, including a collection of hundreds of gowns, handbags, and more than 1,000 pairs of shoes. The new president of the Philippines, Corazon Aquino, charged the Marcoses with attaining their vast wealth through illegitimate means, while Marcos's response has always been that her husband, who died in 1989, was a successful gold trader.

> I did not have three thousand pairs of shoes, I had one thousand and sixty.
>
> IMELDA MARCOS

Today, Imelda Marcos is infamous around the world for her shoes, which to many observers visibly signified the extravagance and greed of the couple when most of their own citizens were living in poverty. Marcos's shoes, size eight-and-a-half, were almost entirely designer brands, including **Ferragamo**, Givenchy, Chanel, Christian Dior, and Charles Jourdan, as well as shoes made by Filipino designers. They included **stilettos**, **pumps**, **slippers**, **boots**, and **sandals**. She was wearing black **espadrilles** when she and her husband fled the country.

Reports of the number of shoes that were left in Imelda's closet—actually, five rooms of the palace were said to be devoted to housing her shoes—in Malacanang Palace vary, with some reports placing the number as high as 3,400 pairs (the figure listed in the *Guiness Book of World Records*). In any case, the number was not only high; it was so high as to boggle the mind of the average person and overshadowed other equally ostentatious figures, such as the tons of gold, billions of dollars, millions of dollars worth of jewels, hundreds of priceless paintings, and numerous homes and palaces owned by the couple. Shoes, because they often symbolize a woman's materialistic nature and vanity, were the items that were seized on the most by the public. One reason may be because it seems clear that she could never wear all of the shoes, making their acquisition even more wasteful.

The possessions of the Marcoses were seized by the new government of the Phillipines after the revolution, and the couple was banned from entering the country. President Aquino briefly put many of the shoes on display in Malacanang Palace to show the greed and extravagance of the former dictator and his wife.

A shoe bearing the name of former first lady Imelda Marcos, widow of former strongman Ferdinand Marcos, is displayed at the Malacanang Presidential Museum in Manila on September 29, 2005. At the height of her power, Imelda gained notoriety for shopping trips to the world's swankiest boutiques, glitzy parties, and lavish beautification projects in the midst of the Philippines's grinding poverty. [AP Photo/ Aaron Favila]

However, Marcos has said that she did not buy many of the shoes, but that they were gifts from designers and that it was her duty as first lady to be a "star" to average Filipinos.

Imelda Marcos was allowed to return to the Philippines in 1991. In 2001, the mayor of Manila opened a museum dedicated to the "shoe capital" of the Philippines, the Marikina district of Manila, in order to bring in tourism. The museum was initially called the Footwear Museum of Marikina and includes displays on the 100-year history of the shoe district as well as more than 700 pairs of Imelda Marcos's shoes, along with those of other famous Filipinos. Marcos was present for the opening of the museum, now known simply as the Shoe Museum, and was able to handle her shoes for the first time in 15 years. Marikina City also possesses the world's largest pair of shoes, which are 18 feet long, seven feet wide, and six feet high.

Imelda Marcos now lives in an opulent apartment in Manila, and, after having been elected to the country's Congress in 1995 and having run for president in 1992 and 1998, she is now retired, but has discussed designing a fashion line. She has said that she now has more shoes than she ever had while First Lady.

See also: Class; Gender

Further Reading Bonner, Raymond. *Waltzing with a Dictator: The Marcoses and the Making of American Policy*. New York: Times Books, 1987; Ellison, Katherine W. *Imelda, Steel Butterfly of the Philippines*. New York: McGraw-Hill, 1988.

MEN'S SHOES

While today women's and men's shoes, with the exception of **athletic shoes**, are strongly differentiated by style, for much of human history this was not the case. Until the Middle Ages and even the Renaissance, men's shoes and women's shoes were more similar than they were different. Additionally, while today women tend to own and wear more pairs of shoes than men, and shoe design is almost entirely focused on women's shoes, this has also not always been the case. Throughout history and across cultures, upper-class men's shoes have often been highly ornamental while commoners wore practical shoes.

For example, pointed-toe shoes known as *poulaines*, which were inspired by shoes worn in the **Middle East**, became fashionable among European noblemen starting in the twelfth century and reached their height of popularity in the fourteenth and fifteenth centuries. Also known as *krakows*, these shoes had toes a third or more longer than the foot; some had toes as long as 24 inches, and only the very wealthy could wear the very long toes, so toe length became a sign of status for well-to-do men. Women's shoes at this time were relatively conservative, and poor European men primarily wore **clogs**.

Another extravagant men's shoe was known as the duckbill or bear paw. These were low-cut slippers with very wide, square toes, and became popular in the sixteenth century, again among European nobility. The fabric on the toes of these shoes was slashed to reveal the brightly colored lining or fur inside the shoes. Because of the extravagance, both duck bills and poulaines were the subject of **sumptuary laws** that were enacted to restrict the extravagance of the shoes and to ensure that only elite men could wear them.

In addition, **high heels** were not initially worn by women. They were first worn by European noblemen, whose riding **boots** were heeled (as were riding boots in other parts of the world, such as the Middle East, from where the practice emerged). Starting in the sixteenth century, it became popular for men in the European courts to wear heeled shoes as indoor wear.

Through the seventeenth and eighteenth centuries, wealthy men throughout Europe were wearing high-heeled shoes, and Louis XIV wore five inch red heels during his reign. It goes without saying that high heels were not only unaffordable but also impractical for working peo-

Men's dress shoes. These Oxfords are conservative and well made, both features associated with men's shoes today. [Copyright 2008 Jupiterimages Corporation]

ple. Heels went out of fashion after the Revolutionary era at the end of the eighteenth century, and when they returned at the end of nineteenth century only women wore them. Men's shoes have had heels of about an inch or less since this time.

In fact, men's shoes since the nineteenth century have been almost exceptional in their plainness. **Cowboy boots**, which have heels of up to two inches, and dance shoes known as Cuban heels, which are worn by male ballroom dancers, are both exceptions to this rule, but both kinds of shoes are worn in specific contexts, and the heels serve a specific purpose. The other exception was during the 1970s, when high-heeled **platform shoes** became fashionable, first among rock stars, pimps, and disco aficionados and finally among hip urban men.

Today, however, men's shoes, whether worn by upper or lower classes, tend to be relatively practical and basic in appearance. Working men's shoes, especially, are made to be functional and comfortable, allowing their wearers to move easily and to do a variety of things, while women's shoes are designed and worn primarily for aesthetic reasons.

Working-class men have always worn practical shoes that are appropriate for their occupations, from the clogs of European peasants to the cowboy boots worn by cowboys and ranchers to the work boots worn many working men today. Boots, however, emerged in Europe as the footwear of upper-class men, who wore them first for riding and later as officers in the military, and for whom boots were a sign of status.

The military is a good example of this. Historically, in Europe, officers wore tall, shiny boots that evolved from riding boots, and had to be polished by servants. Jack boots, Hessian boots, and **Wellington boots** are all examples of the boots favored by officers in many European armies. Because narrow feet were associated with high-bred status, these boots were also quite narrow. Soldiers, on the other hand, wore wide ankle boots known as Blücher boots, which were often poorly made and ill fitting.

Today, middle-class and upper-class men wear shoes that signal their status via their workmanship and the quality of their materials, but not their ornamentation. Men, like women, are often judged based on the quality of their shoes, and a well-made shoe shows that the wearer is a man of good judgement and taste. Upper-class men in particular wear shoes that demonstrate their taste and elegance, but which are understated. Men's shoes tend to be conservative, well made, and functional. Men who collect shoes and who wear fancy shoes are often maligned as gay or feminine, since coveting shoes and wearing ornamental shoes is seen as a female and trivial pursuit.

Men's shoe styles change very slowly, as opposed to women's shoes, which see new styles released multiple times per year. When men's shoes do change, the changes tend to be utilitarian and not strictly for the purposes of fashion.

See also: Boots; Cowboy Boots; Gender; High Heels

Further Reading Breward, Christopher. "Fashioning Masculinity: Men's Footwear and Modernity," in Rielle, Georgio and Peter McNeil, eds. *Shoes: A History from Sandals to Sneakers.* London: Berg Publishers, 2006; McNeil, Peter, Giorgio Riello. "The Male Cinderella: Shoes, Genius and Fantasy," in Rielle, Georgio and Peter McNeil, eds. *Shoes: A History From Sandals to Sneakers.* London: Berg Publishers, 2006; O'Keeffe, Linda. *Shoes: A Celebration of Pumps, Sandals, Slippers & More.* New York: Workman Publishing, 1996.

MIDDLE EAST

The Middle East refers to the region of the world that includes the countries of North **Africa** and Western Asia, which surround the Mediterranean Sea, as well as the countries of and near the Arabian Peninsula. With the exception of Israel, most countries in what we think of as the Middle East are predominantly Muslim, although there is a substantial number of Christians in those countries as well.

Religious and cultural beliefs about feet and shoes in the Middle East often revolve around the idea of purity and impurity.

In **Islam**, it is customary to remove one's shoes before entering a mosque, and Muslims remove their shoes before praying, whether in a mosque, at home, or anywhere else. This is the practice throughout most of the countries of the Middle East today. In addition, Muslims must wash their feet as well as hands, hair, and face before praying, a practice called *wudhu*. Because Muslims pray five times a day and thus must pray when at work, at school, and in public spaces, public foot baths are common features in Middle Eastern countries.

Feet are also considered unclean in many Middle Eastern countries. Therefore it is often considered disrespectful to show the soles of one's feet (or shoes) to others. Westerners traveling in Middle Eastern countries are often warned to sit with their shoes on the floor so that the soles of their feet are not pointed at other people. These practices may stem from cultures in which people's feet got dirty from either going barefoot or wearing **sandals**. On the other hand, women in many Middle Eastern societies take great care of their feet, decorating them with **henna** and adorning them with jewelry.

Stilt sandals decorated with mother-of-pearl inlay. These sandals were used by ladies in Turkish baths in the late nineteenth century, sparing the feet from the hot marble floors. [Photo courtesy of Shoe Icons]

In addition, shoes are considered impure in many Middle Eastern countries. Throwing shoes at Muslims is often seen as a grave offense, and in Iraq after the fall of Saddam Hussein media accounts showed countless images of Iraqis hitting statues and portraits of Hussein with their shoes as a way of insulting and degrading his memory. If shoes are in contact with the ground, which is dirty, and if shoes have to be removed before entering a holy space, then hitting someone with one's shoe is a way of directing symbolic and literal pollution at one's enemy as was the case when an Iraqi journalist threw his own shoes at President George Bush in 2008 to protest the Iraqi war.

Prior to the advent of Islam in the seventh century and the unification of the region under the Arab Caliphates from the seventh to the twelfth centuries, the Middle East was a vast, politically and culturally diverse region. The oldest civilizations in the Middle East were **Egypt**, Mesopotamia, and Persia.

Egypt is one of the oldest civilizations on the planet, dating from the 3000 BCE. Egyptian footwear reflects both the physical environment in which Egyptian people lived as well as their social and cultural beliefs and practices. Sandals, made of woven vegetable matter like papyrus leaves, were probably the earliest type of footwear

This shoe has a metal heel and dates to seventeenth century Persia. [Photo courtesy of Shoe Icons]

in Egypt. Later, sandals were most likely made from a combination of **leather**, papyrus, and/or palm. Only elite Egyptians wore dyed, adorned, or otherwise decorated sandals. In addition, fashionable sandals with upturned toes could only be worn by elites. Later, simple shoes and **boots** were also developed, with the characteristic pointy, upturned toe.

The cultures of ancient Mesopotamia—Assyrians, Babylonians, and Sumerians—were farmers and sheep herders. The Sumerians wore sandals with leather soles, with toe loop and heel guard, starting in perhaps 2600 BCE. The Assyrians and the Babylonians wore similar sandals (sometimes with upturned toes), and knee-high boots were also worn by Assyrians for riding chariots.

Cultures in which horseback riding was an important part of the culture typically wore leather boots. For example, the Hittites, from about 1900 BCE to 1200 BCE, were sheep herders who lived in what is now Turkey, and they wore leather shoes and boots with upturned toes. The Persians, who lived in what is now Iran and whose empire lasted from about 700 BCE to 330 BCE, were conquerors who eventually took over much of the ancient world and who wore boots with upturned toes, curved heels, and soles covered with hobnails. Because of the influence and reach of the Persian Empire, fashions from this area extended throughout the ancient world, even beyond the end of the empire and well into the Middle Ages. (Many scholars think that high heels, in fact, originated among ancient Persian horseback riders, who wore heels to hold their feet in their stirrups while riding. Others locate the origins of the European practice of wearing heels with Mongolian invaders.) Ancient Armenians too wore ankle boots, which were worn for riding and to negotiate the mountainous terrain. The Scythians, who were nomads living in the region of Iran from about 1500 BCE to the second century AD, also wore leather boots. Bedouins today continue to wear boots, made of camel skin, for riding horses and camels, with sheikhs wearing fancier half boots.

Many of the cultural attributes of modern Middle Eastern countries date to the Middle Ages and the advent of Islam and the dominance of the Arab Caliphates. This includes the wearing of shoes with upturned toes and open-backed mules. Boots, which predate this period, continue to be worn today as well.

Because shoes are removed before entering a mosque, there are a great variety of shoes available in the Middle East that are easy to slip on and off, such as open-backed **slippers** known as mules, starting with the rise of the Byzantine Empire in the fourth century. *Khussas*, for example, are traditional slippers worn by both men and women throughout the Middle East. Originally made of wood, but today made of leather or cloth and often highly decorated with embroidery and beading, khussas are most popular in rural regions. Elites wore finely made leather slippers with beautiful embroidery

Throwing Shoes at the Statue of
Saddam Hussein

In Iraq after the fall of Saddam Hussein in April 2003, media accounts showed countless images of Iraqis hitting statues and portraits of Hussein with the soles of their shoes, or throwing shoes at these representations, as a way of insulting and degrading his memory. Throwing shoes at Muslims is generally seen as a grave offense because, in many Muslim countries such as Iraq, shoes are considered impure due to their contact with the ground and the fact that they are associated with the lowest part of the body. This is why shoes must be removed before entering a mosque or engaging in prayer. On the other hand, Al Jazeera reported that the shoe throwing was not a sign of Iraqis spontaneously expressing their joy at the overthrow of their leader, but that the American military had bussed in Shias from other parts of Iraq to deface the statue of Hussein. (During Saddam Hussein's reign, Shias were a persecuted minority in Iraq.) Regardless, this incident indicates that while throwing shoes is indeed an insult in Iraq, it may not be the case that most Iraqis (or at least most Sunnis) wanted to insult Hussein.

An Iraqi man hits with a shoe on the statue of former Iraqi President Ahmed Hasan al-Bakr during a demonstration against the Baath Party in Baghdad May 18, 2003. The statue was then beheaded, then felled by the protesters. Al-Bakr, the Baath Party leader in 1968, became president after a bloodless coup and was succeeded by Saddam Hussein in 1979. [AP Photo/Ali Haider]

and jewels on them. Moroccan slippers with folded down backs, or *babouches*, were worn throughout the region, and only Muslims could wear yellow ones.

Open sandals have also long been popular in Middle Eastern countries. The *niaal* is a simple sandal made with a thick camel hide sole and straps of leather, cloth, or even metal forming the upper.

Stilted sandals, known as *Kipkaps*, *kubkubs*, or *qabqabs*, were high wooden **clogs** worn by high-status women during the Ottomon Empire that may date back as far as the sixth century, along with babouches at home. (The Turkish version is called a *nalin*.) They stood on two stilts and like the Venetian *chopines* or Japanese *geta*, were often extremely high—as high as two feet for shorter women and young brides. The uppers were made of leather, silk, or velvet and were often intricately decorated with embroidery, inlaid wood, mother of pearl, and other precious materials. Special-occasion shoes were decorated over the entire shoe. Designed to keep a woman's feet clean and dry while outdoors or in the bath house, they became items of status among the wealthy urban women who wore them. Like wooden clogs found in other cultures, such as **Korea**, **China**, and **Japan**, these shoes were known for the distinctive sound that they made while walking, and from which the name is derived. While women primarily wore stilted sandals, men wore simple versions while in the bath house.

See also: India; Classical Civilizations

Further Reading Gulevich, Tanya. *Understanding Islam and Muslim Traditions: An Introduction to the Religious Practices, Celebrations, Festivals, Observances, Beliefs, Folklore, Customs, And Calendar Systems of the World's Muslim Communities, Including an Overview of Islamic History and Geography*. Detroit: Omnigraphics, 2004; Stillman, Yedida Kalfon. *Arab Dress from the Dawn of Islam to Modern Times*. Leiden: Brill, 2003.

MILITARY SHOES AND BOOTS

Military shoes refer to shoes and **boots** worn by soldiers during combat. Since ancient **Greece**, men in the military have worn specialized footwear geared toward the demands of the military, including walking long distances, a variety of climates and topography, and fighting.

While the Spartans went barefoot during regular life as well as battle, most Greek soldiers, at least in the later periods, wore **leather** ankle boots, open-toed shoes, or **sandals** with leather leggings. Some of these shoes had hobnailed soles to make them last longer. Roman soldiers also wore a variety of foot coverings, including sandals that laced partway up the leg, open-toed shoes, closed shoes, and both ankle and knee-high boots, again, often with hobnailed soles.

In Europe in the Middle Ages, soft top boots or Cavalier boots became popular in the thirteenth century among the nobility, both for riding and for military pursuits. These boots finally gave way in the eighteenth century to stiff leather boots. Known as **jack boots**, these were often cut away behind the knee, to allow the knee to bend, and were worn by wealthy men and officers during battle. Later came the Hessian boots, another variety of hard leather boot worn during battle, which was replaced in England

Military and police surplus supplies in a section of the marketplace outside Joint Security Station Bab al Sheikh, located in Eastern Baghdad, Iraq, May 27, 2008. [U.S. Army photo by Staff Sgt. Brian D. Lehnhardt/Released. Photo courtesy of Department of Defense]

by **Wellington boots**, shorter, more comfortable boots named after the Duke of Wellington.

Tall stiff riding boots were worn by the calvary in most of the European armies from the eighteenth to twentieth centuries. In particular, jack boots were worn in the French and German armies until the twentieth century, with jack boots being worn, infamously, by the Nazis in World War II. They were also worn by soldiers in the Soviet army and are still worn in the Russian army for dress purposes.

Soldiers have some specific needs when it comes to footwear. Since Roman times, soldiers have been expected to march long distances, sometimes through difficult terrain. For that reason, shoes need to be both sturdy and comfortable. They also need to be waterproof, yet must allow for the foot to breathe, and should be able to withstand mud, sand, and dirt.

But the shoes worn by officers and by soldiers throughout history have often differed, with soldiers' shoes being more practical and officers' shoes being more fashionable. Throughout the eighteenth and nineteenth centuries, officers wore shiny jack boots, Hessians, or Wellingtons, which had to be polished by servants. Because narrow feet were associated with being high bred, these boots were also quite narrow.

Soldiers, on the other hand, with the exception of the calvary, wore regular shoes. Starting in the early nineteenth century, Prussian General Gebhard von Blücher invented wide ankle boots after realizing that his soldiers had a hard time pulling on and off their high jack boots. "Blüchers" were short boots with two flaps below the ankle that could be easily slipped on and off and which laced through the flap. Like the Roman military shoes, these had hobnails on the soles to make them more sturdy and were often worn with gaiters to protect the lower leg.

Blüchers were worn until 1913, and were replaced by the trench boot, worn during World War I by Allied soldiers. Trench boots had an iron plate attached to the heel, replacing the hobnails. Because it wasn't waterproofed, many soldiers also wore rubber Wellingtons while in the trenches to keep their feet dry.

Until the twentieth century, soldiers' shoes were made poorly and often fell apart, especially under the trying conditions of warfare, and in addition were only made in a handful of sizes, making them painful for soldiers with nonstandard foot sizes.

Military shoes improved by World War II, and were stronger and more durable. American soldiers in that war were issued service shoes, which were worn with canvas leggings, and, starting in 1943, ankle-high combat boots with rubber soles and ankle flaps that buckled close; these boots did not have to be worn with leggings. But because they were so stiff, soldiers often developed painful blisters when breaking them in. These boots were worn by American soldiers throughout the Korean and Vietnam wars, although shiny black boots were also introduced in the 1950s.

Soldiers working in different conditions today wear very different forms of footwear. Soldiers stationed in the Pacific theater during World War II wore jungle boots, while paratroopers who jumped out of airplanes were issued special jump boots, designed with extra ankle protection. Tanker boots were worn by soldiers working on tanks and had straps instead of laces. Rubber Wellies were also worn by Allied soldiers during World War II when stationed in the flooded fields of the Netherlands. British soldiers wore desert boots made with suede uppers and crepe soles (like **Hush Puppies**) while serving in North Africa. They wore them a size bigger than their feet, allowing for a greater surface area while walking on the sand. After the war, these boots evolved into creepers, the American version of the suede shoes made famous in the song, "**Blue Suede Shoes.**"

In the last couple of decades, military shoes have gotten lighter and more comfortable, making them more wearable by soldiers who often have to carry more than 100 pounds of gear when walking in extreme environmental conditions. Combat boots today borrow design features from hiking boots, such as the use of breathable fabrics. They are also available in a variety of styles for different conditions and needs, including desert boots, jump boots, jungle boots, and dress shoes for ceremonial occasions. But members of the U.S. Army today are still assigned the standard Army Combat Uniform, which includes tan combat boots to be worn in all environments.

Since the 1960s, combat boots have been popular among punks, skinheads, and members of other subcultures in the United States and England, who purchase their boots in army surplus stores.

See also: Boots; Europe; Jack Boots; Wellington Boot

Further Reading David, Alison Matthews. "War Wellingtons: Military Footwear in the Age of Empire," in Rielle, Georgio and Peter McNeil, eds. *Shoes: A History From Sandals to Sneakers*. London: Berg Publishers, 2006; Knötel, Richard, Herbert Knötel, and Herbert Sieg. *Uniforms of the World: A Compendium of Army, Navy, and Air Force Uniforms, 1700–1937*. New York: Scribner's, 1980.

MOCCASINS

Moccasin refers to a shoe made of a piece of soft **leather** or animal skin that is sewn into a shoe. It is, along with the **sandal**, perhaps the oldest forms of footwear worn by humans and dates back thousands of years. Moccasins are typically made with a single piece of material that makes both the sole and the upper. The word moccasin comes from the Algonquian word *makasin* or *makisina*, for shoe or deerskin shoe.

The simplest moccasin is constructed with a single piece of skin that is wrapped around the entire foot and tied or sewn together along the top. This efficient shoe was the primary form of footwear throughout **Native America** for thousands of years. Hard-soled moccasins, on the other hand, are made with two pieces of skin: a piece of

These ankle-high moccasins are made of deer skin and are beaded around the entire vamp and quarter. [2008 copyright Richard Nelson. Image from BigStockPhoto.com]

untanned skin, or rawhide, for the sole, sewn to a separate piece of softer, tanned, and smoked skin, for the upper. Hard-soled moccasins are worn in areas where the terrain is more difficult and feet need additional protection, as in the American Southwest, while soft-soled moccasins were worn among eastern American tribes whose environment was primarily forested. Soft-soled shoes allowed their wearers to approach an enemy or prey without being heard and could be worn in a **snow shoe** in northern climates or in boats used by coastal groups.

Native American moccasins are constructed with either one or two pieces, and were traditionally sewn with threads made of animal sinew, either in a center seam down the center of the top of the moccasin or along a single side, using whip stitching or running stitching, with knots placed on the outside of the shoe for comfort. The top of the leather was then folded over at the top, at the ankle. The skin used depends on the animals available: elk, buffalo, deer, moose, or even rabbit. Single-piece moccasins are made out of an oval piece of animal skin, which is wrapped around the foot and sewn together, often forming the iconic puckered u-shape over the top of the foot. Two-piece moccasins include a vamp sewn into the top of the upper. Many moccasins also include collars or cuffs at the ankle.

Moccasins are often highly decorated, especially along the top seam, using beads, vegetable dyes, animal hair, ribbons, embroidery, applique, porcupine quills, and metal decorative cones. Often the decorations are created separately on a loom and then sewn onto the finished shoe. Sometimes shoes are decorated only along the collar, or along the vamp, or over the entire upper. Decorations, which include animals, plants, spirits, or geometric designs, indicate the skill of the maker as well as cultural affiliations like

These motorcycle boots have buckles on the side. [Copyright 2008 Jupiterimages Corporation]

tribe and clan. Some tribes had special moccasins to be worn when dead, to carry the wearer into the afterlife.

After the Europeans arrived in North America, some began wearing moccasins themselves. In some cases, they did this because they could not yet import European shoes, but in other cases some wore them because of their comfort and practicality. Europeans changed the Native moccasin by adding a hard leather sole.

Today, since most Native Americans do not wear traditional clothing for everyday wear, moccasins are worn most often at ceremonial events. They have also had surges of popularity among Euro-Americans over the past 30 years and can be purchased both at Native American retailers as well as at mainstream American stores.

See also: Native America; Plains Indians; Southwest Indians

Further Reading Elder, Alan C. In the Steps of Our Ancestors: An Exhibition of Native North American Footwear. Toronto: Ontario Crafts Council, 1989; Paterek, Josephine. Encyclopedia of American Indian Costume. Denver, Colo: ABC-CLIO, 1994.

MORTON'S NEUROMA. See Neuroma.

MOTORCYCLE BOOT

Motorcycle boots, also known as engineer boots, are knee-high black leather **boots** made to be worn while riding motorcycles. They derive in style and function from **jack boots**, which were tall boots made of hard leather, popular in Europe in the seventeenth and eighteenth centuries, worn by calvary soldiers until the twentieth century, and worn by German soldiers during World War II.

Motorcycle boots are made of hard, waterproofed **leather** and are usually 11 inches high. They are designed to protect the leg from being burnt against the motorcycle's tailpipe and to protect the feet, ankles, and legs in the case of an accident. Because they are made of waterproofed leather, they also keep the legs and feet dry during poor weather. Motorcycle boots are low heeled with thick rubber soles. Like horseback riding boots, heels on a motorcycle boot are functional: they help the rider to grip the footpeg and to control the brake and gear shift. In addition, the rubber sole is used to grip the ground when the rider is stopped. They generally pull on because laces or other **shoe fasteners** can get caught in the moving parts of the engine. Some motorcycle boots have a steel toe, and most are lined with additional padding in the upper.

Modern biker boots have their origins in the Chippewa Engineer boots created by the Chippewa Shoe Company in the 1930s. Chippewa opened in 1901, and originally made boots for loggers, but soon expanded to make other kinds of boots. The engineer boots were made on a last used for English riding boots. These boots have changed very little in the 70 years since they have been made, except that they have shrunk from about 17 inches high to the current 11 inches.

While motorcycles were first invented in the nineteenth century, they were not popularized until the early twentieth century, after Harley-Davidson, Indian, and Triumph began making motorcycles. It wasn't until after World War II, however, that motorcycle culture, or biker culture, emerged in the United States. War veterans formed biker clubs, which by the 1960s evolved into an outlaw movement with its own fashion sense, language, and lifestyle. Motorcycle boots are not only functional but also complete—along with tattoos, long hair, and skull rings—the wardrobe for many American bikers.

See also: Boots; Jack Boots; Military Shoes and Boots

Further Reading Steele, Valerie. *Shoes: A Lexicon of Style*. New York: Rizzoli International Publications Inc., 1999; Thompson, Hunter S. *The Harley-Davidson Reader*. St. Paul, MN: Motorbooks, 2006.

NATIONAL PODIATRIC MEDICAL ASSOCIATION

The National Podiatric Medical Association (NPMA) is one of two national associations for podiatrists in the United States. Unlike the **American Podiatric Medical Association**, however, the NPMA has as its primary focus increasing the representation of minorities in **podiatry**. It is a 501c3 nonprofit organization and was founded in 1973.

The NPMA achieves this goal through actively recruiting members of ethnic minorities and otherwise disadvantaged members of society into podiatry, through recruiting minority students into podiatric medicine programs, providing partial funding for minority students, and working to help place graduates into postgraduate positions.

The NPMA also sponsors a student arm of the organization, the Student National Podiatric Medical Association, which was founded in 1973 and has a chapter in each of the nine recognized colleges of podiatric medicine. The SNPMA is primarily a support group for minority students, with a newsletter. The NPMA works to retain minority podiatrists by providing continuing educational opportunities and scholarships. It hosts a meeting every year with exhibits and speakers, during which scholarships are given out to worthy students.

Like the APMA, the NPMA also educates the public on issues regarding feet and foot care, but with a particular focus on the foot disorders that are most likely to affect minority communities. Finally, the organization also informs its members about legislative issues affecting the profession.

See also: Podiatry; American Podiatric Medical Association

Further Reading Alexander, Ivy, *Podiatry Sourcebook*. Detroit: Omnigraphics, 2007; Chang, Thomas, *Master Techniques in Podiatric Surgery*; Philadelphia: Lippincott Williams & Wilkins, 2004.

NATIVE AMERICA

Footwear in the **United States** prior to and after colonization reflected vast differences in the cultures of the Native American communities as well as variations in environment and economy. The discussion that follows focuses primarily on footwear as it was worn when Europeans first colonized North America.

The primary form of footwear for Native American tribes was the **moccasin**, although **sandals**, **boots**, and leggings were also worn. A moccasin is, in its simplest form, a shoe made of a single piece of animal skin, held around the top of the foot with a piece of animal hide. Native American one-piece moccasins were made with a single piece of **leather**, pulled up and around the sides of the foot and sewn together, using sinew, with one seam running from the toe along the upper instep, creating the iconic u-shaped vamp over the instep. Sometimes moccasins were made with two or more pieces, including extra pieces for a vamp, while other tribes made their moccasins with a separate sole and upper. Two-piece moccasins generally have a high collar at the ankle.

Each tribe has different construction methods, designs, and adornment styles, reflecting cultural differences as well as differences in local environment, climate, and resources availability, and many people could recognize different moccasin styles and the tribe from where they derived. Two-piece moccasins were common among Plateau and **Southwest Indians** as well as among Southeast tribes, while one-piece moccasins were more commonly worn among Northeast and Great Lakes tribes, and hard soles were more common among Southwest tribes. Even methods of embroidery and stitch styles were distinguishable between tribes.

> Great spirit grant that I may not criticize my neighbor, until I have walked a mile in his moccasins
>
> NATIVE AMERICAN PRAYER

Moccasins were made with the tanned skins of the animals that were available, including deer, elk, moose, buffalo, or caribou. Moccasins made with a separate hard sole were usually made with rawhide rather than tanned skin. Making moccasins was and is a valuable skill that is passed on from generation to generation. Generally, women are responsible for preparing and tanning the hides, cutting and sewing the moccasins, and the adornment as well. Animal hides are first scraped and then the skin is soaked in a solution of water and lime or lye, and then stretched and dried, and sometimes also smoked. The skin was then softened by treating the hide with the liver, fat, and brains of the animal, a process known as *chamoising*, and then dried again.

Moccasins were often decorated with vegetable dyes, animal hair, and quill-work embroidery using porcupine quills. Decorations usually cover the central seam on the front as well as the collar of the two-piece moccasins. Starting in the mid-eighteenth century when European glass beads became available, beading was utilized as well as other European materials like tin and cloth and manufactured dyes. In addition, after European contact, some tribes incorporated European techniques like embroidery with thread.

A Plains legend tells the story of why Indians wear moccasins. According to the story, a chief had tender feet and hobbled because of the pain of walking. He asked his medicine man to solve the problem of his tender feet. First, the medicine man had the women weave reed mats, which he had young men carry and place before the chief wherever he walked. When that proved inefficient, he used animal skins to create paths on which the chief would walk. When that proved insufficient and the medicine man was about to be killed for his lack of success, he came up with the idea of covering the chief's feet with coverings of animal skin. " 'Big Chief,' the medicine man exclaimed joyfully, 'I have found the way to cover the earth with leather! For you, O chief, from now on the earth will always be covered with leather.' And so it was."

The Woodland tribes lived in semipermanent villages from New England to the Great Lakes region, and much of their clothing and shoes came from the forests where they made their living from hunting and gathering as well as simple farming. The primary footwear of the Woodland tribes like the Shawnee and the Iroquois was moccasins made out of the skins of animals like deer. Because of their location at the time of colonization, Woodland tribes had more contact with Europeans than other groups and traded with them, acquiring new materials with which to make clothing and shoes. Traditionally, they wore soft-soled moccasins made out of a single piece of skin sewn together with a single center-seam and puckering around the instep. Woodland tribes decorated their moccasins with animal or flower designs along the instep or tongue as well as around the ankle cuff, which was often adorned with beading or porcupine quillwork as well.

The Indians of the Southeast lived in the southeast corner of the United States, from Florida to the Gulf of Mexico, and include the Cherokee, Choctaw, and Seminole tribes. They were hunters and gatherers who enjoyed a very mild climate. Starting in 1831, many members of Southeastern tribes were forced by the U.S. government to move to Oklahoma, where they were placed on reservations. The moccasins worn by Southeast Indians were made of deer skin and were often dyed with walnut pulp and other natural dyes and decorated with beads, quills, fringe, or turkey spurs.

The **Plains Indians** live in the central plains states of the United States and include the Shawnee, Cheyenne, and Sioux. Originally hunters and gatherers, their footwear suited their nomadic lifestyle. Hard-sole moccasins, for example, were worn by Plains Indians in order to protect their feet from the harsh environment of the western plains. Plains Indians often decorated their moccasins with beads and quills along the top, the instep, and near the sole. Moccasins to be worn at a wedding were decorated more elaborately, as well those worn by the dead for burial. Boots, made with moccasins sewn to thigh-high leggings, were also worn.

The Great Basin Indians or Plateau Indians include the Nez Perce, Yakima, and Shoshoni, who lived in the Rocky Mountain states. Living as nomadic hunters and gatherers, they picked up shoe construction techniques and forms of adornment from other tribes that they came in contact with. For example, Plateau Indian beadwork includes techniques borrowed from Crow, while their use of flowers in their design is derived from the Metis.

The Southwest Indians live in the states of New Mexico, Arizona, and southern Colorado and Utah and include the Pueblo Indians, the Navajo, and the Apache. Prior to colonization, the Pueblo Indians made their living farming and hunting, while the Navajo and Apache were nomadic hunters and gatherers. The earliest inhabitants of the region, the ancestral Pueblo people (once known as Anasazi) who lived in the four corners region of Colorado, Utah, Arizona, and New Mexico, wore sandals made of woven yucca fibers. Later, the Puebloan people of the region adopted the moccasins worn by other Indians throughout North America. Because of the harsh desert environment, hard-soled moccasins were preferred to protect the feet from cactus and sharp rocks. Many Southwest Indians dyed their moccasins using vegetable dyes, and shoes were decorated with beads, fringe and, after European contact, decorative tin cones.

Indians of the Pacific Northwest Coast live in the coastal regions of Oregon, Washington, and British Columbia and include the Tlingit, Kwaikutl, and Haida. They wore footwear that was well adapted to the temperate climate and activities, which centered around fishing, hunting, and gathering. Many people went barefoot much of the time. The most common form of footwear was similar to that worn by most other Native tribes as well as by the Inuits of the north, from whom Northwest coast Indians probably borrowed it: the soft-soled moccasin. Made with a single piece of skin sewn together with a side seam, moccassins were decorated with totemic designs and included animals, spirits, and plants. Those Indians living in the far northern regions of the northwest coast wore warmer moccasins, designed to be worn in much chillier climates. Here, men and women would wear a moccasin trouser, made of hide with the fur left on, and extending from the foot up the legs. These were worn with **snow shoes** and were, in the nineteenth century, replaced by boots. Snow shoe hare skins were also worn inside of boots and shoes to keep the feet warmer.

In 2007, **Nike** introduced a new shoe that was developed with Native Americans in mind. Because of the high rates of obesity and diabetes among Native Americans, Nike created the Air Native N7 in order to encourage physical fitness and reduce the incidences of disease. Designed to better fit Native Americans' feet, which are on average wider than European's feet, the shoes are also designed to resemble the traditional moccasins. They were sold exclusively to tribal schools for $43 a pair.

See also: Moccasins; Snow Shoes

Further Reading Elder, Alan C. *In the Steps of Our Ancestors: An Exhibition of Native North American Footwear*. Toronto: Ontario Crafts Council, 1989; Paterek, Josephine. *Encyclopedia of American Indian Costume*. Denver, Colo: ABC-CLIO, 1994; Utah Museum of Natural History, Kathy Kankainen, and Laurel Casjens. *Treading in the Past: Sandals of the Anasazi*. Salt Lake City: Utah Museum of Natural History in association with the University of Utah Press, 1995.

NEUROMA

Neuromas are bundles of thickened nerves that develop from pressure to the nerves. The most common type of neuroma is a Morton's neuroma, which affects the region between the third and fourth metatarsal bones, causing pain in the ball of the foot due to the swelling in the digital nerves.

Morton's neuromas are most commonly caused by constant pressure on the foot and are frequently the result of wearing tight shoes. Women are much more prone to neuromas than men for this reason, since fashionable women's shoes tend to be narrow in the toe box, and **high heels** also cause compression of the toes. In addition, other conditions like **hammer toe**, flat feet, and bunions can make it more likely that one will be afflicted with a neuroma, as can activities involving repeated pressure on the balls of the feet, like running. Neuromas cause pain and can interfere with normal activities when untreated.

With too much continuous pressure, the nerves not only swell but through pinching can become permanently damaged. When still in the early stages, the condition can be reversed through wearing wider shoes, restricting repetitive activities, and also massaging the ball of the foot. Ice and heat can also sometimes help. Once the condition has progressed, however, wearing wider shoes can alleviate the symptoms and keep the condition from getting worse, but the bundle of nerves will still persist between the metatarsals.

People with Morton's neuromas can treat the pain by wearing cushioned insoles, metatarsal pads, or dancer pads. Pads are worn underneath the ball of the foot, behind the neuroma, to separate the bones and disperse the pressure to other areas of the foot. In addition, arch supports or custom **orthotics** can help by taking the weight off the ball of the foot and are especially called for in cases of flat foot, and anti-inflammatory drugs can reduce the swelling. In more serious cases, steroids injections may be used to reduce swelling; if that does not work, some doctors may also try injections of alcohol, which is intended to harden the nerve. Finally, surgery may also be warranted if the condition does not improve. Surgery involves cutting into the deep transverse metatarsal ligament, which relieves the pressure on the nerves and thus relieves the pain.

See also: Disorders and Injuries; Foot Care Products; Orthotics

Further Reading MacDonald, Ann. *Foot Care Basics: Preventing and Treating Common Foot Conditions*. Harvard health letter special report. Boston, MA: Harvard Health Publications, 2007.

NEW BALANCE

New Balance is an **athletic shoe** and apparel manufacturing company headquartered in Boston, Massachusetts. New Balance was started in 1906 by a waiter named William Riley who wanted to create arch supports for waiters, police officers, postal workers, and others who were on their feet all day. His company, The New Balance Arch Company, sold his arch support design as well as **orthopedic shoes** primarily to local customers. The company continued to sell these products until 1961, when they were replaced by a new focus on athletic shoes.

Riley designed a **running shoe** in 1925 for a group of Boston runners and began making custom shoes for a variety of sports in the 1930s, which the company continued to provide through the 1960s. In 1961, the company released its first running shoe to the general public, the Trackster. One of New Balance's innovations is creating running shoes in different widths, which began with this shoe. New Balance did not aggressively market the shoe, so the Trackster did not have high sales but instead sold by word of month, from runner to runner.

New Balance was bought in 1972 by James Davis, a salesman who wanted to own his own business. He saw in New Balance the potential for a lot of growth and bought the company for $100,000. Thanks to both the boom in jogging in the **United States** in the 1970s and the new ownership's commitment to marketing, New Balance's sales exploded in that decade. By the mid-1970s, New Balance was the leading seller of running shoes in the United States, and one of its shoes was awarded the best running shoe in the world in 1976 by *Runner's World* magazine. Because New Balance continued its commitment to making well-made shoes in a variety of widths, and because it kept its production facilities in New England, the shoes were heavily favored among runners.

The company suffered financially in the 1980s as it struggled to compete with new companies **Nike** and **Reebok**, and it saw other companies moving their production facilities overseas to cut costs. New Balance focused instead on improving production and quality in the American factories as well as speed of delivery of finished product, resulting in increased sales during the 1990s.

In the late 1990s and 2000s, New Balance began acquiring other companies, such as Dunham, PF Flyers, Aravon, Warrior, and Vital Apparel Group, which allowed it to expand into outdoor shoes, lacross equipment, hockey equipment, sports apparel, and orthopedic shoes. The New Balance name is also used to license a variety of products like eyewear, home exercise equipment, sports monitors, and socks, and they company released a line of children's shoes. Also during the 1990s, New Balance finally opened new manufacturing facilities in Taiwan and shifted 30 percent of production overseas.

Today, New Balance continues to maintain factories in Massachusetts and Maine as well as international locations in **China** and Vietnam. The company employs 4,100 people worldwide and had $1.63 billion in sales in 2007. New Balance remains the only American athletic shoe company to make some of its shoes in the United States (although only about 25 percent are still made in the United States).

New Balance is also unusual in that it does not use expensive endorsement deals with high-profile celebrity athletes to sell its products. Instead, the marketing campaign focuses on the technology and performance of the shoes, which are called by their batch number rather than by a fancy name.

See also: Athletic Shoes; Shoe Sizes

Further Reading Burfoot, Amby. *Runner's World Complete Book of Running: Everything You Need to Know to Run for Fun, Fitness, and Competition*. Emmaus, Pa: Rodale Press, 1997.

NIKE

Nike is a leading producer of **athletic shoes**, apparel, and accessories. Once known primarily as a maker of running shoes, Nike is now the biggest American athletic shoe maker in the world. Nike has 20,700 employees and generates sales of $15 billion per year. The company is headquartered in Beaverton, Oregon.

Founded by former college runner Phil Knight in 1962 as Blue Ribbon Sports, the company originally imported and sold Tiger running shoes from **Japan**; at that time, the major companies selling running shoes in the United States were the German firms **Adidas** and **Reebok**. In 1964, Knight created a partnership with his former track coach, William Bowerman, and the two opened their first store in 1966.

Their first shoe was the Cortez, released in 1968, based on Bowerman's design. In 1971 the company trademarked its Swoosh logo and created the Nike name, but the company was still known as Blue Ribbon Sports until 1978. The first Nike-branded shoe was a soccer shoe, also released in 1971.

Nike's success in the athletic shoe industry can be traced to the rise in fitness and in jogging in particular in the 1970s, combined with the company's technical innovations and creative and celebrity-driven **advertising** campaigns.

One of Nike's major contributions to the athletic shoe industry is the technical innovations that the company pioneered. For example, in 1967 Bowerman invented the cushioned wedge heel. Also in 1967, the company began to use nylon on the uppers of their shoes, and in 1968 developed a cushioned midsole. Perhaps the two biggest innovations, however, were the rubber waffle sole created by Bowerman using a waffle iron in 1972 and Nike's air cushioning technology in 1979. This patented system uses gas that is trapped in polyurethane and is used in the midsole of all Nike air shoes since the Tailwind, introduced in 1979.

In this March 16, 2008, file photo, Seattle SuperSonics center Johan Petro wears a pair of Nike basketball Shox shoes while facing the Denver Nuggets in the third quarter of the Nuggets's 168–116 victory in an NBA basketball game in Denver. [AP Photo/David Zalubowski]

Nike began sponsoring athletes and promoting their products at sporting events with the 1972 Olympic trials, and by the 1976 Olympic Games prominent athletes were wearing Nike shoes, with the first Olympic gold medal won wearing Nike shoes occurring in 1980. By the end of the decade, Nike was selling half of the **jogging shoes** in the United States, and it continues to dominate the market today. As jogging's popularity began to wane, Nike continued to prosper, because of its focus on other shoes, such as those used in basketball, tennis, aerobics, and soccer.

In 1979 the company began releasing clothing, but in the early 1980s sales began to drop, leading Nike to restructure the company, close down the last U.S. manufacturing facilties, and fund an aggressive advertising campaign, spending millions of dollars per year, and in 1985 signing **Michael Jordan** as the most prominent face of the company.

The late 1980s saw more financial troubles and more restructuring, although the air shoes remained profitable. Nike began its "Just Do It" marketing campaign in 1988, encouraging average consumers to "just do it" and become athletes. The "Just Do It" campaign, launched with a $10 million advertising blitz, helped bring the company back. Advertising costs in 1989 alone were $45 million.

Nike's success increased through the 1990s as the company expanded, opening NikeTown locations and outlets around the world and manufacturing sports equipment as well. Also at the end of the 1990s Nike began expanding into extreme and youth sports.

Besides technological innovations, Nike's other major contribution to the athletic shoe industry is its aggressive and creative marketing and use of celebrities to promote Nike products. The company has also led the industry in signing deals with sports teams around the world in which the shoes and uniforms worn by all the athletes were produced by Nike.

Even more successful is the use of celebrity athletes to endorse Nike products, beginning in 1972 with the signing of Romanian tennis star Ilie Năstase. But Nike's first major deal was with basketball player Michael Jordan in 1985. Jordan signed an initial deal worth $2.5 million, which included a shoe named after the basketball star, the Air Jordan. One of Nike's most successful shoes, the Air Jordan, released in 23 different incarnations since 1985, and the commercials featuring Jordan and often co-starring director and actor Spike Lee, played a major role in Nike's success during the 1980s and 1990s. Other popular advertising campaigns in the 1980s featured Bo Jackson and John McEnroe.

In 1995, golfing phenomenon Tiger Woods signed a 20 year, $40 million deal, which is now worth more than $100 million. Woods even wears Nike-branded clothing and shoes when shooting commercials promoting other products. Even more remarkably, in 2003 the company signed a lucrative deal with basketball player LeBron James worth $90 million; what made the deal remarkable was that James had not, at the time of the signing, played a single NBA game. He had just graduated high school and was soon drafted into the Cleveland Cavaliers. Nike spends more money on endorsement deals than any other company in the world.

Nike has been criticized for the way that it uses popular athletes, often African American, to target young, often low-income, urban consumers. The Michael Jordan campaign in particular has been aimed at urban communities in which the shoes are an important status symbol and sign of upward mobility, even when the consumers can't necessarily afford them. Using minority athletes who have "made it" is a way to not only sell shoes but to sell the lifestyle and promise of success symbolized by the athlete. And because the shoes are so expensive—up to $140 per pair, which represents a hefty profit margin considering the low production costs—the cost for purchasing that hope is steep.

Heaven's Gate

Heaven's Gate was an apocalyptic religious cult and Web-development company that gained its fame from a mass suicide in March 1997, in which the dead members were all found wearing matching pairs of new black-and-white Nike Cortez shoes. Cult members followed the leadership of Marshall Applewhite, who preached that the end of the world was near and would be attained by leaving this earth; an occurrence that coincided with the arrival of the Hale Bopp comet. The members were then living in a home in Rancho Santa Fe, California, and the photos of the suicide scene at the home were widely distributed in the aftermath of the event. In the photos, the 39 members, who died from having ingested Phenobarbital and vodka, are seen lying on beds, all wearing identical black clothing and black shoes, covered with purple shrouds, with packed suitcases under their beds. Two months later, another two members, dressed the same as the original group, tried to kill themselves in a Holiday Inn, with one surviving. (He ultimately succeeded in killing himself a few months later.) In 2008, it was rumored that Nike would be releasing a pair of black and purple high tops called the Nike Dunk High. Designed by Todd Jordan, he has been quoted as saying that the design was inspired by the Heaven's Gate tragedy. Sneaker aficionados are already dubbing the shoe the Heaven's Gate. As of this writing, Nike has not released a black and purple version of the Dunk High, and it is also rumored that the shoe will not be released because of its connection to Heaven's Gate. Alleged prototypes of the black and purple sneakers are available on eBay, and as of this writing one is being auctioned for $3,000.

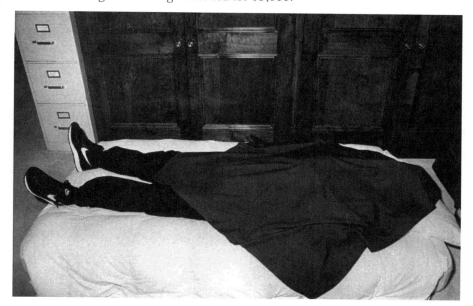

A photograph provided by the San Diego County Sheriff's Dept. shows the position of some of the 39 bodies discovered on March 26, 1997, in Rancho Sante Fe, California, as a result of an apparent mass suicide, at a news conference on March 27, 1997, in Del Mar, California. The photograph was made by the Sherriff's Dept. inside the home. [AP Photo/HO]

In addition, signing celebrity athletes is also risky because consumers are purchasing, in part, the celebrity's personality. If the athlete's public persona and activities don't match the corporate image, the company can suffer, as Nike did when basketball player Kobe Bryant, initially signed to a lucrative deal, was accused of rape in 2004. When football star Michael Vick was convicted on charges of dog fighting and dog killing in 2007, Nike quickly canceled its contract with Vick, just a day before People for the Ethical Treatment of Animals was scheduled to stage a protest outside of the company's Nike Town stores.

One important Nike success was the way it reached out to women, both through products aimed at women and creative advertising that focused on both celebrity and non-celebrity female athletes. Ad campaigns like the "I Can" and "There Is No Finish Line" campaigns celebrate women's athletic power, providing the message that "I can be anything." These campaigns are intended to empower women and have played a major role in the sales of Nike shoes bought by women.

Nike started outsourcing its production early, in 1971, and today all products are produced by overseas subcontractors. In the late 1990s, Nike found itself the focus of a great deal of public protest regarding the working conditions of workers in the company's overseas plants, forcing Nike to change the way it dealt with contractors by the end of the decade. It was revealed in a number of reports that workers—primarily young and female—making Nike products in **China**, Vietnam, Indonesia, and Mexico were earning as little as 15 cents per hour. After a barrage of bad publicity and a handful of lawsuits, Nike now expects contractors to offer a minimum wage and adhere to minimum environmental standards, child protection laws, and independent inspections of factories.

Nike also sells products under the Cole Haan and Bauer names, and in 2003 it bought **Converse** for more than $300 million.

See also: Athletic Shoes; Advertising; Celebrity Endorsements; Converse; Jordan, Michael; Jogging Shoe; Sneakers

Further Reading Garcia, Bobbito. *Where'd You Get Those?: New York City's Sneaker Culture: 1960–1987*. New York: Testify Books, 2003; Papson, Stephen, Robert Goldman. *Nike Culture: The Sign of the Swoosh*. London: Sage Publications, 1998; Vanderbilt, Tom. *The Sneaker Book: Anatomy of an Industry and an Icon*. New York: The New Press, 1998.

"THE OLD WOMAN WHO LIVED IN A SHOE"

"The Old Woman Who Lived in a Shoe" is an English nursery rhyme, known as a Mother Goose story, first published in 1765 by John Newbery in a collection titled *Mother Goose's Melody*.

It reads:

> There was an old woman
> who lived in a shoe.
> She had so many children
> she didn't know what to do.
> She gave them some broth
> without any bread.
> Then whipped them all soundly
> and put them to bed.

Mother Goose tales, known at least as far back as the seventeenth century, are thought to be part social commentary and part children's stories. At least some of them are clearly political and dealt with serious issues like the plague and workers' rights.

In the case of "The Old Woman Who Lived in a Shoe," it is said that this rhyme refers to the inability of Great Britain to control her colonies in the nineteenth century, with the old woman representing Parliament, King James representing the whipping, and the children representing the unruly colonies. The shoe itself, usually a boot, represents the islands of Great Britain. Another interpretation is that the old woman represents King George II who was called the old woman by his constituents, or his wife Caroline, who had eight children. Another interpretation is that this story is grounded in reality and is based on the story of an eighteenth century English woman with 20 illegitimate children, many conceived during her career as a prostitute. It is said that her children formed the "Shoe Gang" that stole wealthy people's shoes, which were then traded for food and liquor. Others think that there was a real person named Mother Goose (Elizabeth Vergoose of Boston) who indeed had too many children, and told her children stories in order to calm and entertain them. Many interpretations focus instead on the fact that she had so many children and that it was a warning rhyme to children to keep them from going down that path.

Another way of understanding the rhyme is to focus on the shoe, which can mean a number of things. One interpretation looks at the historical association of the shoe with marriage, weddings, and fertility. The shoe here can represent the multiplicity of children, or it can represent the fact that the woman is presumably not married, since no husband is present in the tale. Perhaps she was once married, and the shoe is the shoe that she brought with her into her wedding (or which was thrown after her), and now that her husband is gone she is left along with just the shoe and the children.

Another interpretation focuses on the connection between shoes and wealth. Shoes in many cultures represent wealth, freedom, and opportunity, with the very poor unable to afford to wear shoes. The irony for the "Old Woman Who Lived in a Shoe" is that, in this tale, the woman is obviously terribly poor, because she cannot afford to live in a house. Yet a shoe, a symbol of prosperity, is her home.

See also: Beliefs; Fairy Tales

Further Reading Opie, Iona Archibald, and Peter Opie, eds. *The Oxford Dictionary of Nursery Rhymes*. Oxford, England: Oxford University Press, 1977.

ORTHOPEDIC SHOES

Orthopedic shoes are shoes designed to relieve the discomfort of a variety of foot and ankle disorders and, in many cases, to resolve the problem altogether. Orthopedic shoes are worn by both children and adults.

Orthopedic shoes are worn for a number of conditions, including **blisters, bunions, calluses, and corns**, **hammer toes**, **neuromas**, plantar fasciitis, heel spurs, and other problems caused by the wearing of **high heels** or tight shoes. They are also worn by people with **diabetes**, people with legs of different lengths, and people with problems with fallen arches.

Orthopedic shoes are made differently than regular shoes. They have a low heel, tend to be wide, especially in the toe box, have a firm heel counter to provide support to the heel, have a removable, cushioned insole (to be replaced by special **orthotics**, if needed), and have a fairly rigid shank to provide good arch support. They are made of breathable materials that allow the foot to breathe and stay dry and are made to absorb shocks. Many orthopedic shoes are also designed without seams inside, which can cause blisters or other injuries.

Orthopedic shoes are specially designed for a variety of foot and ankle disorders, whether genetic, caused by injury, or caused by wearing inappropriate footwear. They are available in the form of closed shoes, **boots**, **clogs**, **slippers**, and **sandals**.

People who walk with excessive pronation have a gait in which the foot rolls inward as one walks; someone with a supinated walk has a tendancy for the foot to roll outward. In both cases, excessive pronation or supination results in an unnatural walk, which stresses the ligaments, muscles, and tendons of the foot and leg and could cause fallen arches and other conditions as well. Excessive pronation or supination will also cause uneven wear and tear on one's shoes. Pronation or supination can be aided with the use of orthotic inserts, which provide side stability and arch support, or by wearing orthopedic shoes, which are more stable and provide more arch support than regular shoes. Orthopedic shoes made for these conditions have flared outsoles to counteract the foot's tendency to roll and heel stabilizers to stabilize the heel.

Orthopedic shoes are also made for people with two legs of unequal lengths. These shoes are deeper than normal and have removable insoles to allow for the foot on the longer leg to sit deeper in the shoe, while the foot on the shorter leg can rest upon insoles or orthotic inserts or **lifts**. If the legs are extremely unequal in length, the outsoles can be modified as well.

Diabetics generally have poor circulation, which can damage

These old fashioned orthopedic sandals are designed to provide stability to the foot, arch support, and ankle support. [2006 Copyright Krzysztof Nieciecki. Image from BigStockPhoto.com]

the feet. Diabetics often wear orthopedic shoes and boots, which are specially designed with extra depth to accommodate orthotic inserts and are made of special materials to allow the feet to breathe and to keep the feet dry. They are made in a variety of widths to provide extra room in the toes. Some diabetics suffer from diabetic neuropathy in which the feet experience nerve damage, which can lead to the loss of feelings in the foot. Orthopedic shoes (which are often lined with soft materials) and seamless socks are made to alleviate problems associated with this condition and have extra ankle, heel, and arch support to avoid pressure points that can cause blisters or calluses. Diabetic shoes are also designed to reduce stress on the bottoms or sides of the foot and to accommodate disorders such as hammer toes or amputated toes.

Arthritis, in which the joints become inflamed, can also affect the feet, resulting in the need to wear orthopedic shoes that are specially made to accommodate foot swelling and foot pain. Cushioned insoles, soft inner linings, and support for the arches, heels, and toes are all features found in orthopedic shoes that could benefit people with arthritis. In addition, Velcro closures allow for patients with arthritic fingers to more easily put on and take off shoes.

Bunions don't normally require orthopedic shoes, but instead can be healed with the use of bunion pads, arch supports, and other orthotic devices. Nevertheless, orthopedic shoes with wide toe boxes, shoes lined with soft fleece, and stretchable shoes can mitigate the pain of bunions and prevent them from occurring. Stretchable shoes are also recommended for other conditions, such as diabetes, epidermolysis bullosa, hammer toes, foot and toe deformities, and neuromas. Shoes made from stretchable fabrics will alleviate the pain caused by these problems and can keep them from getting worse.

Other conditions for which orthopedic shoes might be warranted could be metarsalgia, high arches, fallen arches, and plantar fasciitis. Orthotic devices—in particular, orthotic insoles—are also prescribed for these conditions. Finally, orthopedic shoes known as wound care shoes are available to patients recovering from **amputations**, injuries, or operations.

There are also specially made orthopedic and diabetic sandals on the market that have wider straps, better shock absorption, and greater arch support than regular sandals. **Birkenstocks**, with their anatomically designed footbed and toe, heel, and arch support, are also popular among people who want to wear sandals but need extra care. In addition, orthopedic sandals tend to have deeper footbeds and removable insoles to allow for the insertion of orthotic inserts. Diabetic sandals have all of the above features and are seamless on the inside, to prevent friction. While the wearing of **flip flops** is generally frowned upon by podiatrists, today there are orthopedic flip flops available that provide arch support and prevent pronation.

Orthopedic shoes are known for being ugly, heavy, and unfashionable, and indeed orthopedic shoes once were, and many still are today. However, many companies are making orthopedic shoes with fashion in mind, partly due to the aging of the Baby Boom generation, and now orthopedic shoes can be purchased in a wide variety of styles and colors. However, there is controversy within the pediatric community over the need for orthopedic shoes for children's conditions, with some doctors taking the position that many children's feet problems (such as flat feet or pigeon toes) will correct themselves over time and that, in fact, going barefoot is the most healthy condition for children's feet.

See also: Blisters, Bunions, Calluses, and Corns; Diabetes; Disorders and Injuries; Hammer Toe; Orthotics

Further Reading Munzenberg, K. Joachim. *The Orthopedic Shoe: Indications and Prescription.* Weinheim, Germany: VCH, 1985.

ORTHOTICS

Orthotics, often called arch supports, are devices that are made to wear inside the shoe in order to support the foot. Orthotics are worn to alleviate problems associated with a number of foot conditions and are also worn by people who spend a great deal of time on their feet, or those who are overweight, to provide additional support. Athletes are another group of people who benefit from orthotics. Orthotics are worn to correct gait problems, provide additional support, relieve pressure and pain, and provide motion control.

Most people do not need artificial arch support because normal arches are able to support the weight of a person naturally. However, certain medical conditions can impair the ability of the arch to support the weight of the body, causing the arch to fall. Other conditions that can cause this problem include weight gain and excessive pronation or supination. Orthotics can either be used to provide support, reduce shock and stress, or change the function and movement of the foot.

Orthotic arch supports are used to support the foot's natural arch and allow the muscles and ligaments of the foot and leg to heal. They are related to, but are different from, foam insoles that can be purchased at the drug store, which provide support and cushioning in the shoe but are not designed to provide serious support. Insoles, arch supports, and heel cups can all be purchased from drug stores or online, while custom orthotics are made for an individual foot and are prescribed by a podiatrist or other doctor. Custom orthotics are made in a variety of ways, such as casting a plaster mold of a person's foot or molding the foot in foam, and today computers are used to model the foot and the gait in order to produce an insert that is truly geared towards that foot.

Functional orthotics are made of hard material such as plastic in order to better control the motion and position of the foot. They are used to correct problems in the function of the foot due to structural problems, too much weight, physical activity, or deformity, as well as excessive pronation or supination. These devices are inserted into the shoe to correct the gait and reverse the pronation or supination, aligning the foot and leg, and reducing pain. Functional orthotics are also used for people with high arches (known as cavus foot), which do not absorb shock well; the orthotic redistributes weight, allowing the entire foot to support the weight of the body. Finally, fallen arches are another condition that is helped by a supportive arch, which redistributes the weight and keeps the bones from becoming deformed and prevents bunions and hammer toes from developing.

Supportive orthotics, on the other hand, are made of softer materials and are primarily used to minimize stress and absorb shock, rather than to correct abnormalities. These are generally purchased from drug stores, although they can be prescribed by a doctor as well. These are used for arthritic patients for whom the protective fat on the feet is gone, and for diabetics, especially those who have lost sensation in the feet. In both of these cases, the orthotic is primarily used to protect the feet and to reduce pressure.

Orthotic inserts are also helpful for pain under the ball of the foot caused by metatarsalgia or neuromas. Metatarsalgia is a condition in which the long bones of the feet become stressed, causing pain in the ball of the foot. **Neuromas** are bundles of pinched nerves that occur between the third and fourth toes, which also cause pain in the ball of the foot. Metatarsal pads help this condition, as do flexible arch supports, which take the weight off the ball of the foot. People with pain in the arch of their feet caused by heel spurs, plantar fasciitis, weight gain, or by standing on their feet too long can alleviate this pain with orthotics. Rigid arch supports and arch cradles can be placed into the shoe, providing additional support and relieving pain.

Even problems like bunions or **hammer toes**, often caused by wearing tight shoes or **high heels**, can be partially alleviated through the use of orthotic insoles that redistribute weight inside the shoe, relieving the pain of both of these conditions. Another condition that affects the foot is *hallux rigidus*, which is a stiffening of the big toe and is caused by arthritis, excessive pronation, or fallen arches as well as injury or heredity. Orthotic inserts can help this condition as well.

Finally, orthotic insoles are used for unequal leg length as well. In this case, orthopedic shoes are worn, which are deeper than regular shoes. The devices are worn in the shoe of the shorter leg to provide additional height and support to that leg.

See also: Disorders and Injuries; Flat Feet and Fallen Arches; Hammer Toe; Orthopedic Shoes

Further Reading Lusardi, Michelle M., and Caroline C. Nielsen. *Orthotics and Prosthetics in Rehabilitation*. Boston: Butterworth-Heinemann, 2000; Shurr, Donald G., and Thomas M. Cook. *Prosthetics and Orthotics*. Upper Saddle River, N.J.: Prentice Hall, 2002.

OVERSHOES

People have worn overshoes for thousands of years to protect their shoes from rain, mud, and dirt. Common overshoes include pattens, **clogs**, **galoshes**, and spats.

Wooden clogs were often worn by peasants in Europe and Asia as they were working in the fields to keep their feet from getting dirty or muddy, or by wealthy elites who wore them outdoors to, again, protect the feet and clothing from dirt, mud, or water. Clogs could either be carved out of a single piece of wood or could be made from a carved piece of wood attached to a separate upper made of cloth or **leather**. While clogs were worn alone as standalone shoes by peasants, many forms of clogs were designed to be worn over shoes.

In Medieval **Europe**, many people wore pattens, which were elevated wooden soles, sometimes on wood or metal stilts, with leather straps to fit over the feet. They evolved out of the European clog. For instance, the Venetian platform *chopine* was made with a wooden or cork platform, with a fully enclosed fabric or leather upper. These were worn as outershoes to protect the shoes of the wealthy from becoming soiled. In Asia, too, elevated wooden soles acted as overshoes, as in the Japanese *geta*, with a wooden stilted sole and a simple thong upper, or the Middle Eastern stilted sandal. Both **China** and **Korea** had overshoes made either with a wooden stilted base or in the shape of a wooden clog.

Galoshes are another form of overshoe worn over shoes in inclement weather to protect one's shoes. Like pattens, galoshes date to Medieval Europe and were originally a form of clog, made of carved wood, with a simple upper strap, and later, a fully formed but open-backed upper made of fabric or leather. The modern galosh emerged in the early twentieth century as a **boot** made of waterproofed leather combined with a rubber bottom, but today most galoshes are made entirely out of rubber or PVC.

Another form of rubber overshoes are waders, chest-high boots made for wading in water or other fluids. They are waterproof and were originally made of rubber, although today they are often made of synthetic materials such as PVC or neoprene. They are worn over boots and sometimes have boots attached on the inside. Waders are worn by anglers, some hunters, and are also worn in occupations that involve wading in water, human or animal waste, or chemicals.

New England Overshoes are a brand of overshoes designed to be worn over shoes in cold or wet weather. They are boots made of nylon and enclose the entire shoe and lower leg, with a strap that tightens across the instep, and protect the shoes and keep the feet insulated. They can also be worn over an ankle or lower leg cast in the winter to protect the bare foot.

Spats were coverings for men's shoes that were popular at the turn of the twentieth century. They were made of cloth and covered the upper of the shoe. They attached to the shoe by a loop under the sole and buttoned up the sides. Spats were primarily associated with military shoes and were worn by French, Italian, and Japanese soldiers as well as Scottish

These overshoes from the 1930s were made by U.S. Rubber for women's high-heeled shoes. [Photo courtesy of Shoe Icons]

infantry. Today, spats are still part of a number of countries' military uniforms, including Portugal, **India**, Pakistan, and Finland. While spats are often used for decorative reasons, they also have a safety function in that leather spats are worn by welders and other people who work with hot or molten metals to protect the ankles, as well as by operators of dangerous machinery like chainsaws.

Gaiters are related to spats in that they are a covering for the shoe, but extend much higher on the leg than spats, typically to the knee, but sometimes above it. They are made of leather, canvas, or cloth and attach to the shoe by means of a strap that wraps under the sole. Like spats, they once were a part of military uniforms and were worn by American soldiers during World War II. Gaiters are primarily worn to protect the legs and ankles, and today are commonly worn by horseback riders.

Snow shoes are another form of overshoe. They are large, flat devices in which the shoe-clad foot is strapped; the large size of the snow shoe distributes the weight of the wearer, which keeps the person from sinking into the snow. Traditional snow shoes were made with a wooden frame and sinew or hide lacing. Wearing a moccasin or animal-skin boot, the person's foot is strapped onto the frame with more laces. They were worn by Native Americans, Inuits, and native Alaskans, as well as European trappers and explorers. Today, snow shoes are made out of aluminum and other metals and are worn recreationaly for people who enjoy hiking in the snow.

See also: Boots; Clogs; China; Europe; Galoshes; Japan; Snow Shoes; Wellington Boot

Further Reading Grew, Francis and Margrethe de Neergaard. *Shoes and Pattens: Finds from Medieval Excavations in London*. Woodbridge: Boydell, 2006.

P

PARKER, SARAH JESSICA

Sarah Jessica Parker is an actress who is most famous for her role as Carrie, a New York City sex columnist obsessed with fashion, in the HBO television show *Sex and the City*, which ran from 1998 to 2004.

Thanks to *Sex and the City*, Parker is now a fashion icon, and what she wears to special events and movie openings is heavily covered by the fashion press. She started her own low-cost fashion line named Bitten in 2007 and has been featured in other companies' fashion advertisements, such as the Gap. Bitten features shoes as well as clothing, all costing under $10 a pair.

Fashion designer Patricia Field chose the outfits worn by Carrie and the other characters on *Sex and the City*, and her unique style and taste shaped the look and feel of the show and also influenced Parker's style outside of the show. Field chose a mixture of vintage and flea market pieces combined with high-end designer pieces by Fendi, Dior, Roberto Cavalli, Chanel, Dolce and Gabbana, and Prada. In real life, too, Parker is known for her daring fashion choices and was awarded the Style Icon Award in 2004 from the Council of Fashion Designers of America.

One of the most notable aspects of the show and of Parker's own wardrobe is the focus on shoes. Parker, both on the show and in real life, is known for wearing high-end designer shoes, and, in particular, **stilettos**. **Manolo Blahnik**, Christian Laboutien, and **Jimmy Choo** are the names most associated with Parker's wardrobe, and her character spent hundreds to thousands of dollars for each pair of the hundreds of designer shoes in her walk-in closet. Parker has been photographed wearing designer mules, **pumps**, stilettos, and platforms, all of which were also featured on the show. She has said that as a child, she loved shoes and shoe stores and began wearing Manolo Blahnik shoes in the 1980s. Still, Parker has also said that filming *Sex and the City* in high-heeled shoes for 18 hours a day damaged her knees, so she no longer wears **high heels** around the clock. Evidently many of the high-end shoes that she wears on the red carpet today are borrowed from designers, and she has noted that she does not, in fact, own a huge collection of shoes as did Carrie. Photos of Parker in public with her family, for instance, generally show her in flats or **Uggs**.

See also: Blahnik, Manolo; Choo, Jimmy; *Sex and the City*

Further Reading Akass, Kim, and Janet McCabe. *Reading Sex and the City*. London: I.B. Tauris, 2004.

Actress Sarah Jessica Parker poses in New York on May 2, 2008, during the movie junket for "Sex in the City." [AP Photo/Rick Maiman]

PATENT LEATHER

Leather is the tanned skin of animals and usually refers to the skin of cows. Leather is one of the oldest, and is the most common, material used in the construction of footwear. Patent leather, developed in the nineteenth century, is leather that has been coated with plastic to make it shiny and waterproof.

The process for creating patent leather was invented in 1799 by an English leather salesman named Edmund Prior who figured out how to waterproof leather by painting bark-tanned leather with black dye (known as Prussian blue), boiled linseed oil, and varnish. While patent leather (or japanned leather) became very popular in England, and later continental **Europe**, the process did not reach the **United States**. However, in 1818, an American inventor named Seth Boyden was shown a piece of patent leather from Germany and tried to replicate it. He came up with a process that involved layering coats of linseed oil on leather, whereby the leather was coated with boiled linseed oil, which was rubbed in and exposed to sunlight to set the finish; there could be up to 15 coats of linseed used before the final patent leather was ready. He began selling his leather in 1820 and sold the business in 1831.

One of the earliest uses for patent leather during the nineteenth century was **dance shoes** for men and women to wear to balls. But because of all the coats of linseed oil and the baking that set it, patent leather during this period was stiff, and the shoes made with it were uncomfortable. Most American patent leather in the nineteenth century was made from tanned cow skin with the finish coated on the flesh side of the skin. By the mid-nineteenth century, most patent leather arrived from Germany and was made from calf skins, but in 1896, Benjamin Baker, a tanner from Maryland, improved upon the process by using chrome-tanned leather, which left the leather softer even after the periods of baking in the sun. He also coated the grain side, rather than the flesh side, and needed only a single coating of linseed oil, which left the material more flexible. Baker released his first product, patent goat skin in 1899, followed by colt skin, which was eagerly purchased by **shoemakers**. Soon after the introduction of Baker's new leathers, imports of German patent leather slowed down and eventually stopped entirely.

Today, patent leather is made with cow skin and is treated not with linseed oil but with polyurethane and acrylic, which were once sprayed on the leather but are now coated with a machine and then machine dried. Today, only three coats are applied; the first two coats include the dye and the third coat is clear. After the leather is finished, it is sold and then turned into shoes, bags, or other products.

The classic patent leather item is a shoe or handbag in black, although today patent leather can be found in any color; the most common, besides black, are white and red. Formal footwear remains the most popular use of patent leather in shoes. Men's formal shoes, to be worn with tuxedoes, are almost always made from patent leather, as are little girls' Mary Janes, which are also worn on special occasions. Dance shoes are still made from patent leather, and today casual shoes can also be made out of patent leather. Another iconic patent leather shoe is the **go go boot**, either made from patent leather or synthetic pleather.

Patent leather is also popular among fetishists, who wear **boots** and **high heels** made of patent leather, as well as shiny PVC and pleather. Vegetarians and vegans who do not want to wear leather have a number of products to choose from that simulate the look and feel of patent leather.

See also: Fetishes; Go Go Boots; Leather

Further Reading Thorstensen, Thomas C. *Practical Leather Technology*. Huntington, NY: Robert E. Krieger Publishing Co., 1976.

PAYLESS SHOE SOURCE

Payless Shoe Source is a national discount **shoe store** chain. It is the largest footwear dealer in the Western Hemisphere, with 4,500 stores in the United States, Canada, Central and South America, and the Caribbean.

The company was founded in 1956 by cousins Louis and Shaol Pozez. Originally called Pay-Less National, then Volume Shoe Corporation, and then Volume Distributors, Payless Shoe Source was the name given to the company's retail stores in 1978. Prior to that time, the stores went by different names in different regions. In 1991, the company's name was formally changed to Payless Shoe Source.

The cousins' vision was to create a shoe store in which customers could pick out and try on the shoes themselves without having to rely on shoe salespeople to help them, and their first stores, opened in Topeka, Kansas, featured all of the shoes placed on shelves for customers to browse through. Payless took the self-selection concept in shoe stores, which had emerged after World War II, and used it in all of its outlets, which helped propel the company to success. By the end of the 1950s, the company had stores in Kansas, Oklahoma, Nebraska, and Texas. The company kept prices low by reducing overhead, opening its earliest stores in former supermarkets, staffed by only one or two clerks. In 1962, the company went public and raised enough money to fund the opening of a dozen new stores a year throughout the decade, and it bought a number of other shoe stores as well.

Initially, Payless purchased shoes from a wide range of both American and foreign shoe manufacturers. Rather than focus on one company or brand, Payless chose to buy from a broad range of suppliers. By the 1960s, however, Payless began having shoes specially made for its stores, beginning the process of creating in-house brands for the company for the first time, beginning in the 1970s.

Payless's success stems from the combination of low prices and a variety of specialty brands that appeal to different demographics, including American Eagle, Champion, Dexter, Disney, American Ballet Theatre, and Airwalk, and the designer collections Abaete, Lela Rose, and alice & olivia. They also occasionally work with designers such as Patricia Field, the designer for the HBO television show *Sex and the City*. Shoe prices range from $10 at the low end to $48 at the high end and are primarily aimed at women and girls. Payless also derives much of its success from its store locations, emphasizing mall stores and stores located in busy shopping centers.

In 1979, the company was purchased by May Department Stores Company, which eventually spun Payless off into its own company in 1996. Throughout the 1980s, the company continued to expand, and by the mid-1980s, Payless had more than 1,000 stores around the country, all of which were supplied by the company's distribution center in Topeka, Kansas. As the decade progressed, Payless bought more of its shoes from Asia and opened its first office in Taiwan in 1983 to coordinate manufacturing and shipment. Today, most of Payless's shoes are made in **China**.

The Pozez brothers eventually retired in the early 1980s, while the company continued to expand, reaching more than 3,000 stores by 1990 and covering all

A Payless Shoe Source sign points customers to a store located east of a Target Superstore parking lot, July 4, 2003, in Lawrence, Kansas. Increased competition from mass merchandisers like Target and Wal-Mart raised questions about the Topeka-based Payless's future. [AP Photo/Orlin Wagner]

50 states with its first store in Alaska. In 1997, Payless bought Parade of Shoes, a chain of more than 200 stores selling mid-priced shoes, and opened its first store in Canada. Throughout the decade, the company not only bought new stores but closed unprofitable stores and began selling through it Web site for the first time in 1999. That year also marked the year that Payless began selling shoes in ShopKo Stores in the Midwest.

During the 2000s, Payless began expanding into Central and South America and the Caribbean, eventually opening 200 stores in Latin America. In 2004, the company, facing competition from big box retailers like Wal-Mart and Target, went through a restructuring and closed down hundreds of outlets, including the Parade of Shoes chain. Sales continued to fall throughout the first years of the decade, and Payless responded by closing more stores, including those in South America. Today, Payless is owned by Collective Brands, a holding company for Payless and Stride Rite as well as Collective Licensing International, which produces Airwalk and other shoe and accessory brands.

In 2008, Payless announced that it was launching an affordable "green" line of shoes in 2009, to be made with sustainable and environmentally friendly materials like hemp, recycled materials, and organic fabrics. Unlike other eco-friendly shoes, however, Payless's will sell for $30 or less.

To keep costs low, Payless sells a large number of shoes made with synthetic and non-leather materials. Because of this, Payless is one of the most popular sources for **vegan shoes** in the United States.

In 2001, **Adidas** sued Payless for copyright infringement, saying that Payless was selling athletic shoes with two and four stripes, which are based upon Adidas's trademarked three-stripe design. Adidas won the lawsuit and was awarded more than $300 million, the largest trademark infringement award ever. Payless's profits in 2007 were $42.7 million.

See also: Shoe Stores

Further Reading Michman, Ronald D., and Edward M. Mazze. *Specialty Retailers: Marketing Triumphs and Blunders*. Westport, Conn: Quorum Books, 2001.

PEDICURE

A pedicure is a treatment for the feet that typically involves trimming, filing, and painting the toenails, filing calluses, and often involves a foot bath and/or a foot massage. Pedicures are offered at professional nail salons that also offer manicures, which are treatments for the hands and fingernails. Pedicures can also be done at home. A man-pedi is a manicure-pedicure combination.

A traditional pedicure is focused on the **toenails**, just as a manicure is focused on the fingernails. In a traditional pedicure, the toenails will be filed and shaped, and then painted with nail polish. A "medicure" is a medical pedicure, or a pedicure in which, in addition to the toenails being attended to, the entire foot is treated. This is becoming more popular today as women, and increasingly men, are looking for intensive foot treatments. While traditional manicures and pedicures take place in nail salons and are given by manicurists or pedicurists (or nail technicians), full pedicures are given in spas and luxury salons, and the cost is much higher than for a regular pedicure. Full pedicures are given by people sometimes called aestheticians or skin care specialists.

The full pedicure generally begins with the pedicurist removing the person's nail polish and soaking the feet in a foot bath to soften the calluses and massage the feet, followed by rubbing oil into the nails and cuticles to soften them. Toenails are then filed and shaped, and the pedicurist uses a callus file or pumice stone to scrape away the dead skin on the foot. A licensed aesthetician can also do more advanced procedures such as slicing away corns or treating **ingrown toenails**, although podiatrists generally advise against having non-doctors treat calluses, corns, or any other problem. Finally, the cuticles are pushed back (or cut), and the nails are buffed and polished. Other practices could include wrapping the feet in heated towels, applying a mask to the feet, and a **foot massage**.

Pedicures are most popular during warm weather months, or in places like Southern California and Florida where the weather is mild all year round and where women frequently wear sandals, exposing the toes and feet to scrutiny.

For many women, smooth, perfectly groomed feet are seen as a status symbol, demonstrating that their feet are not exposed to hard work or filth and that they have the money to invest in professional treatments. Women's feet, in particular, are valued when they are smooth and well-cared for. On the other hand, many men are now getting pedicures as well. In the last few years, as "man-scaping" has become more popular and metrosexual has become a household term, many men are taking care of their feet, investing in pedicures, foot massages, and even wearing sandals.

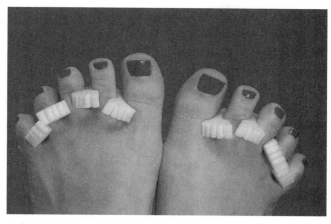

Pedicure. Foam toe spacers like these are often used during pedicures to keep the toenail polish from rubbing off on the toes. 2008. [Copyright Joe Belanger. Image from BigStockPhoto.com]

Professional salons offering pedicures and manicures are regulated by the state, and professional pedicurists should have a cosmetology license provided by the state. In addition, salons and spas are licensed and are periodically subject to visits by the state cosmetology board. Because the tools, including nail clippers, nail files, scissors, and callus files, are used on multiple clients and can sometimes cut skin, they must be sterilized between use. Another aspect of the pedicure is the foot bath, in which the customer's feet soak in a bath of warm, pulsating water. Foot baths, too, need to be sterilized between customers, and fresh water should be used for each customer. Many salons also give the nail polish bottle to the customer after the procedure rather than reuse it on a new customer.

Customers have gotten infections from manicures and pedicures in which the equipment was not clean, a particular concern for patients with preexisting problems such as diabetes, and one woman in Texas evidently died after an infection caused by a pedicure. Some customers try to protect themselves by bringing their own tools to the salon. While this is probably not necessary in a professional salon, podiatrists generally advise people to not have their cuticles cut during a manicure or pedicure because cutting the skin can invite infection. In addition, in many states, pedicurists are not allowed to slice or pierce the skin, and any tools that can cut the skin have been prohibited.

Each country has a different set of regulations regarding manicurists and pedicurists. But even where professional salons are regulated, that doesn't mean that there aren't unregulated people giving pedicures or manicures. For instance, in some African countries, street manicurists offer to paint nails and trim and file finger and toenails. In professional nail salons, the tools used by manicurists are regularly sterilized; street manicurists, on the other hand, do not sterilize their tools, which are then used on multiple people and kept in unhygienic conditions.

One of the newest trends in pedicures is the fish pedicure. This involves soaking one's feet in a foot bath in which tiny, toothless carp are swimming (after first washing the feet in a separate bath). The fish then eat dead skin and calluses off of the customer's feet. This practice began in the summer of 2008 when a nail salon in Virginia began offering fish pedicures. By the end of the year, two states have banned the practice for health reasons, as the same fish are being used to clean multiple customers' skin, and the tanks in which the fish live cannot be truly sterilized.

See also: Blisters, Bunions, Calluses and Corns; Disorders and Injuries; Toenails

Further Reading Toselli, Leigh. *A Complete Guide to Manicure & Pedicure*. London: New Holland, 2005.

PLAINS INDIANS

The Plains Indians are a group of Native American tribes who live in the central plains states of the **United States**, from the Mississippi River to the Rocky Mountains. Tribes include the Shawnee, Cheyenne, Crow, Comanche, Blackfoot, and Sioux. Originally nomadic hunters and gatherers, like other Native Americans, their primary footwear was the **moccasin**. After the Europeans arrived, Plains Indians began to ride horses, which changed not only their subsistence methods but allowed for greater leisure time to devote to arts and crafts, leading to new innovations in moccasin construction and decoration.

Plains Indians traditionally wore hard-soled moccasins made with two pieces (a sole and an upper) that protected their feet from the harsh environment of the western plains. Boots, made with moccasins sewn to thigh-high leggings, were also worn by some, including the Arapaho and Comanche. Because bison was the primary animal resource for many Plains Indians, bison hides were used in the construction of the moccasins throughout the region. Among northern Plains Indians, however, moose was the primary animal used.

After a bison, deer, or other animal was killed, the women prepared the skins to be used in clothing and shoes. Once the hide was prepared, the design was cut and sewn together using animal tendons.

Plains Indians traditionally decorated their moccasins with porcupine quills, which they acquired through trading with other tribes. The quills were dyed and flattened and embroidered with sinew into elaborate patterns and then sewn onto the top, instep, and soles of the shoes. Locally made beads were also used, and fringing was also popular with southern Plains tribes. Finally, hides were dyed with vegetable dyes to create different colors of moccasins. After Europeans began trading with Native American tribes, glass beads were used by Plains Indians starting in the eighteenth century, in some cases supplanting the use of porcupine quills. By the late nineteenth century, intricate beadwork became the hallmark of Plains Indian moccasins.

Plains women not only made the moccasins but were responsible for decorating them, and the decorations reflected not only cultural traditions but the skill and personality of the maker. Moccasin making was a skill that brought respect and prestige to women, and mothers passed their techniques down to their daughters.

Shoes were decorated with images and symbols relevant to the people, like bison, horses, thunderbirds, or bears. Images of eagle feathers, arrows, tipis, peyote buttons, and flowers were also popular designs. Bison, or buffalo, were so important to so many Plains tribes that their use in moccasin decoration went well beyond just images of the animal itself. Buffalo jumps and corrals, bison tracks, bison trails, and even representations of bison intestines were used in beadwork.

Lakota women were well known for their beadwork and quillwork, and special occasion shoes often had fully beaded soles. Cree moccasins were beaded heavily on the entire upper, while Blackfoots used appliques of trade cloth along with beading in their designs. Omaha moccasins were embellished with pom poms, and Sioux shoes used horsehair tufts on the tongues. Other groups' styles reflected trade relationships with non-Plains Indians, like the Iowa whose beading techniques were borrowed from Europeans, the Fox whose beading reflected the styles of Woodland Indians, and the Dakota beadwork, which included flower designs borrowed from the Metis.

After European contact, the lives of the Plains Indians changed forever, which was reflected in their footwear. Not only did decoration styles shift from the traditional porcupine quills to European glass beads, but some Indians began to design moccasins in western styles and motifs.

See also: Moccasins; Native America

Further Reading Elder, Alan C. *In the Steps of Our Ancestors: An Exhibition of Native North American Footwear*. Toronto: Ontario Crafts Council, 1989; Paterek, Josephine. *Encyclopedia of American Indian Costume*. Denver, Colo: ABC-CLIO, 1994.

PLANTAR WARTS

Plantar warts are lesions that erupt on the bottom (or plantar surface) of the feet and are most commonly found underneath the ball and heel where pressure is greatest. They are caused by certain varieties of the HPV virus and, for most people, are relatively harmless. But because humans walk on our feet, the warts are forced by the pressure of the body weight to grow up into the feet, causing pain.

The infection is most commonly picked up in public areas like swimming pools, public showers, and locker rooms, where people go barefoot and where infections can be easily transmitted, and is found more often on women than on men and on children and teenagers. They can also, occasionally, spread onto other areas of the body.

Some plantar warts disappear on their own, but if they do not the typical treatment is to have the warts frozen or burnt off of the feet, both to relieve pain and to keep them from spreading to other people. Rarely, untreated plantar warts can become cancerous.

One of the most common treatments for plantar warts involves freezing the warts with liquid nitrogen, known as cryosurgery. This often takes multiple treatments to be effective. Another option is cauterization, or burning the wart off. Prescription and nonprescription creams and pads, known as keratolytic agents, made with salicylic acid are also an effective treatment. **Dr. Scholl's** Wart Remover and Compound W are two very common products. With this option, the patient applies the medicine daily, covering with a bandage, and then uses a pumice stone to file away the dead skin. Other chemicals that can be used are formaldehyde and silver nitrate.

Patients can also elect to have their warts removed surgically or with a dye laser treatment, available as an outpatient procedure at their doctor's office. Even then, often plantar warts can reappear or spread, necessitating more treatment. Treatments for plantar warts do not kill the virus itself, which cannot be cured or treated with antibiotics. Instead, treatment simply kills the warts.

See also: Disorders and Injuries; Foot Care Products; Dr. Scholl's

Further Reading MacDonald, Ann. *Foot Care Basics: Preventing and Treating Common Foot Conditions*. Harvard health letter special report. Boston, MA: Harvard Health Publications, 2007.

PLATFORM SHOES

Platform shoes, or platforms, are shoes that sit on elevated soles, made of cork, wood, or other natural materials. They have been popular throughout history and in a variety of cultures.

Platforms are really a derivation of the **clog**, a carved wooden shoe worn in many cultures around the world. Worn to keep one's feet elevated in order to protect the feet and the clothing from dirt, mud, and water, clogs in many cultures became status symbols for the elites. The first elevated shoes in the West may have been the elevated boots known as *cothornai* worn by actors in Greek and Roman theater. (Elevated shoes were also worn by actors in English theater centuries later, by boys playing women.) Greek, Etruscan, and Roman women also wore elevated **sandals**, and these sandals may have led to the development of the stilted sandal or *kabkab* worn in the **Middle East** throughout the Ottoman Empire. Other early platform shoes were the Chinese "flower pot" shoes, worn by elite Manchurian women, the Japanese *geta* sandals, and the Indian *paduka* toe knob sandals. In the case of the geta, paduka, and the stilted sandal, these shoes had two to four stilts underneath the sole, making them different from the simple Greco-Roman platform, which has one large sole.

These glittery platform slides were worn in the 1970s. [2007 copyright Monica Boorboor. Image from BigStockPhoto.com]

Chopines, elevated clogs to be worn over shoes, were the first European version of the platform and were worn by wealthy women when going outdoors. With platforms made of wood or cork and upholstered in velvet or leather to match the shoes, they eventually ranged from six to 30 inches in height. Platforms became unfashionable in the seventeenth century, and women's shoes in Europe began to emphasize daintiness, which was associated with femininity.

Platforms in the modern sense—high-heeled shoes that sit on an elevated platform—were created in the 1930s by Italian shoemaker **Salvatore Ferragamo**, who experimented with new materials for his shoes as a result of wartime rationing during World War II. Made with cork or wood rather than stacked leather heels because of the rationing of leather and rubber, platforms quickly became popular in the **United States** and Europe. Some were heeled, but some used the wedge heel, also invented by Ferragamo, which became popular thanks to its sturdiness and comfort. Other notable platform designers included Andre Perugia and David Evins. Platforms traveled to the United States in 1941 and were popular among women who found them comfortable and fashionable. Platforms fell out of fashion after the war and were replaced by **stillettos** as the new fashionable heel for women.

They became popular again in the 1970s, when very high—up to two-inch soles and five-inch heels—platform shoes and boots emerged in the disco era. Platform tennis shoes, sandals, and boots were all sold, with platforms made of cork as well as rubber and plastic. **Candie's** high-heeled slides were a version of platforms because the sole of the foot sat on a slightly elevated platform base. Even men in the 1970s wore platform shoes and boots, associated with disco and also pimp fashion. John Travolta wore them in *Saturday Night Fever*, they were featured in all of the Blaxploitation films of the era, and rock stars like David Bowie, the members of KISS, and **Elton John** routinely wore them. Platforms during the 1970s were often ostentatious, like so many other fashions of the period, and one model had a live goldfish inside of the clear platform. Platforms eventually became so high that doctors worried about injuries arising from men and women falling off of their shoes.

Since the 1990s, platforms have once again experienced a resurgence in popularity, although they've never again become as colorful, gaudy, or high as in the 1970s. Lucite heels are another example of platforms today and are associated with hookers and strippers.

See also: China; Europe; Ferragamo, Salvatore; High Heels; Japan; Korea; Middle East; Sumptuary Laws

Further Reading Ellsworth, Ray. *Platform Shoes: A Big Step in Fashion*. Atglen, PA: Schiffer Pub, 1998; Pedersen, Stephanie. *Shoes: What Every Woman Should Know*. Cincinnati: David & Charles, 2005; Ricci, Stafnia. "Made in Italy: Ferragamo and Twentieth-Century Fashion," in Rielle, Georgio and Peter McNeil, eds. *Shoes: A History From Sandals to Sneakers*. London: Berg Publishers, 2006; Vianello, Andrea. "Courtly Lady or Courtesan? The Venetian Chopine in the Renaissance," in Rielle, Georgio and Peter McNeil, eds. *Shoes: A History From Sandals to Sneakers*. London: Berg Publishers, 2006.

PODIATRY

Podiatry (also known as chiropody in English-speaking countries outside of the **United States**) is the medical specialty that deals with the feet and ankles. Podiatrists have specialized training in the **disorders and injuries** of the feet. They treat minor problems such as corns, calluses, and bunions, **ingrown toenails**, **plantar warts**, and **hammer toes**. They also treat structural problems like fallen arches, plantar fasciitis, and excessive pronation or supination, and injuries such as those to the **Achilles** tendon. Diabetics and others with serious conditions that affect their feet also see podiatrists. Podiatrists diagnose and treat injury, disorders, or illnesses, and perform surgery. They also prescribe the use of **orthopedic shoes** and **orthotics**. Finally, podiatrists educate patients and the general public on proper foot care.

Prior to the twentieth century, people who worked on feet were known as chiropodists and were not trained alongside of other doctors. Instead, they were trained and licensed separately. (During Medieval Europe, while doctors treated patients with a variety of medical complaints, barbers performed surgery, including **amputation**.) Today, podiatrists are still trained separately, but in formal schools of podiatry. Podiatrists receive a Doctor of Podiatric Medicine, or DPM, degree.

The first formal school of podiatry, the New York School of Chiropody, was opened in 1911, followed by the Illinois College of Chropody and Orthopedics in 1912, which was opened by William Scholl, of the **Dr. Scholl's** brand.

Today, there are eight such schools in the United States, all of which are accredited by the Council on Podiatric Medical Education. In the United States, students must first earn a bachelor's degree from an accredited college, and then, after passing the MCAT, take a four-year program at a school of podiatry, followed by a residency of two to three years. Podiatrists learn many of the same thing that medical students learn, but with an emphasis on feet and legs. They also must pass national and state

This engraving shows a barber-surgeon treating the foot of a man who sits on the right. Engraving by C. Vischer after A. Brouwer. [Photo courtesy of the National Library of Medicine]

podiatry exams in order to receive a license to practice in a particular state, or they can take the exam of the National Board of Podiatric Medical Examiners for the state license.

Some podiatrists specialize in certain procedures, such as surgery, or certain types of practice, such as dermatology, geriatrics, sports medicine, or diabetic foot care. Podiatrists can be board-certified in some of these specialties, which involves additional training and both oral and written tests specific to that specialty. Podiatric surgeons who want to be board-certified for surgery are certified by the American Board of Podiatric Surgery, for example, which involves a three-year residency at minimum. (Orthopedic surgeons also specialize in operating on the feet.)

There were approximately 12,000 podiatrists working in the United States in 2006.

See also: Blisters, Bunions, Calluses and Corns; Diabetes; Flat Feet and Fallen Arches; Foot Care Products; Hammer Toe; Ingrown Toenails; Neuroma; Orthotics; Orthopedic Shoes

Further Reading Alexander, Ivy, *Podiatry Sourcebook*. Detroit: Omnigraphics, 2007; Chang, Thomas, *Master Techniques in Podiatric Surgery*; Philadelphia: Lippincott Williams & Wilkins, 2004.

POLYDACTYLY

Polydactyly refers to a condition of having more than five fingers or toes. It is found in humans as well as in other mammals. The condition is congenital and can be caused by a single mutation or by other syndromes such as Carpenter syndrome, Trisomy 13, or Rubinstein-Taybi syndrome. In the United States, it is much more common in African Americans than any other ethnicity. About two-thirds of polydactyly cases affect the feet, and about one-third are passed down from family members.

Polydactyly is related to syndactyly, or webbed fingers and toes. During normal fetal development, the hands and the feet are shaped like paddles, and as gestation progresses the digits begin to separate. In fetuses carrying the genes for these two conditions, the digits don't fully separate, leaving either webbed toes or fingers or an extra digit or piece of tissue. Sometimes the two conditions can also occur together. In feet, the most common type of polydactyly is post-axial polydactyly, in which the extra digit grows on the outside of the foot, next to the pinky toe.

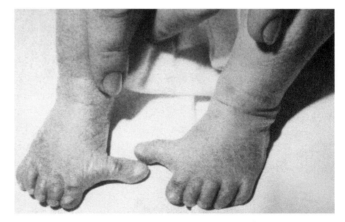

This newborn is displaying the birth defect known as polydactylia involving both feet. Polydactylia, a congenital abnormality involving the occurrence of extra fingers or toes, is due to errors in the process of fetal development and can usually be corrected by surgery. Dr. James Hanson. 1974. [Photo courtesy of Public Health Image Library, CDC]

People with polydactyly usually have a sixth digit, which is only rarely fully functional. In animals, however, those with the condition usually have a fully functional sixth digit, as in the case of the famous six-toed cats who once belonged to Ernest Hemingway and whose descendents still live at his residence in Key West, Florida.

Extra toes and fingers can be removed surgically, and surgery is more common in cases of additional fingers, as additional fingers often impair the function of the hands. (Polydactyly cats, however, often experience greater function, since the extra digits sometimes give them the ability to grasp objects with their paws.) For people with extra toes who have not had them removed, finding footwear that fits is often difficult. **Orthopedic shoes**, which are often wider in the toe than regular shoes, is often a solution.

See also: Disorders and Injuries; Orthopedic Shoes; Webbed Toes

Further Reading Chen, Harold. Atlas of Genetic Diagnosis and Counseling. Totowa, NJ: Humana Press, 2006.

"THE PRINCESS AND THE GOLDEN SHOES." See *"Cinderella."*

PROSTHETICS

Prosthetics are artificial limbs worn by amputees or those with congenital conditions in which a limb is missing. A transtibial prosthetic replaces a lower leg and foot and transfemoral prostheses replace the entire leg and foot. For upper limbs, transradial and transhumeral prostheses replace the arm, with the former replacing a missing lower arm and hand and the latter replacing the entire arm and hand.

Feet and legs are two of the most common appendages that are replaced with prosthetics today. **Diabetes** is the most common reason in the United States for feet to be amputated, and at least 15,000 people lose feet or legs to land mines in former war zones every year. (Cambodia is the world leader in numbers of lost limbs due to land mines, with an estimated 43,000 people having lost a limb since 1979.) In addition, thanks to the wars in Iraq and Afghanistan, hundreds of soldiers and an unknown number of noncombatants have lost legs and feet from war trauma. (Iraq soldiers lose lower limbs at twice the rate of soldiers in World War I and World War II primarily because of the heavy use of improvised explosive devices by the enemy. In addition, because medical care is better today, many more soldiers survive what would have been fatal injuries in previous wars.) Other reasons for the loss of feet and legs include congenital conditions, disease (such as cancer), and industrial or car accidents. People who have lost a leg above the knee have a much more difficult time walking and otherwise using their leg and foot than those who have lost only the foot or the leg below the knee.

Simple artificial limbs have been worn for thousands of years. Wooden or iron rods were attached, usually with straps, to the stump of the leg, allowing those missing a foot or part of a leg to continue to walk. With the **classical civilizations**, medical procedures had improved and amputations were done more often, necessitating prosthetic limbs. In the Middle Ages, both peg legs and hooks for arms became available for amputees.

With the rise of the Renaissance, techniques and materials for prosthetic devices improved, and artificial limbs were constructed out of iron, copper, steel, and wood. In the sixteenth century, French barber-surgeon Ambroise Paré developed new techniques for **amputation** that involved tying off arteries rather than cauterizing them. He also invented the first mechanical hand and the first artificial leg with locking knees. Paré was also the first doctor to document the phenomenon of phantom pain in an amputated limb. Also at this time, new materials were being used to create lighter limbs, like leather and paper. In the seventeenth century, Dutch surgeon Pieter Verduyn developed a new fashion for attaching artificial legs to the body, a process still commonly used today, as well as the first non-locking, below-knee prosthesis.

In 1800, James Potts invented an artificial leg made out of wood that included artificial tendons (made from cat guts) that allowed for the movement

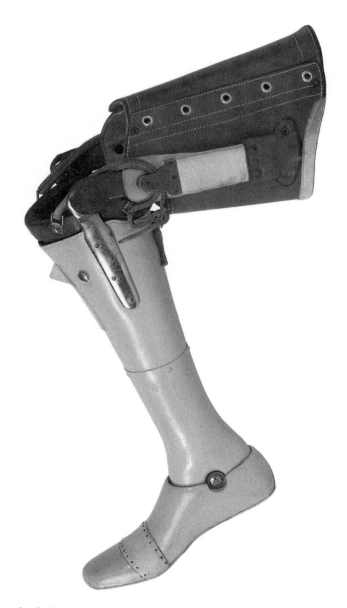

This below-knee prosthesis has a jointed ankle and connects at the knee. [Copyright 2008 Jupiterimages Corporation]

of the foot. Other early attempts at creating artificial limbs that could move included an 1812 artificial arm that was attached with straps to the opposite shoulder, allowing the wearer to move the artificial arm with his shoulder movements. In 1898, an Italian doctor named Vanghetti invented an artificial arm that could be controlled through movements of the muscles.

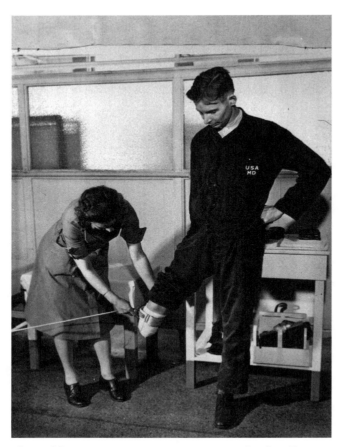

This soldier is receiving exercises on weighted pulleys to strengthen his leg for a prosthesis. Photo taken at Percy Jones General Hospital, Battle Creek Michigan. [Photo courtesy of the National Library of Medicine]

Technological improvements in artificial limbs developed during the Civil War, when tens of thousands of soldiers lost limbs. In addition, the development of anesthesia in the 1840s allowed for longer amputation surgeries, which led to better rates of patient survival and better use of prosthetics after surgery. Also in the 1840s, surgeon James Syme developed a new technique for amputating at the ankle rather than the thigh, which allowed for many more people to keep their legs. New companies opened to make artificial limbs after the end of the war. For instance, J. E. Hanger, a Confederate soldier and engineer who lost a limb during the Civil War, opened a factory for artificial limbs in 1861. One influential manufacturer of artificial limbs during this time was A. A. Marks. His company made artificial arms and legs with rubberized hands and feet and patented a number of new inventions related to artificial limbs from 1854 to 1898.

In 1917, the Artificial Limb Manufacturers and Brace Association was formed in Washington, D.C., in order to encourage an increase in production of artificial limbs to meet wartime demand during World War I. Still, until the development of plastics for artificial limbs, they were still primarily made of carved wood, metal, and leather, making them heavy and difficult to use. Artificial hands, for example, were either simple steel hooks or heavy molded rubber hands attached to a wooden and steel arm. In 1909, an amputee named D. W. Dorrance invented the first hook that opened and closed and was operated by flexing the muscles on the opposite shoulder.

The first and second world wars created a huge need for artificial limbs in Europe, with hundreds of thousands of injured soldiers needing limbs. American companies that formed after the Civil War tried to meet the demand, but it wasn't until after World War II that the modern developments in artificial limbs really picked up. The Artificial Limb Program was started by the National Academy of

Sciences in 1945 to do research in prosthetics and to develop new artificial limbs, and the Veterans Administration gave grants to private corporations like Northrop Aircraft to develop new artificial limbs rather than weapons. The result was new devices that replaced the old wood and leather limbs and new methods of attaching and fitting prosthetics to those who needed them. After the war, this specialized training resulted in the formation of the American Board for the Certification in Orthotics and Prosthetics, an organization that set standards for training in the manufacture and fitting of prosthetic devices.

Starting in the twentieth century, using plastic, silicone, or PVC in artificial limbs has allowed for prosthetics that look and feel more lifelike, and are stronger and lighter than old-fashioned artificial limbs. Today, modern prosthetics are made of plastic (usually polypropylene), which covers the internal structure and which is attached to the stump using straps and a sock that cushions the stump and protects it from pressure. Artificial feet are still made in part with wood, although they also include foam and plastic.

The first biomechanical limb, using "myoelectricity," was developed in the 1940s but became available in the 1960s. These prosthetics are attached to the body in a way that allows for electrical signals to travel from the muscles of the body into the prosthetic, causing movement in the prosthetic. The nerves in the arm or leg are surgically modified to control movement in a muscle that has been affixed with biosensors. The biosensors can pick up the movement in the muscle, send it to a controller in the prosthetic, and, when flexed, the muscle then forces the prosthetic to move. The new frontier in prosthetics technology today is developing an artificial limb that can be controlled by the brain of the amputee.

Most artificial limbs are attached to the body with a socket that is then strapped or attached through suction to the stump of the arm or leg. The prosthetic is then removed for sleeping, showering, or other activities. A new way to attach limbs to the body is through screwing a titanium bolt into the bone of the stump; the bolt is then attached to an abutment, which then gets attached to the artificial limb. This causes the patient less pain because it relieves the pressure of the stump and also allows for more muscle control of the artificial limb. Prosthetics are prescribed by a doctor and are custom-fitted to the patient by a prosthetist. Patients then undergo physical therapy to learn how to use the device, and it generally takes weeks for patients with artificial lower limbs to learn how to walk, drive, or do other activities.

Artificial legs and feet are in many ways much more simple than those substituting for arms and hands because feet don't need to be able to grasp and manipulate objects. On the other hand, because feet and legs bear the weight of the body and allow for locomotion, there are specific needs that lower limb prosthetics need to meet.

Athletes who are missing lower limbs can now wear specialized devices to help them run. Made of carbon fiber and shaped like sickles, these devices, known as Cheetah blades, do not try to replicate the look or feel of legs or feet but are specially designed to allow for running. As this technology has improved, it has created a controversy among professional and amateur athletes, many of whom feel that it gives disabled athletes an unfair advantage over athletes who run on their own legs. Oscar Pistorius, for example, is a double amputee who wears Cheetahs, and he petitioned the International Olympic Committee to be able to compete at the 2008 Beijing Games while wearing his prosthetics. He was ultimately turned down and has also been disqualified from competing in any track event sanctioned by the International Association of Athletics Federation because the Cheetah is thought to provide an unfair advantage.

Artificial limbs cost thousands, and sometimes tens of thousands, of dollars, so they are unaffordable for many people, particularly in the developing world. A number of organizations make prosthetics available to low-income people around the world, especially to those who were the victims of war. In Iraq, doctors report that the greatest number of surgeries performed on Iraqi citizens today are amputations of lower limbs.

See also: Amputation; Diabetes

Further Reading Ott, Katherine, David Harley Serlin, David Serlin, Stephen Mihm. *Artificial Parts, Practical Lives: Modern Histories of Prosthetics.* New York: NYU Press, 2001; Shurr, Donald G., and Thomas M. Cook. *Prosthetics and Orthotics.* Upper Saddle River, N.J.: Prentice Hall, 2002.

PROVERBS

A proverb is a popular saying that expresses a basic truth. Some proverbs are popular around the world, while others are culturally specific. There are a number of proverbs in which feet and footwear play a major role.

Straw sandals are useful only if they fit your feet.

KOREAN SAYING

Many proverbs about feet and shoes relate to travel. For instance, throwing a shoe at someone when they are setting off on a trip was once a good luck tradition in English-speaking countries. The ability for feet and shoes to travel is also used metaphorically in proverbs, as in the Irish saying, "Your feet will bring you to where your heart is." In addition, sayings that refer to "grass under one's feet" have to do with not moving, as in the saying, "so lazy that grass grows under your feet." Not moving is sometimes considered a positive trait, as in the many phrases that discuss finding happiness in one's own backyard, such as "the best manure is under the farmer's foot."

Whether or not feet are on the ground is also associated with not losing control, so "keeping one's feet on the ground" indicates not letting fame, wealth, or power "go to one's head." "Dragging one's feet," on the other hand, means not wanting to take action on something, while getting "cold feet" means not wanting to commit to something. Feet, then, can hold one back from accomplishing something. And finally, walking is a slow way of travel, compared, for example, to horseback, so phrases that compare the two forms of locomotion are common, such as "sickness comes on horseback but goes away on foot." This refers to the speed with which we get sick and the length of time it often takes to heal.

Feet often metaphorically indicate one's position, either with respect to movement or settling in. "Sit a beggar at your table and he will soon put his feet on it" means that if you invite a beggar to your house, he will make himself at home and not leave. "Better wear out shoes than sheets" means that it is better to work than to sleep in. "Put your best foot forward" means to show your best side in public. This last expression is most likely related to the fact that shoes are an indication of status, so putting one's best foot forward also means to wear good shoes.

Many proverbs reflect the idea that shoes are connected to the soul, so wearing someone's shoes, for example, tells you what they are like and what they have experienced. "Never judge someone until you have traveled a mile in their shoes," for instance, means that wearing their shoes allows you to experience their experiences. Another expression is "to step into another man's shoes," which means to take his office or position. This is related to the phrase, "following in your father's footsteps," which refers to continuing in your father's profession. This phrase probably derives from the fact that it was once common to leave one's shoes at death to one's children since shoes were prohibitively expensive for the poor. Another possible origin was the ancient European tradition by which when a man adopted a son, the son put on his adopted father's shoes.

In addition, the phrase "to die with one's shoes (or boots) on," while it originally meant being hanged, is now taken to mean dying while working or during combat. It reflects the idea that the person is so hardworking, self-sacrificing, or heroic that he never stopped working and died without taking a break.

How a shoe fits is often metaphorically used to indicate whether a particular task or occupation suits a person. "If the shoe fits, wear it," for instance, indicates that if something pertains to you, you need to accept it. On the other hand, "every shoe fits not every foot" means that one may not be well suited to every task. "A shoemaker must not go beyond his last" means that no matter how skilled one is, one should not strive to do something beyond one's means and talents. Other proverbs use well-worn shoes to make a point. "Old shoes and old friends are best," for example, implies that the older and well worn a shoe is, the better it feels, and that old, comfortable shoes are better than new and unknown shoes, or friends. Another similar expression is "old shoes are easiest."

In cultures around the world, small feet are considered more attractive in women than large feet because female vulnerability indicates femininity and sexuality. The Sena of Malawi and Mozambique say "never marry a woman with bigger feet than your own" and "don't marry the one with big feet because she is your fellow male." These are similar to the Chinese proverb, "the woman with the long feet ends up alone in the room." Here again, a woman with big feet is both undesirable and also mannish. A similar saying is found in **India**, "if a girl develops long feet, she will be in trouble after marriage." This indicates that she will speak outside of her place.

Shoes in proverbs also represent status because in many cultures and for much of history, the wearing of shoes was associated with high status. So the ancient Hebrew saying, "I do not desire a shoe that is larger than my feet" means I do not want a wife who is a higher class than my own. The proverb "a shoe too large trips one up" can indicate that one has taken on too much and cannot handle it all.

On the other hand, the common phrase, "I cried because I had no shoes; then I met a man who had no feet" or "better a bare foot than no foot at all" compares the lack of status associated with having no shoes to having no feet at all. This means that even if one thinks one's own situation is terrible, there is always someone in a worse situation than you. In addition, the Chinese proverb, "a man in boots will not speak to a man in shoes," refers to the fact that high-status men do not speak to low-status men.

A number of proverbs regarding shoes or feet do not really have to do with shoes or feet. For instance, the popular phrase, "the shoemaker's son always goes barefoot" (other variants include "who is worse shod than the shoemaker's wife?" and "the cobbler always wears the worst shoes") just means that many times a person only cares for others, and cares for himself and his family last.

See also: Beliefs; Shoe Etiquette

Further Reading Brewer, Ebenezer Cobham, and Ivor H. Evans. *The Wordsworth Dictionary of Phrase & Fable*. Hertfordshire, England: Wordsworth Editions, 1994; Schipper, Mineke. *Never Marry A Woman With Big Feet: Proverbs From Around The World*. New Haven: Yale University Press, 2003.

PUMPS

The term pump refers most commonly to heeled women's shoes, and most specifically, professional shoes that are worn in the office. They are seamless, closed, usually made of leather, do not have fasteners, and are generally cut low on the upper to reveal a bit of "toe cleavage." However, the term can also be used to refer to ballet flats or **athletic shoes** in England. In England, the American usage of pump goes by the name court shoe.

Pumps derive from the high-heeled shoes worn initially by courtly men in sixteenth century France, and later popularized by King Louis XIV in the seventeenth century. Prior to this time, wealthy men wore riding **boots** while outdoors, and both men and women wore flat **slippers** indoors.

Women began wearing heeled pumps in the mid-sixteenth century after the Duchess of Orleans wore them at her wedding in 1533, and the trend soon spread to other European courts. Heeled shoes remained fashionable through the seventeenth and eighteenth centuries, and even middle-class women with money began wearing heels, albeit low ones, during the eighteenth century. Heeled pumps went out of fashion after the revolutionary era at the end of the eighteenth century and were replaced by flats and low-heeled shoes (still called pumps). When high heels once again became fashionable at the end of the nineteenth century, only women wore them, and they were often decorated with bows and buckles. Men still wore pumps, but by this time they were low-heeled and largely without ornamentation.

Pumps have been worn by women throughout the twentieth century. In the early decades of the century, ornately decorated heeled pumps were part of every well-dressed woman's wardrobe, alongside fancy boots. By the 1940s, platform heels and strappy heeled **sandals** began to compete with pumps, but pumps were still the classic women's shoe. The 1950s saw the development of the **stiletto**, which changed the shape of pumps, making them more streamlined and less chunky. After the war, too, embellishments returned to women's shoes, and pumps became fancier in terms of materials and decorations. While the 1960s and 1970s brought new shoes into fashion, such as **go go boots** and platforms, pumps remained popular. In the 1980s, as women began working alongside men in white-collar jobs, pumps became the standard footwear for professional women.

These black pumps are part of every professional American woman's work wardrobe. [2006 copyright Justin Miller. Image from BigStockPhoto.com]

Today, pumps are just one of the many shoes in most women's wardrobes and are associated primarily with dressy wear and formal situations. They are most often worn with dresses, skirts, and formal trousers and signify conservative good taste and professionalism. They are also often worn by female ballroom dancers. Heels can be chunky or stilletto, depending on the era.

See also: High Heels; Platform Shoes

Further Reading Lawlor, Laurie. *Where Will This Shoe Take You? A Walk Through The History Of Footwear*. New York: Walker & Company, 1996; O'Keeffe, Linda. *Shoes: A Celebration of Pumps, Sandals, Slippers & More*. New York: Workman Publishing, 1996; Steele, Valerie. *Encyclopedia of Clothing and Fashion*. Farmington Hills, MI: Charles Scribner's Sons, 2005; Yue, Charlotte and David. *Shoes: Their History in Words and Pictures*. Boston: Houghton Mifflin, 1997.

"THE RED SHOES"

"The Red Shoes" is a **fairy tale** written by Hans Christian Andersen in 1845. Andersen, born in 1805 in Denmark, originally wanted to be a poet, playwright, and novelist. The son of a shoemaker who died when Hans was 11 years old, he spent much of his childhood playing in the old women's ward of the poor house and heard the women tell stories of trolls and fairies and ghosts.

"The Red Shoes" tells of a little girl named Karen whose poverty forces her to go barefoot in the summer and to wear wooden **clogs** in the winter. After her mother's death, Karen is adopted and her adopted mother buys her a pair of shiny red shoes that she cannot stop thinking about, even wearing them to church, which is highly inappropriate. She then meets an old man who magically makes her shoes dance until she removes them. When her adopted mother falls deathly ill, Karen chooses to go to a ball in her red shoes rather than care for the woman, and the shoes once again begin dancing until she must have an executioner chop off her feet and make her a set of wooden feet. Karen ultimately cannot return to church because her chopped-off feet will not allow her to enter; she only gets forgiveness after working as a maid in the church and praying for repentance.

Because "The Red Shoes" is an original story, it does not have variants around the world like "**Cinderella**" and other popular folk tales. However, it does have a number of features that are found in other folk tales, most especially a magical pair of shoes.

Red shoes have a long history in Europe, being associated with the Catholic Church, with power and wealth (partly because red shoes were expensive to obtain until the mid-nineteenth century when inexpensive dyes were created), and also with sex, sin, and prostitution. The pope traditionally wears red **slippers**, signifying Imperial authority and the blood of the martyrs. Red heels are associated with royalty and were once worn exclusively by the King Louis XIV and his court, and, before that by Roman emperors. Finally, red shoes are often worn by prostitutes and bad girls.

It is no surprise then, that to illustrate Karen's sin of pride and vanity, that Andersen would have her wear red shoes, which, in her case, represent not only pride and vanity, but also sexuality and passion via the uncontrollable dancing. Andersen's background is illustrative here, as he was not only the son of a shoemaker; he was a virgin and was evidently afraid of sex, while his aunt ran a brothel. His own sister Karen was the illegitimate child of his mother, a product of sin herself. By cutting off the fictional Karen's shoes, Andersen could be thought

This red Mary Jane shoe is a popular shoe for young girls. [2008 copyright Emin Ozkan. Image from BigStockPhoto.com]

to have been de-sexualizing her, and by returning her to the wood shoes she once wore (in the form of wooden feet), she can no longer be vain again.

Clearly, red shoes signify the sin of pride. Originally, Karen fell in love with red shoes after seeing them on a princess; because red shoes signify royalty as well, Karen's wearing of the shoes can be interpreted as her attempt to step above her station, which **sumptuary laws** of the time were in place to prevent. In addition, as a child, Andersen once watched his father make a pair of red dancing shoes for a wealthy customer, who ultimately spurned the shoes and insulted the shoemaker's work.

"The Red Shoes" shares some similarities with the **Wizard of Oz**, which also features a pair of magical red shoes. In both cases, the shoes can't be removed from the heroine's feet, and with them she travels magically. Also, as with the *Wizard of Oz* there is a lesson to be learned from the shoes. In the case of the *Wizard of Oz*, that lesson is that home is always within the heart, and happiness should not be sought externally. In the case of "The Red Shoes," however, the lesson is to learn humility. While Karen is dancing uncontrollably, she encounters an angel who tells her "Dance in your red shoes until you are pale and cold . . . and wherever there are children proud and vain you must knock at the door till they hear you, and are afraid of you. Dance you shall. Dance always."

The dancing shoes of this tale are similar to shoes in other tales as well, such as **"The Shoes That Were Danced to Pieces."** In this tale, 12 princesses are under a spell that makes them go dancing every night in the underworld, wearing their dancing slippers out every night. Here, it's not the shoes that force the princesses to dance, but the shoes certainly play a role in their leaving their castle and traveling to the underworld palace where they dance till their shoes are worn out, causing their father a great deal of suffering.

See also: "Cinderella"; Fairy Tales; *The Red Shoes*; "The Shoes That Were Danced to Pieces"; *The Wizard of Oz*

Further Reading Braekstad, H. L., Translator. *Hans Christian Andersen's Fairy Tales*, translated New York: Beekman House, 1978; Davidson, Hilary. "Sex and Sin: The Magic of Red Shoes," in Rielle, Georgio and Peter McNeil, eds. Shoes: *A History From Sandals to Sneakers*. London: Berg Publishers, 2006.

THE RED SHOES

The Red Shoes is a 1948 film that was directed by Michael Powell and Emeric Pressburger and starring Moira Shearer. It tells the story of a ballerina who must choose between dance and love and who eventually loses her life due to the conflict.

The Red Shoes is based on the Hans Christian Andersen **fairy tale**, "**The Red Shoes**," in which a girl named Karen becomes obsessed by her shiny red shoes, choosing to go dancing in them rather than to care for her dying adopted mother. The girl is punished for her pride and selfishness when the shoes take on a life of their own and force Karen to dance until she must chop off her feet to make them stop.

In the film, Vicky is a young aspiring dancer who is discovered by Lermentov, a ballet company director, who recognizes her passion for dance and hires her. However, Vicky must promise that she will focus on dancing and must maintain that "dance is more important than life itself," unlike the previous prima ballerina who was fired after she got married. Vicky becomes a famous dancer, but at the same time falls in love with Julian, the composer of the ballet, to Lermentov's chagrin, who forces her to choose between dancing or her love for Julian. She chooses Julian and quits dancing, but is invited back to dance "The Red Shoes," and accepts, in effect choosing dancing over her now-husband Julian. Again, she is given an ultimatum, this time by Julian, and kills herself. The movie ends with Julian cradling Vicky's dead body, and with Lermentov going ahead with the evening's performance without his lead dancer.

The film is intended to set Vicky up as the parallel to Karen in the fairy tale. In both cases, the heroine is compelled to dance—Karen by virtue of the fact that her shoes are magical thanks to her sins of pride and vanity and Vicky because of her love of dance and the influence that Lermentov holds over her—and in both cases this compulsion leads to disaster. In both the film and the story, the heroine must repent, as Karen does by fervent prayer and as Vicky does by acknowledging, as she lay dying, her error to Julian and asking that he remove the shoes. Lermentov himself says, when explaining the story of "The Red Shoes" to Julian, "time rushes by, love rushes by, life rushes by, but the red shoes dance on," but he could just as easily have been talking about Vicky.

However, the reality is that Vicky has not sinned like Karen and hardly deserves the same fate. In fact, part of the film's appeal lies in something that many audience members can sympathize with or, at least, admire: the consuming desire to devote oneself to art. However, placing the film in the context of the times when it was made, in post–World War II Britain, the message of the film begins to make more sense. As in the United States, many British women had joined the workforce during the war but after the war ended, they were asked to stay home once again. The movie's message might be that Vicky's sin is found in her desire to pursue her art, rather than staying at home with her husband, as society demanded.

The British film, made with real ballet dancers rather than actors, did not do well on its initial British release, but it became a huge success in the United States. *The Red Shoes* was also made into a Broadway musical in 1993, but the show closed after only five performances.

See also: "The Red Shoes"

Further Reading Connelly, Mark. *The Red Shoes: Turner Classic Movies British Film Guide*. London: I.B. Tauris, 2005.

RED WING

The Red Wing Shoe Company is a family-owned company that makes work shoes and outdoor shoes. Founded in 1905, the company has 2,500 employees and annual sales of more than $400 million.

The Red Wing Shoe Company was founded in 1905. Named after the city in which it was founded, Red Wing, Minnesota, the company was founded by a **shoe store** owner, Charles Beckman, who began making shoes for farmers, loggers, miners, blacksmiths, and railroad workers, none of whom had been specifically targeted by the footwear industry at that time. During World War I, Red Wing made the Munson Last, the standard boot for American soldiers, which the company continued to sell after the war. (It manufactured hundreds of **military shoes and boots** for World War II as well). In 1914, J. R. Sweasy joined the company, bought it in 1920, and his family continues to own the company today.

In the 1930s, Red Wing began making steel-toe boots and shoes for industrial workers and oil-resistant boots worn by oil field workers. In addition, in the 1930s the company introduced a new rubber sole, replacing the original leather sole, and not only led the industry in the use of synthetic materials but lowered the costs on its shoes enough to keep the company profitable during the Great Depression.

The brand is primarily known as a maker of durable men's work shoes, but with changes in the U.S. economy in the 1980s, resulting in a reduction in the industrial sector of the economy and a rise in female workers, Red Wing changed its focus. Rather than making "work shoes," the company now makes "shoes for work," including shoes for the service industry, for women, and shoes for outdoor recreation. Red Wing had actually begun making outdoor shoes as early as 1965 under the Vasque name, which became a big part of the company's success in the 1970s when hiking became a popular American pastime. During the 1970s, the company got an unlikely boost as steel-toe work boots became popular with American punks, who began wearing work shoes like **Dr. Martens** and Red Wings.

Today, Red Wing continues to make industrial work boots and shoes, but it has expanded into areas like health care and food service and other professions that involve standing for long periods of time. Because so many employees in these fields were women, the company developed the Lady Red Wings line that took the safety and comfort features of the men's shoes and combined them with styles and shapes to appeal to women.

The 1980s and 1990s saw the company take its marketing into new directions, including a campaign in the 1990s through which customers were sent thank-you notes after their purchase and a six-month follow up communication. In 1998, the company introduced the WORX line of low-cost work boots, which are manufactured overseas and sold directly to companies via the Red Wing Industrial Program, which provides shoes and boots based on a company's workforce and needs.

Unlike most American shoe companies, Red Wing continues to manufacture most of its shoes in the **United States** and remains headquartered in Red Wing,

Minnesota, with additional factories in Missouri and Kentucky. Red Wing now sells more than 300 styles of shoes and boots, under the names Red Wing, Lady Red Wing, Vasque, Irish Setter (which makes sports and hunting boots), and WORX. The four U.S. factories together produce about 22,000 pairs per day. Red Wing shoes are sold in more than 4,000 locations in the United States alone. Still, union workers in the United States are critical of the fact that Red Wing makes some shoes overseas.

In 2005, to mark the company's centennial, Red Wing had a size 638 boot made, based on the iconic Red Wing product, the 877 Work Boot.

See also: Boots; Military Shoes and Boots

Further Reading Red Wing Shoe Company. *100, Red Wing Shoes: 1905–2005*. Red Wing, MN: Red Wing Shoe Company, 2004.

REEBOK

Reebok International Limited is the oldest manufacturer of **athletic shoes** in the world. Founded in 1895, the company gained American prominence first in the 1970s with tennis shoes and then in the 1980s by making athletic shoes geared towards women. Reebok now sells athletic shoes, fitness apparel, and sportswear and owns a number of brands, including Ralph Lauren, Rockport, and Polo Sport. Today, Reebok is owned by **Adidas**.

Reebok began as J. W. Foster and Sons, a small shoe company making spiked shoes for runners in Bolton, England, after its founder, runner Joseph Foster, took a pair of shoes and added **spikes** to them for his own use in 1893. After other runners expressed an interest in his shoes, he began making them to sell, and eventually his shoes were worn by runners at the 1924 Olympics. In 1958, two of Foster's grandsons, Joe and Jeff Foster, formed their own company called Reebok, named after the rhebok, an African gazelle. Reebok ultimately took over J. W. Foster and Sons.

Reebok shoes were introduced to American audiences after American outdoor goods distributor Paul Fireman began distributing them in the United States. He incorporated Reebok USA in 1979, and in 1981 he opened up a factory in **Korea** to produce the shoes.

When they were first sold in the **United States**, Reeboks were the most expensive athletic shoes available, and competitors like **Nike** and Adidas had already cornered the primary athletic shoe market. So Reebok USA focused on targeting specific markets, like women, and created shoes for a brand new market, aerobics, starting in 1982. The company released the first aerobics shoe called the Freestyle that year, which was worn not only for aerobics but for casual wear as well. Because they were made with women in mind, the shoes were more colorful and fashion-forward than most athletic shoes on the market and became wildly popular for the company.

With the company's success in the United States, Reebok USA bought Reebok International and diversified by making other types of athletic shoes like tennis shoes. By the mid-1980s, Reebok was making $90 million in profits per year, and the shoes were more popular than ever, until the decline in the aerobics trend led to a loss in sales of the company's flagship shoe.

Reebok began making other athletic shoes in the mid-1980s, like basketball shoes, as well as sportswear and accessories, and began competing with Nike, Adidas, and **Converse** for a share of those markets. It bought other shoemakers like Rockport and Avia, which also made aerobics shoes, and Frye Boots, both of whichReebok later sold. Keeping the female customer base in mind, Reebok also introduced volleyball shoes and walking shoes, which, like the aerobics shoes, became huge sellers for the company.

Through the 1980s, Reebok's focus and public image centered more around fashion than on performance, and it found sales dropping as Nike began to dominate the athletic shoe market, especially with the heavy focus on athletic performance and Nike's aggressive advertising.

Reebok experienced a comeback of sorts with the introduction in 1989 of the Pump, a basketball shoe with an air pocket sewn into the collar that was inflated using a tiny pump in the tongue. While the pump technology did not increase the performance of the shoes, the gimmick was extremely popular and the phrase "Pump it up" became a well-known expression. Reebok incorporated this feature into its other shoes, and the company's profits increased. In the early 1990s, Reebok had an advertising slogan, "Pump Up, Air Out," which promoted the Pump technology at the expense of Nike's Air Technology.

In the 1990s, Reebok introduced other shoes like baseball and football shoes, making the transition from fitness and fashion-oriented shoes to performance-oriented footwear, and dozens of professional athletes began wearing the company's shoes. In 1993, Reebok signed an endorsement deal with golfers Greg Norman and Jack Nicklaus and created **golf shoes** named after them. The company also signed an endorsement deal with Shaquille O'Neal and created a basketball shoe named after him, the Shaq Attack, but it was unsuccessful, and the extra expense of creating performance shoes hurt the company's bottom line. The company struggled financially throughout the decade, but sales picked up in the twenty-first century with a new focus on professional sports and an embrace of hip hop culture.

In the 1990s, Reebok gained a name for its promotion of human rights after it was publicaly criticized for its relationship with the apartheid regime in South Africa and for labor problems in its Korean factories in the 1980s. The company now sponsors the Human Rights Award, an annual award given to civil rights activists, and works to improve working conditions for laborers in overseas apparel and shoe factories.

Today, the Freestyle aerobics shoe is still a profitable shoe for the company and is worn by cheerleaders and aerobics dancers. But Reebok, while maintaining its focus on women and fitness, is now much more involved in professional sports. Reebok sponsors a number of international sports teams, and in the past few years has signed deals to provide the official apparel or merchandise for most major sporting organizations in the United States. For example, Reebok is the official shoe and apparel supplier for the National Football League, and the company supplies the merchandise and apparel for the National Basketball Association and the jerseys for the National Hockey League.

Reebok shoes, like shoes made by Nike and Adidas, have long been popular among urban African-American youth. Capitalizing on that market, in 2002, Reebok released Rbk, a new line of shoes and clothing that are said to be inspired by street fashion, and in 2003 the company partnered with rappers Jay-Z and 50 Cent to create Rbk shoes and clothing. By signing deals with celebrities (and nonathletes) like Jay-Z, Reebok has been able to reach more urban teenage males, a segment of the population long dominated by Nike.

In 2006, Adidas acquired Reebok for $3.8 billion. The combined sales of Reebok and Adidas now stand at $12 billion annually, compared to Nike's $14 billion.

See also: Adidas; Athletic Shoes; Celebrity Endorsements; Nike

Further Reading Garcia, Bobbito. *Where'd You Get Those?: New York City's Sneaker Culture: 1960–1987.* New York: Testify Books, 2003; Gill, Alison. "Limousines for the Feet: The Rhetoric of Trainers," in Rielle, Georgio and Peter McNeil, eds. *Shoes: A History From Sandals to Sneakers.* London: Berg Publishers, 2006; Vanderbilt, Tom. *The Sneaker Book: Anatomy of an Industry and an Icon.* New York: The New Press, 1998.

REFLEXOLOGY

Reflexology is a holistic health practice by which pressure is placed on the feet and hands in order to promote health and well being. In particular, reflexology is used to diagnose illness, reduce stress, and treat illness.

Reflexology proponents maintain that reflexology was practiced in ancient **Egypt**, **Greece**, **India**, **China**, and **Japan**, but there is no evidence that when foot therapies were practiced in these cultures, they were related to the modern understanding of reflexology "zones." Reflexology was first practiced in 1913 by a doctor named William Fitzgerald, who called it "zone therapy" and who came up with the idea that the body is broken into zones that correspond to specific areas of the hands and feet. It was promoted by Eunice Ingham, a nurse, in the 1930s and 1940s, but it did not become popular until the 1990s.

According to proponents, by placing pressure on specific areas of the hands and feet, this will affect the corresponding body parts and result in better blood flow to the affected regions. In that sense, reflexology is like **acupuncture**, which finds that acupuncture points correspond to areas of the body, and by inserting a needle into a particular point, healing will occur.

In reflexology, the body is broken into 10 zones, with five on each side of the body. The left foot (and hand) is linked to the left side of the body, while the right foot or hand is linked to the right side. Further, the region from the arch of the foot to the toes represents the body above the waist while the area from the arch to the heel represents the body below the waist. The big toe, for instance, corresponds to the head, brain, and the pituitary gland. The ball of the right foot corresponds to the lungs and heart, while the ball of the left foot corresponds to the lungs, and the top of the instep corresponds to the lower back and hips.

The principle behind reflexology is that humans have pressure sensors in the hands and the feet that allow us to detect danger, and which are connected to internal organs that are then put into motion when a danger arises. By pressing the correct zone, stress is released in the corresponding area of the body, unblocking blockages and increasing blood flow.

Reflexology practitioners are trained to use their fingers and thumbs in a particular way when manipulating the hands and feet. Foot rollers can be used too. Unlike acupuncture, reflexology is not regulated and can be practiced by anyone, including lay people, massage therapists, or nurses and other medical practitioners. Most reflexologists do get some training, however, at locations like the International Institute of Reflexology. A standard course lasts six months and offers 200 hours of training. The American Reflexology Certification Board (ARCB) has, since 1991, offered certification to reflexologists in the United States, who have concluded at least 110 hours of training and can pass the organization's written and practical tests. According to the ARCB, which provides demographic information on practitioners, the average reflexologist in the United States is white, female, in her 40s, and practices reflexology part time.

These wooden reflexology slides have wooden bumps that correspond to 68 points on the feet, which correspond to other areas of the body. [2008 copyright Jamalludin Aabu Seman. Image from BigStockPhoto.com]

Reflexology is said to reduce stress, and some practitioners claim that reflexology can cure illness. It has been claimed that reflexology can reduce wrinkles, help in weight loss, improve circulation, reduce toxins, balance energy, and bring the body into equilibrium, not to mention treat virtually every illness and disorder. For many practitioners, however, it is primarily used to treat stress and is promoted as an adjunct to western or eastern medicine and not as a substitute for it. Sessions last for 30 to 60 minutes and are not focused on particular body parts, as in acupuncture; instead, the whole foot is worked.

Reflexology is also used to assess stress levels, as the presence of calluses, bunions, or **hammer toes**, for example, is said to indicate stress in other parts of the body.

A number of studies have been conducted in the last 10 years on the benefits of reflexology, and none appear to demonstrate a relationship between receiving reflexology treatments and improvements in health, or in the reflexology diagnoses and accurate medical problems. On the other hand, reflexology, like massage, has been shown to relax patients, leading to a temporary reduction in stress.

The benefits of reflexology can also be attained through wearing reflexology **sandals** or walking on special reflexology paths. Reflexology sandals are slides with rubber or plastic nubs molded into the sole, which stimulate the feet when walking. Reflexology sandals are only intended to be worn for about 20 minutes per day. A reflexology path is a path laid with stones placed in a particular pattern; walking on the stones will stimulate the reflexology points and thus improve health and relieve stress. Reflexology paths are common in many Asian countries and can also be found in the **United States**.

See also: Acupuncture; Foot Massage

Further Reading Kunz K, Kunz B. *The Complete Guide to Foot Reflexology*. Albuquerque, NM: Reflexology Research, 1993; Sachs J, Berger J. *Reflexology: The A-Z Guide to Healing with Pressure Points*. New York: Dell Publishing, 1997; Soble, Michelle. *Podiatry for the Reflexologist*. Yellville, AR: Whitehall Publishing Company, 2002.

ROME. *See* Classical Civilizations.

RUNNING SHOE. *See* Jogging Shoe.

SABOTAGE

Sabotage refers to a destructive act that takes place while at work or at war. It is intended to disrupt the activities of the workplace or the enemy. The term sabotage refers to the French term, *sabot*, for shoe, and specifically, to the carved wooden **clogs** worn by peasants and workers. *Saboteur* is a French word that means "to make a loud clattering noise with sabots," and sabotage means both to destroy machinery as well as to work poorly, or to "spoil through clumsiness."

There are a couple of different explanations for the origin of the term, which may be anecdotal. One explanation says that during a French railroad strike in 1910, the railroad workers destroyed the sabots, or railroad ties, which kept the trains from running. Another explanation instead says that French textile workers in the nineteenth century threw their own clogs into the looms, shutting them down, as a form of workplace disruption and as a way of expressing rage at the rapid industrialization of their craft.

A third explanation claims that when workplaces were disrupted due to a strike that factory owners brought in scabs, or replacement workers, from the countryside, who wore sabots, or clogs, and that the term refers to the use of such scabs, who worked slowly due to lack of training, during strikes. This explanation would turn the modern use of the term sabotage on its side, as the use of the sabots, or peasants, was not intended to disrupt work but instead intended to maintain workplace continuity. Finally, a fourth interpretation refers again to the practice of peasants wearing clogs and demonstrating their anger at the mechanization of agriculture during the nineteenth century by throwing their shoes into the threshing machines.

There is no historical proof of any of these events actually taking place, although they certainly may have occurred, but without documentation. It certainly makes sense that the term would have originated in a workplace disruption by sabot-clad workers, and most of the accounts locate its origins in the rapidly industrializing nineteenth century, which was certainly a time for worker anxiety, especially among the skilled crafts such as textile workers.

The irony of the term is that while it was once used to refer to a loud form of workplace disruption, sabotage is generally used today to refer to covert, and quiet, acts of sabotage. In addition, the term can be used to imply that the workers themselves, through the wearing of their clunky shoes, are responsible for workplace slowdowns and that replacing them with industrial machines is a good thing. A similar term in English, although without the intentional overtones, is "slipshod," which means to do something poorly and is also derived from a shoe-related term (wearing loose shoes or **slippers**).

Calls for sabotage were common during the early decades of the twentieth century, in Europe and in the United States, when workers were beginning to organize and the seeds of unionization were taking hold. Sabotage, as it came to be used in the United States, referred to any form of workplace disruption or destruction to machinery, intended to allow the workers to demonstrate their unhappiness and try to have their demands met by the factory owners without having to risk calling a strike.

See also: Clogs

Further Reading Green, Harvey. *Wood: Craft, Culture, History*. New York: Penguin, 2007; Veblen, Thorstein. *On the Nature and Uses of Sabotage*. New York: B.W. Huebsch, 1921.

SANDALS

Sandals, along with **moccasins**, are most likely the oldest form of footwear. Sandals keep feet cool in a hot environment, yet also protect the feet from hot sand, rocky soil, or other impediments. Sandals were not commonly worn in Northern **Europe** or North America prior to the twentieth century, however, because of the cold weather.

At its simplest, a sandal is simply a sole made of **leather**, rubber, woven vegetable matter, or wood or metal that is attached to the foot with a simple strap made out of leather or fiber. Sandals can be extremely simple or extremely elaborate. Sandals were the predominant footwear in much of the classical world, as well as in **Africa**, Latin America, **India**, and much of the **Middle East** prior to colonization. They are also popular in societies in which it is common to remove one's shoes before entering a home, and are thus found throughout Asia.

The classical civilizations from North Africa, the Middle East, and southern Europe all favored sandals as the most common form of footwear when outdoors. Indoors, in most cultures during this period, people went barefoot. Sandals, made of woven vegetable matter like papyrus leaves and palm fibers, were probably the earliest type of footwear in **Egypt**. For thousands of years, Egyptians wore sandals—at their most basic, a sole with a thong that attaches between the toes—with elites and commoners wearing different forms of this basic footwear. Only elite Egyptians wore dyed, adorned, or otherwise decorated sandals, and only the Pharoah and members of his court could wear gold or jeweled sandals. The Sumerians also wore sandals with leather soles, with a toe loop and heel guard, as did the Assyrians and the Babylonians, sometimes with upturned toes. The ancient Hebrew people wore footwear that was similar to that of other groups in the Middle East.

The cultures of ancient **Greece**, beginning with the Minoans of Crete, also wore sandals outdoors, made of simple soles strapped to the foot with straps of thongs. Sandals or *krepis* were the most common sandal in ancient Greece, made with a leather sole with leather thongs going between the toes and over the instep. Other sandals had a central strap down the middle of the top of the foot, with additional straps coming out of the central strap, and others known as *pedila* had straps that wrapped partway up the calf. Sandals and open-toed shoes and **boots** were common in **Rome** as they were in Greece. Sandals, called *solae*, could range from simple and practical to highly adorned with gold and other precious materials. Generally, they were made with a sole of leather attached to the foot either with a simple toe strap (over the second toe; unlike the Greeks who wore the toe strap over the big toe) or a number of leather straps. Courtesans and elite women both in Greece and Rome also wore elevated sandals.

These simple Chinese sandals are made from rice straw, and may be one of the oldest types of footwear. [2006 copyright Heng Kong Chen. Image from BigStockPhoto.com]

Because Africa is made up largely of tropical and desert habitats, the climate tends to be warm or hot for most of the year throughout much of the continent. For this reason, sandals are the most common traditional foot covering throughout much of Africa. Made of leather, wood, pods, or bark, and often decorated with shells, straw, or beads, sandals provide protection from the ground yet keep the feet cool. Today, many African sandals are made with soles of recycled rubber from automotive tires.

Simple sandals of woven grass or wood are the original form of footwear in much of India. *Kapula*, for example, refers to sandals made of woven grasses that are still worn today in the Himalyan region. Because the cow is sacred to Hindus, wearing leather is still relatively uncommon for most Indians. For that reason, sandals are often made of wood, plant fibers, and metals. One of the oldest forms of footwear still being worn in India is the *paduka*, a simple thong sandal made with a wooden sole and a knob on a post between the big toe and second toe. With the development of Buddhism in India in the third century, Indians were wearing wooden sandals with straps, and royals wore sandals adorned with jewels. Another Indian sandal is the *chappal*.

Sandals are commonly worn in a number of Asian and Middle Eastern countries in which it is common practice to remove one's shoes before entering a building. The *niaal*, for example, is a simple sandal made with a thick camel hide sole and straps of leather, cloth or even metal forming the upper, and is worn in many Middle Eastern countries.

The oldest shoes still worn in **Japan** are sandals made of rice straw, twisted into ropes and plaited to form the sandal's sole, with the ropes acting as straps. Known as *waraji*, these were traditionally worn by peasants, and were probably introduced from **China** in the eighth century. The *zori* is the modern Japanese version of the straw sandal, traditionally made with plaited straw soles with a straw rope thong between the toes, and originally worn by the upper classes. Another shoe that developed at the end of the eighth century is the *geta*, a wooden thong sandal with a cloth thong, generally with one to three stilts underneath.

Like Africa, much of Latin America is warm to hot, so sandals are the traditional form of footwear for much of the region. **Huaraches** are Mexican sandals made with a recycled tire outersole, a leather insole, and a woven leather upper. They have been worn in much of Central and South America and are extremely long-lasting sandals. Mayans, for instance, wore sandals made of untanned hides and laces made of plant fiber, which laced up the leg. Aztec peasants often went barefoot, but nobles wore sandals made of leather and woven plant fiber straps, often decorated, while in South America the Incas wore sandals made of woven fiber soles and uppers made of either fiber or llama skin.

Even in North America, where the **moccasin** was the dominant form of footwear, Indians living in the Southwest once wore sandals made out of woven yucca fibers. These sandals were designed to protect feet from rocks, cactuses, and other obstacles common in the Southwest. In addition, the soles were designed for traction and were waterproof so they could be worn in the rivers running through the area.

Today, sandals are no longer a simple form of protection for the bottom of the feet. They have evolved into an infinite variety of styles, from flat sandals to platform sandals to high-heeled sandals. Andre Perugia, a designer for Paul Poiret, made sandals popular among fashionable Europeans, tying the concept to vacations on the French Riviera, in the 1920s. (They were briefly popular in Europe at the end of the eighteenth century, but the fad did not last.) In the 1930s, high-heeled sandals emerged thanks to the invention by **Salvatore Ferragamo** of the metal arch support, which allowed for high-heeled shoes without closed toes to hold the feet in. Painted **toenails** became popular at this time because women could now display their carefully manicured nails in their high-heeled sandals.

Ferragamo is also responsible for the modern platform sandal as well as the wedge heel, both of which are still being used in both shoes and sandals. Finally, it was Ferragamo who was also at least partly responsible for popularizing (if not inventing) the steel **stilletto** heel, allowing for another iconic high-heeled sandal. Designers like **Manolo Blahnik**, Christian LaBoutien, and **Jimmy Choo** have become famous through their stiletto sandals.

The twentieth century was the century in which sandals went from practical footwear to fashion. Besides the stiletto, platform, and wedge, other iconic sandals were released in the twentieth century, such as **Birkenstocks**, **flip flops**, and **sport sandals**. Today, sandals are more than functional. They can be sexy because the foot is almost naked, covered only with a few simple straps. This is seen especially in the slide, another form of sandal popularized in the twentieth century. The slide is a sandal with a wooden sole and a single, wide strap as the upper. Slides derive from the sixteenth century Venetian *chopine* and in the twentieth century were reintroduced as orthopedic sandals from **Dr. Scholl's** or sexy high-heeled slides from **Candie's**.

See also: Africa; Clogs; Europe; Ferragamo, Salvatore; Huarache; India; Japan; Stilettos

Further Reading Ricci, Stafnia. "Made in Italy: Ferragamo and Twentieth-Century Fashion," in Rielle, Georgio and Peter McNeil, eds. *Shoes: A History From Sandals to Sneakers*. London: Berg Publishers, 2006; Utah Museum of Natural History, Kathy Kankainen, and Laurel Casjens. *Treading in the Past: Sandals of the Anasazi*. Salt Lake City: Utah Museum of Natural History in association with the University of Utah Press, 1995.

SEX AND THE CITY

Sex and the City was an American television show that ran on the cable network HBO from 1998 to 2004. It was based on the 1997 book of the same name by Candace Bushnell and starred **Sarah Jessica Parker**, who played a sex columnist named Carrie, and her three best friends, played by Cynthia Nixon, Kim Cattral, and Kristin Davis. The show prominently featured the high-fashion clothes and shoes that the characters loved and is well known for popularizing designer shoes in general, and **Jimmy Choo**, and **Manolo Blahnik** shoes in particular. *Sex and the City* was also made into a feature film in 2008.

Fashion designer Patricia Field chose the outfits worn by the characters on the show, and her unique style and taste shaped the look and feel of the show and also influenced American fashion trends. Field, who won an Emmy for Best Costume Design for the show, chose a mixture of vintage and flea market pieces combined with high-end designer pieces, especially for Carrie, whose character had the most unique fashion style. One of the most notable aspects of the show is the focus on shoes. Manolo Blahnik and Jimmy Choo are the names most associated with the women on the show (although the film also featured shoes by Azzedine Alaia, Christian Dior, and Proenza Schouler), and the characters—Carrie in particular—were often shown spending hundreds to thousands of dollars for their designer shoes. While some viewers found the focus on extreme materialism

> "You have to learn to wear his shoes. It doesn't happen overnight. But now I can race out and hail a cab. I can run up Sixth Avenue at full speed. I've destroyed my feet completely but I don't care. What do you really need your feet for anyway?"
>
> CARRIE BRADSHAW, SPEAKING ABOUT MANOLO BLAHNIK SHOES

offensive, most viewers loved seeing the extravagant fashions, and brands like Jimmy Choo soon became household names, even if most women could still not afford them.

Not only do the characters on *Sex and the City* wear expensive and impractical shoes, they talk about them, shop for them, and throw brand names around. Some episodes featured shoes more than others, such as in an episode in the sixth season titled "A Woman's Right to Shoes" in which Carrie attends a baby shower and finds that her $485 Manolos have been stolen by a guest at the party. The loss of the shoes, and Carrie's grief, caused her to wonder whether she chose the right lifestyle—that of a single woman who spends hundreds of dollars on shoes, compared to a married woman with children. She ultimately decides that it's a woman's right to choose shoes and decides to throw herself a bridal shower (celebrating her marriage to herself) and receives a replacement pair of Manolos as a gift.

In an episode from Season Four titled "Ring a Ding Ding," Carrie finds that she's about to be evicted from her apartment after breaking up with her boyfriend, and says, after realizing that she's spent $40,000 on all her shoes, "I will literally be the old woman who lived in her shoes." She realizes that she has to make a choice between spending all of her money on shoes and other frivolous items and planning for her future. Another episode in which shoes featured was in the third episode entitled "What Goes Around Comes Around" in which Carrie got mugged and the thief made off with her favorite pair of Manolos. She shows her allegiance to her shoes by telling him, "You can take my Fendi baguette, you can take my ring and my watch, but don't take my Manolo Blahniks." Carrie again shows her love for her shoes in "The Good Fight" in Season Four when Carrie leaves Aidan after his dog Pete chewed on a pair of her Manolos. One episode, titled "La Douleur Exquise" from Season Two, features Charlotte, who finds that she is able to get beautiful shoes for free from a shoe salesman with a foot fetishist, who asks her to try on shoes for him.

Manolo Blahnik credits "Sex and the City" for his success in America, acknowledging that he wouldn't have had the success he has gained without the show's promotion of his shoes. Other shoes featured on the show have experienced similar levels of success. For instance, in "Baby, Talk is Cheap" in Season Four, Carrie wears a pair of **Dr. Scholl's** exercise sandals; by the end of the next day, that sandal sold out on the Dr. Scholl's Web site.

Carrie's love of expensive, frivolous, yet beautiful shoes can be seen as a sign of shallowness and materialism, not to mention immaturity and misplaced priorities, but can also be read as a sign of her power. Carrie is a successful single woman who carries out her life (even running to catch a cab) in five-inch **stiletto** heels, and while she and her friends spend a great deal of time obsessing over men and fashion, ultimately she is successful on her own terms, and wearing very **high heels**, for Carrie as well as for other women, is a sign of that power. Sarah Jessica Parker once told a reporter that while shooting the show, the director would often tell her that she could remove her shoes for a close-up, but she always kept them on because "the expression of a woman in flats is totally different from one in heels." A woman in heels is a powerful woman, and this is one of the reasons for the show's enduring popularity among women.

See also: Blahnik, Manolo; Choo, Jimmy; Parker, Sarah Jessica; Stilettos

Further Reading Akass, Kim, and Janet McCabe. *ReadingSex and the City*. London: I.B. Tauris, 2004.

SHOE CARE AND REPAIR

Shoes need to be cared for in order to keep them looking their best and to make them last a long time. As shoes break down, they can be repaired by professionals who were once known as cobblers and are now called shoe repairmen. Because we are often judged by how our shoes look, keeping shoes looking good ensures that we will be seen in a good light.

Throughout much of human history, shoes were extremely expensive and only available to those who could afford them. Prior to the Industrial Revolution—when shoe production became mechanized, making inexpensive shoes available to the masses—those who could afford shoes often wore the same pair of shoes for years, and even handed them down to their children. For this reason, caring for shoes was essential and repairing them as they became worn was critical.

Military shoes and boots, in particular, need to be maintained and kept in good condition. In wartime, in particular, when both shoes and the materials for shoes like **leather** are limited, soldiers are expected to keep their shoes in good condition, and civilian shoe repairmen often played an important role in warfare by repairing soldiers' shoes during war. During World War II, shoes that were too worn to be repaired were given to German and Japanese prisoners of war. According to military records, American soldiers fighting during this war wore out two pairs of shoes per year.

Dress shoes, especially expensive shoes worn by the wealthy, also demand special care and protection. Pattens, a form of **overshoe** worn in Medieval **Europe**, allowed elites to protect their **pumps**, often made from materials like silk brocade and velvet, from water, dirt, and mud when outdoors. Chopines and **galoshes** were also worn for this same purpose. These overshoes fell out of fashion in the eighteenth century, as the development of sidewalks in Europe made walking outdoors less hazardous.

Shoe repairmen, known formally as cobblers, were once common craftsmen throughout Europe since the Middle Ages and the **United States**. (Cobblers both repaired shoes and also remade, and sold, old shoes with old leather and other materials.) Like **shoemakers**, or cordwainers, cobblers either worked in their own shops in villages and towns or traveled from town to town, repairing shoes as they went. Replacing worn heels and soles was, for centuries, the most commonly requested service from a cobbler.

In both Europe and the United States, shoe repair shops were once found in every town, and after World War II, large numbers of shoemakers and shoe repairmen immigrated to the United States and opened up shoe repair shops since many European shoe factories were bombed during the war. At the same time, many Americans began repairing their shoes themselves, rather than bringing them to shoe repair shops, in order to save money, starting the decline in shoe repair shops in the United States.

Today, shoes are cheaper than ever—both in the sense that they are less expensive, since most shoes are now made in Asia using very low paid labor, and also because many shoes today are made poorly, with poor-quality materials. In addition, shoe fashion is governed by the same forces that shape the fashion industry, making many styles of shoes unfashionable after just a season or two. For these reasons, many people treat shoes as expendable items; they are purchased, worn for a brief time, and then discarded rather than repaired. In addition, as new materials like rubber and plastic became more commonly used in shoes, the ability to repair shoes made with those materials has been hampered, in part because many shoes today are molded, rather than created with separate pieces on a last, making it impossible to replace soles or heels.

Today, there are approximately 7,000 shoe repair shops in the United States (down from at least 100,000 in the 1930s), many of which also offer shoe shine services and non-related services like key-cutting. As the economy in the United States crumbled in 2008, shoe repairmen have found more business, as budget-minded customers are choosing to have their shoes repaired rather than replaced. Indeed, Kiwi Brands, the world's leading shoe polish company, maintains that when people make more of an effort to care for their shoes, this indicates that times are hard economically; an economic upswing, on the other hand, is marked by people paying less attention to the care of their shoes. As in the past, resoling shoes and replacing heels remain the most common ways to repair old shoes.

Leather shoes are also maintained via shoe polish, which dates to the eighteenth century and is used to keep leather shoes waterproof and shiny. Polishing leather shoes not only keeps leather shoes looking their best, but can mask scuffs and other damage, thus extending their life as well. While some people continue to have their shoes professionally shined at a shoe shine and repair shop, most people simply buy shoe polish from the drug store and clean and polish their shoes themselves. Suede shoes cannot be polished, but can be treated with a waterproof spray to protect them from water damage. Athletic shoes and other cloth and rubber shoes can often be washed in the washing machine when dirty.

Shoe storage is another important aspect of keeping shoes well cared for. Shoe trees, racks, cabinets, and boxes can keep shoes in good shape. By providing a safe, designated space for shoes, they stay in better shape because they are not sitting on top of each other. This is particularly important for men's and women's dress shoes, which can not only be scuffed from being poorly stored, but can become misshapen. Using a shoe horn to put shoes on is another way to keep them from being misshapen.

See also: Shoe Shine and Polish

Further Reading McGowan, James. *The Shoe Shine Buff: The Professional Shoe Care Book*. Huntingdon: CAW Pub, 1996.

SHOE ETIQUETTE

Shoe etiquette refers to the cultural rules that govern what can or should be done with shoes. The most common rule is that shoes should not be warn indoors, and especially in private homes. This practice is found throughout much of Asia and the **Middle East** and was observed in the civilizations of **Egypt**, **Greece**, Israel, and **Rome**. Because shoes are in contact with the ground, shoes are considered impure in many cultures, which explains the norm of removing one's shoes before entering a home or sometimes a public or sacred space.

While it is normal to wear shoes inside people's homes in much of the west, it is still considered impolite to place one's shoes on top of tables, couches, or other furniture. In public places, in particular, such as in movie theatres, it is considered bad form to place one's feet on the seats. Some folk **beliefs** about the unluckiness of shoes (as when one puts shoes on a table or places them higher than one's head) are related to this custom.

Feet, whether shod or barefoot, are often considered impolite to point towards, or touch, other people. In **India**, parts of **Africa** and the Middle East, and parts of Asia, touching one's foot or shoe to another person, and especially to their head, is very rude.

Removing one's shoes in the presence of a person of higher status was once a common practice and was a way of showing humility and respect and demonstrating one's subordinate status. This was common in **Japan** during the Imperial period and in Africa prior to colonization.

On the other hand, it is considered impolite to remove one's shoes in the presence of other people in some cultures, and in particular in the West there is a concern about **foot odor**. Another reason for the practice of keeping one's shoes on is that removing shoes for many westerners is an intimate act and doing so in front of strangers or acquaintances is seen as untoward.

Shoes are often given as a gift to mark certain occasions and are especially associated with a number of rites of passage around the world. Marriage is the most important occasion associated with shoes, and some cultures had practices that involved giving a new pair of shoes to the bride, having the bride's father give the bride's shoes to the groom, or the groom placing a new pair of shoes onto the bride's feet at the wedding. Alternatively, the bride herself could make her own **wedding shoes**, sometimes her mother will make her wedding shoes, or else the bride is expected to make shoes for the members of her husband's family.

Birth and death are also occasions in which a person might get a new pair of shoes. In **China**, for example, babies are given shoes at their one-month birthdays, and the dead wear longevity shoes, embroidered with special designs, in order to carry them to the afterlife. In addition, the close relatives of the dead will wear white clothing and shoes to the funeral. Traditional Jewish custom demands, instead, going barefoot (or foregoing leather shoes) during the seven-day mourning period after a death.

See also: Beliefs; China; Class; Classical Civilizations; Japan; Judaism; Middle East; Wedding Shoes

Further Reading Cleary, Meghan. *The Perfect Fit: What Your Shoes Say About You.* San Francisco: Chronicle Books, 2005; Monger, George. *Marriage Customs of the World: From Henna to Honeymoons.* Santa Barbara: ABC-CLIO, 2004.

SHOE FASTENERS

Throughout history, there have been a range of ways of fastening shoes to the foot. Shoes today can be fastened to the foot with a range of materials, from Velcro fasteners to shoelaces. For much of world history, shoes were relatively simple and included **sandals**, **moccasins**, or **slippers** made out of one or two pieces of animal skin, and **boots** made of a sole combined with a larger piece of skin to cover the leg. In addition, wooden **clogs** or wooden-soled shoes were also popular footwear throughout **Africa**, Asia, the **Middle East**, and **Europe**.

With respect to early moccasin-style shoes and boots, the earliest form of fastening would have been strips of **leather** or woven plant fiber. The hide or leather was wrapped around the foot and ankle, and strips of hide either wrapped around the ankle and upper, or were threaded through holes poked into the upper. This was the most common way that closed shoes were fastened in the classical world and Medieval Europe. Native American moccasins, on the other hand, utilized both leather laces as well as stone, bead, or metal buttons or conches, around which the laces tied.

In Medieval Europe as turned shoes replaced these earlier slippers, fastening systems changed. Instead of simply wrapping a piece of leather around the foot, turned shoes involved cutting and sewing together, using animal sinew or thin strips of leather, pieces of leather and then turning the finished shoe inside out in order to wear. Turned shoes were made in the Roman Empire and Europe starting in about the fourth century, but were reserved for members of the upper classes. Turned shoes could be fastened with a number of devices, including metal buckles from about the thirteenth century, laces made of leather, ribbon, or cord from at least the twelfth century, leather toggles from about the twelfth century, and buttons made of bone, wood, or metal, from about the fourteenth century. Lace holes were punched into the leather using an awl, and often a reinforcing piece of leather was sewn behind the lace holes for extra support.

It wasn't until the development of the welted shoe, in the fifteenth century, that other means of constructing and fastening shoes became available. With welted construction, shoes are made right side out on a wooden last, with the pieces sewn together, using sinew or leather strips in the early Middle Ages, and linen, flax in the later Middle Ages, in the shape of the shoe directly on the last. Fastenings after the Middle Ages included buckles, lacing, and buttons. By the end of the sixteenth century, shoes with closures largely replaced slip on shoes for those who could afford them.

Regardless of the fastening, latchets were needed on shoes to provide a place for the upper pieces to come together. Latchets or straps, which emerged around 1570, are an extension of the material from the two-quarters of the shoe that are pulled together to allow for the shoe to close over the tongue. It is on the strap that buttons or buckles would be attached; the latchet is used for laces. Occasionally, well-made shoes had reinforcements of wire around the lace holes. Some latchet shoes had openings on the side between the quarter and the vamp, while others were entirely closed, and by the late seventeenth century latchet shoes were always closed.

While fasteners such as buttons and buckles were partly functional, shoe buckles, which became popular during the reign of Louis XIV in the sixteenth century, were worn by noblemen and were often highly lavish, made of precious metals and adorned with jewels and a variety of decorative motifs. Buckles continued to get larger and more elaborate throughout the eighteenth century, and by the 1770s, both men's and women's shoes featured such large buckles that they became a source of social satire. Shoe buckles gradually got smaller and were eventually replaced by shoe laces at the end of the eighteenth century, and when they are worn today, are for the most part functional rather than decorative. On the other hand, women's sandals, and especially high- heeled sandals, are still fastened with tiny metal buckles.

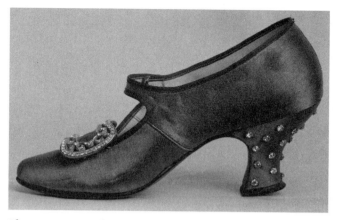

This satin pump has a rhinestone buckle on the vamp as a decoration. Photo taken 1909–1914 by Harris & Ewing. [Photo courtesy of the Library of Congress Prints and Photographs Division]

In the nineteenth century, buttons were popular closures on shoes and boots, and boots were also closed using lacing. Some boots, which were extremely popular during this century, were made with elastic cloth panels known as gores; these boots did not need a closure because they stretched when they were put on or removed. Buttons and laces both continued to be used through the early twentieth century, when laces finally overtook buttons, which fell out of style.

Modern shoelaces of cord with a metal or plastic aglet, to help thread the lace through the holes and keep them from unraveling, were developed at the end of the eighteenth century. Today, there are elasticized shoe laces as well as decorative items like charms that can be attached to shoelaces. Decorative lacing is an important feature in certain shoes, such as **espadrilles** and ballet slippers, both of which are held onto the feet with satin ribbon (as in ballet slippers) or cloth ribbons.

Modern closures for shoes include zippers and Velcro. Zippers developed from the slide fastener that was invented in 1893, but they were not used for shoes until the twentieth century when the B. F. Goodrich Company sold rubber **galoshes** with slide fasteners called Zips in 1923. Zippers weren't really available through the rest of the world until after World War II, however, and are used primarily on boots, rather than shoes.

Velcro was invented in 1941 but was not commercially produced until the 1950s and was marketed as a "zipperless zipper" to be used to fasten clothing. While its usage in clothing is primarily limited to certain kinds of sturdy clothing and uniforms, it has become a popular closure in **athletic shoes**. A more recent innovation in athletic shoes is the Boa lacing system, which replaces conventional shoelaces and is used in running shoes, ski boots, and snowboard boots. It involves titanium wires that are run through a wheel; the wearer cranks the reel to tighten the laces, which allows for much quicker lacing and ensures that the laces will not come undone when active.

Some shoes are not fastened at all and slip on the feet. **Pumps**, **cowboy boots**, riding boots, **motorcycle boots**, and slippers and clogs do not need fasteners, nor do flip flops and other forms of sandals. For boots, shoe horns are often necessary to pull the boot onto the foot, and some boots include a bootstrap, a strap, or tab at the top of the boot to aid in pulling the boot on.

See also: Foot and Shoe Adornment

Further Reading Friedel, Robert. *Zippers: An Exploration in Novelty*. New York: W. W. Norton, 1994; Pedersen, Stephanie. *Shoes: What Every Woman Should Know*. Cincinnati: David & Charles, 2005.

SHOEMAKERS

Shoemakers are craftspeople who make shoes. While many people use the term cobbler for shoemaker, technically cobblers use old **leather** and primarily repair shoes, while shoemakers use new leather and make shoes. The traditional English term for shoemaker is *cordwainer*, which derives from the French term *cordonnier* and is related to the Spanish city Cordoba, known for its fine leather. The term cordwainer was first used in the twelfth century.

Starting in the eighth century in **Europe**, shoes evolved from simple **moccasin**-like shoes made of one or two pieces, sewn together with either a center seam or side seam, into turned shoes made inside out, of a number of pieces. Starting in about the twelfth century, new construction techniques developed, and shoemaking became yet more specialized. Also at this time, **shoemakers' guilds** first emerged in Europe.

From the Middle Ages until the Industrial Revolution, shoemakers in Europe and the Americas were an important cottage industry, and every town had a shoemaker. Shoemakers generally worked at home or in very small shops. In rural areas that could not support a full-time shoemaker, shoemakers often traveled from village to village, carrying their workbench, lasts, and tools with them and making shoes for local families using leather from local tanneries. Often the shoemaker would visit the same families once a year to make new shoes for the family members.

Shoemakers trained as apprentices to master shoemakers until they learned the craft well enough to practice on their own. Those working in small towns, villages, and the colonies did not make fashionable shoes; shoes were functional. Urban shoemakers and those that catered to wealthy clients, on the other hand, looked to the European courts to find out what was fashionable at the time. The first trade school for shoemaking was Cordwainers College, established in London in 1887. (Today it is known as the London College of Fashion.)

The first shoemakers arrived in North America in the early seventeenth century and were found in the first permanent English settlement on the continent, Jamestown, Virginia. Virginia remained the source of leather and shoes throughout the seventeenth century until the other New England colonies started tanning their own leather and making their own shoes.

In the mid-nineteenth century, with industrialism, the craft of shoemaking changed, allowing for semiskilled workers to replace highly skilled craftsmen, especially in North America, where these technologies were first developed. By the end of the nineteenth century, most shoes being made in the **United States** and Canada came from mechanized shoe factories rather than traditional shoemakers.

This young apprentice is nailing a heel onto a shoe under the guidance of a shoemaker. Reproduction of painting by Emile Adan, copyrighted by Braun & Company, New York, 1914. [Photo courtesy of the Library of Congress Prints and Photographs Division]

There are still shoemakers and bootmakers who make shoes by hand. Cowboy boot makers continue to make **cowboy boots** by hand and according to nineteenth century techniques, and custom shoemakers (or bespoke shoemakers) can still be found in Europe and in some cities in the United States. These shoemakers use machines when necessary, but do much of their work by hand.

Saint Crispin and his brother Saint Crispinian are the patron saints of shoemakers; they were Roman shoemakers in third century Gaul who converted to Christianity and made shoes for the poor. October 25 is St. Crispin's Day, known as the Shoemaker's Holiday.

See also: Shoemaking; Shoemakers Guilds

Further Reading Swann, June. *Shoemaking*. Princes Risborough: Shire, 1986.

SHOEMAKERS' GUILDS

Shoemakers' guilds are professional guilds of **shoemakers**. Guilds of craftsmen were formed in Medieval Europe in order to protect trade secrets and control their trades and were derived from Roman craft organizations. Guilds were recognized by the king and were also involved in religious and charitable activities.

Guilds were presided by a governing body of some kind and were only open to master craftsmen. Apprentices and journeymen could not join until they had risen to the level of master craftsmen, which would generally take a number of years;

guild membership was subject to the approval of the guild members. Craftsmen who could not demonstrate honorable breeding or who came from professions that the guild disapproved of would be rejected.

The first European shoemakers' guilds, or cordwainers' guilds, were established in the twelfth century as shoemaking techniques advanced and the trade became professionalized. The first English shoemakers' guild was formed in Oxford in 1131, followed by a London guild a few years later. The earliest German guild was formed in 1158. While the term cordwainer originally referred to anyone who worked with **leather**, tanned leather, or made leather goods, it eventually became restricted to shoemakers, while other leather craftsmen were organized into their own guilds. In addition, a division of labor emerged among shoemakers whereby most shoemakers no longer had to tan and prepare their leather; those activities were done by a separate occupational group. Guild rules also assured that cobblers would only be allowed to work with old leather while cordwainers could work with new leather. (In the sixteenth century, however, the London Cordwainers' guild merged with the cobblers.)

In areas under the control of a guild, craftsmen could not work in a craft without being members of the guild. In addition, the guilds could petition the king to restrict the number of craftsmen working in a certain area in order to keep competition to a minimum. In rural areas, however, shoemakers often operated outside of the reach of the established guilds.

Guilds began to decline in the eighteenth century, and by the nineteenth century, with the rise of industrialism and demands for free trade, guilds fell out of fashion for most trades. Still, shoemakers' guilds in Europe did survive, and by the end of the nineteenth century began to act in an educational and advisory capacity, even though their control over the shoemaking trade had disappeared. The Cordwainers' Company, for example, established a trade school in London in 1887 that trained students in shoe design and manufacture.

See also: Shoemaking; Shoemakers

Further Reading Farr, James Richard. *Artisans in Europe, 1300–1914*. Cambridge: Cambridge University Press, 2000.

SHOEMAKING

Shoemaking, since the Middle Ages, is a craft involving dozens of steps, from tanning the **leather** to be used in the shoes, to the final assembly of the materials. Prior to that time, the most common forms of footwear in the world were **moccasins** and **sandals**, both of which involved relatively simple tools and techniques to create.

Starting in the eighth century in **Europe**, shoes became more elaborate and shoemaking became a more complicated craft, as foot coverings evolved from moccasin-like shoes made of one or two pieces, sewn together with either a center seam or side seam, into shoes made of a number of pieces.

The first innovation in shoe construction in the Middle Ages was the introduction of turning, in which a shoe is made inside out, with an upper and sole sewn together with thong and later linen thread, and then turned back outside with the seams hidden. At this time, shoes were mostly ankle-high booties, and either slipped on, or were fastened with a simple toggle or thong. Because the leather had to be soft in order for the shoe to be turned inside out, turn shoes were made with very soft soles, making them wear out very quickly.

As new shoe styles emerged, new construction techniques developed as well, including the welt or rand, which was a piece of leather sewn into the shoe between the upper and the sole. By the fifteenth century, welted construction emerged as the newest technique to make shoes. Here, shoes are not made inside out, but the uppers are made rightside out on a last and then are sewn together with a welt to the insole, and then the sole is finally attached to the welt, holding the shoe together. Also, shoes began to be made from smaller pieces that were sewn together, using linen thread, to make the entire shoe. Since they are not turned, the sole could be made of much stiffer leather, making welted shoes much more sturdy. The other development that emerged thanks to this new construction technique was heels, which were devised to keep the rider's foot in the stirrup, and became a feature of riding **boots** after the thirteenth century.

Lasts, introduced first in Europe in the late fifteenth century (although a form of metal last was used by Romans in earlier eras), were carved wooden models

These men and boys are learning to make shoes in an American trade school. Photo taken by Frances Benjamin Johnston, 1899. [Photo courtesy of the Library of Congress Prints and Photographs Division]

in the shape of a foot, on which the upper for a shoe or boot was constructed. (Today, they are made of plastic.) Lasts, from the time that they were introduced until the mid-nineteenth century, were known as "straight lasts" and were the same for the right and left foot. In the Middle Ages, shoemakers would only own a few lasts, in a handful of sizes, and in one basic style. It wasn't until heeled shoes emerged in the sixteenth century that lasts needed to be made in different styles in order to give sufficient strength to the shoe for the heel to be mounted on it. Lasts are still used for shoe construction today and remain probably the most important innovation in shoe construction in history.

From the Middle Ages until the Industrial Revolution, **shoemakers** in Europe and the Americas were an important cottage industry, and every town had a shoemaker. (Cobblers, on the other hand, are by definition those who repaired shoes, but did not actually make them.) Shoemakers could either make "bespoke shoes," for a particular customer, or standard shoes to be sold to whoever wanted to buy them. For bespoke shoes, the shoemaker would measure the feet and select the appropriate last. For a foot that was wider than his standard last sizes, he would add layers of leather around the last to create a wider size. Using the last and his patterns, the shoemaker would cut the pieces of leather, and assemble them, using a pincer, on the last, after soaking and stretching the leather. (Softer pieces of leather are used for the uppers while a harder piece is used for the sole.) The pieces are then tacked to the last where they dry in place, and are then sewn together and are attached to the sole. Prior to industrialization, it took two to three days to make a pair of shoes.

Shoemakers' tools until industrialization included a selection of lasts to make uppers, and all of the tools to cut and sew the leather and other materials, including saws, knives, scrapers, punches, nippers, scissors, pincers, hammers, awls, carvers, needles, burnishing tools, lapstone, and thread. All of these, plus his lasts and patterns, were stored in the workbench.

The invention of the rolling machine in 1845—which quickly compacted leather and replaced the lapstone and hammer—combined with the sewing machine—which was invented in 1846 and which made sewing the uppers easier—both made shoes faster and easier to produce. In 1858, a new machine was developed that allowed for the soles to be machine-sewed to the uppers, further simplifying production. Once these machines, known as McKay machines, became widely used by shoemakers, shoes became less expensive and much more widely worn. Also, new styles could be created with frequency, leading to a surge in new shoe styles. Also at this time, the "crooked" last finally became widespread, which allowed for different shoes to be made to fit the right and the left foot.

Other machines such as the buttoning machine, and, in 1889, the lasting machine which replaced hand shaping with a pincer (and can last 1,200 shoes per day), further mechanized the industry, allowing for semiskilled workers to replace high-skilled craftsmen, especially in North America, where these technologies were first developed. By the end of the nineteenth century, most shoes being made in the **United States** and Canada came from mechanized shoe factories.

Because the United States led the world in the industrialization of shoe production, American shoes overtook European-made shoes.

Custom handmade shoes, or bespoke shoes, were still popular among the wealthy until the mid-twentieth century, when bespoke shoes began to be replaced by designer shoes, first in Europe and then in the United States. At this time, shoemakers with wealthy clientele began designing shoes with aesthetics in mind, and not for individual customers. Their shops eventually supplanted the small custom-made shoemakers and began the trend of designer brands.

Today, shoes are either made by designer shoemakers or, much more commonly, by mass-production techniques, and shoes are often designed on computers using computer-aided design programs that allow a designer to see the proposed shoe in three dimensions. But the basic methods developed in the Middle Ages remain: after the design has been finalized, a last is made for each shoe style and for each size that will be made. From the last, a pattern is made, also for each size. The various parts of the shoe are cut out of the leather or other material, using the patterns, and are machine-stitched or glued together. Once the upper is assembled, it is pulled over the last in a modern lasting machine, shaped to the last, and attached to the sole. Today, however, soles are created with three separate parts: the insole, the midsole, and the outer sole, all of which must be separately combined, with the insole being inserted last into the finished shoe.

Making shoes can be environmentally destructive today. Because inexpensive shoes (and many high-end shoes as well) are now made in third-world countries to take advantage of cheap labor and lax environmental laws, industrial runoff and pollution from the toxins in shoe production is often released into the environment with little oversight. Shoes today are made with a variety of synthetic materials like plastic and vinyl that emit chemicals during production and, once they are disposed of, when they decompose in a landfill. The cushioning materials used in modern insoles and midsoles, such as polyurethane, are also filled with chemicals that leach toxins into the earth and water. The process of tanning leather is also extremely environmentally destructive, and the glues and solvents that hold shoes together are also hard on the planet. The good news is that many companies are working to create more environmentally friendly shoes today, and some companies have programs that will recycle used shoes in order to keep them out of landfills.

See also: Shoemakers Guilds; Europe; Shoemakers

Further Reading Skyrme, Tim. *Bespoke Shoemaking, A Comprehensive Guide to Handmade Footwear*. Agnes Water, Queensland: Artzend Publications, 2006; Swann, June. *Shoemaking*. Princes Risborough: Shire, 1986.

SHOE SHINE AND POLISH

Shoe polish is a product that is used to polish shoes. Shoe shine refers to the practice of polishing shoes. Certain types of shoes have historically been the focus of shoe polish. Military boots worn by both officers and soldiers are one example.

The rise of **athletic shoes** and the decline in the wearing of boots have both contributed to the decline in popularity of boot polish since the 1970s.

Shoe polish was designed to be used to polish **leather** shoes, although it can also be used to polish synthetic, non-leather shoes. It is intended to restore the shiny appearance of leather and to correct scars in the surface.

Shoe polish was once made of wax, animal tallow, and lampblack, and it became popular to blacken one's shoes when shiny leather **boots** like **jack boots** became fashionable, in the eighteenth century. Commercial shoe polish products were not available until the nineteenth century, and it wasn't until the early twentieth century that boot polish was widely available, as boots became more widely worn by the general public, thanks to the Industrial Revolution, which both made the production of boots cheaper and also led to the rise of work boots for industrial workers.

World War I and World War II also influenced the popularity of boot polish for soldiers and officers. Officers had subordinates shine their boots for them and soldiers had to shine their own shoes, and would be penalized if their boots were not glossy enough. An Australian product called Kiwi, released in 1904, was the first major boot polish on the market, and was heavily used by English soldiers in both world wars. American soldiers, on the other hand, did not have access to Kiwi polish until the second world war. Kiwi is still the biggest brand of shoe polish in the world, and is now owned by Sara Lee.

Man shining a girl's shoes along the street in New York City, September 13, 1911. [Photo courtesy of the Library of Congress Prints and Photographs Division]

Today, shoe polish is made of a combination of chemicals intended to provide both color and shine, including dyes, tupentine, and gum arabic. Shoe polish is applied to the shoes with a brush or cloth, and the polish is rubbed into the surface, sometimes with a bit of saliva, which results in a "spit shine." Modern shoe polish often comes with its own sponge applicator attached to the bottle.

Shoe shiners are people, usually men or boys, who shine shoes in public places for money. Shoeshining is an occupation that takes little skill and little initial output—the shoeshiner must buy a seat for the customer, and the polish, cloth, and other tools for the job—so it is a popular job for poor people in both developing and developed countries around the world.

Shoeshiners either set up shop on their own, in subway stations or other public places, and sometimes work in shoe shine parlors in big cities. Through much of the twentieth century, shoe shine parlors in the United States often employed immigrant boys looking to make some money for their families and the parlors were often run by other immigrants. The owners of the parlors often sent money back to their home countries in order to pay for new arrivals, who would then work off their debt at the shoe shine parlor. Other shoe shine parlors hired largely African-American men. For many Americans of a certain age, the shoe shine parlor is a relic of pre-Civil Rights America, an era when white businessmen cared about the shine of their shoes and African Americans were relegated to the informal economy. They are also reminiscent of a time when adults did not wear **sneakers** (at least in public), and men and women bought shoes to last and did not throw them away when they became worn out.

As the shoe shine's popularity faded, many shoe shine parlors began repairing shoes as well, eventually evolving, if they survived, into modern shoe repair stores.

See also: Men's Shoes; Military Shoes and Boots

Further Reading Stumpf, Doug. *Confessions of a Wall Street Shoeshine Boy*. New York: Harper Collins, 2007.

SHOE SIZES

Shoe sizes refer to how shoes are sized to fit different people's feet. Shoe sizing systems differ by country, sometimes by type of shoe or type of wearer, and have changed historically. During much of European history, for instance, shoes were offered in a very small number of sizes, and most people were accustomed to wearing shoes that did not really fit their feet.

In the **United States**, shoe sizes are different for men, women, and children. Women's shoe sizes range from 5 to 15 ½, and men's range from 3 ½ to 14. American shoe sizes go up in increments of one half. Men and women can both wear each other's shoes (or children's shoes if their feet are small enough), but a women's size is

> Almost every woman is not only conscious of her feet, but sex conscious about them.
>
> ANDRE PERUGIA

always 1 ½ sizes greater than the equivalent men's size. Children's sizes differ by age, with infants, toddlers, and children having a different sizing system.

Shoe sizes are primarily based on the length of the foot. Prior to the early twentieth century, all ready-to-wear shoes came in one width; although longer shoes were wider than shorter shoes, each shoe size did not come in a variety of widths. This changed in 1905 when **Dr. Scholl's** began offering shoes in a variety of widths, generally from narrow to extra wide. Not all manufacturers today offer shoes in multiple widths, however.

Since the 1920s, feet have been measured at shoe stores by shoe salesmen using a metal device known as the Brannock Device. (Prior to this time, shoes were measured with a ruler called a Ritz Stick.) Invented by Charles Brannock in 1925 for his father's shoe store, it remains the industry standard in the United States for measuring feet. The customer stands in stocking feet on the Branock Device, and the device measures both the length and width of the customer's foot. While different brands of shoes often are sized differently, for the most part this measure can be safely used by the customer when trying on and buying shoes. Brannock marketed his device to shoe manufacturers and retailers, as well as to the U.S. Navy. He later made a specialized Army Brannock Foot Measuring Machine for the Army for use in World War II, since the Army's shoes were made on special lasts.

Shoes, on the other hand, are sized on the basis of either the length of the average foot that could fit that shoe, the length of the inside of the shoe, or the length of the last on which the shoe was made. Shoe sizes in the United States are based on the length of the last, and the increments are measured in "barleycorns," which is a third of an inch. The English system is the same as the American, but the English system (which is the source of the American system) is one (for men's) or one-and-a-half (for women and children) size smaller than the American. It begins with a "hand" for children, which is four inches in length, and two hands for adults. The international system is also based on the length of the last, but the increments are measured in "Paris points," which is two-thirds of a centimeter. Other countries, such as **Japan** and Australia, have their own systems as well, generally based on the length of the foot.

Today, anyone can measure their own foot with a pencil, paper, and ruler. Simply trace the outline of your foot on a piece of paper, and then draw a rectangular box, with the ruler, around the outline. Write down the length of the rectangle, and do the same with the width. Using a shoe conversion chart (specific to one's country and gender, and easily found on the Internet) will then tell you what size feet you wear, based on how long your feet are. Using a width chart will then tell you whether your feet are narrow, regular, wide or extra wide.

See also: Shoe Stores

Further Reading Sterlinglast Corp. *The True Story of Shoe Sizes*. Long Island City, NY: Sterlinglast Corp., 1980.

SHOE STORES

Shoe stores are stores dedicated to selling shoes. They may also sell shoe accessories such as **socks**, stockings, shoe polish, and shoe horns, and today often sell handbags. Shoes are sold in dedicated shoe stores as well as department stores and discount stores as well as through the Internet.

Prior to the nineteenth century, shoes were not sold in stores. Instead, **shoemakers** made shoes for individual wearers, and sometimes also sold ready-made shoes from their workshops. Larger shoemakers who employed a staff of shoemakers in big towns could sometimes afford to keep an inventory of shoes in stock, which they sold to customers who came to their doors. In Massachusetts in particular, the center of shoemaking in the **United States**, some shoemakers could keep dozens or even hundreds of pairs of shoes in stock.

But it wasn't until the Industrial Revolution in the late nineteenth century that shoes were made in large enough numbers to be sold in a different fashion. With the large shoe manufacturers that were established in the United States and England in the late nineteenth century came the need to distribute shoes on a wider basis: through retail shoe stores.

Shoe stores in the United States thrived in the first decades of the twentieth century, and as more Americans could afford to buy shoes, stores opened in every big city in the country. The Great Depression and World War II slowed sales considerably, but since the end of the war, shoe stores have continued to expand, and as the fitness craze hit in the 1970s, specialty **athletic shoe** stores opened, and profits for the industry soared. Also in the 1970s came the shopping mall, and with it shoe stores got even more exposure and benefited from shoppers who bought shoes even when they may not have intended to go shoe shopping. Other shoe stores found success in strip malls, where only a single shoe store is located, alongside of grocery stores and other specialty retailers. In the 1990s, shoe stores began to suffer thanks to competition from discount retailers like Wal-Mart and Target as well as large discount shoe retailers like **Payless Shoe Source** and Famous Footwear. These big box stores continue to take a larger percentage of the retail shoe market.

Prior to the development of self-service shoe stores, customers who visited a shoe store had a shoe salesman or saleswoman wait on them. The clerk would measure the customer's feet and would show them samples of shoes on the showroom floor. The clerk would then go into the back and find the shoes in the right size and put them on the customer's feet. With the rise of self-service shoe stores after World War II, customers would instead browse the shoes, which are displayed openly on racks throughout the store, and would both size their feet and try on the shoes themselves. Payless Shoe Source popularized the concept, which cut the costs of buying shoes at those retailers who adopted it, but at the same time angered many full-service shoe stores and department stores, which saw their sales being cut.

Shoe stores have always relied on **advertising** to sell their products. In the early decades of the twentieth century, newspapers were the primary place that shoe stores would advertise sales and attract interest in their products. Today, the trend is for shoe manufacturers to nationally advertise their shoes on television and in magazines. Big shoe store chains, however, continue to advertise in local markets.

Condoleezza Rice Shopping for Shoes after Hurricane Katrina

On September 1, 2005, three days after the levees broke in New Orleans during Hurricane Katrina, it was reported in the *New York Daily Post*'s "Page 6" gossip column and on the *Drudge Report* that Secretary of State Condoleezza Rice was seen shopping at Ferragamo in Manhattan, where an angry fellow shopper shouted at her for buying expensive shoes (she was said to have spent "thousands of dollars") while people were dying in New Orleans. While there is some doubt as to whether this altercation occurred (although there is no doubt that Rice did shop there that day), the rumor traveled quickly over the Internet and fed into the American public's anger at the Bush administration's lack of attention to New Orleans during and after the disaster. Rice was later depicted in a political cartoon dressed as Marie Antoinette, surrounded by Manolo Blahnik shoes, saying "Let them eat shoes." Secretary of State Rice is known to have expensive taste in footwear, including Ferragamos and Manolo Blahniks.

Today, shoe stores are both stand alone, individually owned stores, or part of regional or national chains. Specialty shoe stores sell only certain types of products, such as athletic shoes or women's shoes, or they focus on a price range, with some stores tailored to low-end purchasers and other stores to high-end purchasers. Consumers can also buy shoes at department stores, clothing stores, sporting good stores, big box discount stores, and through mail order catalogues. Factory outlet stores, too, sell name-brand shoes at a discount.

See also: Payless Shoe Source; Shoe Sizes

Further Reading Michman, Ronald D., and Edward M. Mazze. *Specialty Retailers: Marketing Triumphs and Blunders.* Westport, Conn: Quorum Books, 2001.

SHOE STRUCTURE

Modern shoes have a relatively straightforward structure. Shoes are fashioned out of a sole, insole, upper, tongue, heel, quarter, and vamp. Most shoes also have a lining inside the shoe. The sole of a shoe is the part of the shoe that lies between the bottom of the foot and the ground. It generally consists of the outsole, which touches the ground, the insole, which lies inside the shoe and supports the foot, and the midsole, which are the materials between the insole and the outsole.

Shoe soles are traditionally made of **leather** or rawhide. Early shoes did not have a separate insole or midsole, while modern shoes often have orthopedic or removable insoles for extra comfort. The insole often breaks down before the shoe gets old, but today, this can be replaced. Outsoles, too, because they are in contact with the ground, often break down and lose their surface texture. Finally, the midsole is the area of the shoe that modern technology focuses on. Made today of foam, many athletic shoe companies also have their own patented cushioning systems like air cushions or gel that are inserted into the midsole.

The shank is a piece of metal found in some shoes, which lies between the sole and the insole and provides support to the arch of the foot. Shanks are necessary in high-heeled shoes.

The heel is the attached to the bottom of the outsole, under the heel of the foot. Traditionally made of stacked leather, today heels can be made of wood, cork (for **platform shoes**), plastic, and steel (for **stilettos**).

The quarter is the part of the upper that lies behind the heel of the shoe and encapsulates the rear of the foot. The heel counter is a piece of stiff material, above the heel of the shoe at the back of the upper. It lies between the inner lining and the quarter and stabilizes the foot and maintains the shape of the shoe.

The upper is the part of the shoe that attaches to the sole and covers the entire foot. The most traditional material for shoe uppers is leather, followed by cloth. Today, uppers can be made from canvas (as in athletic shoes), leather, cotton, rubber, or a variety of synthetic materials, as in **vegan shoes**.

The vamp is the part of the

"Banned" Running Shoes

Spira Footwear makes running shoes equipped with one-inch springs in the heel and under the toe, which are technically prohibited by the organizations that oversee track and field events around the world. According to the company, these springs allow wearers to exercise longer with less impact on the feet, knees, and legs and with less overall stress on the body. In addition, the springs do not wear out or break down the way that other types of cushions do, such as foam and rubber. The shoes were released in 2002, but according to Spira the United States Association of Track and Field prohibits the wearing of springs in shoes, and the International Association of Athletics Federations prohibits using technology that provides an unfair advantage to the wearer, effectively prohibiting Spira shoes in competition events. However, neither organization has penalized runners who have worn the shoes in competition events, and both have publicly stated that the shoes are not banned. (In fact, a number of runners have worn Spira shoes in competitions, many winning or placing in marathons or other events, and in 2008 an Angolan runner was the first person to wear Spira shoes in an Olympic event.) Still, the company nevertheless has done much to publicize the "outlaw status" of its shoes, and in 2006 it offered a $1 million bounty to any runner who won the Boston Marathon wearing a pair of Spira shoes.

upper that covers the front of the foot from the middle to the toe, and where the shoe laces, buckles, buttons, or Velcro are found. In front of the vamp lies the toe box, which surrounds and protects the toe.

The toebox is the front of the vamp that covers the toes. In some shoes, the toebox is reinforced, as in steel-toe shoes for industrial work, or pointe shoes for ballet dancers. Because narrow feet are often preferred for women, toeboxes are often more narrow than the toes are, causing corns, bunions, and hammer toes to develop.

The tongue is featured in modern shoes that lace or connect on the front of the upper. The tongue is the separate piece of leather or cloth that lies between the two separate pieces of the upper, and over which the laces tie.

Shoes are fastened through a variety of means. Shoes that are fastened with shoe laces, which can be made of materials like cloth, sinew, twine or leather, have holes in the shoes for the laces to pass through. Today these are called eyelets. Modern cloth shoelaces have a plastic coating at the tip of the laces called aglets, which make it easier for the laces to pass through the eyelets. Other methods of shoe closure are buttons, snaps, buckles, and, today, Velcro.

See also: Shoemaking; Shoemakers

Further Reading Swann, June. *Shoemaking*. Princes Risborough: Shire, 1986.

"THE SHOES THAT WERE DANCED TO PIECES"

"The Shoes That Were Danced to Pieces" is a Grimm's **fairy tale**, also known as "The Twelve Dancing Princesses." It is classified by folklorists as Aarne-Thompson Tale Type #306: "the danced out shoes." Unlike a lot of other fairy tales popularized by the Grimm brothers starting in 1812, it is relatively recent and has a relatively narrow distribution. It may only date to the seventeenth century, and has just over a hundred variants, primarily in Central Europe.

The story tells of a king with 12 daughters whose shoes were found to be "danced to pieces" each morning, even though the king locked the daughters in their room each night, barring them from going out. In order to find out where the daughters went each night, he makes a proclamation that any man who can solve the riddle of his daughters' nightly disappearance would be able to marry the daughter of his choice, while any man who failed would lose his life, either by beheading or hanging (some variants have humiliation, rather than death, as a punishment). After a number of men (often 12) tried and failed to solve the puzzle, a poor soldier (in some variants, he is a cowherd or an impoverished nobleman) shows up at the castle to try his hand. But first, he meets an old woman who advises him not to drink any wine that may be offered and gives him a cloak of invisibility, allowing him to follow the princesses as they leave for a magical castle in which they dance the night away (perhaps under enchantment) with 12 princes. After the soldier reveals their activities to the king, he is given the oldest (or sometimes the youngest) daughter as his bride.

Most French variants of the tale have one daughter wearing out 12 pairs of shoes each night (she actually meets 11 other princesses each night), rather than 12 daughters found in the German tales, and other variants have three daughters dancing the night away. A related tale is "Katie Crackernuts," in which the hero is a girl named Katie who has to save a prince from a curse that forces him to attend a ball in an otherworldly environment every night, leaving him sickly.

"The Shoes That Were Danced to Pieces" has a number of important motifs, which show up in most versions of the tale. The wedding motif is common in fairy tales around the world, in which the lowly hero marries the princess (L161). Of course weddings and shoes are associated in folk beliefs around the world, so it is not surprising that in this case solving the puzzle of the shoes leads to the marriage of the princess and the hero. The old woman (N825.3.1.) who gives the hero a magical device (a cloak of invisibility AT DI36i.i2) is also a common element, as well as the hero's need to stay awake and resist the poisoned wine. The "do or die" test is common in folktales, whereby the hero must either perform the task adequately or forfeit his life; this element was eliminated from Victorian versions of the tale, so as not to negatively impact the children reading the tale. Other motifs found in this tale include a king as the father, 12 daughters, "each more beautiful than the other," the notion that beauty equals virtue, and the fact that the girls all sleep together and are locked up together in their room each night. Other common elements include the reward for the hero is marrying the princess, the fact that the hero follows the princess for three days and three nights, and the fact that the hero brings a token with him back as proof of his journey.

Many of the motifs in this story harken back to the myths and tales of the ancient classical world. For example, the castle where the princesses danced is clearly found in an underworld, which is accessed through a passageway underneath the girls' bed, which is similar to accounts of Hades for the ancient Greeks. The trees in this other world were made of silver, gold, and diamonds, which is very similar to the trees in the underworld found by Gilgamesh in the ancient Sumerian epic. The princesses must cross a great lake in 12 little boats; in Greek mythology, the dead are ferried across the river Acheron, the River of Woe, in a boat that takes them to Hades. While there, the princesses drink wine, which could be the source of their enchantment; in Greek myths, if one were to eat or drink in Hades, one could never leave.

Shoes are obviously an important motif in this tale, providing both the means of escape for the princesses, and, through solving the riddle of the shoes, the hero gains his reward, which is to marry one of the princesses. In addition, during the nineteenth century when this tale was popularized, wealthy women (like the princesses) wore delicate silk slippers to balls, and they were quickly worn out from the outdoor wear, so the basis of the tale is found in reality.

See also: "Cinderella"; Fairy Tales; "The Red Shoes"

Further Reading Bettelheim, Bruno. *The Uses of Enchantment: The Meaning and Importance of Fairy Tales*. New York: Vintage Books, 1975; Opie, Iona and Peter. *The Classic Fairy Tales*. New York: Oxford University Press, 1974; Propp, Vladimir. *Morphology of the Folktale*. Austin: University of Texas, 1968; Tatar, Maria M., ed. *The Classic Fairy Tales*. New York: W. W. Norton, 1999; Thompson, Stith. *The Folktale*. New York: Holt, Rinehart, and Winston, 1946; Zipes, Jack, ed.*The Oxford Companion to Fairy Tales*. Oxford: Oxford University, 2000.

SIMPSON, O.J.

O. J. Simpson is a former professional football player and actor who was charged with killing his estranged second wife, Nicole Brown Simpson, and her friend, Ronald Goldman, in 1994. He was acquitted of the murders in criminal court but was later found liable for their deaths in civil court.

One of the most damning pieces of evidence against Simpson at Simpson's murder trial had to do with a trail of bloody shoe prints found at the scene of the crime. Police found more than 65 distinct footprints left in Nicole Simpson's blood, on both the front porch and the back walk of Nicole's condominium. The shoe prints were made by size 12 Bruno Magli "Lorenzo" shoes. Nicole's body was found between the front gate and the front steps, where she was killed, while

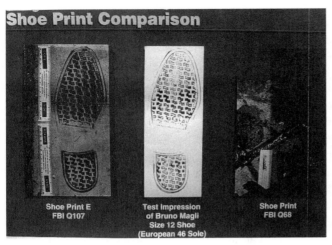

Shoe Print Comparison

Shoe Print E
FBI Q107

Test Impression
of Bruno Magli
Size 12 Shoe
(European 46 Sole)

Shoe Print
FBI Q68

This is a photograph of exhibit 403 in the wrongful death civil suit against O.J. Simpson that shows a test shoe print of a Bruno Magli shoe and shoe prints from the crime scene. This copy was released to the media following testimony by FBI shoe print expert William Bodziak, November 21, 1996 at Los Angeles County Superior Court in Santa Monica, California. Bodziak claims to have found 18 points of similarity between the shoes in a 1993 photograph of Simpson on the sidelines of an NFL game allegedly wearing Bruno Magli shoes, shoe prints at the murder scene, and a model pair of Bruno Magli's used by the FBI for the investigation. [AP Photo/Susan Sterner]

Goldman's body was found in an enclave off the walkway. The killer is thought to have walked through the pools of blood left by both victims, leaving the bloody footprint trail. In addition, Nicole's dog Kato also walked through the blood himself, leaving his own footprints for police to find. Further, a bloody Bruno Magli footprint was found in Simpson's Ford Bronco as well.

Bruno Magli is a brand of Italian high-end, handmade men's and women's shoes. Today, Bruno Magli men's shoes start at about $200 and go up to $780 at the high end. (The Lorenzo sold for $160 during the mid-1990s. That model is no longer made by the company.) They are worn by fashionable men who favor craftsmanship and luxury and who spend a lot of money on their clothes and shoes.

While Simpson, during the trial, initially claimed that he never owned a pair of Bruno Magli shoes (he famously called them "ugly ass" shoes during his testimony), the jury was shown photos of him wearing a pair of Lorenzos (which the defense claimed were doctored; later, during the 1997 civil trial, more photos emerged of Simpson wearing the shoes). The prosecution noted that only 299 pairs of Lorenzos had ever been sold in the United States and alleged that Simpson purchased the shoes at Bloomingdale's in New York, where he often shopped. While Simpson was not convicted of the crime, and the shoes were never found, many observers felt that this was a compelling piece of evidence against him.

In addition, the police recovered a dark sock from Simpson's home with blood found to be from Nicole. The blood was both found in a glob in a spot that would normally have been covered by shoes, but was also found sprayed on the top of the sock. One explanation for the bloody glob is that Simpson, after killing Nicole and Ron Goldman, removed his shoes after getting into his Bronco and returning to his home, and that while removing his bloody shoes, accidently got some blood on one of his socks. Upon returning home, he removed the socks, where the police later found them. The spray would have been caused by Simpson walking in the blood and the blood spraying up at him.

Sales of Bruno Magli shoes went up by 30 percent in the year following the trial, and the company's brand recognition shot upwards. More than 10 years later, Bruno Magli shoes are still associated with O. J. Simpson and the murder trial.

See also: Men's Shoes

Further Reading Bosco, Joseph. *A Problem of Evidence: How the Prosecution Freed O. J. Simpson*. New York: William Morrow & Company, 1996.

SKATEBOARDING SHOES

Skateboarding shoes, also called skate shoes (or "sk8 shoes"), are low-top **sneakers** designed for skateboarding. The uppers are made of **leather**, canvas, or other materials, and the soles are made of a rubberized, nonskid material that allows for traction on the board.

Skateboarding became popularized in the United States during the 1960s and emerged out of the surfer culture of Southern California in the 1950s. The original skateboards were most likely made from scooters (rollerskate wheels attached to a board, and connected to a push bar), with the push bars removed. The first users were probably surfers who wanted something to ride when they could not surf, and riding a board on wheels provided the feeling of riding a wave.

The first true purpose-made skateboards were being sold by the end of the 1950s, and the sport took off in the 1960s. During the 1970s, skateboarders began developing some of the tricks that would mark the sport, and skateboard technology improved with the development of urethane wheels replacing the old clay wheels, which allowed better maneuverability. Skateboarders also began skating in empty swimming pools, which became the model for the skateparks that would emerge later. During the 1980s, the sport had its first stars and skateboarding started to become commercialized, with top skateboarders getting endorsement deals from **athletic shoe** and apparel companies. For skateboarding pros, skateboarding is considered an "extreme sport" today, although many people ride skateboards as a form of transportation or just for fun. It's now included in the X Games.

Skateboarders, or skaters, wear low-top, retro-style sneakers when skateboarding. Skateboard style is connected to both surfing and punk style and draws from both subcultures. In addition, because skateboarding is not a mainstream sport, its adherents tend to favor clothing and products that are less corporate and more homegrown. On the other hand, skater shoes are chosen because of more than their style.

These sneakers work well for skateboard tricks like ollies. [Copyright 2008 Jupiterimages Corporation]

They must also be well-designed for the sport, which means they need good traction and heavy reinforcement on the front edges, known as the "ollie area," named after the first skateboard trick. They need to be flat on the bottom in order to hold onto the grip tape on the top of the skateboard. Older brands favored among skaters include flat-bottomed retro **Adidas** and **Vans**, which, when combined with the baggy jeans and loose-fitting tee shirts, completes the iconic skater look. (Some skaters, on the other hand, wear tighter-fitting clothes.)

Since skateboarding has become professionalized, with small and large companies offering products specifically designed for skateboarding, specialty shoe brands have emerged, including Etnies, Emerica, and DC. Skateboarders continue to favor Vans (Vans now makes special skate shoes, since the slipons popular in the 1960s and 1970s are not practical for skateboarding) and skate shoes made by skater-owned companies like Emerica. When **Nike** began to make skateboard shoes in 2002, many skaters rebelled, refusing to buy the shoes, and a coalition of angry skateboarders and snowboarders began a "Don't Do It" campaign aimed at encouraging skaters and snowboarders to resist allowing Nike to profit off of their sports. (One of the critiques is that Nike began sponsoring skaters in order to foster "street cred" and also sold the shoes in artificially low numbers in skateboard stores, hoping to create demand.)

Today, skater-owned companies like Etnies continue to thrive, selling to skaters and non-skaters, while new skater-owned companies like Emerica and Lakai have become established. Most major skateboarding shoe companies sponsor skate teams.

Skateboard fashion and style, including the style of shoes, has influenced youth fashion and culture. Kids today, whether or not they skateboard, often favor the baggy clothes and skater shoes worn by skateboarders, and when Sean Penn's character wore Vans in 1981's *Fast Times at Ridgemont High*, kids everywhere began wearing the same checkerboard slip-on shoes.

See also: Adidas; Nike; Sneakers; Vans

Further Reading Brooke, Michael. *The Concrete Wave: The History of Skateboarding*. Toronto: Warwick Publishing, 1999; Vanderbilt, Tom. *The Sneaker Book: Anatomy of an Industry and an Icon*. New York: The New Press, 1998.

SKATES

Skates refers to footwear worn while either roller skating or ice skating. People have been ice skating for thousands of years, with the oldest evidence for ice skating found in Scandinavia and the Netherlands. The oldest skates were made from animal bones, which were shaved flat, drilled with holes, and tied to shoes, and allowed the wearer to glide across the ice, using sharpened poles (as in cross country skiing) to gain momentum. This may have been followed by the use of wood rails worn underneath shoes. In the fourteenth century in the Netherlands, the first metal blades were created. At this time, iron runners were attached to a wooden platform; the skate was like a patten or **overshoe** and then strapped onto regular shoes using straps or laces. In the late sixteenth century, the first sharpened, double-edged steel blade was invented in the Netherlands, and the use of poles was discontinued because skaters could use the edge of the blades to push off and gain momentum. Also at this time, blades were curled at the front, and from the late sixteenth century through the next two centuries, the blade became longer, lower, and more curled in front, so that it resembled a *poulaine*. Because of the cold winters in Northern Europe in the seventeenth century, ice skates were commonly owned and used by a great many people. With the invention of the sharpened steel blade, skaters now cut into the ice as they skate, rather than glide on top of it. It wasn't until the eighteenth century that ice skating was introduced into England and then the rest of **Europe**, followed by the American colonies.

Ice skates began to change again in the mid-nineteenth century. By this time, in Holland a few different forms of

Skates like these are worn for both recreational skating and for figure skating. [Copyright 2008 Jupiterimages Corporation]

ice skates existed, including the "Linschoten" model with a long curled steel blade, the "Warga" model with a long steel blade supported by wood, the "Bergambacht" skate with a taller blade and taller platform, and an English model with a tall but short blade with a very slight curl. By the end of the century, a new skate had appeared, with a heavier platform, and the loss of the steel curl (although they retained a wooden curl in the front). Different varieties were available based on whether they were used for speed skating or recreational skating. By the early twentieth century, all metal skates had emerged, ultimately replacing the wood and metal Dutch skates. Around 1890, the metal skate had merged with the **boot**, and the modern ice skate boot had emerged.

Also during the nineteenth century, there were a number of American inventions that changed ice skates. In 1848 a steel clamp was invented to replace the leather straps that held the skate onto the boot. And in 1865, American skater

Jackson Haines invented a two plate, all metal blade, which attached directly to the boots, allowing for a variety of moves that had not been performed prior to that time. In 1870, Haines also invented the first rake or toe pick, the jagged saw-like edge on the front of the blade that allows for many of the moves found in modern figure skating. And in 1914, John Strauss made skates lighter with his invention of the closed-toe blade made from a single piece of steel, which allows for the performance of many of today's figure skating jumps.

Originally, ice skating occurred out of doors and was a way that people in icy areas traveled, using frozen rivers or lakes. Besides the use of ice skating as transportation, frozen lakes and ponds were natural ice skating rinks and were areas where people came to skate recreationally. In Scandinavia and the Low Countries, ice skating was popular for all classes, but as it got introduced into the rest of Europe starting in about the seventeenth century, it became a recreation for the upper classes. In the **United States**, 300,000 people a day skated on Wollman Rink in Central Park when it first opened in 1949. The first refrigerated ice rink, however, was in London in 1876, called the Glaciarium. Indoor, refrigerated ice rinks are typically found in warm climates where outdoor ice skating is impossible.

These quad skates are rented and worn in roller rinks across the country. [Copyright 2008 Jupiterimages Corporation]

Early ice sports included barrel racing, speed skating, and curling, with the first organized speed skating race held in 1763 in England. Skating clubs formed in Europe in the seventeenth century and in the United States in the mid-nineteenth century. Other ice skating sports include ice hockey and figure skating.

Ice hockey is a Canadian sport involving two teams of players who use sticks to force a puck into a goal. It is based on field hockey and was brought to Canada by British soldiers as a game called shinty. By 1860, Canadian players had substituted a puck for a ball and modern ice hockey was born. Bandy and ringette are both related sports that also involve using sticks to shoot a puck, ball, or ring into a goal. Ice hockey players wear plastic ice hockey boots.

Figure skating has its origins in the eighteenth century when skating technology improved to the extent that skaters were able to perform turns and other moves on the ice. Figure skating is also made possible by the inventions of American skater Jackson Haines in the nineteenth century, which allowed for many of the modern figure skating moves, and for joining together dance moves with skating, creating what is now known as the International style of figure skating. Figure skating today involves individuals and pairs of skaters who perform athletic moves, including jumps and spins, set to music. Figure skaters wear leather skating boots.

The first roller skates, known as dry land skates, were based on ice skates and were probably invented by someone who wanted to ice skate in the summer. It is thought that this first occurred in the Netherlands where people would ice skate through the canals in winter. In 1760, a Belgian inventor named Joseph Merlin invented a pair of boots with metal wheels. The first patented roller skate, however, was in 1819, invented by a Mr. Petitbled of Paris. This skate had three wheels in a straight line attached to a piece of wood that was then strapped to a shoe. Subsequent patents were issued throughout the nineteenth century for other versions of inline roller skates, and in 1828 a patent was issued to August Lohner who invented a skate using three wheels—two in back and one in front. In 1863, James Plimpton invented the first "quad" skate with four wooden wheels set in two parallel rows at the front and back of the skate. The pairs of wheels were attached to a "truck," which was then affixed to the plate of the skate, allowing the sets of wheels to move independently of each other. The skate itself then was then worn like a patten, strapped to a regular shoe with two leather straps. This design would remain unchanged for almost a 100 years.

Another important design was in 1866 when Everett Barney invented a metal clamp used to fasten skates onto shoes. In 1876, the toe stop was patented, and in the 1880s ball bearings began to be used in wheels, but it wasn't until the early twentieth century that metal wheels replaced wooden wheels. Other wheel materials included aluminum for speed skaters and fiber composition wheels for indoor rink skating. In the 1930s, Lucite and brake fiber were used as well for the wheels.

The earliest roller skates included just the skate assembly attached to a plate with straps. The first combined boot and skate assembly, the "shoe skate," was invented in about 1900, but was initially only used by professional skaters; the general public continued to skate using Plimpton's design.

Roller skates were seen in a number of ballets and operas in the nineteenth century in which they substituted for ice skates, including The Artist or Winter Pleasures in 1818 in Berlin, Le Prophete in 1840 in Paris, the Meyerbeer in Paris in 1849, and Plaisier de Hiver in the 1850s.

Originally, roller skating was practiced at skating rinks. The first public skating rink opened in France in 1828, followed by London in 1857. The first American roller rink was opened by James Plimpton in 1866 in Rhode Island, followed by the Coliseum in Chicago in 1902, and Madison Square Garden in 1908. The sport exploded during the early decades of the twentieth century, with recreational skating as well as competition skating, including ballroom roller dancing, speed skating, and roller polo.

Roller skating exploded again in the 1970s when disco and roller skating combined, and roller discos opened up across the country. In the 1960s, polyurethane wheels were developed, making skating much smoother and allowing for the possibility of skating outdoors on rougher surfaces. The 1970s also saw the release of a number of roller skating movies like *Rollerball* and *Roller Boogie*. The 1970s were the last decade of popularity for roller skating, which lost much of its popularity due to the rise of roller blading.

In 1978, roller blading got its start. A hockey player named Scott Olson found an antique pair of roller skates with the wheels in one line, and, with his brothers, designed a new pair of inline skates, using three polyurethane wheels attached to ice hockey boots. (In the mid-1990s, the hard ice hockey boot was replaced by a softer boot.) Olson thought that other hockey players like themselves would enjoy skating in the off season, using skates modeled on the ice skates that they regularly wore. Olson quit playing hockey and bought a patent for a similar skate from Chicago Rollerskate in 1981 and incorporated Ole's Innovative Sports in 1982 in order to sell the new skates, which he called Rollerblades. By 1988, the company, by then named Rollerblade Inc., had sold $10 million worth of Rollerblades, but Olson was no longer with the company, having sold out in 1985 in order to pay off debt. Today, thanks to the dominance of the Rollerblades brand, most people still think of all inline skates as Rollerblades, even though other companies have now entered the market, including two companies founded by Scott Olson. Rollerblading was a major American trend in the 1980s, and, while not as popular as it was during its height, remains a popular sport today.

Today, roller skating continues to be a recreational activity in which people go to roller rinks, rent skates, and skate in a rink to music. Some people also skate outdoors, usually with inline skates. Roller skating also forms the basis of a number of competitive activities, such as roller dancing (introduced in 1910), speed skating (which dates to the 1890s) rollery hockey, roller derby, and aggressive skating. Another form of recreational skating is known as free skating and involves outdoor skating with tricks.

Rollery derby began in 1935 as an endurance sport in which participants skate around a rink thousands of times; it later changed into the modern sport involving two teams that skate around a rink, passing other players, and involving shoving and aggression. It was popular during the 1970s and featured in films like *Rollerball*, but fell out of fashion in the 1980s. It was recently resurrected after the A&E television show *Rollergirls* aired in 2006. Roller hockey, first introduced in 1878, is played with both quad and inline skates; the original game features quad skates and is based on field hockey, while the inline version of roller hockey is based on ice hockey. And aggressive roller skating uses tricks and techniques borrowed from skateboarding. All of these types of skating have specialized skates for it, such as derby skates, jam skates, quad racing skates, and artistic skates.

Heelys refer to a type of roller shoe that resembles a shoe but that is equipped with a hidden, detachable wheel underneath the heel. Heelys were first released in 2000 and are extremely popular with kids, although in the last year their popularity has been declining. Their popularity has led to them being banned in shopping malls, schools, and other indoor places. They are also controversial with doctors because of the numbers of injuries seen in children who wear Heelys.

nese simple slippers are worn only in the house and are nerally worn with pajamas. [Copyright 2008 Jupiterimages orporation]

See also: Snow Shoes

Further Reading Gutman, Dan. *Ice Skating, From Axels to Zambonis.* New York: Penguin Books, 1995; Turner, James, Zaidman, Michael. *The History of Roller Skating.* Lincoln, NE: National Museum of Roller Skating, 1997.

SLIPPERS

Slippers are, at their most basic, shoes that slip on and off of the feet, and are not held on the feet with any sort of **shoe fasteners** like laces, buttons, bows, or zippers. The term is also used to refer to shoes made with soft materials which have a thin, soft sole. Slippers in the West are associated with pajamas and other night clothes, but they are common indoor footwear in much of the world.

Slippers are a common form of footwear in much of Asia and the **Middle East** because in those cultures it is normal to remove one's shoes when entering a home. In these cultures, slippers are outdoor shoes that have a hard leather sole but are slipped off and on easily. When indoors, individuals either go barefoot or wear socks on their feet. For instance, in the Middle East and **India**, open-backed mules known *mojaris, juttees, khussa,* or *babouche* were worn as far back as the fourth century. These could be made of embroidered **leather** or cloth, and are often elaborately embroidered and beaded.

Ballet slippers are a form of slipper that are worn by ballet dancers when they perform. Made today out of leather and covered in satin, ballet dancers once wore the heeled shoes worn in the European courts. But in the early eighteenth century, ballet slippers lost their heel. Soft, heelless slippers became standardized for ballet, and later were adopted by wealthy women in the nineteenth century who wore them to balls, and Empress Josephine wore taffeta slippers with silk ankle ties for her coronation in 1804. The fairy tale, "**The Shoes That Were Danced to Pieces**" is based on the idea of wealthy women wearing delicate silk slippers to balls, which quickly wore out from the use. In "**Cinderella**," too, the noblewomen who attended the balls wore fancy slippers of silk and brocade.

When slippers are worn out of doors, they are primarily associated with the wealthy because of their often fragile construction and delicate materials which make it impossible for them to be worn for work. The pope, for example, wears red slippers of velvet or silk, but in modern times popes have often chosen to forego the traditional slippers when traveling or outdoors, and instead have begun to wear regular footwear. On the other hand, the Chinese have been wearing straw slippers for outdoor work for centuries. Two thousand years ago, cloth slippers began to be worn, and cloth and silk slippers began to replace straw slippers.

In many cultures, slippers are the shoes worn indoors after one's outdoor shoes are removed. When slippers are made to be worn indoors, they are soft soled and comfortable. In **Japan**, guests are offered either a pair of *zori* **sandals** or slippers when visiting, to replace their outdoor shoes.

Even in cultures in which it is not customary to remove one's shoes when entering a home, many people wear slippers or houseshoes as comfortable indoor footwear. Slippers have been worn in the bedroom for thousands of years, and because of this, are linked with intimate activities. In ancient **Rome**, for example, Roman women wore slippers, known as *socci*, indoors, making them erotically charged; only prostitutes wore them in public. In **China**, it was traditional for brides with bound feet to have special sleeping slippers to be worn to bed. Even after **foot binding** was no longer practiced, wearing red sleeping slippers was and is still a common bridal practice.

Mules, or slippers made with just a vamp and no quarters, arose in the Middle East and were favored by Egyptians, Greeks, and Romans. The term mule comes from the Latin *mulleus calceus*, which indicated the red slippers worn by Patricians. Mules, known as *pantofles*, were adopted by French women by the sixteenth century as bedroom slippers. By the end of the seventeenth century, wealthy French women began wearing high-heeled, highly adorned mules in public, and even King Louis XIV wore them. In fact, many wealthy men wore mules throughout Renaissance Europe, perhaps because they are classic indoor shoes and are generally worn by the leisure classes. But revealing one's naked heels in public was, for many, scandalous, and by the nineteenth century the mule retreated back to the bedroom.

Today, high-heeled mules are still considered extremely sexy and are popular among shoe fetishists. Mamie Van Doren and Marilyn Monroe were both photographed in high-heeled mules, and **Frederick's of Hollywood** has sold mules since 1961 and popularized marabou-trimmed mules for a generation of American housewives. **Candie's** brought mules back into fashion in the **United States** in the 1970s and they remain sexy today.

Slippers are now associated with children. Children's slippers, and some women's slippers, come in a variety of styles, patterns, and colors, including in the shape of plush animals. Men's slippers tend to be more conservative and are found in very simple shapes and colors. Some cover the whole foot, while others are open-backed. Modern Western slippers are made of soft, comfortable materials such as synthetic fur and terry cloth.

See also: Candie's; China; Japan; Middle East; India; Europe; Ballet Shoes; Dance Shoes

Further Reading DeJean, Joan. *The Essence of Style: How the French Invented High Fashion, Fine Food, Chic Cafes, Style, Sophistication, and Glamour*. New York: Free Press, 2005.

SNEAKERS

Sneakers are a nickname for **athletic shoes** of all kinds, made possible thanks to the innovation of **vulcanization**, which allowed for the bonding of a rubber sole to a canvas upper in the late nineteenth century. The term is most commonly used, however, to either refer to generic athletic shoes, or to court shoes like

ese high-top sneakers are staple items in many young men's rdrobes. [Copyright 2008 Jupiterimages Corporation]

basketball shoes. Gym shoes are another term for generic sneakers, and boat shoes are often referred to as sneakers, although they are in fact a specialty shoe.

Sneakers are made primarily out of breathable fabric (usually canvas) or **leather** on the upper, with, most importantly, rubber soles. The first true sneakers were **Keds**, created in 1917, and called sneakers because the rubber sole allowed the wearer to sneak up on another person, but sneakers owe their presence to their predecessors: croquet and cricket shoes worn by the British during play. Made with canvas and leather uppers, these shoes had rubber soles, which later became the distinguishing feature of sneakers.

Today, someone who calls their shoes "sneakers" most likely does not wear them for any athletic activity, other than perhaps skateboarding. Instead, they are favored by young people (and increasingly, older people as well) who want comfortable shoes to wear that are also cool or hip.

The iconic sneaker is the **Converse** All Star, released by the Converse Rubber Shoe Company in 1917, the same year that Keds released its first sneaker. The All Star was geared towards basketball players, but, after former basketball player Chuck Taylor endorsed his own model of All Stars and began selling them himself to athletes, soldiers, and kids, their popularity among the general population skyrocketed. By 1955, Converse shoes were the best-selling shoes in the **United States**. During that same period of time, popular stores like Montgomery Wards and Sears sold canvas and rubber sneakers as everyday shoes to children and adults, adding to their ubiquity in culture. As sports in the United States became more democratic, with millions of Americans engaging in after-school and weekend leisure activities, Keds and Converse sneakers became part of the wardrobe of every American.

Popular culture since the 1950s has played a major role in popularizing certain kinds of sneakers, especially for youth. Actors, musicians, and athletes wearing particular brands or types of sneakers made them even more popular. Kurt Cobain's devotion to Converse One Stars propelled the brand to greater popularity among young fans of the grunge scene and even led to a special "Converse Chuck Taylor Kurt Cobain" sneaker in 2008. Jeff Spicoli wore **Vans** slip-ons in 1981's *Fast Times at Ridgemont High*, creating a new trend among surfers, skateboarders, and those who wanted to emulate those lifestyles. Johnny Ramone of the Ramones famously wore Vans, All Stars were worn by the cast of

West Side Story, Baby wore Keds in *Dirty Dancing*, and rappers Run-DMC wrote a song called "My **Adidas**" about their shoes.

Sneakers are also associated with gang culture and drug culture. It is commonly thought that sneakers strung over urban utility lines indicate that drugs are available there or that a gang is active in that location. While there are a number of alternative theories, there doesn't appear to be any proof for any of them. However, given that police report that dangling sneakers are at their most common during summer break and school holidays, the possibility is strong that it is just an indication that bored kids are present.

Sneakers have definitely been associated with violence, though. During the 1980s and 1990s there was a rash of killings of young kids for their high-priced sneakers (usually **Nike**), a period known as the shoe wars. Critics pointed out at the time that Nike and other companies marketed their expensive shoes primarily to inner-city youth who had little money but seemed willing to spend what they did have on shoes. Those who did not have the opportunity to buy the shoes instead robbed other kids (known as sneakerjacking) for them. Only big-name brand shoes like Nikes were stolen in the sneaker wars; "clones" that look like a brand-name sneaker but are instead produced by stores like Kmart, were not targeted.

Another trend involving sneakers began in the 1980s. As American women began to enter the professional workforce in greater numbers, many began to wear sneakers to work and to carry their pumps in a bag with them. The "sneaker brigade" refers to large numbers of female commuters wearing sneakers to and from work, which got its start during the New York City subway/transit strike in 1980.

Today, sneakers are more than ever a sign of youth cool and status. Many are now decorated with wild colors, sequins, and designs, and in 1993, LA Gear made a sneaker with flashing lights on it. Sneakers entered high fashion in the 1980s when designers brought out wedge-heeled sneakers and when platform sneakers were introduced in the 1990s. Today, older sneakers are purchased by collectors who favor vintage sneakers from the past; Nikes, Pumas, and Adidas from the 1970s are especially collectible.

See also: Adidas; Athletic Shoes; Converse; Nike; Skateboarding Shoes; Vans

Further Reading Garcia, Bobbito. *Where'd You Get Those?: New York City's Sneaker Culture: 1960–1987*. New York: Testify Books, 2003; Gill, Alison. "Limousines for the Feet: The Rhetoric of Trainers," in Rielle, Georgio and Peter McNeil, eds. *Shoes: A History From Sandals to Sneakers*. London: Berg Publishers, 2006; Haven, Kendall. *100 Greatest Science Inventions of All Time*. Westport, CT: Libraries Unlimited, 2006; Papson, Stephen, Robert Goldman. *Nike Culture: The Sign of the Swoosh*. London: Sage Publications, 1998; Vanderbilt, Tom. *The Sneaker Book: Anatomy of an Industry and an Icon*. New York: The New Press, 1998.

SNOW SHOES

Snow shoes are large flat **overshoes** that are attached to shoes and are worn while walking in the snow. The large size of snow shoes allows the wearer's weight to be dispersed to a larger surface area and keeps the feet from sinking into the snow. This allows the wearer to walk on top of deep, soft snow. Snow shoes have been worn by people like Native Americans, Inuits, residents of the **Arctic region**, and early Europeans, and probably allowed for the expansion of humanity into snowy northern regions.

The traditional snowshoe is made with an open wooden frame made of a single branch of hard wood bent into a circle, through which another piece or two of wood is crossed to provide stability. Inside of the frame, animal hide thongs (from caribou or deer) are tightly woven into a netting, and then the whole device is attached to a boot or shoe with straps of hide. Many snow shoes are turned up at the front to keep the snowshoe from digging into the snow. Snow shoes like this are primarily worn by the residents of the Arctic Circle and Inuits and other native peoples living in **Alaska** and northern Canada.

The oldest snowshoe found by archaeologists was found with "Oetzi the Iceman," a mummy found in the Italian Alps who lived more than 5,000 years ago. Archaeologists found a hazelwood frame and lime-bast strings that were most likely the pieces of the snowshoe, as well as a pair of **leather** shoes with straps attached that were most likely used to attach to the snowshoe. While this is the oldest extant snowshoe that has survived today, simple snow shoes were most likely being used by humans who lived much earlier and most likely were invented in Europe or Asia during the coldest periods of the Upper Paleolithic. Other early snow shoes may have been made out of a solid piece of wood or animal hide, attached to a **moccasin** or **boot**. As humans migrated out of Eurasia into North America, they would have brought that technology with them. It is thought that in **Europe**, snow shoes evolved into skis, which then became the dominant mode of transportation through snowy environments throughout Europe.

In North America, snow shoes were primarily used by natives of the northwest coast and the Woodland tribes of the Great Lakes region. These groups perfected the classic snowshoe design using a wooden frame with animal skin webbing inside. The native people of Alaska wore snow shoes that were either oblong or triangular shaped, and were worn most while traveling through open territory. For the most part, though, snow shoes were not as common among those living in Alaska as among those living in other parts of what would become Canada and the **United States**, because native Alaskans were able to travel on ice or densely packed snow.

Snow shoes were critical for Indians living in wooded or mountainous areas. The Cree and Ojibwa of Canada and the Great Lakes region made long, narrow snow shoes, with upturned points at both the front and the back that were good for crusty snow. Other Great Lakes groups like the Iriquois wore shorter ones, designed for use in the forest. One variety used in the Great Lakes region and Eastern Canada by groups like the Huron was the beavertail, which was round in front with a tail or point in back. The beavertail design is useful for areas where the snow is deep and powdery and travels well on open trails. Another design used in this region was the bear paw, a short oval design with no tail, which was more useful in rocky or wooded areas where a longer snow shoe would be cumbersome. Plains Indians like the Sioux, too, used snow shoes to hunt buffalo. Finally, the Northwest Coast Indians used a longer, narrower

This snow shoe is made the traditional way, with wood and leather straps. [Copyright 2008 Jupiterimages Corporation]

snow shoe, like those found in Alaska. Generally, the men made the frames and the women made the netting. In all cases, the wearers strapped their moccasins or boots into the snow shoes with leather straps. These three styles—the oval bear paw, the teardrop shaped beaver tail, and the long and narrow Alaskan—remain the three most popular snowshoe styles today.

After the colonization of North America, snow shoes were worn by French and English settlers in Canada, and especially by hunters, fur trappers, traders, and explorers traveling through snowy regions starting in the early seventeenth century. The French in particular borrowed the Native styles that they found and used them to their advantage in both conquering Native territories and their battles with the English. By the eighteenth century, the English-Americans had begun equipping their own soldiers with snow shoes, which allowed them to better control and expand their territories. Some European men married Native women, both to create alliances with the tribes with whom they traded, and also because Indian women had the skills and the knowledge to find food, cook, and, importantly, make snow shoes.

Snow shoes until the 1950s were made by hand, both by native groups and by Euro-Americans, of wood with animal skin webbing. To make the traditional snow shoe, the wood is soaked first to make it flexible, and then is bent into the shape of the frame, which is then dried to fix the shape. Strips of treated or untreated animal hide are then used to create the webbing. Traditionally, in North America, the snow shoes were attached to moccasins, but Europeans used their own shoes and boots.

In the 1950s, new materials like magnesium and polycarbonate were first used for the frames, creating lighter snow shoes. Nylon-coated neoprene or steel were both introduced to create the laces, even for wood framed snow shoes. In the 1970s, new materials were again developed for the frame, including lighter metals like aluminum and the replacement of the webbing with a solid decking. Today, the deck, or base of the snow shoe, is usually solid, rather than webbed, and is made of polyurethane or other plastics, as are the bindings that attach the snow shoe to the boot. Modern snow shoes have crampons on the bottom, for traction. New styles have emerged, too, for different uses, with small, narrow snow shoes being worn for racing and larger, wider shoes being used for hiking. Most people wear hiking boots with their snow shoes, or jogging shoes if running. Modern snow shoes are made in factories today.

Recreational snowshoeing began in the eighteenth century in Quebec, with the formation of snow show clubs. These clubs, which were also found in the Great Lakes and New England areas, were made up of generally upper-class men and women who got together to hike and to race on snow shoes and were popular until the 1930s. Races were both long and short distance and sometimes included obstacle courses, hurdles, and hill-sliding. While the popularity of the sport waned in the 1930s, it was revived in the 1970s with the fitness craze in America, and again in the 1990s. Snow shoes are worn today by outdoor enthusiasts who wear them while hiking in the snow, or by anyone who needs to walk through the snow. On the other hand, wooden snow shoes with leather webbing are still made and are preferred by many because they don't freeze, are quiet, and have more "floatation" than metal snow shoes. Today, snow shoes are worn for racing and running, for recreational hiking, and for long distance hiking, with the smallest snow shoes used for racing and the biggest shoes used for long distance snow shoeing.

See also: Alaska; Arctic Region; Moccasins; Native America; Plains Indians

Further Reading Edwards, Sally, and Melissa McKenzie. *Snowshoeing*. Champaign, Illinois: Human Kinetics, Inc., 1995; Prater, Gene. *Showshoeing*. Seattle: The Mountaineers, 1997; Vaillancourt, Henri. *Making the Attikamek Snowshoe*. Greenville, N.H.: Trust for Native American Cultures and Crafts, 1987.

SOCKS. *See* Hosiery.

SOUTHWEST INDIANS

The Southwest Indians live in the states of New Mexico, Arizona, and southern Colorado and Utah, and include the Pueblo Indians, the Navajo, the Zuni, and the Hopi. Pueblo Indians include the tribes living along the Rio Grande who are descended from what once were called the Anasazi, or ancestral Pueblo people. Prior to colonization, the Pueblo Indians made their living farming corn, beans and squash, while the Navajo and Apache and other groups were nomadic hunters and gatherers. After European contact in the mid-eighteenth century, the Navajo began raising sheep and goats.

Archaeological evidence shows that thousands of years ago, pre-Pueblo peoples living in the Four Corners region wore **sandals** made of woven yucca leaves. By the time of Spanish contact, however, Southwest Indians were wearing **moccasins**, borrowed from other Native American tribes. Because of the harsh desert environment, Southwest tribes wore hard-soled moccasins to protect the feet from cactus and sharp rocks, rather than soft-soled moccasins. These were made with two pieces of skin, with the hard sole sewn onto the softer upper, rather than a single piece. Three-piece moccasins were also made, using two pieces of skin for the upper—one for the back of the foot and the second for the front and top of the foot.

Moccasins were made of tanned deer skin as well as buffalo skin, which may have been acquired through trade. Skins were tanned by men, first scraping off the flesh and tissue, removing the hair, and soaking the skin in a bath of ashes and water. For the heavy soles of the moccasins, no further manipulation was done, but for the softer leather used for the uppers, the skin would be rubbed with a mixture of animal organs and fat in order to soften the **leather** before stretching and soaking the skin further. Like other groups, the skin was often smoked as the final step. (Sometimes the soles were made instead from the thick neck skin of the deer.) Moccassins were custom-made for an individual and cut to fit that person. Traditionally, the moccasin, after it is cut and sewn, would be soaked in wet sand and allowed to dry on the wearer's foot.

Knee-high moccasins were worn by both men and women and were made with a sole cut out of thick rawhide, which is sewn to a an upper that includes a longer piece of skin that is then wrapped around the leg and secured with leather thongs or silver Navajo conches. Many Pueblo tribes also wore leggings out of deerskin or, after colonization, cotton, often for ceremonial purposes, but also to keep the legs warm in cold weather. They were held up by woven garters. In addition, tribes who lived in areas with cold winters also wore **snow shoes** over their moccasins.

Like other tribes, the moccasins worn by Southwest Indians were often elaborately decorated. Many Southwest Indians dyed their moccasins using mineral and vegetable dyes in colors like red, black, white, yellow, and turquoise. In addition, Southwest tribes adorned their shoes with beading, probably borrowed from Plains Indians, fringe, and the silver Navajo buttons known as conches. Moccasins to be worn during ceremonial events were fancier than those worn for everyday use, such as the white moccasin with black soles worn by Puebo Indians for dances.

See also: Moccasins; Native America; Plains Indians

Further Reading Elder, Alan C. *In the Steps of Our Ancestors: An Exhibition of Native North American Footwear*. Toronto: Ontario Crafts Council, 1989; Paterek, Josephine. *Encyclopedia of American Indian Costume*. Denver, Colo: ABC-CLIO, 1994; Utah Museum of Natural History, Kathy Kankainen, and Laurel Casjens. *Treading in the Past: Sandals of the Anasazi*. Salt Lake City: Utah Museum of Natural History in association with the University of Utah Press, 1995.

SPICE GIRLS

The Spice Girls were a British pop group formed in 1993, made up of Melanie Brown, Melanie Chisholm, Emma Bunton, Geri Halliwell, and Victoria Adams (now Beckham). The Spice Girls released their first album in 1996 and eventually released three albums plus a greatest hits collection; they went on two world tours and released a movie before disbanding in 2000. (Geri Halliwell left the group in 1998.) In 2007, they reunited for a world tour that was completed in 2008.

The Spice Girls, who were given "spice names" in 1996 (Scary, Sporty, Baby, Ginger, and Posh), appealed to young girls who emulated the group's dancing, "girl power" philosophy, and fashion. The Spice Girls were well known in the 1990s for the fashion trends that they set and for the over-the-top clothing and shoes they wore. One major footwear trend that they popularized was the return of **platform shoes**, in the form of platform **sneakers**, platform **boots**, and platform **sandals**. For four years, the Spice Girls were seen wearing super high, super chunky platforms, including the glittery purple platform boots worn by Baby Spice and the red, white, and blue Union Jack platform boots worn by Ginger Spice. Girls and women everywhere began wearing platforms again during this time.

One controversy over shoes had to do with Sporty Spice. Because she was the "athletic" one, she often wore athletic clothing and shoes. In particular, Sporty wore **Nike**, bringing criticism for her endorsement of a company that was embroiled in controversy for the working conditions at their Asian factories.

See also: Platform Shoes

Further Reading Golden, Anna Louise. *The Spice Girls*. New York: Ballantine Books, 1997; Sinclair, David. *Wannabe: How the Spice Girls Reinvented Pop Fame*. London: Omnibus Press, 2004.

SPIKES. *See* Cleats and Spikes.

SPORT SANDALS

Sport sandals are **sandals** designed to be worn for outdoor activities like rafting, hiking, and boating. They first became popular during the 1980s with the brand Teva, and are now one of the best-selling types of **athletic shoes**.

While athletic shoes are most associated with athletic activities today, this was not always the case. The ancient Greeks, for example, used to run barefoot and competed in the ancient Olympic games with bare feet, but with the expansion of the Greek Empire, many athletes began to wear sandals for track and field events. Roman athletes also wore sandals, and borrowed the use of hobnails from the Etruscans, making their sandals more durable and also giving the athlete more traction. In the New World, sandals were worn during all activities throughout Central and South America. For instance, in the Inca Empire of Peru, runners, known as *chasqui*, were employed to relay news and messages throughout the region and completed their task wearing sandals.

In the 1970s, the **Dr. Scholl's** Exercise Sandal was extremely popular among American women. While this sandal was not designed to be worn while exercising, it was devised to provide exercise as the wearer walks because the toes had to grip the raised toe crest. But it was not until 1982 that the first sandal was designed in the West expressly for the purposes of athletic use.

Designed by Mark Thatcher, an outdoorsman, river guide, and unemployed geophysicist, the Teva sandal emerged out of his interest in designing a pair of shoes to be worn while engaging in water sports such as boating. He found that normal athletic shoes got soaked, while regular sandals and **flip flops** did not stay on the feet or provide adequate support. Thatcher ended up taking a flip flop and adding another strap to it, around the ankle, to hold the sandal onto his foot. As other river guides saw his new design, they began asking him to make them a pair, and he realized that he could go into business. His new sandal had a foam flip flop sole combined with nylon straps and was called Teva. Thatcher began selling the Tevas, which he had produced by California Pacific, to outdoor retailers in the southwest. After a court battle with California Pacific over the rights to the product, Thatcher approached Deckers Outdoor Corporation, a sandal and beachwear maker, in 1985, who began making and distributing Tevas. The sandal was wildly popular during the 1990s, not only with outdoors enthusiasts but with college students and other young people.

Sandals like these are designed to be worn during a variety of activities like hiking, water sports, or running. [Copyright 2008 Jupiterimages Corporation]

Made of a thick foam sole that floats in water, the original Teva had a nylon toe strap, an ankle strap, and a strap connecting the two. Later models had a more advanced sole that had a molded footbed, grippier outsole, and straps made of nylon, leather, or synthetic leather, with Velcro closures. In addition, the thong toe strap disappeared, replaced by a strap going across the toes. Since Teva's arrival, a variety of companies have released their own sports sandals, including **Nike**, **Reebok**, and **Adidas**.

See also: Adidas; Athletic Shoes; Native America; Nike; Reebok; Sandals; Uggs

Further Reading Hoffman, Frank, William Bailey. *Fashion and Merchandising Fads.* New York: Haworth Press, 1994; Vonhof, John. *Fixing Your Feet: Prevention And Treatments for Athletes.* Berkeley, CA: Wilderness Press, 2006.

STILETTOS

Stiletto refers to the thin spiked heel found in some high-heeled shoes, and to the shoes themselves, known as stilettos. Stiletto heels are made of steel, and they are named after the stiletto dagger.

High heels emerged in the West when European noblemen began wearing **boots** with heels, an innovation borrowed from the Mongol riders who invaded **Europe** during the thirteenth century. By the sixteenth century, noblemen began wearing these heels on their indoor, court shoes, as well as on their boots, and by the end of the century, noblewomen adopted the practice as well. In the seventeenth century, the French King Louis XIV popularized high-heeled **pumps** for men with thick, curved, Louis heels. With the fashion set by the King and his court, heels would be worn by noblemen and noblewomen until the French Revolution. Once heels became fashionable again, in the late nineteenth century, only women wore them, and high heels became firmly associated with femininity.

Heel height and thickness in high-heeled shoes has always been limited by the materials used to make them. Heels were traditionally made of stacked leather or wood and could not be too high nor too narrow, or else the shoe would not have enough support. Prior to this time, very high shoes were only possible with the platform **clogs** and elevated **sandals** that were popular throughout Asia, the **Middle East**, and parts of **Africa**. The Japanese *geta*, the Turkish stilted sandal, the Chinese "flower pot shoe," and the Indian *paduka* were all sandals or shoes that sat on very high platforms made of wood. The *chopine*, first popularized in the fifteenth century, was the Southern European version. In all cases, the height of the shoes was possible through the very thick platform, made either of a solid piece of wood or layers or wood or cork. Once high-heeled shoes were popularized in the sixteenth and seventeenth centuries, the heel was elevated higher than the rest of the foot and sat on relatively wide leather heels for support.

The stiletto was made possible through a number of innovations, starting in the nineteenth century, but especially during the twentieth century. For instance, in 1854, Francois Pinet patented the Pinet heel, a straighter, thinner heel, and in 1885 he introduced the hourglass heel. These heels were early predecessors to the twentieth century stiletto, but until the 1950s heels remained, for the most part, relatively low and wide.

Salvatore Ferragamo, during World War II, experimented with innovative materials as a way of coping with wartime restrictions of leather and other conventional **shoemaking** materials. He invented the chunky platform and the wedge heel, both of which were popular through the late 1930s and into the early 1940s. The platform went out of style after the end of World War II, however, and with the end of rationing shoe designers could once again use the materials that were unavailable to them during the war, such as leather and steel. Feminine fashions were popular, including clothing that emphasized the waist, hips, and breasts, and high heels that emphasized the curve of the legs and ankles became fashionable.

Ferragamo paved the way for the stiletto heel with his invention of the steel arch, which allowed for heels to be much higher. The actual invention of the stiletto is less clear, with some historians crediting Ferragamo and some Charles

These black patent stilettos are both sexy and intimidating. [2008 Copyright Igor Terekhov. Image from BigStockPhoto.com]

Jourdan. Other designers associated with popularizing the stiletto were André Perugia and Roger Vivier, both French designers, and Italian designers Armando Albanese and Alberto Dal Co. In any case, the stiletto made its first European runway appearance in 1954 and quickly became popular in Europe and the **United States**.

In the 1950s and early 1960s, stilettos were worn by Hollywood celebrities like Marilyn Monroe, Gina Lollabrigida, Brigitte Bardot, Sophia Loren, Lana Turner, and Marlene Dietrich and were associated with high glamour. They were also associated with bad girls like Jayne Mansfield and were worn by Playboy Bunnies at the Playboy clubs during the 1960s. Stilettos paired with a tight pencil skirt and a cigarette were the icons of the 1950s bad girl.

Stilettos fell out of fashion in the 1960s, replaced by **go go boots**, platforms, and later pumps, and did not return until the 2000s, when designers like **Jimmy Choo** and **Manolo Blahnik** resurrected them, making them more popular than ever. The HBO television show, *Sex and the City*, also played a major role in popularizing stilettos for a new generation of women.

Stilettos range from one inch (short stilettos are known as kitten heels or Sabrina heels) to about five inches, although higher heels are possible, especially when combined with a platform sole. Stilettos are extremely thin, which is only possible when they are made of steel. Other high heels are made out of molded plastic with or without metal inside to reinforce the heel.

Stiletto heels are thought to be the sexiest of all high heels. Because of their height, the wearer's posture and gait is transformed. With stilettos, the spine curves, the hips and buttocks are thrust out, the breasts are thrust forward, the legs are elongated, and the gait changes. Because of this, it's not surprising that stiletto **sandals** and **boots** are the most popular form of footwear among both Bondage Discipline Submission Masochism (BDSM) aficionados as well as foot and shoe fetishists. In fact, extraordinarily high shoes were featured in fetish art such as the 1940s–1950s bondage magazine *Bizarre* even before the modern stiletto heel became a reality.

Another reason that stilettos are popular among those in the BDSM world has to do with the fact that extremely high heels render the wearer more vulnerable, since she cannot run well in them. Fetish shoes, for example, are so high that the wearer cannot walk without assistance.

On the other hand, many people find the wearing of very high heels empowering. Stilettos make the wearer taller, and many women feel powerful wearing them. Stilettos, because of the noise that they make while a woman walks, also announce her presence as she enters a room, which is a far cry from the days when women were expected to be quiet. Stilettos make their wearers feel like leaders rather than followers, and are not worn by the meek. Stilettos can be elegant and, when combined with a power suit, emblematic of power, and also vulgar, when worn by prostitutes or bad girls, as was the case when Sandy in *Grease* traded in her saddle shoes and poodle skirt for a pair of patent stilettos and skin-tight pants. In the BDSM community, too, stilettos are worn by dominatrixes who use their height and lethal heels to dominate men.

Stilettos, because of the extremely narrow heel, can damage wooden and lino-leum floors. Heel protectors are available and are worn over stiletto tips to keep them from damaging floors. They are also hard to wear on the grass, as the heels will sink into the soil. Stilettos, like high heels in general, are also associated with a whole host of health problems for women, from bunions to corns to **hammer toes** to fallen arches, and even to hip and back problems.

See also: Clogs; Eroticism; Ferragamo, Salvatore; Fetishes; High Heels

Further Reading Benstock, Shari and Suzanne Ferriss, ed. *Footnotes: On Shoes*. New Jersey: Rutgers University Press, 1994; Cox, Caroline. *Stiletto*. New York: Harper Design, 2004; Danesi, Marcel. *Of Cigarrettes, High Heels, and Other Interesting Things: An Introduction to Semiotics*. New York: St. Martin's Press, 1999; Davidson, Hilary. "Sex and Sin: The Magic of Red Shoes," in Rielle, Georgio and Peter McNeil, eds. *Shoes: A History From Sandals to Sneakers*. London: Berg Publishers, 2006; Ricci, Stafnia. "Made in Italy: Ferragamo and Twentieth-Century Fashion," in Rielle, Georgio and Peter McNeil, eds. *Shoes: A History From Sandals to Sneakers*. London: Berg Publishers, 2006; Semmelhack, Elizabeth. "A Del-icate Balance: Women, Power and High Heels," in Rielle, Georgio and Peter McNeil, eds. *Shoes: A History From Sandals to Sneakers*. London: Berg Publishers, 2006; Steele, Valerie. *Fashion and Eroticism: Ideals of Feminine Beauty from the Victorian Era to the Jazz Age*. New York: Oxford University Press, 1995; Steele, Valerie. *Fetish: Fashion, Sex and Power*. New York: Oxford University Press, 1996; Steele, Valerie. *Shoes: A Lexicon of Style*. New York: Rizzoli International Publications Inc., 1999; Walford, Jonathan. *The Seductive Shoe: Four Centuries of Fashion Footwear*. New York: Stewart, Tabori and Chang, 2007.

SUMPTUARY LAWS

Sumptuary laws are laws that place restrictions on clothing, food, or luxury con-sumption. They are often used to maintain **class** distinctions in stratified societies by restricting certain luxury items to elite classes, and clothing and footwear are common targets for sumptuary laws. They were common in **Europe** from the thir-teenth century into the eighteenth century, in Imperial **China** and **Japan**, and pre-colonial **Africa**. One of the earliest documented sumptuary laws dates from the third century BCE in **Rome** and restricted the amount of gold that women could wear and the color of their tunics. Sumptuary laws regarding clothing generally dealt with the types of fabrics, amount of fabric, and fabric colors that could be worn by members of different classes.

One reason for laws that aim to restrict the wearing of certain clothing and shoes is that governments (and the Church in Medieval Europe) often saw exces-sive spending on lavish fabrics to be both a sign of moral decay and vanity, but also a waste of money. The English in particular worried that the excessive spending on foreign materials like silk was problematic for society and for the local economy. Another reason for these laws is that prices could be regulated by establishing restrictions on the amount of fabric that can be used in a product. Finally, the laws ensured that the lower classes did not appear to be striving to be "above their station." Of special concern, evidently, was that prosperous merchants or craftsmen might be able to dress in clothing finer than members of the nobility.

Sumptuary laws were found in the classical world, restricting the wearing of certain items of clothing, jewelry, and footwear as well as the consumption of food and drink. In Ancient **Egypt**, for example, only elites could wear dyed, adorned, or otherwise decorated sandals, and only the pharoah and members of his court could wear gold or jeweled sandals. Greek citizens were allowed to wear sandals decorated with specific adornments, which were prohibited for non-citizens. Roman law dictated the type and color of shoe that could be worn by the classes; free men wore pale colors, senators wore black, and emperors wore red shoes and boots encrusted with precious stones. In addition, only high-status Roman women could adorn their shoes with gold or jewels.

In Africa, some cultures had laws that forbade certain classes from wearing certain types of footwear or wearing footwear at all. After colonialism, shoes became less expensive and more easily available, but it wasn't until the twentieth century that African elites lost their control over footwear and the sumptuary laws were overturned.

These kinds of laws were also common throughout Asia. Imperial China restricted certain types of footwear, colors, or materials to certain classes or contexts. For instance, red (or pink) shoes were worn at weddings and other celebrations, bright yellow shoes could only be worn by the emperor and empress, only seniors wore black shoes, and white shoes were worn during mourning. At one time, merchants had to wear one black and one white shoe to distinguish them from other citizens.

Korea had these laws as well, which restricted the wearing of certain colors to the wealthy, while commoners could only wear white and pale colors. In addition, men and women were expected to wear different kinds of shoes, and occupational distinctions were bound by law as well.

In Imperial Japan, sumptuary laws ensured that only elites could wear cloth shoes, while peasants had to wear straw shoes. In addition, laws were passed that prohibited the wearing of lacquered *geta* because of their ostentatious nature, although courtesans continued to wear them.

Europe, from the Middle Ages through the Renaissance, had a number of laws passed regulating the types of shoes and materials that could be used for different classes of people, including the clergy. Legislation passed in the fifteenth century in England classified the citizens into as many as 39 different social groups, from noblemen to doctors to unmarried daughters of laborers, all with different categories of dress appropriate for them. Both French and English laws from the fourteenth to the seventeenth century limited the types of fabrics that different social classes could wear, and both Italian and French law restricted gold embroidery on shoes or clothing to nobility. Men and women throughout Europe had different laws pertaining to them, and within the sexes, social status was generally explicitly noted. It was also common in Europe to restrict certain items of clothing to prostitutes or courtesans or to restrict prostitutes from wearing certain items. For instance, an Italian law restricted the wearing of **slippers** in public to courtesans.

Sumptuary laws were issued in England in 1363 that restricted very long toes on *poulaines* only to upper-class men, allowing lower classes to wear shoes with shorter toes. (Noblemen could wear shoes that extended 24 inches beyond the toes; gentlemen could wear 12 inches; merchants could wear 6.5 inches; and commoners could only wear two inches of toes.) Poulaines were eventually replaced in the sixteenth century by wide-toed, duckbilled shoes, which were also the focus of legislation. Laws were enacted to restrict the width of the toes (they got as wide as eight inches by mid-sixteenth century, necessitating a law restricting them to six inches), and Mary I eventually outlawed them in order to appease the Catholic Church.

Women's shoes, too, were the focus of restrictive legislation. *Chopines*, wooden soled, open-backed platform **clogs**, were status symbols for Venetian women from the fifteenth to seventeenth centuries and eventually ranged from six to 30 inches in height. Because of the danger to women (who sometimes fell off of them), the excessive amount of material used to make them, and the association with courtesans, who originally popularized them, a series of laws were passed to restrict their height, materials, and usage. For instance, in the late fourteenth century men were forbidden from wearing chopines, and in the sixteenth century laws were passed forbidding the use of certain materials like gold and silver on shoes, but especially on chopines. In 1430, Venice passed a law restricting their height to three inches, but the law did not take, as women continued to wear taller and taller shoes throughout the century.

As middle-class Europeans began to purchase and wear fashionable clothing or shoes, sumptuary laws began to be enacted in order to control the wearing of luxury items by non-elites. For instance, legislation was passed by Louis XIV that restricted the wearing of red heels to members of the court. After the French and American revolutions, sumptuary laws in Europe began to disappear.

In the modern era, laws regulating footwear are rare but can still be found. "No shirt, no shoes, no service" signs are common in businesses and restaurants throughout the **United States**, and while those are not legal regulations, they reinforce the idea that only a certain class of person is welcome in those establishments. School uniforms represent another form of sumptuary law, aimed at public or private school children. In addition, since the 1980s a number of schools and school districts have banned some items of clothing and shoes in order to ensure that gang clothing or colors are not worn in the schools and also because certain items of clothing or footwear are thought of as disruptive, such as high-heeled shoes, red and black Air Jordans, Heelys, or even black shoes.

See also: Africa; China; Class; Europe; Japan

Further Reading Baldwin Francis Elizabeth. *Sumptuary Legislation and Personal Regulation in England*. Baltimore: John Hopkin Press, 1926; Dewald, Jonathan. *Europe 1450 to 1789: Encyclopedia of the Early Modern World*. New York: Charles Scribner's Sons, 2004; Kovesi Killerby, Catherine. *Sumptuary Law in Italy 1200–1500*. New York: Oxford University Press, 2002; Wiesner, Merry. *Early Modern Europe, 1450–1789*. Cambridge: Cambridge University Press, 2006.

"THESE BOOTS ARE MADE FOR WALKIN"

"These Boots Are Made for Walkin" is a pop song written by Lee Hazlewood and first released by Nancy Sinatra in 1966. It has since been covered by dozens of artists and achieved new popularity after it was recorded by Jessica Simpson in 2005 for the film *The Dukes of Hazzard*.

Nancy Sinatra is the daughter of singer and actor Frank Sinatra, and "These Boots Are Made for Walkin" was her most popular song. Released on her 1966 album "Boots," it became a number-one hit. Sinatra is often thought of as a "one hit wonder" because she never had another number-one hit.

The song tells the story of a woman who rejects the advances of a man who lies to her, makes promises that he doesn't keep, and cheats on her. The chorus, "these boots are made for walkin, and that's just what they'll do, one of these days these books are gonna walk all over you," is the woman's way of telling the man that she's going to leave him, and make him suffer in the process. Sinatra was told by Hazlewood, who also produced the hit, to sing the song as if she were a 16-year-old girl being taken advantage of by her 40-year-old boyfriend, and her version became something of a feminist anthem to women. In the music video accompanying the song, Sinatra wore a pair of black **go go boots** with medium chunky heels, and her backup dancers wore mid-calf length black boots with **stiletto** heels. "These Boots" was also a popular anthem among American soldiers in the Vietnam war.

In Jessica Simpson's 2005 version, Simpson wears red **cowboy boots** and "Daisy Duke" cut-off shorts, and the music video and accompanying lyrics provide a more overtly sexual image than Sinatra's version. The video seemed to offer a mixed message: the lyrics, which were rewritten for the movie, still include some of the "empowering" feelings of the original song, but Simpson's appearance (in particular, the final scene where she soaps up the movie's car, the General Lee, in a pink bikini) and demeanor in the video appeared to be aimed at soliciting male attention.

In 1993, during the 51-day standoff between the FBI and an apocalyptic cult known as the Branch Davidians at their compound in Waco, Texas, the FBI played Nancy Sinatra's version of the song, over and over, at very loud volumes as a form of "psychological warfare" intended to force the Davidians to surrender to authorities. Some people believe that the government planned on setting the fires that ultimately killed the Davidians based on the final stanza of the song, which ironically warn the listener against "thinkin' that you'll never get burnt."

See also: Go Go Boots

Further Reading Pedersen, Stephanie. *Shoes: What Every Woman Should Know.* Cincinnati: David & Charles, 2005.

TOENAILS

Toenails are the primate equivalent of a claw or a hoof on another animal and grow from the end of a primate's toes. They are made of protein and continuously grow throughout one's lifetime. In primates, toenails and fingernails allow the hands and feet to be more useful in terms of grasping; in other animals, even those with prehensile digits, claws can get in the way. In humans, because toes are no longer used to grasp objects, toenails have lost much of their function and instead are both a focus of adornment and a potential area for disease and injury.

Toenails grow from a nail bed on the toe, and like fingernails they are considered dead material; because the nail plate has no nerve endings, nails can be cut or otherwise damaged without pain or damage to the body. Because nails grow continuously at a rate of about a half inch per month, most people file or trim them. However, the nail bed itself does have nerve endings, and damage to the nail bed can cause serious pain and injury. The cuticle is the skin at the side of the toenail or fingernail, and it too can experience damage, most commonly by tearing or cutting the nail too close to the nail bed.

While nails grow at a rate of about a half an inch per month, their growth depends in part upon environmental and genetic factors. In addition, illnesses can cause deformities to the fingernail, can cause the nail to become discolored, and can create grooves across the nail. Poor diet can leave the nails thin, split, or brittle, and the use of drugs can also cause changes in the condition of the nails.

Because the health of the toenails or fingernails is often linked to health or illness in the rest of the body, nail health is often used as an indicator of overall health or illness. For instance, fingernail diagnoses are used in traditional Chinese medicine; abnormal ridges or colors are then associated with various meridians in the body. In Western medicine, too, whether nails are extra thick or thin, strangely shaped or colored, or smooth, groove, or pitted can all indicate a possible health problem. In addition, Western medical professionals will sometimes test the color of a nail to see whether a patient is in shock.

There are a number of conditions that affect toenails and can cause them to become inflamed, malformed, discolored, brittle, or even fall off. Such causes include infection, injury, fungi, other diseases, reactions to drugs or chemotherapy, or dietary deficiencies. Some conditions, on the other hand, are hereditary, and some may indicate cancer. In other cases, nails could become inflamed or malformed due to allergies or reactions to household chemicals. In addition, toenails can become infected when getting a **pedicure** if the pedicurist does not sterilize his or her tools or from a reaction to the chemical agents used in nail polish or nail remover. Finally, nails also simply get more brittle and will tend to split and become discolored as people age.

Toenails can easily become injured, most commonly by dropping something heavy on the toes or by wearing shoes that are ill fitting. **Ingrown toenails** are one example in which the side of a toenail grows into the toe bed, which can cause pain and infection. It can be caused by wearing tight or high shoes, by an injury to the toe or trimming the toenails into a rounded shape, or the shape of a person's toenails. With an ingrown toenail, the skin will grow around the nail, causing inflammation, redness, pain, discharge, and, when left untreated, an infection. Dropping a heavy object on a toenail, on the other hand, most commonly will cause a hematoma, which is a discoloration and swelling of the toenail, with a pocket of blood trapped inside.

Keeping toenails healthy involves wearing clean **socks** and well-fitting shoes, since ill-fitting shoes can cause injury to toes and toenails and dirty or wet socks can invite infection. In addition, wearing protective footwear like safety shoes is a way to protect feet from injury when working in a dangerous environment. Keeping toenails trimmed is a way to prevent hangnails and ingrown toenails and the infections that can result from them. Finally, wearing shoes or **sandals** when walking in wet or dirty environments is another way to protect both toes and toenails from infection.

Toenails are a major site of adornment in cultures around the world. While they have not experienced as much adornment as fingernails, many women around the world (and increasingly, men) do lavish a great deal of attention on the appearance of their toenails.

Toenail painting is the most common form of toenail decoration and usually involves purchasing nail polish from a drug store, department store, or supermarket, and painting one's nails oneself. Nail polish colors, like makeup, change seasonally, with new colors becoming fashionable in a given season. However, many women get their nails professionally painted, shaped, and cared for by pedicurists at nail salons. One popular look is the French manicure in which white polish is painted on the white part of the nail that protrudes beyond the nail bed, and then a nude color is painted along the entire nail.

Another way of decorating the nails is by creating special effects on the nails. Some manicurists paint designs on both finger and toenails, and today a variety of kits are available to purchase that include stencils, stickers, and glue-on jewels and charms to decorate nails. Some artists also airbrush designs on nails, with or without stencils. Individuals can also paint images on their own nails, using just a toothpick dipped in nail polish. Temporary tattoos can also be applied to nails once they have been polished. Today, some women have their toenails pierced, either using a needle or pin or by purchasing a simple nail piercing tool. Specialized fingernail and toenail jewelry is now available to wear in the piercings.

Even people who do not paint or otherwise decorate their toenails often take special care of them, treating themselves to pedicures on a regular basis. A pedicure involves having a professional file, trim, polish, and sometimes paint one's toenails. It also involves trimming the cuticles, filing or scraping the calluses off of the feet, rubbing lotions onto the feet, and a foot massage. While pedicures, like manicures, are primarily used by women, many men today get pedicures as well, although it is still uncommon to find a man with polished toenails.

See also: Disorders and Injuries; Foot and Shoe Adornment; Ingrown Toenails; Pedicure

Further Reading Copeland, Glenn, Stan Solomon, and Mark Myerson. *The Good Foot Book: A Guide for Men, Women, Children, Athletes, Seniors*. Alameda, CA: Hunter House, 2005; Vonhof, John. *Fixing Your Feet: Prevention and Treatments for Athletes*. Berkeley, CA: Wilderness Press, 2006.

TORTURE

Torture refers to using pain or the threat of pain to cause someone to give in to their captor or tormentor. It has historically been used by state and religious authorities to extract confessions or incriminating information from alleged criminals or prisoners of war who otherwise would not speak. It has also been used to convert unwilling participants to a new religion and to indoctrinate and "reeducate" political prisoners or political activists. Torture is also used to dehumanize those being tortured and as a form of punishment for those accused of extremely serious crimes, such as heresy. During the European witch hunts of the fifteenth to eighteenth centuries, torture was also used to get the accused witches to confess because authorities felt that a voluntary confession was invalid. Roman slaves, too, could not be trusted to confess voluntarily and were tortured for this purpose. Finally, torture has been used by sadistic killers, often serial killers, who take pleasure in watching their victims suffer before killing them.

Methods of torture have included forced exercise, the breaking of bones, removal of the nails or teeth, binding the body, roasting the soles of the feet over hot coals, branding, flogging, burning, castration, cutting, water torture, foot whipping, knee capping, the removal of limbs, rape, starvation, tongue removal, as well as various forms of psychological torture. In Medieval Europe, a number of specialized tools were created to torture victims, including the rack, the boot, the breaking wheel, the lash, padlocks, the stock, the thumbscrew, and the Iron Maiden.

There are a number of different torture techniques focused specifically on the feet. Torturing the feet is an especially good technique for torture because the victim must then walk on his feet (assuming he survives), causing pain and often permanent debilitation long after the end of the torture. In addition, where torture focused on the feet is used in the **Middle East**, it is also a method of humiliation because the victim's feet are displayed, which is a sign of shame.

The "boot" was a technique popular in Medieval Europe that was used to crush the feet and lower legs. While there have been multiple variants of the boot, the basic premise is that it is a casing made of iron, planks of wood, or other material that is placed tightly around the foot and lower leg and slowly tightened in order to crush the bones. The Chinese version of the boot was known as *kia quen*, which involved placing wooden boards around the victim's feet and tightening them either sharply or slowly.

The boot is similar to *kittee*, a British form of torture used by tax collectors in colonial **India**. In kittee, two wooden boards are used to flatten or crush an area of the body, such as the breasts, hands, or feet. Another British form of punishment was picketing or pictoning, in which the victim is forced to stand on a pointed stake.

Bastinado is a Chinese torture technique that involves caning the soles of the feet (or the buttocks) over a long period of time, which is intended to cause immense suffering. In a much less severe form, bastinado has also been used as a form of corporal punishment for children in **China**. An equivalent form of torture is known as the *falaka* or *falanga*, which refers to a device used to immobilize the feet so that they can be lashed. Popular in Muslim countries, once a person has been tied to the falaka, which is essentially a long pole, the soles of the feet are beaten with crop, stick, or pipe. Beatings done with the falaka are much more intense than bastinado but are used for both punishing criminals and disciplining children.

Self Mortification. Close-up of a devotee's leg at the Hindu celebration Thaipusam, celebrating Lord Murugan's conquest over evil. [2008 copyright Wong Szefei. Image from BigStockPhoto.com]

Toenails, like fingernails, are also often the subject of torture, via either smashing them with a hammer or pulling them out of the skin. In addition, burning the soles of the feet with cigarettes or other lighted objects is a low-tech form of torture. Finally, there have been instances of torture involving the tickling of the feet, such as in China or **Rome** where supposedly the victim's feet are coated with a sweet substance like honey, which is then licked off by a domestic animal. It is difficult to know whether this ever occurred or whether the reports are simply apocryphal.

Lightly flogging feet is also practiced among adherents of bondage, discipline, sadism, and masochism. Here, the pleasure of the activity derives from the binding of the "victim," (i.e., the submissive) and the dominant's ability to see the pain in the victim's face. Fetishists also collect photos and videos of (usually) women being bound and having their feet lashed. Other forms of foot torture popular among foot fetishists include using clothespins to bind the toes, piercing the toes with needles, forks, or other sharp objects, or simply binding the feet very tightly. Some people go further, burning the bottoms of the feet and cutting them with knives or needles to cause more damage. On the other hand, tickle torture is used by some in the BDSM community.

Self torture, or self-mortification, is another practice that often involves feet. Self-mortification refers to the practice of punishing oneself, either in a religious context or to atone for wrongdoing. Self-mortification often involves inflicting pain on one's own body by whipping, branding, cutting, or other means. A number of different religious traditions encourage the practice of self-mortification either for their members or their priests. Hindu holy men, for example, often engage in self-mortification, including fasting, self-flagellation, laying on a bed of nails, and other practices. Wearing **sandals** in which the soles are made up of dozens of sharpened nails (on which the feet rest) is one such practice and ensures that the penitent will suffer with every step.

See also: China; Crush Videos; Fetishes; Middle East

Further Reading Foucault, M. *Discipline and Punish*. Harmondsworth: Penguin, 1979.

TRANSGENDER SHOES

The term transgender refers to men or women who adopt the behaviors, roles, and appearances of the opposite gender. Transgendered people include transvestites who cross-dress, those who choose to be androgynous in appearance and/or behavior, and people who feel that they were born in the wrong body, such as transsexuals. The terms also refers to drag queens, who are typically gay men who dress like women (i.e., dress in drag) for performance purposes.

> Look to the heel young man, the sex is in the heel.
>
> LOLA, THE DRAG QUEEN IN *KINKY BOOTS*

Transgendered men, or transmen, are more common in many cultures than women and generally wear women's clothing. Finding well-fitting clothing and footwear is often a challenge for transvestites, drag queens, and transexuals.

Because men are generally larger than women, their feet are usually larger, and sometimes much larger, than women's feet, making it hard for transmen to find shoes. For that reason, there are a number of companies today that specialize in shoes for transmen and sell them over the Internet. (Prior to the Internet, these companies sold primarily through mail-order catalogues.) These companies provide feminine footwear in sizes up to men's size 17, although many such companies do not sell a wide variety of practical shoes, catering instead to drag queens and others who want to dress up, but not dress regularly as women. For that reason, **high heels** are the most common footwear offered by companies making shoes for transmen.

Transgender shoes are not only larger (and wider) than regular women's shoes, but they are often specially made as well, with extra reinforcement and cushioning to support a heavier wearer, and often thicker **leather** as well.

Because many men have not had much experience wearing high heels, transmen often have to learn how to walk in heels without hurting themselves and so that they look graceful. There are videos and courses available to help transgendered men to move and walk in a more feminine fashion, and to walk in heels. For instance, Miss Vera's Finishing School for Boys Who Want to Be Girls is a cross-dressing academy that covers dressing, walking, and acting feminine. Some experts also recommend starting with wedge platforms, kitten heels, or **espadrilles** as a way to transition to high heels. Open-toed **sandals** are also easier on men's feet than closed-toed **pumps** because they provide a bit more room for the toes. Some transmen prefer **boots** to shoes because they hide masculine ankles and emphasize the curve of the calves.

Determining one's **shoe size** is not always easy for transgenders, and since most transmen purchase their shoes online, they cannot try them on before purchasing them. Most companies offer conversion charts on their Web sites to help their customers buy the right size shoe.

See also: Eroticism; Fetishes; High Heels; *Kinky Boots*

Further Reading Lomas, Clare, Peter McNeil and Sally Gray. "Beyond the Rainbow: Queer Shoes," in Rielle, Georgio and Peter McNeil, eds. *Shoes: A History From Sandals to Sneakers*. London: Berg Publishers, 2006; Steele, Valerie. *Fetish: Fashion, Sex and Power*. New York: Oxford University Press, 1996; Vera, Veronica. *Miss Vera's Cross-Dress for Success: A Resource Guide for Boys Who Want to be Girls*. New York: Villard, 2002.

UGGS

Ugg is a brand of soft Australian boot that was extremely popular in the early part of the twenty-first century in the United States, and the term "uggs" also refers to generic sheepskin boots.

Sheepskin boots have long been worn among shepherds and others in rural Australia and New Zealand and have also been popular in cold climates

> "If the shoe fits, it's ugly."
> ANONYMOUS

because the wool lining keeps the feet and legs warm. Originally, the boots, known as uggs for ugly boots, were made of two pieces of sheepskin in the shape of a boot, sewn together with a seam going up the front and back, and without a separate sole. During World War I, Allied airline pilots wore boots called fug boots for warmth while flying.

But it was surfers who popularized the boots in the late twentieth century. Australian surfers in Perth began wearing sheepskin boots in the 1960s to keep themselves warm after getting out of the cold water. They were made of merino sheepskin, first with linoleum and then rubber soles. The boots were the iconic footwear of Perth surfers, followed by surfers on Australia's west coast, and later, American surfers. Perth was, and still is, the host of a number of Uggs manufacturers.

In the late 1970s, surfers Brian Smith (from Australia) and Doug Jensen (from the **United States**) trademarked the name Ugg and began selling the boots to American surfers. They were soon sold in surf shops throughout California and were primarily worn by swimmers and surfers.

Jensen soon left the company that he cofounded, Ugg Holding, but Smith remained until 1995, when Deckers Outdoor Corporation (which also makes Teva **sport sandals**) bought the company. Today the company is called Ugg Australia, a division of Deckers Outdoor. Ugg Australia fought, unsuccessfully, to keep the term Uggs as a trademarked term after the Australian Supreme Court ruled that the term should be public domain. Today, in Australia, other companies are free to use the term, but in the United States Uggs is still trademarked and thus protected. The Uggs made by Ugg Australia are no longer made in Australia; today, like so many other shoes, they are made in **China**. Besides Ugg Australia, there are a number of other companies making sheepskin boots, some of which are knockoffs of the Uggs brand, and others that were being made before Uggs was trademarked, but only Ugg Australia can use the Ugg name in the United States.

Uggs are made of sheepskin, with the woolly side on the inside and the tanned skin side on the outside, and a sole made of ethylene vinyl acetate. The wool insole keeps the feet and legs so warm that socks are not needed when wearing them. The most popular Uggs are the classic short boots that extend to the mid-calf and can be worn with the top folded down to expose the fleece inside.

Uggs became popular beyond the surfing crowd in the United States starting in the late 1990s, thanks to Decker's promotion of Uggs as luxury footwear, leading to celebrities wearing them. Their popularity skyrocketed after Oprah Winfrey bought 350 pairs that she gave to her audience in 2000. However, it is a handful of celebrities like Mary Kate and Ashley Olson, Pamela Anderson, Britney Spears, Kate Hudson, and Sienna Miller who really made Uggs a household name and must-have fashion item, often wearing the boots in warm-weather Los Angeles with short skirts or shorts. Ironically, Anderson, who began wearing Uggs with her bathing suit while filming the television show *Baywatch* from 1992 to 1997, only realized in 2007 that Uggs are made of sheepskin. A vegetarian, animal rights advocate, and spokesperson for People for the Ethical Treatment of Animals, Anderson was embarrassed to be caught wearing animal skin shoes and quickly repudiated them, asking her fans to wear vegetarian boots instead.

Today, Ugg Australia makes dozens of styles of shoes, slippers, and boots (some of which sell for more than $300) and is expanding into accessories as well. Decker reported that Uggs sales generated more than $300 million in 2007.

See also: Boots; Crocs

Further Reading Koleff, George. *How to Make Ugg Boots: The Manual*. Pasadena, South Australia: Encyclotel, 1991; McIntosh, Sue. *The Killer Ugg Boots from Down Under*. Whorouly East, Victoria: S. McIntosh, 1988; Vejlgaard, Henrik. *Anatomy of a Trend*. New York: McGraw Hill, 2008.

UNITED STATES

Footwear in the United States has gone through a huge variety of changes since the first Europeans arrived. This section will treat only Euro-American footwear; Native American shoes are treated in a separate section.

The first European **shoemaker**, Thomas Beard, arrived in the United States on the Mayflower in 1629, with a selection of hides and **shoemaking** tools. Shoemakers like Beard ended up making up one of the largest trades in the new colonies. They generally worked at home, in small shops, or worked as itinerant shoemakers, traveling from village to village, making shoes for local families. Most were located in urban areas.

Lynn, Massachusetts was the center of the shoemaking industry in North America during the colonial period, with the majority of the **leather** tanning and shoe production occurring there, and by 1778, American-made shoes were being exported to colonies in the West Indies as well.

Most colonists, unless they were wealthy, did not wear fashionable shoes inspired by European fashions. Instead, they wore practical shoes made by local shoemakers. Rural residents often spent a lot of time outside, so their shoes needed to be durable and able to handle the extremes of weather. Leather **boots** and strong leather shoes were common for men, and women often wore low leather or fabric boots without heels and, again, sturdy leather shoes. Some Americans, especially those from Spain or France, even adopted the **moccasins** worn by local Native American communities for everyday wear. Those who could afford it also had shoes that could be worn to social occasions, such as silk shoes for women or **jack boots** (starting in the mid-seventeenth century) for men. Some Americans also wore pattens when outdoors to keep their dress shoes clean. Children, especially during the earliest years of colonization, mostly went barefoot, and when shoes were warranted during the cold months they wore hand-me-downs from their parents. Where regional differences occurred, those were both reflective of local conditions in America as well as differences in the countries from which the colonists came.

> All women, whether virgins, maidens, or widows, who shall after this Act impose upon, seduce or betray into matrimony any of His Majesty's male subjects by virtue of high heel shoes would be subject to the same severe punishment meted out to suspected witches.
>
> SEVENTEENTH CENTURY MASSACHUSETTS LAW

Wealthy Americans, and in particular English Americans, on the other hand, had their shoes delivered from **Europe** throughout the colonial period and were able to wear the latest European styles, which included high-heeled **pumps** made of silk, brocade, or velvet in the eighteenth century and delicate **slippers** in the nineteenth century. Wealthy men wore heeled shoes with decorative buckles and stiff leather boots. Wealthy Americans wore their European shoes and clothing to the balls that became popular in large cities in the nineteenth century. Some of the colonies passed **sumptuary laws** to ensure that **class** differences would be preserved through fashion and footwear choices.

It wasn't until the nineteenth century that American shoemakers began making fashionable shoes that satisfied the most upper-crust American, and it wasn't until halfway through the century that many Americans could actually afford them.

Shoemaking, and shoe wearing, changed in the United States starting in the mid-nineteenth century with the development of machines that replaced much of the hand labor that previously went into making shoes. With the development of machines for compacting leather, sewing uppers, sewing uppers to soles, and even shaping leather onto lasts, more people could afford shoes and more shoe styles were created. By the end of the nineteenth century, most shoes being made in the United States came from mechanized shoe factories.

With mechanized shoe production, shoes became affordable for far more Americans, who could now buy them at shoe stores rather than from shoemakers, and the styles of shoes popular in Europe became popular, and widely worn, in the United States as well, including flat slippers for women and

military shoes and boots for men. Materials for making shoes expanded as well as the garment industry in the United States developed, allowing for the availability of many new fabrics. While European women who wore fashionable European shoes were not working women, many American women wearing those same shoes did do a lot of work in their homes, making European fashions less practical in the American context and creating new foot disorders that were previously unknown in this country. Women, for the most part, wore shoes that were aimed at indoor wear and leisure, while men wore shoes that were appropriate for outdoor use. In addition, in the nineteenth century small feet became fashionable for women, so shoes became smaller, causing additional problems with women's feet.

The nineteenth century also saw the beginning of the women's suffrage movement in the United States, which impacted shoe design. Shoes became available that were less confining and more practical, which suited America's newly independent women.

Industrialization changed both shoe production as well as clothing production, stimulating the development of a new **fashion industry** centered in New York City. By the end of the nineteenth century, the garment industry exploded in New York, creating both ready-to-wear clothing for average Americans as well as high-end clothing, still based on European designs. It wasn't until World War II, when American clothing and shoe manufacturers could no longer have easy access to European designers, that American shoe and clothing designers emerged in their own right, creating the American fashion industry that eventually spawned influential American shoe designers like Beth Levine.

The "Shoe Bomber"

Richard Reid was arrested on December 22, 2001, after he was caught on American Airlines Flight 63 from Paris to Miami trying to light a fuse on a bomb that was placed in his shoe. Known since then as the Shoe Bomber, Reid had been trying to blow up the plane, and according to the FBI the homemade bomb in his shoe had enough explosives in it to do the job. He was thwarted by two flight attendants who smelled the lit match and then restrained him with the help of passengers. Reid is an English citizen who spent time in prison for petty crimes and converted to Islam while incarcerated, taking the name Abdul Ra'uff. In the 1990s, he began associating with members of al-Qaeda and became enchanted by the promise of jihad. By the summer of 2001, in concert with other al-Qaeda members, he had decided to bomb Flight 63. He was convicted of trying to blow up a plane in 2003, and has been in a maximum security prison in Florence, Colorado, since that time. Reid's bomb was made out of plastic explosives and was inserted into the sole of his shoe. After his arrest, TSA screeners began asking airline passengers to remove their shoes when going through airport screening, so that they could be screened for explosives residue. Today, it is not only common practice for passengers to walk barefoot or in socks through airport screening, but it has become customary for travelers to wear easy -to-remove shoes while traveling so as not to hold up the line at security. In addition, airport screeners are expected to be on alert especially for thick-soled shoes, as these can more easily conceal explosives or other dangerous items. It is unknown what kind of shoes Reid was wearing.

Shoes in twentieth century America changed along with changes in American culture. In particular, as women's roles changed, footwear changed as well. The 1920s saw women achieving the vote and radical changes in fashion as dresses got shorter and Victorian style and morality largely disappeared. Women's footwear reflected these changes, with both practical shoes emerging to be worn while dancing as well as sexy shoes worn with short skirts.

The 1930s was marked by the Great Depression, and America moved towards war, but Hollywood movies showcased glamorous fashion and shoes. **Salvatore Ferragamo**, shoemaker to Hollywood royalty, invented cork **platform shoes**, which were popular in the late 1930s in the United States. His invention of the steel arch also allowed for the development of high-heeled **sandals**, which became popular during the 1950s. During the second world war, American designers (like European designers) had to cope with a lack of materials due to wartime rationing and designed shoes made with new materials like reptile skins and nylon mesh. Wartime laws limited heel heights to one inch and colors were limited to six basic choices. Since nylon and silk were both needed for the war effort, women couldn't wear stockings, and many painted a seam down the back of their legs.

With the 1950s, a great variety of shoes came into fashion, from fashionable **stilettos** for nighttime and saddle shoes and sneakers for recreation. Flat ballet slippers also became fashionable, warn with capris. During the 1960s, counterculture influences hit fashion and footwear, and **go go boots** and earthy sandals like Birkenstocks became popular. The 1970s saw the rise of disco, which brought back the platform shoe, and the fitness movement, which spurred the explosion of **athletic shoes** as lifestyle shoes. Fitness and self-improvement continued to be popular throughout the 1980s, and athletic shoes continued to remain extremely popular. Designer brands became popular in the 1980s and 1990s, and television shows like *Sex and the City* influenced women to spend hundreds of dollars on status brand shoes. The last two decades have also seen women joining the workforce in enormous numbers, leading to the rise of women's power **pumps** in the office.

See also: Europe; Native America; Shoemakers; Shoemaking

Further Reading Burns, William E. *Science and Technology in Colonial America*. Westport, CT: Greenwood Publishing Group, 2005; Morse Earle, Alice. *Two Centuries of Costume in America, 1620–1820*. Rutland, VT: CE Tuttle Company, 1971; Rexford, Nancy. "The Perils of Choice: Women's Footwear in Nineteenth-Century America," in Rielle, Georgio and Peter McNeil, eds. *Shoes: A History from Sandals to Sneakers*. London: Berg Publishers, 2006.

VANS

Vans is a maker of athletic shoes, primarily skateboard shoes, but also shoes for snowboarding, surfing, BMX, and other extreme sports. It also makes clothing and accessories like helmets and pads through its Pro-Tec label. The classic Vans shoe is a canvas and rubber slip-on, although today there are dozens of styles of Vans.

The Van Doren Rubber Company was founded in 1966 by Paul Van Doren, a shoe manufacturer. Van Doren and his partners wanted to make shoes and sell them directly to the public, which they did when they opened their first store in Anaheim, California, selling three styles of shoes, which were called Vans. The shoes were basic **leather** or canvas deck shoes that were made for men, women, and children.

When Van Doren and his partners first opened their store, they didn't stock it with ready-made shoes. Instead, the store showcased the shoe models, and customers picked the style and color they wanted, which the staff then made for the customers. As the shoes became more popular, the partners opened dozens of new stores throughout Southern California, catering to schools, sports teams, and other groups that wanted special colors or patterns on their shoes.

Vans shoes were originally made with canvas or leather uppers and a rubber sole with a diamond pattern across the bottom. Later, the design changed to one that features six-sided stars, for better grip. Because skateboarders were among the earliest customers in some of their stores, in 1976 Vans began making a shoe specifically for them: the checkerboard-patterned Era, designed by skateboarders Tony Alva and Stacy Peralta. The checkerboard design came about because skateboarders were coloring their shoes themselves in a checkerboard pattern. It was padded in the back and sides and had a label that read "Off the wall" on it, and protected skaters' feet when they fell. At that time, Vans also began sponsoring skateboarders, paying them a few hundred dollars to wear their shoes while competing.

1979, Vans introduced its first slip-on, which became the iconic Vans shoe. After the checkerboard slip-ons were worn by Sean Penn in the 1982 movie *Fast Times at Ridgemont High*, their popularity skyrocketed among skateboarders and kids in general, and Vans began selling the shoes in department stores, shoe stores, as well as in Vans retail locations. Also in the 1970s, Vans introduced shoes made for BMX riders, making Vans the shoe of choice for BMX as well as for skateboarding.

The company's profits fell in the 1980s as competition increased from low-cost competitors and interest in slip-on shoes waned, forcing Van Doren to file for bankruptcy in 1984. After a corporate restructuring, Vans once again gained popularity in the late 1980s and took advantage of its American manufacturing to deliver shoes to retailers in just five days after order.

In 1988, Van Doren sold the company, now called Vans Inc., to McCown De Leeuw and Company, but the 1990s saw further financial struggles for the company as it struggled with overseas competition, which forced the company to move manufacturing facilities to **Korea** in 1995 and to introduce new lines of footwear as well as specialty shoes such as snowboarding **boots**. The company also began designing a number of shoes named after professional athletes, boosting brand recognition further among athletes and fans. The company opened its first Vans skateboarding park in Orange, California, in 1998, and today it has eight skate parks. It also sponsors sporting and music events in order to create more brand recognition among the target demographic. Besides its sponsorship of music events, Vans shoes have been famously worn by a number of rock stars like Johnny Ramone. Vans have had two hip hop songs written about them, and the company has created special shoes for bands like Motorhead and Iron Maiden.

In 1999, Vans and Pacific Sunwear combined their companies to form VanPac, which makes clothing and accessories. Today, Vans are most popular among skateboarders, surfers, snowboarders, and other athletes as well as youth in general who are interested in the Southern California surfer/skater lifestyle. The company is a major leader in the youth sportswear market, with **Converse** and **Nike** as the primary competitors. Vans is now a subsidiary of VF Outdoor Inc., which is a subsidiary of VF Corporation, a multibillion-dollar apparel company.

See also: Athletic Shoes; Skateboarding Shoes; Sneakers

Further Reading Brooke, Michael. *The Concrete Wave: The History of Skateboarding.* Toronto: Warwick Publishing, 1999.

VEGAN SHOES

Vegan shoes, also known as vegetarian shoes, are shoes that are made without **leather** or other animal products. Worn primarily by vegetarians, vegans, and animal rights advocates, vegan shoes are becoming extremely popular today.

Most vegans, and many vegetarians, choose not to wear leather or other animal skins. Leather refers to the skin of animals, generally cattle, and today most leather used in shoes is a by-product of the meat and dairy industries, with millions of cows per year dying for consumption in the United States alone. The skin of these cows is then used by clothing, shoe, and accessories manufacturers as well as makers of furniture, car seats, and more. In addition, many high-end shoes and **boots** today are made with the skins of "exotic" animals like snakes, ostriches, and crocodiles, which are either raised on ranches or hunted in the wild.

Many vegetarians, vegans, and animals lovers are not comfortable wearing shoes or clothing made with animal products because of the cruelty involved in the raising and slaughtering of the animals. For years, conscientious vegetarians sought out non-leather shoes made of fabric, rubber, and synthetic materials, often purchasing their shoes through low-cost retailers like **Payless Shoe Source**. Some brands of shoes have been made without leather for years, such as **Converse** All Stars, but fashion-conscious consumers did not have a great deal of choices when it came to choosing chic shoes without leather.

Today, this situation has changed, as companies like Moo Shoes, Alternative Outfitters, and Ethical Wares sell fashionable vegetarian shoes and other big retailers like Zappos dedicate a sizeable portion of their product line to non-leather shoes. Heartland Products was the first major retailer of non-leather shoes, opening in 1986 and offering **cowboy boots**, **athletic shoes**, dress shoes, and casual shoes through mail order, and it is still in operation today. While most vegan shoe companies sell their products online, there are a handful of retail locations that specialize in non-leather shoes and accessories, such as Moo Shoes in New York City, Otsu in San Francisco, or All Vegan in San Diego. These companies sell shoes made by a variety of designers, some of whom make both leather and non-leather shoes, like **Birkenstock** or **Nike** (which ironically made a non-leather shoe called the Air Carnivore).

There are a number of companies today, on the other hand, that design and manufacture exclusively vegetarian shoes, bags, belts, and accessories. These include Rinaldi, Neurara, and Novacas. Beyond Skin is a British company that produces made-to-order vegan shoes that are hand-stitched and hand-lasted, made of fabrics like satin and synthetic leather, and Mink is an Italian company that also offers handmade non-leather shoes made with denim, linen, and cotton. Fashion designer Stella McCartney, daughter of Paul McCartney and a vegetarian herself, makes a line of luxury shoes and boots with prices in the hundreds of dollars, and actress and vegetarian Natalie Portman also makes a line of limited-edition vegetarian shoes for the company Te Casan.

Many animal activists have encountered problems because of the availability of beautiful, high-quality non-leather shoes that often mimic the look and feel of leather perfectly. Activists often report being accused of hypocrisy when wearing what appear to be leather shoes,

> Socially, shoes send a signal, a way of recognizing one type of person from another ... shoes can tell something about what we are like, sometimes even who we are aspiring to be, the persona we are trying out.
>
> CLARISSA PINKOLA ESTES

and some have even gone so far as to wear stickers on their shoes that say that they are not made of leather in order to reduce confusion.

See also: Leather; Payless Shoe Source

Further Reading Williams, Erin E., Margo DeMello. *Why Animals Matter: The Case for Animal Protection*. Amherst, NY: Prometheus Books, 2007.

VULCANIZATION

Vulcanization refers to the technology developed by Charles Goodyear in 1839 that allows for the molding of rubber. Without vulcanization, **athletic shoes** as we know them would not exist today, nor would **galoshes** or other rubber **boots** and shoes.

Vulcanization allowed for the creation of light, flexible shoes and waterproof shoes and boots. Prior to the use of rubber in shoes, shoes could only be waterproofed by treating the **leather** with oil, which resulted in shoes that were only partially waterproof and which lost much of their flexibility and softness. Prior to the use of rubber in shoes, elevated **clogs** or pattens were worn to protect feet, shoes, and clothing from water, dirt, and mud. Similarly, without rubber-soled shoes, athletes wore heavy leather shoes or boots for sports like soccer, tennis, and croquet.

The first person who tried to use rubber to waterproof clothing was Charles Macintosh, after whom the Mackintosh raincoat was named in 1823. Macintosh was able to create thin sheets of dried liquid rubber that he then sewed onto fabric to make into clothing, but the early garments were stiff, did not smell good, and could not withstand changes in temperature.

In 1844, Charles Goodyear, who had spent 20 years and much of his income studying the properties of rubber, finally patented a process that involved heating a mixture of natural rubber and sulphur, which allowed for the molding of rubber into a durable, flexible, and lightweight substance that did not melt in hot weather or harden in cold weather. Goodyear saw that his invention could allow for the production of waterproof shoes and boots as well as other products and, indeed, his invention has allowed for thousands of rubberized products to be created, including rubber boots and rubber-soled athletic shoes as well as tires. Ironically, the Goodyear Tire and Rubber Company that is today known for tires but that also made early athletic shoes was not founded by Charles Goodyear; it was simply named after him. Goodyear himself died 30 years prior to the founding of Goodyear Tire and Rubber, in $200,000 worth of debt.

Rubber has allowed for not just waterproof boots and athletic shoes but also has played an important part in workplace safety. Rubber-soled shoes are worn by professionals such as nurses, food service workers, and housekeepers, where protection against slipping on slick floors is critical. In addition, rubber shoes offer protection from falling objects and protect the foot from being splashed with blood, chemicals, or other unpleasant materials in many workplaces. Finally, slip-on toe protectors made of rubber are one of the newer safety innovations in the workplace, replacing for many workers steel-toe safety shoes, with rubber overshoes combined with interchangeable toe protectors.

See also: Athletic Shoes; Galoshes; Wellington Boot

Further Reading Haven, Kendall. *100 Greatest Science Inventions of All Time*. Westport, CT: Libraries Unlimited, 2006; Slack, Charles. *Noble Obsession: Charles Goodyear, Thomas Hancock, and the Race to Unlock the Greatest Industrial Secret of the Nineteenth Century*. Hyperion, 2003.

WEBBED TOES

Webbed toes, known (along with webbed fingers) as *syndactyly*, is a condition in which a person retains skin between some or all of the toes or fingers (although most commonly between the second and third toe), causing the toes to appear to be fused. This skin is present in the fetus during gestation but typically disappears during the first six weeks of development. When the skin does not disappear during gestation, the child is born with webbed toes.

Webbed toes occur regularly in waterfowl and some amphibians, but it is relatively rare in humans. It occurs in one of every 2,000 to 3,000 human births and is a heritable condition caused by inheriting a set of recessive genes from both parents. Because it is heritable, it is common to find that a person with webbed fingers or webbed toes has close family members with the same condition—at the very least, family members will often carry the gene in the heterozygous condition, although they won't express the trait.

Webbed toes and fingers can also be a symptom of a larger disorder, such as Down Syndrome, which is caused by inheriting an extra 21st chromosome as well as a handful of other genetic disorders.

There are different degrees of the condition, with some people having toes that are only partly connected and others with the condition having their toes fully connected. Webbed toes can be surgically corrected, but surgery is much more common with webbed fingers since impaired functionality is more important with fingers than with toes. Most people with webbed toes have no loss of function or sensation, and they do not cause pain or discomfort, although some people are embarrassed to have them. On the other hand, many people are proud of their webbed toes and show them off in public. Body modification aficionados even get the webbing between their toes pierced as a form of foot adornment. In addition, there is a subculture of foot fetishists who are attracted to webbed feet.

People who are concerned about this condition can be genetically tested to see if they carry the trait, which would indicate whether they could pass the gene onto their offspring.

See also: Disorders and Injuries; Polydactyly

Further Reading Moore, Keith L., and T. V. N. Persaud. *Before We Are Born: Essentials of Embryology and Birth Defects*. Philadelphia: Saunders, 1998.

WEDDING SHOES

It is very common in cultures around the world for shoes to be associated with weddings, brides, and marriage. For instance, shoes bring luck at weddings. Tying shoes behind a newly married couple's car brings luck in England and the **United States** and fertility in Transylsvania. Throwing shoes after the couple as they leave the church will also bring them good luck, as would placing a coin into the bride's shoe. Further, if a bridesmaid gets one of the shoes, she will marry next. Bridegrooms in France often put coins in their shoes prior to their weddings as a way of preventing impotence via sorcery. It is no accident that the fairy tale "**Cinderella**" has as its central symbol the glass slipper, which will, for Cinderella, ultimately represent her chances at happiness, love, and marriage.

There are a number of old English beliefs about shoes and the bridal bed, including the belief that the groom's left shoe should have the buckle removed to keep witches from interrupting the consummation. On the other hand, if the husband buckles the bride's shoe on the day of their wedding, she will control their relationship. In **India** it was once customary for the bride's red

These traditional wedding slippers are red because red is a lucky color and is heavily featured at Chinese weddings. [2005 copyright Jiang Jingjie. Image from BigStockPhoto.com]

shoes to be thrown across the roof to let visitors know that the couple was inside on their honeymoon.

It is thought by many that shoes are such common wedding symbols because they represent the bride's submission to her husband and the passing of the authority over the bride from the father to the husband. Early English marriage custom included, for example, the father removing one of the bride's shoes and giving it to the groom. Another English custom was the groom tapping the bride's shoe to demonstrate his authority over her. In the ancient Jewish tradition, a widow who is expected to marry her brother-in-law can remove a shoe from his foot, releasing him from the obligation. Even the tradition of throwing shoes after the couple (or tying them to the car) can be read as the transfer of authority over the bride from father to son in law.

Marriage also involves, at a more fundamental level, the transfer of a woman from one house to another. In ancient **Egypt**, the bride's father gave the groom's father a pair of her **sandals**, signaling the transfer of the daughter from one family to another. Even today, in many cultures, the bride will be given a new pair of shoes when she leaves for her wedding, as in **China**. In **Greece**, a groom will put the bride's shoes on her feet prior to her wedding, and among the Zuni, a woman's fiancé makes her wedding boot for her. In India, the bride is often given a gift of a new pair of silver shoes for her wedding, and in **Japan** the bride is often given a new pair of *zoris*, which symbolize marital bliss. It has also been customary in many cultures for a young man to make a pair of shoes to give to his beloved; if she accepts the shoes, she accepts his proposal of marriage and the shoes become an important symbol of their love together. Often it is the bride who makes the shoes for the groom, as in Malaysia, where a bride would not only make her own wedding shoes but would make a pair of beaded and embroidered mules for her husband and his family as well. But generally, it is more typical for a woman to make, or receive from her own family, a pair of special shoes to be worn at her wedding and to become part of her possessions as an adult married woman. Shoes, then, in the context of marriage, represent both the physical movement of the bride from one place to another as well as the transfer of authority over her from her father to her husband.

The shoes that a bride wears to her wedding, or to her honeymoon, are often very symbolic. For instance, traditionally in China, a bride wore special **slippers** on her wedding night over her foot bindings, which were embroidered by her or her mother and sometimes had erotic pictures painted inside for the new couple to enjoy.

China has perhaps the most elaborate set of conventions surrounding shoes and weddings. For centuries it was expected for a man to give his intended bride a pair of silk shoes, while the bride would make shoes for her fiancé's grandparents and great grandparents, and her family would make a pair of shoes for their future son in law. Today, it remains customary in many places in China for a woman to make her own pair of bridal shoes—usually embroidered with auspicious flowers and animals—which she would wear at her wedding and to make shoes for all the members of her fiancé's family, which represent the new bride's hopeful new relationship with her future in-laws. It is also still common in some parts of China for the bride to make her husband's first pair of wedded shoes. A bride will only wear her wedding shoes for the first three days of her marriage, and again after she bears her first child, while her husband can wear his shoes indefinitely. Sometimes a bride must put her wedding shoes under the bed to demonstrate to her husband that she will not wed again.

Today, European and American brides primarily wear white dresses and matching white shoes for their weddings. This trend was started in 1840 by Queen Victoria, who wore white to her wedding, breaking from the tradition of wearing blue.

See also: Beliefs; China; Europe; Judaism

Further Reading Monger, George. *Marriage Customs of the World: From Henna to Honeymoons*. Santa Barbara: ABC-CLIO, 2004.

WELLINGTON BOOT

Wellingtons refer to a type of tall **boot** popularized by the first Duke of Wellington in the early nineteenth century as well as to a type of **overshoe**, known as **galoshes**, and popularly known as Wellies.

During the nineteenth century, Hessian boots were popular among European nobility and officers. Hessian boots were tall **leather** boots with cutouts at the rear to allow the knee to bend, and were often ornamented with tassels. They were worn for both riding and combat and were popular amongst officers in European armies.

In the 1840s, the Duke of Wellington asked his **shoemaker** to modify the Hessian boot, which resulted in a lighter boot made of softer leather (which was waxed for durability) that was lower and more closely fitted to the leg. The Duke wanted comfortable boots that could be worn both in combat and indoors. After the Duke wore them, they became popular in England for two decades and were worn by British calvary soldiers in wars throughout the nineteenth century. They were also worn by soldiers in the American Civil War and may have led to the development of the **cowboy boot** in America.

Today, Wellingtons or Wellies refer to galoshes, overshoes made out of PVC or rubber and worn in the rain, but they could be worn as standalone boots as well. Wellies were developed thanks to the invention of **vulcanization** by Charles Goodyear, which allowed for the development of rubber-soled shoes as well as rubber boots. With the ability to mold rubber into a flexible, durable substance that could be used in virtually any climate, the galosh, or Wellie, was invented. The British Rubber Company, founded in 1856, was the first company to start producing rubber boots in England.

These Wellies are worn in rainy weather around the world. [Copyright 2008 Jupiterimages Corporation]

Wellies were worn by British soldiers in World War I to keep their feet dry in trenches, but farmers and workers of all types wore them at work, and they were again used in World War II by soldiers working in the flooded fields of the Netherlands. Today, Wellies are made of synthetic rubber or PVC, come in a rainbow of colors, and are worn around the world by men, women, and children during wet weather and by certain occupations like fishermen and farmers. They are also known as gumboots or Blücher boots in other parts of the world.

See also: Boots; Galoshes; Jack Boots; Military Shoes and Boots; Vulcanization

Further Reading David, Alison Matthews. "War Wellingtons: Military Footwear in the Age of Empire," in Rielle, Georgio and Peter McNeil, eds. *Shoes: A History From Sandals to Sneakers*. London: Berg Publishers, 2006; Edwards, Adam. *A Short History of the Wellington Boot*. London: Hodder & Stoughton, 2006; Haven, Kendall. *100 Greatest Science Inventions of All Time*. Westport, CT: Libraries Unlimited, 2006.

THE WIZARD OF OZ

The Wizard of Oz is a book by Frank Baum, published in 1900, and a movie based on the book that was released in 1939 that starred Judy Garland. It tells of Dorothy, a farm girl from Kansas, who gets knocked out during a tornado and dreams that her house, with her in it, is carried through the tornado to a faraway land known as Oz. While in Oz, Dorothy befriends a lion, a tin man, and a scarecrow, battles an evil witch, and eventually returns home again, when she wakes up from what appeared to have been an elaborate dream.

A central element in the *Wizard of Oz* is the ruby shoes that Dorothy is given after she accidentally kills the Wicked Witch of the East with her house. Those magic **slippers** are to protect her from the Wicked Witch of the West, who wants vengeance on Dorothy for killing her sister, but their real power is revealed at the end of the story when Dorothy finds out that by clicking her heels three times and repeating "there's no place like home," she can return to Kansas.

In *The Wizard of Oz*, the ruby slippers play a critical role in the story. They are first seen on the feet of the dead Wicked Witch of the East as she lies beneath Dorothy's house; they then are magically transported onto Dorothy's feet by Glinda the Good Witch of the North, which angers the Wicked Witch of the West, the dead witch's sister, who says that she's the only one who knows how to

The ruby slippers worn by Judy Garland in the 1939 film "The Wizard of Oz" are displayed during a media tour of the "America's Smithsonian" exhibition, April 10, 1996, in Kansas City, Missouri [AP Photo/Ed Zurga]

use their magic. Later, after her capture by the witch, when the witch tries to remove the slippers, she realizes that she can't touch them without becoming burnt, as the shoes are not only held fast to Dorothy's feet (as in "**The Red Shoes**"), but burn the witch (as in the end of "Snow White" when the evil Queen is forced to wear, and dance in, the red hot shoes.)

As with a number of folk tales such as "**Cinderella**" or "The Red Shoes," it is not surprising that shoes are central to the heroine's journey. Shoes are symbolic of journeys, and magical shoes allow folk heroes to magically travel to distant lands or to accomplish fantastic feats. Unlike many tales, however, Dorothy's slippers do not provide the key to her eventual wedding; in fact, there is no prince or wedding whatsoever in this story. They also did not convey her to Oz (her house did that), although they do bring her home again. In addition, the slippers, like magical shoes and **boots** in other tales, allow Dorothy to travel along the yellow brick road to the Emerald City, where they gain her admittance, and she beseeches the wizard to send her home. Ultimately, of course, it is the shoes that bring Dorothy home and that teach her the central lesson of the film—that home is in the heart.

Even though the shoes in Baum's book were originally not red (they were changed from silver to red for the movie to take advantage of the new technology of Technicolor), both silver and ruby are precious materials, and in **fairy tales** it is common for magical shoes to be made of materials like gold or silver. Indeed, it is often the precious material that gives the shoes their magical quality. Some scholars have interpreted the red slippers to be, instead, representative of Dorothy's growing sexuality and her impending menstruation. Another interpretation is that the slippers represent one's principles and by keeping them on, Dorothy never loses sight of hers. This, however, is an odd interpretation given that red slippers and fancy shoes in general are traditionally associated with pride, vanity, and royalty, as in "The Red Shoes."

There were multiple pairs of ruby slippers made for the film itself, with five surviving today. Designed by Hollywood costumer Gilbert Adrian, the white silk and leather slippers were dyed red and covered with burgundy sequined organza and adorned with leather bows covered with red jewels and beads. The shoes are found in museums—including the Smithsonian, which reports that more than 5 million people see them yearly—and private collections, with one pair selling at auction to a private collector for $666,000 in 2000.

The year 2009 will see the seventieth anniversary of *The Wizard of Oz* film, and for the anniversary a number of shoe designers such as **Manolo Blahnik**, **Jimmy Choo**, and Christian Laboutin are designing their own versions of the ruby slippers, which will be auctioned off to benefit charity.

See also: "The Red Shoes"; Fairy Tales

Further Reading Thomas, Rhys. *The Ruby Slippers of Oz*. Los Angeles: Tale Weaver, 1989.

Resource Guide

ORGANIZATIONS

American Apparel and Footwear Association
1601 No. Kent Street, 12th floor,
Arlington, VA 22209
703-524-1864
http://www.apparelandfootwear.org/

American Podiatric Medical Association
9312 Old Georgetown Road
Bethesda, MD 20814-1621
(301) 581-9200
http://www.apma.org/

National Podiatric Medical Association
1706 E. 87th Street
Chicago, IL 60617
773.374.5300 phone
http://npmaonline.org/index.html

United Shoe Retailers Organization
PO Box 4931
West Hills, CA 91308
PHONE: 818-703-6062
http://www.usraonline.org/

WEBSITES

A Century In Shoes
http://www.centuryinshoes.com/

All About Shoes
http://www.allaboutshoes.ca/en/

Charlie's Sneaker Pages
http://sneakers.pair.com/

Cowboy Boots
http://www.dimlights.com/blogger.htm
Foot Care.org
http://www.foot-care.org/

Foot Talk
http://foottalk.blogspot.com/

Footwear News
http://www.footwearnews.com

Footwear of the Middle Ages
http://www.personal.utulsa.edu/~marc-carlson/shoe/SHOEHOME.HTM

Head over Heels
http://www.headoverheelshistory.com/

Paleopodiatry
http://paleopodiatry.blogspot.com/

Shoe Info.net
http://www.shoeinfonet.com/

Sneaker Blogger
http://www.sneakerblogger.com/sneaker/index.php

Sneaker Freaker
http://www.sneakerfreaker.com/

MUSEUMS

Bally Shoe Museum
Schönenwerd Bally Schuhmuseum
Oltnerstrasse 6
CH-5012 Schönenwerd
Switzerland

Bata Shoe Museum
327 Bloor Street West
Toronto ON
CANADA
M5S 1W7
416.979.7799
http://www.batashoemuseum.ca

Boot and Shoe Collection at the Northampton Art Gallery
Guildhall Road
Northampton NN1 1D
England
01604 838111
museums@northampton.gov.uk
http://www.northampton.gov.uk/site/
scripts/documents_info.php?
categoryID=1482&documentID=135

Brockton Shoe Museum
216 North Pearl St., Rte, 27
Brockton, Massachusetts 02301
(508) 583-1039
http://www.brocktonhistoricalsociety.org/

Clarks Shoe Museum
Clarks Village
High Street
Street BA16 0YA
United Kingdom
01458 842 169

Cordwainers College Historic Shoe Collection
The Library
London College of Fashion
20 John Princes Street
London WIG OBJ
020 7514 8678
http://vads.ahds.ac.uk/collections/
LCFSHOE.html

Deutsches Ledermuseum
D-63067 Offenbach
Frankfurter Str. 86
0049-(0)69829798-0
info@ledermuseum.de
http://www.ledermuseum.de

Ferragamo Museum
Via dei Tornabuoni 2,
50123 Florence.
Italy
+39 055 3360 456/455
http://www.salvatoreferragamo.it/en/
#folderId=/en/themuseum

Fuller Craft Museum
455 Oak Street
Brockton, MA 02301
508-588-6000
http://www.fullercraft.org

High Heel Museum
(online only)
http://www.highheelshoemuseum.com

History of Footwear Museum
Plaza Sant Felip Neri
E-08002 Barcelona
Spain

Japan Footwear Museum
4-16-27 Matsunagacho,
Fukuyama-city,
Hiroshima-prefecture 729-0104
Japan
(084)934-6644

Le Musée Internacional de La Chaussure
2, rue Sainte-Marie,
Romans,
France
04 75 05 81 30

Museo del Calçat
Pç Sant Felip Neri, 5
08002 Barcelona
Spain
34 93 3014533
http://www.barcelonaturisme.com/
Museu-del-Calcat/_vf-SMlY1y
IuKQTV1aq49kAo1OW J1ZmyqjEEp
VjGHybwtDEPsyQxxnBbm
AxikrKhV

Museo Del Calzado
Avda. de Chapí, 32
03600 ELDA (Alicante) España
965383021
Email: info@museocalzado.com
http://www.sho.es/museo/

Museo della Calzatura
Piazza Ducale .
Vigevano 27029 (PV)
Italy
0381-690370 / 0381-299282
http://www.italiavirtuale.info/italy/
ComponiVetrina.php?IdVetrina
=12356&DescCategoria
=Specializzato

Museum of Shoe Production and Industrial History
Turnstraße 5
D-76846 Hauenstein
Germany
06392/915 165
http://www.stadt-pirmasens.de/museen/
Pirmasens_3_Museen_Hauenstein.htm

Museum of Shoemaking
Museum of Southeastern Moravia of Zlin
Obuvnicke museum
Svit 1
760 00 Zlin
Czech Republic
+420 (0) 577 - 522225
http://www.volweb.cz/muzeum/
english.htm

National Museum of Roller Skating
4730 South Street
Lincoln, Nebraska 68506
Phone: (402) 483-7551
http://www.rollerskatingmuseum.com/

National Shoe Museum
Musea Izegem
B. de Pélichystraat 5
8870 Izegem
Belgium
051/31 64 46

http://www.musea.izegem.be/eng/
schoeiselmuseum.asp
Nederlands Leder en Schoenen Museum
Elzenweg 25
5144 MB Waalwijk
Netherlands
0416 - 33 27 38
http://www.schoenenmuseum.nl/

Sexy Art History Museum for Miniature Shoes
(online only)
http://www.schuh.at/

Shoe Icons
(online only)
http://eng.shoe-icons.com/index.htm

Shoes or No Shoes Museum
Vandevoordeweg 2
9770 Kruishoutem
Belgium
+32 9 383 52 87
http://dev.shoesornoshoes.com/main.htm

The Shoe Museum of Marikina
J.P. Rizal Street
Barangay San Roque,
Marikina City
Philippines
(632) 430-9735
http://www.marikina.gov.ph/pages/
shoemuseum.htm

The Temple University School of Podiatric Medicine Shoe Museum
8th and Race Streets,
Philadelphia, PA 19107
215-625-5243
http://podiatry.temple.edu/pages/about/
shoe_museum/shoe_museum.html

Virtual Shoe Museum
(online only)
http://www.virtualshoemuseum.com/
vsm/index.php

Bibliography

Aamidor, Abraham. *Chuck Taylor, Converse All Star: The True Story Behind the Man Behind the Most Famous Athletic Shoe in History*. Bloomington: Indiana University Press.

Adams, Richard. *Prehistoric Mesoamerica*. Norman, OK: Universit of Oklahoma Press, 1991.

Akass, Kim, and Janet McCabe. *Reading Sex and the City*. London: I.B. Tauris, 2004.

Akinwumi, Tunde M. "Interrogating Africa's Past: Footwear Amongst the Yoruba," in Rielle, Georgio, and Peter McNeil, eds. *Shoes: A History From Sandals to Sneakers*. London: Berg Publishers, 2006.

Alexander, Ivy, *Podiatry Sourcebook*. Detroit: Omnigraphics, 2007.

Amato, Joseph Anthony. *On Foot: A History of Walking*. New York: NYU Press, 2004.

Atkinson, Jeremy. *Clogs and Clog Making*. Shire Publications, 2009.

Atkinson, Mary. *Hand and Foot Massage: Massage Taken to the Extremes*. London: Carlton, 2001.

Baker, William. *Sports in the Western World*. Totowa, NJ: Rowman & Littlefield, 1982.

Baldwin, Francis Elizabeth. *Sumptuary legislation and personal regulation in England*. Baltimore: John Hopkin Press, 1926.

Barringer, Janice, and Sarah Schlesinger. *The Pointe Book: Shoes, Training & Technique*. Princeton, NJ: Princeton Book Company, 2004.

Bartel Sheehan, Kim. *Controversies in Contemporary Advertising*. London: Sage, 2003.

Barwick, Sandra *A Century of Style*, London, Allen & Unwin, 1984.

Bata, Thomas John, Sonja Sinclair. *Bata Shoemaker to the World*. Toronto: Stoddard, 1990.

Beard, Tyler. *The Cowboy Boot Book*. Salt Lake City: Peregrine Smith Books, 1992.

Beard, Tyler, and Jim Arndt. *Cowboy Boots*. Layton, UT: Gibbs Smith, 2004.

Benstock, Shari ,and Suzanne Ferriss, eds. *Footnotes: On Shoes*. New Jersey: Rutgers University Press, 1994.

Bettelheim, Bruno. *The Uses of Enchantment: The Meaning and Importance of Fairy Tales*. New York: Vintage Books, 1975.

Blundell, Sue. "Beneath Their Shining Feet: Shoes and Sandals in Classical Greece," in Rielle, Georgio, and Peter McNeil, eds. *Shoes: A History From Sandals to Sneakers*. London: Berg Publishers, 2006.

Bonner, Raymond. *Waltzing with a Dictator: The Marcoses and the Making of American Policy*. New York: Times Books, 1987.

Bosco, Joseph. *A Problem of Evidence: How the Prosecution Freed O. J. Simpson*. New York: William Morrow & Company, 1996.

Bowman-Kruhm, Mary. *The Leakeys: A Biography*. Westport, CT: Greenwood Publishing Group, 2005.

Braekstad, H. L., Translator. *Hans Christian Andersen's Fairy Tales*, translated New York: Beekman House, 1978.

Breward, Christopher. "Fashioning Masculinity: Men's Footwear and Modernity," in Rielle, Georgio, and Peter McNeil, eds. *Shoes: A History From Sandals to Sneakers.* London: Berg Publishers, 2006.

Brewer, Ebenezer Cobham, and Ivor H. Evans. *The Wordsworth Dictionary of Phrase & Fable.* Hertfordshire, England: Wordsworth Editions, 1994.

Brooke, Michael. *The Concrete Wave: The History of Skateboarding.* Toronto: Warwick Publishing, 1999.

Burfoot, Amby. *Runner's World Complete Book of Running: Everything You Need to Know to Run for Fun, Fitness, and Competition.* Emmaus, Pa: Rodale Press, 1997.

Burns, William E. *Science and Technology in Colonial America.* Westport, CT: Greenwood Publishing Group, 2005.

Chaiklin, Martha. "Purity, Pollution and Place in Traditional Japanese Footwear," in Rielle, Georgio, and Peter McNeil, eds. *Shoes: A History From Sandals to Sneakers.* London: Berg Publishers, 2006.

Chang, Thomas. *Master Techniques in Podiatric Surgery.* Philadelphia: Lippincott Williams & Wilkins, 2004.

Chen, Harold. *Atlas of Genetic Diagnosis and Counseling.* Totowa, NJ: Humana Press, 2006.

Christopher Breward. Fashioning Masculinity: Men's Footwear and Modernity. Rielle, Georgio, and Peter McNeil, eds. Shoes: A History From Sandals to Sneakers. London: Berg Publishers, 2006.

Cleary, Meghan. *The Perfect Fit: What Your Shoes Say About You.* San Francisco: Chronicle Books, 2005.

Cole, Kenneth. *Footnotes: What You Stand For Is More Important Than What You Stand In.* New York: Simon & Schuster, 2003.

Connelly, Mark. *The Red Shoes: Turner Classic Movies British Film Guide.* London: I.B. Tauris, 2005.

Copeland, Glenn. *The Foot Book: Relief for Overused, Abused and Ailing Feet.* New York: Wiley, 1992.

Copeland, Glenn, Stan Solomon, and Mark Myerson. *The Good Foot Book: A Guide For Men, Women, Children, Athletes, Seniors.* Alameda, CA: Hunter House, 2005.

Cosgrave, Bronwyn. *The Complete History of Costume and Fashion: From Ancient Egypt to the Present Day.* New York: Checkmark Books, 2000.

Cox, Caroline. *Stiletto.* New York: Harper Design, 2004.

Cox, Marian Roalfe. *Cinderella: Three Hundred and Forty-Five Variants of Cinderella, Catskin and Cap o'Rushes.* London: The Folklore Society, 1893.

Cristian, Adrian. *Lower Limb Amputation: A Guide to Living a Quality Life.* New York: Demos Medical Publishing, 2005.

Danesi, Marcel. *Of Cigarretes, High Heels, and Other Interesting Things: An Introduction to Semiotics.* New York: St. Martin's Press, 1999.

David, Alison Matthews. "War Wellingtons: Military Footwear in the Age of Empire," in Rielle, Georgio, and Peter McNeil, eds. *Shoes: A History From Sandals to Sneakers.* London: Berg Publishers, 2006.

Davidson, Hilary. "Sex and Sin: The Magic of Red Shoes," in Rielle, Georgio, and Peter McNeil, eds. *Shoes: A History From Sandals to Sneakers.* London: Berg Publishers, 2006.

Davies, Owen, and Willem de Blecourt. *Beyond the Witch Trials.* Manchester: Manchester University Press, 2004.

Deal, William. *Handbook to Life in Medieval and Early Modern Japan*. New York: Oxford University Press, 2007.

DeJean, Joan. *The Essence of Style: How the French Invented High Fashion, Fine Food, Chic Cafes, Style, Sophistication, and Glamour*. New York: Free Press, 2005.

de Vaux, Roland. *Ancient Israel: Its Life and Institutions*. New York: McGraw Hill, 1961.

Dewald, Jonathan. *Europe 1450 to 1789: Encyclopedia of the Early Modern World*. New York: Charles Scribner's Sons, 2004.

Dougans, Inge. *The Complete Illustrated Guide to Reflexology: Therapeutic Foot Massage for Health and Well Being*. Boston: Element, 1996.

Dunaway, Wilma A, *The African-American Family in Slavery and Emancipation*. Cambridge: Cambridge University Press, 2003.

Dundes, Alan, ed. *Cinderella: A Folklore Casebook*. Madison: University of Wisconsin Press 1982.

Easton, Timothy. "Spiritual Middens" *Encyclopedia of vernacular architecture of the world* v.1, Cambridge University Press, 1997.

Eastop, Diana. "Garments deliberately concealed in buildings," in: Wallis, R., and Lymer K. (eds.) 2001. *A Permeability of Boundaries? New approaches to the Archaeology of Art, Religion and Folklore*. BAR International Series S936. Oxford: British Archaeological Reports, 79–84.

Edwards, Adam. *A Short History of the Wellington Boot*. London: Hodder & Stoughton, 2006.

Edwards, Sally, and Melissa McKenzie. *Snowshoeing*. Champaign, Illinois: Human Kinetics, Inc., 1995.

Elder, Alan C. *In the Steps of Our Ancestors: An Exhibition of Native North American Footwear*. Toronto: Ontario Crafts Council, 1989.

Ellison, Katherine W. *Imelda, Steel Butterfly of the Philippines*. New York: McGraw-Hill, 1988.

Ellsworth, Ray. *Platform Shoes: A Big Step in Fashion*. Atglen, PA: Schiffer Pub, 1998.

Endres, Stacey, and Robert Cushman. *Hollywood at Your Feet: The Story of the World Famous Chinese Theatre*. Los Angeles: Pomegranate Press, 1992.

Farr, James Richard. *Artisans in Europe, 1300–1914*. Cambridge: Cambridge University Press, 2000.

Fixx, James F. *The Complete Book of Running*. New York: Random House, 1977.

Fleischman, Gary, and Charles Stein. *Acupuncture: Everything You Ever Wanted to Know But Were Afraid to Ask*. Barrytown: Station Hill Press, 1998.

Foucault, M. *Discipline and Punish*. Harmondsworth: Penguin, 1979.

Frazine, Richard Keith. *The Barefoot Hiker: A Book About Bare Feet*. Berkeley: Ten Speed Press, 1993.

Fried, Gil, Steven Shapiro, and Timothy DeSchriver. *Sport Finance*. Champaign: Human Kinetics Publishers, 2003.

Friedel, Robert. *Zippers: An Exploration in Novelty*. New York: W. W. Norton, 1994.

Garcia, Bobbito. *Where'd You Get Those?: New York City's Sneaker Culture: 1960–1987*. New York: Testify Books, 2003.

Gideon Bosker, and Bianca Lencek-Bosker. *Bowled Over: A Roll Down Memory Lane*. San Francisco: Chronicle Books, 2002.

Gill, Alison. "Limousines for the Feet: The Rhetoric of Trainers," in Rielle, Georgio, and Peter McNeil, eds. *Shoes: A History From Sandals to Sneakers*. London: Berg Publishers, 2006.

Glanz Margo, Mercedes Iturbe. *Walking Dreams: Salvatore Ferragamo, 1898–1960*. Spain: Editorial RM, 2006.

Golden, Anna Louise. *The Spice Girls*. New York: Ballantine Books, 1997.

Golden, Mark, and Peter Toohey. *Sex and Difference in Ancient Greece and Rome*. Edingburgh: Edinburgh University Press, 2003.

Gottwald, Laura. *Frederick's of Hollywood, 1947–1973: 26 Years of Mail Order Seduction*. New York: Drake Publishers, 1973.

Grass, Milton. *The History of Hosiery, from the Piloi of Ancient Greece to the Nylons of Modern America*. New York: Fairchild Publications, 1955.

Green, Harvey. *Wood: Craft, Culture, History*. New York: Penguin, 2007.

Grew, Francis, and Margrethe de Neergaard. *Shoes and Pattens: Finds from Medieval Excavations in London*. Woodbridge: Boydell, 2006.

Grimm, Jacob, and Wilhelm Grimm. *Household Tales*. Margaret Hunt, translator. London: George Bell, 1884, 1892.

Gulevich, Tanya. *Understanding Islam And Muslim Traditions: An Introduction To The Religious Practices, Celebrations, Festivals, Observances, Beliefs, Folklore, Customs, And Calendar Systems Of The World's Muslim Communities, Including An Overview Of Islamic History And Geography*. Detroit: Omnigraphics, 2004.

Gutman, Dan. *Ice Skating, From Axels to Zambonis*. New York: Penguin Books, 1995.

Haig, Matt. *Brand Royalty: How the World's Top 100 Brands Thrive and Survive*. London: Kogan Page Publishers, 2004.

Hall Strutt, Daphne. *Fashion in South Africa 1652–1900: An Illustrated History of Styles and Materials for Men, Women and Children, with Notes on Footwear, Hairdressing, Accessories and Jewellery*. Amsterdam: AA Balkema, 1975.

Haven, Kendall. *100 Greatest Science Inventions of All Time*. Westport, CT: Libraries Unlimited, 2006.

Hay, William, Anthony Hayward, Myron J. Levin, and Judith M. Sondheimer. *Current Pediatric Diagnosis & Treatment*. New York: McGraw-Hill Professional, 2002.

Hoffman, Frank, and William Bailey. *Fashion and Merchandising Fads*. New York: Haworth Press, 1994.

Hong Fan. *Footbinding, Feminism, and Freedom: The Liberation of Women's Bodies in China*. London: Cass, 1997.

Jackson, Steven, and David L. Andrews, eds.. *Sport, Culture and Advertising: Identities, Commodities and the Politics of Representation*. London: Routledge, 2005.

Jahss, Melvin. *Disorders of the Foot and Ankle: Medical and Surgical Management*. Philadelphia: Saunders, 1991.

Jeffreys, Sheila. *Beauty and Misogyny: Harmful Cultural Practices in the West*. New York: Routledge, 2005.

Jenkins, J. Geraint, *Exploring Country Crafts*. Wakefield: EP Publishing, 1977.

June, Jennifer, Dwight Yoakam, and Marty Snortum. *Cowboy Boots: The Art and Sole*. New York: Universe Publishing, 2007.

Kassing, Gayle. *History of Dance: An Interactive Arts Approach*. Champaign, IL: Human Kinetics, 2007.

Kennedy, Rick, and Randy McNutt, *Little Labels—Big Sound: Small Record Companies and the Rise of American Music*. Bloomington: Indiana University Press, 1999.

King, J C H, Birgit Pauksztat, and Robert Storrie. *Arctic Clothing of North America: Alaska, Canada, Greenland*. Montreal: McGill-Queen's University Press, 2005.

King, Philip, and Lawrence Stager. *Life in Biblical Israel*. Louisville, KY: Westminster John Knox Press, 2001.

Knötel, Richard, Herbert Knötel, and Herbert Sieg. *Uniforms of the World: A Compendium of Army, Navy, and Air Force Uniforms, 1700–1937*. New York: Scribner's, 1980.

Ko, Dorothy. *Cinderella's Sisters: A Revisionist History of Footbinding*. Berkeley: University of California Press, 2007.

Koleff, George. *How to Make Ugg Boots: The Manual*. Pasadena, South Australia: Encyclotel, 1991.

Kovesi Killerby, Catherine. *Sumptuary Law in Italy 1200–1500*. New York: Oxford University Press, 2002.

Kunz, K., and B. Kunz. *The Complete Guide to Foot Reflexology*. Albuquerque, NM: Reflexology Research, 1993.

Kunzle, David. *Fashion and Fetishism: A Social History of the Corset, Tight-Lacing and Other Forms of Body Sculpture in the West*. New York: Rowman & Littlefield, 1982.

Langer, Paul. *Great Feet for Life: Foot Care and Footwear for Healthy Aging*. Minneapolis: Fairview Press, 2007.

Lawlor, Laurie. *Where Will This Shoe Take You? A Walk Through The History Of Footwear*. New York: Walker & Company, 1996.

Lomas, Clare, Peter McNeil, and Sally Gray. "Beyond the Rainbow: Queer Shoes," in Rielle, Georgio, and Peter McNeil, eds. *Shoes: A History From Sandals to Sneakers*. London: Berg Publishers, 2006.

Lorimer, Donald, and Donald Neale. *Neale's Disorders of the Foot*. New York: Elsevier Churchill Livingstone, 2006.

Luciano, Lynne. "A Culture of Narcissism." In *Looking Good: Male Body Image in Modern America*. New York: Hill and Wang, 2001.

Lusardi, Michelle M., and Caroline C. Nielsen. *Orthotics and Prosthetics in Rehabilitation*. Boston: Butterworth-Heinemann, 2000.

MacDonald, Ann. *Foot Care Basics: Preventing and Treating Common Foot Conditions*. Harvard health letter special report. Boston, MA: Harvard Health Publications, 2007.

Mann, Felix. *Reinventing Acupuncture: A New Concept of Ancient Medicine*. Philadelphia: Elsevier Health Sciences, 2000.

Mason, George Frederick. *Animal Feet*. New York: William Morrow, 1970.

May, Bella. *Amputations and Prosthetics: A Case Study Approach*. Philadelphia: F.A. Davis Company, 2002.

McComb, David. *Sports in World History*. New York: Routledge, 2004.

McDowell, Colin. *Manolo Blahnik*. New York: HarperCollins Publishers, 2000.

McIntosh, Sue. *The Killer Ugg Boots from Down Under*. Whorouly East, Victoria: S. McIntosh, 1988.

McNeil, Peter, and Giorgio Riello. "The Male Cinderella: Shoes, Genius and Fantasy," in Rielle, Georgio, and Peter McNeil, eds. *Shoes: A History From Sandals to Sneakers*. London: Berg Publishers, 2006.

McNeil, Peter, and Giorgio Riello. "Walking the Streets of London and Paris in the Enlightenment," in Rielle, Georgio, and Peter McNeil, eds. *Shoes: A History From Sandals to Sneakers*. London: Berg Publishers, 2006.

Means Lawrence, Robert. *The Magic of the Horseshoe: With Other Folklore Notes*. Boston: Houghton-Mifflin, 1898.

Meldrum, D. Jeffrey, and Charles Hilton, "From biped to strider: the emergence of modern human walking, running, and resource transport." American Association of Physical Anthropologists Meeting. Birkhäuser, 2004.

Michman, Ronald D., and Edward M. Mazze. *Specialty Retailers: Marketing Triumphs and Blunders*. Westport, Conn: Quorum Books, 2001.

Monger, George. *Marriage Customs of the World: From Henna to Honeymoons*. Santa Barbara: ABC-CLIO, 2004.

Moore, Keith L., and T. V. N. Persaud. *Before We Are Born: Essentials of Embryology and Birth Defects*. Philadelphia: Saunders, 1998.

Morse Earle, Alice. *Two Centuries of Costume in America, 1620–1820*. Rutland, VT: CE Tuttle Company, 1971.

Mullin, Bernard J., Stephen Hardy, and William Anthony Sutton. *Sport Marketing*. Champaign, IL: Human Kinetics, 2007.

Munzenberg, K. Joachim. *The Orthopedic Shoe: Indications and Prescription*. Weinheim, Germany: VCH, 1985.

Muzzarelli, Maria Giuseppina. "Sumptuous Shoes: Making and Wearing in Medieval Italy," in Rielle, Georgio, and Peter McNeil, eds. *Shoes: A History From Sandals to Sneakers*. London: Berg Publishers, 2006.

Nahshon, Edna, ed. *Jews and Shoes*. New York: Berg Publishers, 2008.

Nainfa, John Abel. *Costumes of Prelates of the Catholic Church according to Roman Etiquette*. Whitefish, MT: Kessinger Publishing, 2008.

Oakes, Jill, and Rick Riewe. *Alaska Eskimo Footwear*. Anchorage: University of Alaska Press, 2007.

O'Keeffe, Linda. *Shoes: A Celebration of Pumps, Sandals, Slippers & More*. New York: Workman Publishing, 1996.

Opie, Iona, and Peter Opie. *The Classic Fairy Tales*. New York: Oxford University Press, 1974.

Opie, Iona Archibald, and Peter Opie, eds. *The Oxford Dictionary of Nursery Rhymes*. Oxford, England: Oxford University Press, 1977.

Ott, Katherine, David Harley Serlin, David Serlin, and Stephen Mihm. *Artificial Parts, Practical Lives: Modern Histories of Prosthetics*. New York: NYU Press, 2001.

Papson, Stephen, and Robert Goldman. *Nike Culture: The Sign of the Swoosh*. London: Sage Publications, 1998.

Paterek, Josephine. *Encyclopedia of American Indian Costume*. Denver, Colo: ABC-CLIO, 1994.

Pedersen, Stephanie. *Shoes: What Every Woman Should Know*. Cincinnati: David & Charles, 2005.

Perkins, Dorothy. *Encyclopedia of Japan: Japanese History and Culture, from Abacus to Zori*. New York: Facts on File, 1991.

Peters, Erika. *The Complete Idiot's Guide to Walking for Health*. Indianapolis: Alpha Books, 2001.

Prater, Gene. *Showshoeing*. Seattle: The Mountaineers, 1997.

Pratt, Keith, Richard Rutt, and James Hoare. *Korea: A Historical and Cultural Dictionary*. Surrey: Curzon Press, 1999.

Propp, Vladimir. *Morphology of the Folktale*. Austin: University of Texas, 1968.

Red Wing Shoe Company. *100, Red Wing Shoes: 1905–2005*. Red Wing, MN: Red Wing Shoe Company, 2004.

Rexford, Nancy. "The Perils of Choice: Women's Footwear in Nineteenth-Century America," in Rielle, Georgio, and Peter McNeil, eds. *Shoes: A History From Sandals to Sneakers.* London: Berg Publishers, 2006.

Reyna, Ferdinando. *A Concise History of Ballet.* New York: Grosset & Dunlap, 1965.

Ricci, Stafnia. "Made in Italy: Ferragamo and Twentieth-Century Fashion," in Rielle, Georgio, and Peter McNeil, eds. *Shoes: A History From Sandals to Sneakers.* London: Berg Publishers, 2006.

Rielly, Edward J. *The 1960s.* Westport, CT: Greenwood Press, 2003.

Rielle, Georgio, and Peter McNeil, eds. *Shoes: A History From Sandals to Sneakers.* London: Berg Publishers, 2006.

Roberts, Adam. "Crush Videos," in Stallwood, Kim, ed. *A Primer on Animal Rights: Leading Experts Write about Animal Cruelty and Exploitation.* New York: Lantern Books, 2002.

Rogers, Dave. *The Complete Avengers: Everything You Ever Wanted to Know about The Avengers and The New Avengers.* New York: MacMillan, 1989.

Sachs J., and J. Berger. *Reflexology: The A–Z Guide to Healing with Pressure Points.* New York: Dell Publishing, 1997.

Sarrafian, Shahan. *Anatomy of the Foot and Ankle: Descriptive, Topographic, Functional.* Philadelphia: Lippincott, 1993.

Schipper, Mineke. *Never Marry A Woman With Big Feet: Proverbs From Around The World.* New Haven: Yale University Press, 2003.

Schmidt, Mark Ray. *The 1970s.* San Diego: Greenhaven Press, 2000.

Schoeffler, O. E., and Williams Gale. *Esquire's Encyclopedia of 20th Century Men's Fashions.* New York: McGraw-Hill, 1973.

Sebesta, Judith Lynn, and Larissa Bonfante. *The World of Roman Costume.* Madison: University of Wisconsin Press, 1994.

Semmelhack, Elizabeth. "A Delicate Balance: Women, Power and High Heels," in Rielle, Georgio, and Peter McNeil, eds. *Shoes: A History From Sandals to Sneakers.* London: Berg Publishers, 2006.

Shurr, Donald G., and Thomas M. Cook. *Prosthetics and Orthotics.* Upper Saddle River, N.J.: Prentice Hall, 2002.

Sims, Josh, and Mal Peachey. *Rock Fashion.* London: Omnibus, 1999.

Sinclair, David. *Wannabe: How the Spice Girls Reinvented Pop Fame.* London: Omnibus Press, 2004.

Skyrme, Tim. *Bespoke Shoemaking, A Comprehensive Guide to Handmade Footwear.* Agnes Water, Queensland: Artzend Publications, 2006.

Slack, Charles. *Noble Obsession: Charles Goodyear, Thomas Hancock, and the Race to Unlock the Greatest Industrial Secret of the Nineteenth Century.* Hyperion, 2003.

Smit, Barbara. *Sneaker Wars: The Enemy Brothers who Founded Adidas and Puma and the Family Feud that Forever Changed the Business of Sport.* New York: Ecco, 2008.

Soble, Michelle. *Podiatry for the Reflexologist.* Yellville, AR: Whitehall Publishing Company, 2002.

Steele, Valerie. *Fashion and Eroticism: Ideals of Feminine Beauty from the Victorian Era to the Jazz Age.* New York: Oxford University Press, 1995.

Steele, Valerie. *Fetish: Fashion, Sex and Power.* New York: Oxford University Press, 1996.

Steele, Valerie. *Paris Fashion: A Cultural History.* New York: Oxford University Press, 1998.

Steele, Valerie. *Shoes: A Lexicon of Style.* New York: Rizzoli International Publications Inc., 1999.

Steele, Valerie. *Encyclopedia of Clothing and Fashion*. Farmington Hills, MI: Charles Scribner's Sons, 2005.

Steele, Valerie. "Shoes and the Erotic Imagination," in Rielle, Georgio, and Peter McNeil, eds. *Shoes: A History From Sandals to Sneakers*. London: Berg Publishers, 2006.

Stillman, Yedida Kalfon. *Arab Dress from the Dawn of Islam to Modern Times*. Leiden: Brill, 2003.

St. Pierre, Denise. *Golf Fundamentals*. Champaign, IL: Human Kinetics, 2004.

Strauss, Barry. *The Trojan War: A New History*. New York: Simon and Schuster, 2007.

Stumpf, Doug. *Confessions of a Wall Street Shoeshine Boy*. New York: Harper Collins, 2007.

Sumner, Graham, Raffiello, Amato. *Roman Military Clothing*. Oxford: Osprey, 2005.

Swann, June. *Shoemaking*. Princes Risborough: Shire, 1986.

Swann, June. "Shoes concealed in buildings," *Costume: Journal of the Costume Society* No. 30 (1996): pp. 56–99.

Tarlo, Emma. *Clothing Matters: Dress and Adornment in India*. Chicago: University of Chicago Press, 1996.

Tatar, Maria M., ed. *The Classic Fairy Tales*. New York: W. W. Norton, 1999.

Thomas, Dana. *Deluxe: How Luxury Lost Its Luster*. New York: Penguin Group, 2007.

Thomas, John Christopher. *Footwashing in John 13 and the Johannine Community*. Sheffield: JSOT Press, 1991.

Thomas, Rhys. *The Ruby Slippers of Oz*. Los Angeles: Tale Weaver, 1989.

Thompson, Hunter S. *The Harley-Davidson Reader*. St. Paul, MN: Motorbooks, 2006.

Thompson, Stith. *The Folktale*. New York: Holt, Rinehart, and Winston, 1946.

Thorstensen, Thomas C. *Practical Leather Technology*. Huntington, NY: Robert E. Krieger Publishing Co., 1976.

Toselli, Leigh. *A Complete Guide to Manicure & Pedicure*. London: New Holland, 2005.

Tourles, Stephanie. *Natural Foot Care*. Pownal, VT: Storey, 1999.

Tungate, Mark. *Adland: A Global History of Advertising*. London: Kogan Page Publishers, 2007.

Turner, James, and Michael Zaidman. *The History of Roller Skating*. Lincoln, NE: National Museum of Roller Skating, 1997.

United States War Department. *Handbook on German Military Forces*. Baton Rouge: Louisiana State University Press, 1990.

Utah Museum of Natural History, Kathy Kankainen, and Laurel Casjens. *Treading in the Past: Sandals of the Anasazi*. Salt Lake City: Utah Museum of Natural History in association with the University of Utah Press, 1995.

Vaillancourt, Henri. *Making the Attikamek Snowshoe*. Greenville, NH: Trust for Native American Cultures and Crafts, 1987.

Van den Beukel, Dorine. *Traditional Mehndi Designs : A Treasury of Henna Body Art*. Berkeley, CA: Shambhala Publications, 2000.

Vanderbilt, Tom. *The Sneaker Book: Anatomy of an Industry and an Icon*. New York: The New Press, 1998.

Vaughn, R. L. *The Doctrine of Foot Washing*. Mount Enterprise, TX: Waymark Publications, 2006.

Veblen, Thorstein. *On the Nature and Uses of Sabotage*. New York: B. W. Huebsch, 1921.

Veillon, Dominique. *Fashion Under the Occupation*. New York: Berg, 2002.

Vejlgaard, Henrik. *Anatomy of a Trend*. New York: McGraw Hill, 2008.

Vera, Veronica. *Miss Vera's Cross-Dress for Success: A Resource Guide for Boys Who Want to be Girls*. New York: Villard, 2002.

BIBLIOGRAPHY **349**

Veves, Aristidis, ed. *The Diabetic Foot*. New York: Humana Press, 2006.

Vianello, Andrea. "Courtly Lady or Courtesan? The Venetian Chopine in the Renaissance," in Rielle, Georgio, and Peter McNeil, eds. *Shoes: A History From Sandals to Sneakers*. London: Berg Publishers, 2006.

Vonhof, John. *Fixing Your Feet: Prevention And Treatments for Athletes*. Berkeley, CA: Wilderness Press, 2006.

Walford, Jonathan. *The Seductive Shoe: Four Centuries of Fashion Footwear*. New York: Stewart, Tabori and Chang, 2007.

Wardlow, Daniel. *Gays, Lesbians and Consumer Behavior: Theories, Practice and Research Issues in Marketing*. New York: Harrington Park Press, 1996.

Weiner, Jennifer. *In Her Shoes*. New York: Atria Books, 2002.

Welsh, Peter C. *Tanning in the United States to 1850*. Washington, DC: United States National Museum, 1964.

White, Nicola, Ian Griffiths. *The Fashion Business: Theory, Practice, Image*. London: Berg Publishers, 2000.

Wiesner, Merry. *Early Modern Europe, 1450–1789*. Cambridge: Cambridge University Press, 2006.

Williams, Erin E., and Margo DeMello. *Why Animals Matter: The Case for Animal Protection*. Amherst, NY: Prometheus Books, 2007.

Yang, Shaorong. *Traditional Chinese Clothing: Costumes, Adornments & Culture*. San Francisco: Long River Press, 2004.

Yue, Charlotte, and David Yue. *Shoes: Their History in Words and Pictures*. Boston: Houghton Mifflin, 1997.

Zamperini, Paola. "A Dream of Butterflies? Shoes in Chinese Culture," in Rielle, Georgio, and Peter McNeil, eds. *Shoes: A History From Sandals to Sneakers*. London: Berg Publishers, 2006.

Zipes, Jack, ed. *The Oxford Companion to Fairy Tales*. Oxford: Oxford University, 2000.

Index

About the Author

Margo DeMello has a B.A. in Religious Studies from U.C. Berkeley and earned her Ph.D. in Cultural Anthropology in 1995 from U.C. Davis. She currently lectures at Central New Mexico Community College, teaching sociology, cultural studies, and anthropology.

Her books include *Bodies of Inscription: A Cultural History of the Modern Tattoo Community* (2000), *Stories Rabbits Tell: A Natural and Cultural History of a Misunderstood Creature* (with Susan E. Davis, 2003), *Low-Carb Vegetarian*, (2004), *Why Animals Matter: The Case for Animal Protection* (with Erin E. Williams, 2007), *The Encyclopedia of Body Adornment* (Greenwood Press, 2007), and *Teaching the Animal: Human Animal Studies Across the Disciplines* (Forthcoming).

She has had her work published in journals such as *Anthropology Today*, *Journal of Popular Culture*, and *Anthrozöos*, and contributed essays and chapters to *Pierced Hearts and True Love: A Century of Drawings for Tattoos* (Ed Hardy, ed., 1995), *Cultural Anthropology: The Human Challenge* (William Haviland, 2004), *Encyclopedia of Human-Animal Relationships* (Marc Bekoff, ed., Greenwood Publishing, 2007), *A Cultural History of Animals: The Modern Age* (Randy Malamud, ed., 2007), and *Encyclopedia of Animal Rights* (Marc Bekoff, ed., Greenwood Publishing, Forthcoming). She wore orthopedic shoes as a child, has an ongoing neuroma in her foot, and today wears vegan shoes.